BEING DEAD
IS BAD
FOR BUSINESS

BEING DEAD

IS BAD

FOR BUSINESS

a memoir

STANLEY A. WEISS

DISRUPTION
BOOKS

AUSTIN   NEW YORK

This book is a memoir. It reflects the author's present recollections of experiences over time. Some names and characteristics have been changed, some events have been compressed, and some dialogue has been re-created.

Published by Disruption Books
Austin, TX, and New York, NY
www.disruptionbooks.com

Distributed by Disruption Books

For ordering information or special discounts for bulk purchases, please contact Disruption Books at info@disruptionbooks.com.

Cover design, text design, and composition by Kim Lance

Print ISBN: 978-1-63331-012-4
eBook ISBN: 978-1-63331-013-1

10 9 8 7 6 5 4 3 2 1

For Lisa

Contents

PREFACE:
The Atomic Bomb Saved My Life — ix

INTRODUCTION:
A Sunny Town for Shady People — 1

1 The Argument — 11
2 Lessons from Queen Street — 19
3 The Chance — 29
4 Enlisted — 35
5 Learning the Advantages of Partnership — 49
6 First Love — 55
7 Imagine Sisyphus Happy — 65
8 The Spy Who Taught Me — 73
9 Catching the Bug in Mexico — 82
10 Getting Screwed, Getting Serious — 85
11 Manganeso Mexicano — 93
12 *Montaña de Manganeso* — 100
13 Frank Senkowsky — 108
14 The Angel of Independence — 115
15 Falling in Love with the Poppers — 123
16 The Mysteries of Marriage — 133
17 Hans and My Grinding Mill — 142
18 Hans and Gretl — 150
19 New Partners, New Opportunities — 159
20 Ah, San Francisco — 172
21 At Odds — 189
22 Destroyed — 201
23 *Ramparts* — 209
24 Chicago's Fierce Dogs — 222
25 Everything Changes — 229

26   *The Pentagon Papers* and Project Harvest Moon   234

27   Moving to London   238

28   Adrift   244

29   Wild and Crazy in New Hollywood   255

30   My Gstaad   265

31   Gaining Traction   277

32   Turning Fifty   285

33   The Citizens Party   290

34   Seeing What Wasn't There   309

35   Being Dead Is Bad for Business   315

36   Finding My Voice   323

37   Counselor   330

38   There's Something About Charley   338

39   Coming of Age   351

40   Crossing a Ravine on a Rope   361

41   Growing Our Footprint Across the World   372

42   Looking in the Mirror   389

43   Bleeding on the Keyboard   404

44   Finding Gold After All   419

      EPILOGUE:
      Seventy Years to a Better Vocabulary   428

      ACKNOWLEDGMENTS   434

      ABOUT THE AUTHOR   436

The Atomic Bomb Saved My Life

The atomic bombs that America dropped on Japan in August 1945 took more than 200,000 lives. But they probably saved mine.

At the time, I was a young sergeant in the United States Army being readied to participate in the full-scale invasion of Japan. The previous year, I had enlisted in the service just three weeks after my seventeenth birthday, a skinny Jewish kid from South Philadelphia eager to follow my older brother into war.

None of us knew how long the war in the Pacific would last. The reports about the nearly three-month battle for the island of Okinawa were gruesome, with more than a hundred thousand Japanese dead, many by suicide. We didn't know that America had suffered almost fifty thousand casualties, although we'd heard the number was massive. Still, we knew the invasion of Japan would likely begin from this battle-scarred island, and we all assumed that the Japanese homeland would be defended with equal ferocity. It was predicted that the mission would take the lives of more than a hundred thousand American GIs.

But then the bombs were dropped on Hiroshima and Nagasaki. The war ended. And I was spared.

I sometimes think of all the things that wouldn't have happened in my life if the invasion had gone forward. Chasing lovers to Paris and San Francisco. Running from banditos in Mexico. Making my fortune as a treasure hunter of sorts. Getting to know leaders, thinkers, and entertainers through my work as a philanthropist. Visiting all those unforgettable places, from San Luis Potosí to Bali to Rajasthan to Phuket to the Golan Heights.

I think of the experiences I've had over the past seven decades, and of the remarkable people I've been privileged to meet: the slopes in Switzerland where I learned which James Bond didn't know how to ski . . . the salon dinners at my home in London with everyone from Freddie Forsyth to Jung Chang to Dame Edna (Barry Humphries) to Lord Carrington, the last surviving member of the Churchill government . . . the spirited conversations between my Gstaad neighbors and pals John Kenneth Galbraith and Bill Buckley . . . the wild times in San Francisco and Hollywood with my circle of famous friends in the late 1960s, and the nervous hours spent one weekend worrying about the Beat poet who got lost in the snow . . . the thing Jackie Kennedy once said to me that I'll never forget.

I think of the opportunities I've had to create a better world, and the sometimes painful journey I've traveled from being a naïve boy with father issues to becoming a man and a father in full myself. The organizations I founded in Washington, DC. The magazine I tried to control and the political party I tried to start.

Above all, I think about the magical ride I've had with my wife Lisa, the love of my life for more than half a century—who barely escaped the Holocaust with her family—and the extraordinary children we raised together and the incredible fun we continue to have with their children.

I now realize that in the seven decades since the war, I've come full circle—from being a young soldier whose life was saved by an atomic bomb, to becoming an international business executive whose company achieved great success by selling a mineral that made nuclear bombs possible, to emerging as a philanthropist who has spent thirty-five years working to assure that not one nuclear weapon will ever be used again.

I'm not sure if that makes me a success or a hypocrite, an idealist or a realist—part of the solution or part of the problem. You probably aren't sure either, and you probably don't have a preconceived notion about this, because chances are that you've never heard of me.

So, in encountering this story, you may find it to be the embodiment of a generation of Americans now largely gone—a generation, as the historian Arthur Schlesinger once wrote of the young Kennedy administration, that saw "the world as plastic and the future unlimited" and that believed itself capable of shaping and molding the planet as we desired and we dictated, mostly for good. Or you may see it as a story of outsize ambition and influence, one in which big American companies—and the entrepreneurs who lead them—play too large a role in the world and seek to solve the earth's ills only after they've played a role in causing those ills in the first place.

I'm not sure what you'll think of me—all I can do is tell the story and let you be the judge. But wherever you come out, I think you'll agree: that it's an improbable American life.

Stanley A. Weiss
Washington, DC
September 2016

INTRODUCTION

A Sunny Town for Shady People

My life was changed by a movie.

I know a lot of actors and actresses have stories about how their careers went in a different direction after seeing so-and-so on the silver screen, or after getting a big break from such and such that launched them into the stratosphere. But this isn't that kind of story. I'm not an actor. I'm a treasure hunter who literally saw a film and decided on the spot to move thousands of miles away and dig for minerals I didn't know, in a country I'd never been to, facing a language I didn't speak. It was the mother of all impulsive decisions—but it brought more adventure, friendships, and fortune to my life than I had ever thought possible.

And it all started with Humphrey Bogart.

The year was 1951. I was a student at the School of Foreign Service at Georgetown University, nursing a heartbreak, with little idea what I was going to do when I graduated. I had no job prospects and no money, aside from the small stipend I received through the GI Bill after serving in the US Army during World War II.

A friend from back home in Philadelphia, Al Himmelfarb, had come to campus earlier that day. From time to time during the school year, Al visited me to tout one offbeat scheme after another to make money in some exotic place. This time, after several scouting trips to Mexico, he was convinced we could get rich mining something called manganese. I knew next to nothing about Mexico, and I had no inkling what manganese was. I wasn't even sure how to pronounce it. I liked the idea and I'd always been a risk taker, but the thought of mining in Mexico seemed too daunting a challenge.

After Al left, I felt depressed. I decided to go to the movies. I saw a film that had been released a few years earlier, shot by the then-up-and-coming director John Huston. Like his celebrated first film, *The Maltese Falcon*, this movie starred Humphrey Bogart and the director's own father, Walter Huston.

It was called *The Treasure of the Sierra Madre*.

The opening scene of the movie, set in Tampico, Mexico, in the 1920s, hooked me. Two of the characters embodied competing essences of me at the time: one resembled who I was then; the other personified who I wanted to be. Dobbs, a penniless American in tattered clothes, wants to pick up a cigarette butt from a gutter, but a Mexican bootblack beats him to it. This loser, played by Bogart, repeatedly asks another American, dressed in a white suit, to spare him a dime. The opulent American, played by John Huston in a cameo role, gives him a handout three times before telling Dobbs, "From now on, you have to make your way through life without my assistance."

Though I would have denied it then, I must have subconsciously recognized in Dobbs some struggling part of myself, not because I would have ever begged, but because with a newly broken heart and an uncertain future, I was emotionally in the gutter. At the same time, I identified with the guy in the white suit, because he was the man I wanted to become: generous, strong, tough—and rich.

The next big scene ignited the core of the story and grabbed my imagination. Dobbs and another American down on his luck overhear a wizened elderly prospector tell some guys in their flophouse: "Gold in Mexico? Why, sure there is. Not ten days from here . . . a mountain's waiting for the right guy to come along, discover her treasure, and then tickle her until she lets him have it."

It was like the old-timer was speaking directly to me, telling me to seize the one opportunity I had, to begin in earnest pursuing my most rampant dream: to make lots of money. Like Dobbs, I was totally ignorant about mining, and I didn't want to sit around, "waiting for a job" and seeing my "money getting shorter every day."

The movie roused in me an appetite for adventure. I wanted to know the thrill of taking a chance, to get the kick from betting on myself, to discover the grit needed to fight off banditos. I wanted the movie's romance, too: the journey to a new land that was like nothing I had imagined or experienced. When the miners hacked a trail through the jungle—and later, when a windstorm beat them into the desert sand—I fantasized about pushing myself to my limits.

I saw only the allure and shrugged off the movie's grim view of money. The old-timer warned that gold corroded men's souls: "You lose your sense of values and your character changes entirely." But I was sure that whatever treasure I might be lucky enough to find wouldn't change me, let alone drive me crazy like Dobbs.

The twenty-four-year-old boy who walked into that movie theater was impulsive, instinctive, unreflective, ravenous, lusty, ready to leap. And something the man in the white suit said lodged itself deep in my soul: "If you don't take a risk, you can't make a gain."

Before the movie even ended, I had absolutely resolved to go to Mexico to make my fortune mining manganese. The next morning, I learned I could earn credits at Georgetown if I enrolled in a summer course at Mexico City College, and I confirmed that my GI Bill would pay for it. I rushed home to pack. My aunt gave me $600.

A week later, I crossed the bridge over the Rio Grande from Brownsville, Texas, into its neighboring town, Matamoros, and entered Mexico for the first time.

The gas station attendant in Matamoros cackled when I asked him how to get to Mexico City. He sensed I knew nothing about his country and must have relished throwing a scare into a gringo just for fun. He told me to take the high route over the Sierra Madre Oriental Mountains and then make my way south to the capital city, which is 2,500 meters above the sea. I did the math; Mexico City was more than 8,000 feet above sea level. For some reason, this made me break out in a sweat.

So far, the pleasant trip from Philadelphia to Matamoros had relaxed me. I had never been much of anywhere in America, so I'd wanted to take in the lovely Blue Ridge Mountains in Virginia and Tennessee. An easygoing schoolmate, also heading to Mexico City College, rode shotgun and split the cost of the gas. As we drove through the mountains' flowering spring, I relaxed into a haze of rosy optimism. All I had to get me started was a book I had bought, called *How to Look for Minerals and Metals*. Yet I was completely confident I would live a rich, romantic, exciting, and independent life.

I felt quite differently later when I hit the first hairpin bend in the narrow two-lane road, high in the Sierra Madre Oriental range. I had paid no attention to the snickers of the guy at the gas pump when he warned us about the Tommies and Charlies, nicknames for the route's treacherous curves. Tommies was an Americanization of Tamaulipas, the state where we were driving. I never found out where the term "Charlies" came from.

When I arrived in Mexico City, I fell sick with dysentery. I couldn't eat, and became unhealthily skinny and darkly depressed. Worst of all, my bizarre fear of being a mile and a half above sea level filled me with an all-consuming, debilitating sense of dread. I constantly imagined I was going to fall through the floor or the street or my bed or the seat of my car into a suffocating, formless, bottomless space without sound or light or air. It made no sense.

I was too unnerved by my fears to try to figure them out, and anyway, I had no appetite or capacity for self-analysis.

I told myself that I simply had to do or die. My refusal kindled a drive to do whatever it took to realize the "me" I wanted to become. In spite of my physical and psychological exhaustion, a stubborn willfulness—now a familiar part of my character—kicked in for the first time.

⁂

I BEGAN MY SEARCH for gold in the bar at the Hotel Ritz in Mexico City. It was hardly ritzy at the time. The bar was filled with down-and-out prospectors who had spent their whole lives trying to hit it big but had only wound up cadging drinks and smokes. I almost expected one of them to come over like Bogie's Dobbs in *Sierra Madre* and ask me, "Brother, can you spare a dime?"

I struck up a conversation with a real-life old-timer, a nice seventy-three-year-old guy named Malkin. Like Howard, the grizzled veteran in the movie, he was a straight shooter, didn't want anything from me, and seemed to know everything about prospecting. I told him I wanted to look for gold and showed him the manual I had bought to get me started.

Malkin set the book aside and began to tell me what he had learned the hard way, from experience—street wisdom that I never would have found in a guidebook. "Go to a village in a mining area," he said. "You are white and American. Members of the local indigenous tribe will come to you, think you are rich, and take you to where the 'mines' are. You'll need to pay them something. They'll usually try to trick you by showing you some fool's gold, but you might get lucky anyway and strike it rich. Even if you don't, the experience will be worth it, because you'll learn something."

Then he told me the best place to mine was in the southwestern state of Guerrero, but it was dangerous there, and I'd likely be killed.

Looking back, I realize this was the first in a series of conversations in my newly minted career that would eventually give birth to the one cardinal rule that guided my decision making for the subsequent seven decades: If you want to succeed, don't die. What I wanted to be more than anything in life was a success. And unless you are Elvis Presley or Michael Jackson, being dead is bad for business.

Despite Malkin's warnings, I found this heady mix of treasure, danger, and adventure irresistible. The next day, I returned to the Ritz, but I couldn't find Malkin. I met another older guy there who gave me the impression he knew lots about prospecting. He said he could help me find gold in Guerrero. I thought he would be good company, and he told me he would pay his way, so I invited him to join me. We drove due south on a serviceable highway built to ease traffic through Guerrero's very mountainous country to its capital, Chilpancingo. Everything in the area was primitive, and as soon as we got off that road, we had to deal with crude trails barely passable in my Chevy.

My new friend guided me to a village. He said he knew there was a mine nearby where I could find gold. Just as Malkin had predicted, some members of the local indigenous population came to me and offered to take me there. It was clear that the trek was going to be rough, so I left my friend behind and entrusted him with one of the few valuables I had brought: a bottle of scotch.

I stomped around in the wild for more than two days and nights looking for that damned mine, sleeping out under the stars, getting bit by mosquitoes, following the indigenous Mexicans here and there and everywhere. When we finally found a dig, there was nothing there. I realized the locals had no idea where to find gold. They had deliberately run me around in circles.

When I picked up the supposedly savvy old-timer back at the village, he was drunk. By now I knew he too had no idea about mines in Guerrero. My bottle of Johnny Walker Red looked full, but my first swig told me he had already drunk most of it and watered down the rest to try to fool me. He even used dirty water.

⁂

I HAD BETTER LUCK when I headed to the resort town of Cuernavaca, about an hour's drive south from Mexico City, searching for both gold and fun. I was not the first. The town's soothing temperatures and lush breezes had attracted pleasure seekers for centuries. Aztec emperors had summered there. Cortés, the Spanish conquistador, built a palace there. Emperor Maximilian I entertained in the gardens of his summer retreat there. But none of those guys had as much fun there as I did with a female bullfighter who shared my love of adventure.

Cuernavaca's nickname, "a sunny town for shady people," intrigued me. The author Malcolm Lowry revealed its seductive lure in his classic novel, *Under the Volcano*, a book about death, fatalism, and a doomed alcoholic. He reported that "the ghosts of ruined gamblers haunt" bars that once were casinos and "a certain air of desolate splendor pervades." He found the twin volcanoes that watch the city "terrifying in the wild sunset."

I learned that the town's shady people came in many different tints. A set of exiled American communists lived there, doing their best with their stubborn convictions and ruined lives. The locals relished Rita Hayworth's frequent stays and wrapped themselves in her aura of glamour, unbuckled belts, and brutish ex-husbands. The town bragged that the infamous gangster Bugsy Siegel liked to visit, always leaving a whiff of the mob behind.

A smart set, mostly Americans, lived there or made the easy drive from Mexico City. Norman Mailer came to escape the woeful reviews of his second novel. Leonard Bernstein came to visit his sister, Shirley. Movie pooh-bahs and their entourages came down from LA to play. I easily mingled with this mélange of talents. When asked what I did, I said, "I'm a failed prospector." My line—at once mysterious, self-deprecating, and true—never failed to trigger an invitation to join in.

Once again, one of the local tribe members offered to take me to a mine. He showed me an ugly hole in the ground, haphazardly surrounded by piles of dirt a few feet high. Although I found it hard to believe I would find anything of value in such a crude dig, I coughed up enough rough Spanish to ask, "Is there *oro* in there?"

"*Si, señor*," he replied.

I gestured to the man, who was a foot shorter than me, to descend into the dark, mysterious hole first. I wavered for a moment or two, fighting back my fear of falling through the earth. Then I took a deep breath and followed.

We wiggled and wound from one space to another, over and down, a bit at a time, without a ladder, as if we were mountain climbing underground. After working ourselves down about twenty feet belowground, we dropped into a dark, low-ceilinged room. Trickles of light from outside and from the lamp on my miner's helmet dimly lit the chamber. Purplish flecks in the walls gave the room a subtle, magical hue. I had no idea what the rocks were.

"Is this gold?" I asked him.

"No, it's not gold."

"Then what is it?"

"It's amethyst."

At least, that's what I thought he said. But I knew so little Spanish, I couldn't be sure. I couldn't pronounce "amethyst" even in English.

Later I learned that the beautiful color of manganese comes when it combines with other elements. The presence of amethyst meant there could have been a rich manganese deposit nearby, a fact that flew over my head at the time.

I chopped off a piece of the wall with my miner's hammer. Once outside, I knocked off the dross. The rock's blue-violet beauty sparkled in the light. I gave my indigenous guide a dollar and headed back to the Ritz to show Malkin what I had found.

He had been right. I did learn some valuable lessons from my first try. I was thrilled that I had overcome my fears and descended into a mine. I was even more delighted that I had come out unscathed, and relieved that working underground was not as uncomfortable as I had dreaded.

Of course, I was disappointed that the glitter I'd found was not gold. But my first taste of prospecting made me want more.

⚶

I'D BEEN IN CUERNAVACA for a few weeks when a local group of indigenous Mexicans told me the Japanese had dug a tunnel outside a village twenty miles south before the war and left a deposit of manganese no one had worked for over a decade. I went with them to take a look at the mine. They led me to the tunnel, went in and brought out some dark material. No fool, I had them send it to be analyzed. I was delighted when they reported that the assayer said it was high-grade manganese.

I hired them to work in "the Japanese mine," as they called it. The eighty dollars a month I still received from my GI Bill covered their pay. In those days this was a fortune large enough to support lots of the families in the town, so the locals were anxious to keep me around.

I moved into the village, bought a horse, and named him Tom. I wore a sombrero and carried a US Army–issue Colt .45 pistol. Every morning as I rode up to the mine to see how the work was going, I felt the very model of a modern major miner. My transformation from Dobbs to the man in the white suit seemed imminent.

After a few weeks we'd gathered a large stockpile of manganese ore. I continued to insist that the workers regularly test their diggings. The work was going so well that I went to Cuernavaca on the weekends. I had lots of fun with a lovely dancer there. One Sunday I decided to show her my mine to impress her. We drove out to the village, rode up to the mine together on Tom, and went into the tunnel.

The next day the workers refused to work. They told me *la mina*, being feminine, was very angry and jealous because I had taken a woman into the tunnel. They believed the mine's curse made it too dangerous to work there. They wouldn't go back until I got a priest to bless it and lift the hex.

Even though the area was quite anticlerical, I somehow found a priest. He made a living by traveling on horseback from village to village like a circuit rider, and he looked like Friar Tuck from the Robin Hood stories. He insisted I kneel with him on the hard slate in front of the mine while he prayed. It took him hours to bless everything he could think of, above and below the ground. My knees still hurt thinking about it.

When the priest finished, I asked him how I could thank him. He pulled a pistol out of his cassock and challenged me to a shooting contest. I had been a pretty good shot in the army, but I was rusty, and my .45 felt clumsy. I hit nothing. The canny priest, on the other hand, could really shoot. He laughed at me, as did the workers. I joined in and laughed at myself. Everybody was happy. The priest rode off to another village, perhaps to find another victim for another shooting match. The miners went back to work, satisfied that his blessing had soothed the mine's hurt feelings.

Eventually I had almost enough ore for a shipment, and I was ready to make some real money. To make sure I had something to sell, I sent a sample of my own to a lab. I was astonished when they told me that it wasn't manganese. The locals had been conning me, mining pure slate and feeding me fictitious lab reports of high-grade ore.

Even though I was in a peaceable part of Mexico, I thought I might not get out of town alive if I told them what my lab had found. I quietly stole out of the village and never returned.

Back to the gutter I went. But by then, I had caught the fever for adventure. This, I decided, was a life that would suit me, something I could pour my whole heart into, something that could—and eventually would—bring the riches and respect that I craved more than anything. I would be the wealthy man in the white suit—all I had to do was make sure I didn't die in the process. This, it turned out, would be harder than it might seem.

I could hardly imagine the places my career as a treasure hunter would take me in the decades ahead: from grimy holes in the ground to the most glamorous groups of people and places imaginable; from encounters with gunrunners and bandits to audiences with presidents and movie stars; from tunnels that reached toward the center of the earth to a global race for minerals that would put me and my company at the very center of the Cold War between the United States and the Soviet Union.

As I look back, I realize that much of the adventure I sought in life, and my eagerness to live as fully and freely as I could while taking risks way beyond the norm, were to prove I was not like my father—a very decent but weak man. I didn't want to live my entire life so afraid to die that I couldn't live.

ONE

The Argument

I was fourteen years old that night in the fall of 1941 when an argument erupted between my mother and father during dinner. We four children had never heard our parents quarrel or even raise their voices toward each other, so their fight and its ferocity shocked us. Even now, I cringe at the memory of my sweet, gentle mother throwing a fury of complaints, frustrations, and accusations at my father. He winced and tried to dodge her criticisms, and then he gave up and silently hung his head. Their row triggered the end of my boyhood.

Walter J. Weiss was a good man and a good father. He'd sit on the side wall of our front steps, puffing on his pipe as I gathered up neighborhood kids for a game of baseball in the empty lot across Queen Street from our house, which also served as his law office. He'd take off his coat and tie for the game but still be decked out in his distinctive style—golf knickers, silk stockings, and two-tone semi-brogues.

He loved to perform for my friends and me before we played ball. He'd put on his hat, lean against our house, pretend to blow into his thumb, and run his head against the wall. His hat would tilt up, as if it were blowing off his head. We squealed in delight. My friends loved my father's little show. They loved him. And I got to bask in the reflected glow of their delight in him and his affection for them.

But my father was also weak. His mother made him this way.

When Anna Weiss and her husband, my grandfather Benjamin, came to America from Russia in the early 1890s, she had little cash but possessed two exceptional powers: a gift for making money and an iron will. She was a shrewd, tough businesswoman who constantly worked angles, a strategy that must be genetic considering my early follies in business. She found some way to buy several homes on Queen Street, one at a time, and she also bought most of the houses on Kauffman, the next street over, which we called "the little street." We called those homes "Trinity houses" because they were stacks of three tiny, square rooms—the Father, Son, and Holy Ghost.

The Trinity houses were hovels, really, and barely habitable. My grandmother rented them to black families, whom she called by offensive names—a memory that makes me cringe when I think about it today. She charged her vulnerable renters by the head. Once a month she let herself into their homes, put the squeeze on them face-to-face, and extracted whatever meager coin they had to keep a roof over their heads. This was right in the middle of the Depression, which started in Philadelphia months before the stock market crash of 1929. By the mid-1930s, only four in ten workers in the city worked full-time; the rest worked part-time or didn't work at all.

Everyone could see how Anna Weiss dominated her husband. A lovable soul, my grandfather sat quietly next to her on her bench, smoking his Helman cigarette, at peace with his role as a compliant consort. He didn't like to work, so he contented himself with some light maintenance of her houses, a bit of tinkering at most.

My grandmother made more than enough money to spoil her son too, even from his very beginning. When she learned she couldn't have any more children after his birth, she found a soothsayer to bless her baby to ensure he would survive and continue the family line.

My father's shaky habits with money are rooted, I believe, in my grandmother's pampering. She instilled in him a sense of entitlement, the notion that he was a step above other folks in the neighborhood. She underwrote his education at the University of Pennsylvania Law

School and indulged him in his Ivy League taste for snappy clothes, spats, a fedora, and a double-breasted cashmere overcoat.

Still living at home in his twenties and not yet a member of the bar, he ran for Pennsylvania state senator in the Republican primary in 1918, which he couldn't have done without his mother's financial support. I suspect he ran simply because she insisted that he do so. The local Republican bosses, the three Vare brothers, controlled the party's primaries in south Philadelphia. If they endorsed you, you won. If not, you lost. And they expected you to wait your turn. Apparently it wasn't my father's turn—his candidacy was doomed from the start. He lost in the primary.

My father never ran for office again. But thanks to my grandmother's push and venture capital, he had found his profession. He enlisted as a faithful full-time worker in what everyone called the Organization— the Republican city machine. I can see now that his position of subordination in his job echoed the one his mother had imposed on him as a boy. Just like his mother, the Organization would take care of him, as long as he did what he was told.

Later that year, in the best move of his life, my father briefly ventured out of his mother's shadow. In December 1918, he asserted himself and married my mother, Anne Lubin, a woman profoundly different from my grandmother but just as strong.

My father must have been struck to his core when he first saw her, a petite and beautiful woman with a natural grace. I can only imagine his delight when he began to discover the truths of her interior beauty as well. She had lost her mother when she was six years old and then lost her father to his second marriage. She grew up parentless, lived with her older sister, and supported herself as a bookkeeper. She developed her defining inner strengths on her own: her precocious self-possession, her quietude, and her infinite capacity to love. She was a strong, undemanding partner who gave my father what his mother had not. She encouraged him, reassured him, and reinforced his best self.

She also nursed him. That winter after their wedding, my father came down with the infamous Spanish flu. It had raged through Philadelphia in the fall of 1918, killing more people than in any other American city. It hit our part of the city especially hard. My mother took care of her new husband as he suffered chills, fever, coughing, vomiting, nausea, pains throughout his body, and the constant fear of passing the virus to her. Their young marriage, already bonded by love, now was fused forever in the fire of facing death together. My father learned just how strong and brave his bride could be.

By 1925 my father had been drawn back into his mother's shadow. My brother, Howard, had been born in July 1921; my sister Janice, four years later. (I would follow seventeen months after Janice, in December 1926, and my younger sister, Flora, would arrive five years after me.) My parents needed a bigger house for their growing family. They moved to 303 Queen Street, a house I assume my grandmother found and helped finance for her own reasons. I'm sure she was delighted to have her boy ensconced in the handsomest residence in the neighborhood, once again within her grasp.

My grandmother had disdained my mother from the beginning. Her rancor ran the gamut. It was petty: She felt it was demeaning for my father, while courting, to be forced to take three trolleys out to where my mother lived. It was financial: She resented my mother having no money to bring to the marriage. It was tribal: As a Russian Jew, she felt irredeemably superior to my mother, who was a Lithuanian Jew, or Litvak—the people who had led opposition to the strict orthodox teachings of Hasidism. It was the raw hauteur of an adoring mother: She insisted my father's bride simply wasn't good enough and never would be good enough for her beloved son.

The two women most central to my father's psyche would live only a few doors from each other for the rest of my grandmother's life. She incessantly maligned my mother for the next twenty years, and my father was too weak to stand up to her and defend his wife. Although she was as peaceable and gentle as my grandmother was quarrelsome, my mother was too strong and centered to be dominated. For decades my grandmother had bent our neighborhood, my grandfather, and my father to her will, but she had met her match.

MY FATHER DIDN'T LIVE lavishly, but he did live colorfully. He kept his wardrobe spiffed up just as his mother expected. We always had a nice Buick, which he loved to fill with a bunch of kids and whip off to the circus. He had box seats—third row—in the Baker Bowl on Saturdays, which ignited in me a lifelong passion for baseball and the Phillies. Guests were always welcome to join us for a meal cooked and served by Lillian Smith, our black housekeeper. He even took a house on the Atlantic seashore for us each summer, right in the middle of the Depression. He seemed to feel he deserved these perks.

We skirted the harshest consequences of his relaxed habits about money throughout most of the thirties. The Organization provided him with enough income to keep us afloat, rewarding him with a plum patronage position as they did for 85 percent of their other key division leaders who, like him, reliably delivered the vote in their divisions. They made him a city real estate assessor, a job with few duties that paid $5,000 a year, equivalent to about $80,000 today. In addition, the Republican machine would sometimes kick him a lucrative divorce or accident case that needed a lawyer only to help formalize a pregreased settlement before one of their judges.

After six years, however, he was let go.

My parents bitterly blamed Henry J. Trainer, the Third Ward's Republican boss and my father's direct supervisor, for this loss of our primary source of income. It didn't matter to them that the Depression, defeats in city elections, and hostile state and New Deal administrations had greatly reduced the number of such jobs Trainer and the Republican machine could dispense. They believed the boss had enough juice to protect my father if he so desired, and they felt Trainer owed the same loyalty to my father that my father had shown him.

I learned much later that shortly after my father lost his assessor's job, my mother, with nowhere else to turn, asked for help from her well-to-do brother. For more than two years, my uncle, Nathan Lubin, rolled up in his big black car every weekend or so. My cousin Hilly would hop out, and we would run off to play. I had no idea that the primary purpose of these visits was for my uncle to hand my mother enough money to support us for the next week or two. A couple of months before the big argument, my uncle died.

My mother's last resort was gone. Once again we had no income, so that night at dinner she railed against my father's inability to provide. She complained that he didn't have the backbone to collect overdue fees from his clients. She blamed him for not having the strength to stand up to Trainer.

She was also exasperated with his unwillingness to ask for money from his mother. It's not clear to me that my grandmother had ever helped us much in other tight times, and she had become even more hard-edged in her final years, but my mother knew she had more money than we did. And as my mother bemoaned my father's timidity that night, her resentment of his repeated failure to assert himself and to stop his mother's abuse of her over the years welled up and spilled across the table.

Every day my mother struggled with the humiliating, unrelenting reality my father avoided. We were out of cash and out of credit. We were way behind on our mortgage. We had run up a tab with our grocers. We hadn't paid Lillian for ages. My mother simply could not bear the stress alone anymore, and her outburst was a cry from her heart for help from my father.

MY MEMORY OF THEIR argument has had an enduring dark power over me all these years. Until that evening, I had viewed my parents through the rose-colored glasses of a carefree boyhood, but the argument, like the climax of a light comedy that unexpectedly takes a dark turn, revealed their most fundamental characters to me. My instinctive reaction to what I learned about them changed me.

For the first time I had to face the reality that my loving father was a weak and fearful man. His failure to protect our family financially was only one aspect of his weakness. He lived in constant fear, too anxious to assert himself and too timid to take risks. His fear that he would be castigated for making a wrong choice made him indecisive, so he hid instead in the protective custody of his mother and his boss, safely doing whatever they told him.

He also feared dying. His mother never let him forget he'd almost died as an infant. The limp he acquired in a high school football accident likely warned him further of his body's vulnerability. I suspect his near death from the Spanish flu continually preyed on him too. He was a hypochondriac with an infinite list of imagined maladies. By the night of their argument, real afflictions—high blood pressure and too much weight—were making him ill.

The night of the argument was also the first time I became conscious of my mother's strength. She had developed her character as a young woman without parents. She had fearlessly nursed her young husband in the grip of a plague. She had held my grandmother resolutely in check for years. She had asserted herself when we needed help, finding a college scholarship for my brother, Howard—whom we all know as Buddy—a fine high school for me, and money to support our family when there was none. Her strength of character had kept the peace among us and served as the unstated moral center of our home as we grew up.

The argument must have served as a catharsis for her. I never heard her raise her voice again, but from that night on she assumed the ultimate responsibility for our household's security and anchored our family with resolute, uncomplaining courage.

All these years, a vivid picture of my mother's indomitable character has sporadically floated up from my memory and broken my heart. Not long after the argument, she found a job selling corsets door to door. Someone had to pay the bills, and peddling women's undergarments wasn't beneath her. I can still see her packing her sample case every morning, ready to march from house to house, knowing she would face repeated rejections. She'd return home late in the afternoon, exhausted from the heat and difficulty of the day but with her dignity and resolve intact. What a woman!

My mother's struggle marked me in an indelible way. Barely a teen-ager, I pledged to myself that I would do what my father had not: find a way to provide for my mother so she would never want for money or be forced to work in that way again. I would succeed where my father had failed.

It would be a long time before I made money. But over the years, whenever I have recalled this image of my mother's doggedness, it spurred me on.

TWO

Lessons from Queen Street

Queen Street in Philadelphia was where I first learned to love fun. Competitive games were my favorite. I loved winning, and I usually did win. More serious fun came during the 1930s from studying clay modeling with a communist who had recently returned from the Spanish Civil War and learning clarinet from Mr. Gigliotti, an admirer of Mussolini. I grew quite enamored of the clarinet and enlisted four friends to form the Stanley Weiss Orchestra. We never made it big, but we played at my sister Janice's wedding and a couple of bar mitzvahs.

And then there was baseball. Like most kids my age, I was obsessed with the Phillies. Even though they were one of the worst teams in the National League—at one point losing more than one hundred games in six of seven successive seasons—it didn't change the love we felt for them. During summers, a group of friends and I regularly snuck into games through a hole in the fence on the Broad Street side of the Baker Bowl. Wedged into the surrounding neighborhood, the field had some of the most absurd dimensions in baseball, with a cavernous center field and a really short right field, albeit with a sixty-foot wall. As we came into view of the field, my eyes immediately went to my favorite player, the one star the team had during that era: the "Hoosier Hammer," Chuck Klein. A prodigious home run hitter and terrific outfielder, Klein was the National League's Most Valuable Player in 1932. A year later, he won the Triple Crown when he hit .368 with 28 homers and 120 runs batted in. I held my bat like him and ran the bases like him. For most of my childhood, I wanted to *be* him.

Not all my fun happened on Queen Street. I spent a lot of summers as a teen in Arden, Delaware, with my cousin Hilly, my boyhood hero. He was three years older than me, and he was handsome and sophisticated. He played more obscure sports I had hardly heard of, like field hockey, and he taught me how to play racquetball.

His family's thriving restaurant business in Chester, Pennsylvania, brought in enough money for them to have a summer place in Arden, a village and art colony that was as pastoral as Queen Street was urban. There were no city streets, only byways like Pond Road, Pump Path, and Appletree Lane. Its cottages and bungalows spread out irregularly, each in its own plot. Arden offered a village green and a freshwater swimming pool that locals had made by damming the creek and directing the water into a corner of concrete walls.

In Arden, I was as free to chase fun as I was at home. Such freedom for the young was embedded in the town's culture. For years after its founding in 1900, children even voted in its town meetings. The arts-and-crafts soul of the place generated a flood of organized activities for kids, such as parades, fairs, and masquerades. And the midsummer nights invited some unorganized escapades too, such as hiding in the trees to sneak a peek when the girls skinny-dipped.

Arden also offered us kids a rich menu of music and theater, so I brought my clarinet and sat in when someone was jamming. Hilly loved the stage. He performed Shakespeare and Gilbert and Sullivan, and he played in the town's Robin Hood Theatre in the summer stock company, a mix of residents and some of Broadway's biggest on a busman's holiday. One summer he got me cast in *The Wizard of Oz* as the Scarecrow. The part seemed a good fit; I was as skinny as a scarecrow, and I sang "If I Only Had a Brain" as if it had been written especially for me.

I had some of the best times in Arden with Dan Bloch, who became my closest friend. His father's leather goods business had gone bust in the Depression, leaving his family with only their little summerhouse to live in year-round—and leaving his father adrift. Dan and I mostly played pickup softball and hung out at the pool. I swam well, but Dan, a fantastic swimmer, always won our races.

In the summer of 1942 I was offered a job as a waiter at a new camp in the Poconos for Jewish girls, and I arranged for Dan to join me. We said we were seventeen years old, the minimum age to work there. He was sixteen, and it bothered him when I persuaded him to fib. I thought nothing of it. I was fifteen.

The summer promised to be a teenage boy's dream come true, until one night some girls spotted Dan sneaking up to their bunkhouse. They shrieked and awoke the palace guard. Dan was hauled before the owner and almost thrown out. A few nights later, I got caught too, trying to get to a particularly hospitable girl, and was summarily expelled. Dan left with me.

While my recollections of my earliest Philadelphia and Arden friends have mostly faded, Dan Bloch remains an integral character in my memories of those innocent seasons when our young lives seemed so uncomplicated and our fun came so effortlessly.

⁂

I HAD SO MUCH fun on Queen Street and in Arden because my parents let me run free. They didn't monitor me, push me, or hold me accountable. Sometimes my mother would send me to bed early if she felt I had been "bad," whatever that might have meant. But I would sneak out of my bedroom and onto the deck, and slip off into the night until I'd had my fun. I had the feeling that my parents knew exactly what I was doing but pretended not to notice.

My grandfather indulged me too. He would give me a nickel to buy him cigarettes. Sometimes I would put the coin in the drugstore's slot machine instead, betting that I would win a candy ball while getting his money back. When I lost his nickel, he might tell me, "Don't do that again." But then he would tilt his head a little, flash a twinkle in his eye, and give me another nickel.

While my parents granted me all this freedom, they held my older brother, Buddy, on a tight leash. They expected him to shine in every way. My mother frowned on his running around with his own gang of friends, even though they were older and more responsible than mine. She fenced him in, both literally and figuratively. It galled him that she never allowed him to climb the iron fence where we played baseball, even though I did. All of us kids did. She forced Buddy to take piano lessons, which he thought was sissy, and insisted that he practice even when the rest of us were outside playing catch. He would close the curtains and play softly so the guys couldn't hear him. I decided to play the clarinet on my own, because I liked it. And if I hadn't played it, no one would have minded. Buddy did what he was told. I did what I wanted.

My parents especially pressed my brother to excel at school. And he did, spectacularly. He worked hard and graduated from high school at fifteen. My mother insisted that he go to the University of Pennsylvania, like our father, and she secured him a political scholarship from a friendly state senator. Buddy graduated from the Wharton School at nineteen.

I felt no such pressure. No one paid much attention to my schooling, including me. My parents didn't seem to mind that I drifted through grade school, indifferent to the classes, mostly focused on avoiding the toughs who liked beating up on smaller guys like me.

In spite of my mediocre grades, my mother pulled some family strings to get me into Central High, a select school for smart kids. Although Buddy had excelled there, no one insisted that I try to do the same. I looked around at the bookish guys with their neat bow ties and horn-rimmed glasses and thought they were wimps. One day one of these guys stood up and announced, "Egad! The teacher split an infinitive." I thought he was downright weird. Only fuddy-duddy characters in comic strips said, "Egad!"

One history class caught my attention briefly, and one teacher made *Hamlet* real and alive for me for a while, but I was mostly bored with or clueless about the opportunities the school's distinguished faculty offered. I made no effort to develop the critical disciplines of learning:

the close reading of a text and the hard work of writing a clear sentence or grappling with a challenging question. To me, these things just had little value or appeal.

⁂

SINCE MY PARENTS DIDN'T draw any lines for me to rebel against at home, I waged my two feistiest boyhood rebellions further down Queen Street, one at my grandmother's home and the other at Rabbi Borenstein's. Every Friday night my grandmother commanded our family to celebrate Shabbat and eat a traditional Jewish meal with her and my grandfather. She kept a strictly kosher house, and she insisted that we observe the intricate web of Orthodox rules and rituals.

I dreaded these evenings. I found them revolting. The house seemed disgustingly unclean and was filled with a pervasive sour smell. Everything was old and musty, and heavy curtains darkened the rooms. I became sick to my stomach every visit. Years later I learned my nausea was an allergic reaction to buckwheat, the key ingredient in kasha, a Russian Jewish dish my grandmother always served.

My reaction to these evenings was more than physical. I was gripped every Friday with a visceral revulsion to my grandmother's incessant drive to dominate everyone in our family. She convened these dinners under the aegis of religion, and we had no choice but to go, especially since my father was her enabler. Each week she exploited her seat at the table to launch a fresh wave of assertiveness and control over us.

She picked her targets. My sisters should have been easy marks for her. But my grandmother paid little attention to either of them. In Orthodox Jewish life, girls were treated as second-class citizens, so her granddaughters were not important enough for her to waste her energy on.

She saved her ammo for her nemesis, my mother. Every Friday she fired a withering blast of judgments at her, criticizing the way my mother was bringing us up. She complained that my mother was not helping my father when he needed help. Above all she chastised my mother for not being religiously observant enough and for not faithfully keeping kosher. Her mastery of these dietary laws was complete, so she always had a fresh set of accusations to make.

It was hard for me to make any sense of these dramas. I knew that we didn't have a kosher house. We ate bacon and oysters, both of which my father brought into the house. But we gave the impression that we were observant, because my father lacked the strength to stand up to his mother.

My grandmother tried to bring me to heel as well, demanding this and requiring that. I didn't confront her or overtly rebel. Rather, I ignored her and waited for an opportunity to slip away.

She also pressured my father to make me attend our family's Orthodox synagogue every Saturday, but even as a boy, I couldn't stand the certitude, severity, and unbending self-righteousness that I found there, and it didn't seem right to me that my mother had to sit in a separate and inferior place. I would sneak out to listen to the radio and find out how the Phillies were doing. I did the same thing on Yom Kippur, to listen to the World Series. My father let me run. Although he played a prominent role in the congregation, he was more interested in chairing committees and hosting eminent speakers than in dealing with his son.

By contrast, one experience that had a deep impact on me was when Lillian, our housekeeper, took me to her black Baptist church. I had never seen anything like it. From the preacher's impassioned sermon, which got louder and more animated as he went along, to the unapologetic and vocal expressions of praise from the parishioners, to the music that just made me want to sway with the congregation. It was all so real and joyful, I absolutely loved it. This, I thought, was *my* religion—something I never, ever felt in the synagogue.

My grandmother did partly succeed in reining me in, by leaning on my father to make me attend the religious school held in the home of her friend Rabbi Borenstein. It seemed to me like a house of horrors, and I grew to hate it as much as anything I hated in my young life. Every Wednesday afternoon I had to subject myself to the rabbi's Hebrew language drills, his instructions on the Torah, and his boot camp for my bar mitzvah. My grandmother, no doubt, also expected her ally to teach me some discipline while I was under his thumb.

About a dozen of us would meet with the rabbi in a dark makeshift classroom. He would bang his bell—which was almost as large as his ego—to call us to attention. Then he would strut up and down the aisle, celebrating himself in detail. We were supposed to learn about famous Jews, but we mostly heard about Rabbi Borenstein. His narcissism knew no bounds. After every bar mitzvah, he would ask us in Yiddish, "What did they say about the rabbi?" He even asked this of my brother, who had definitely been the star of his own ceremony. He expected Buddy to reply, "Oh, they loved you, Rabbi. They gave you all the credit for my speech."

The rabbi was an ugly little man physically. He was even more repellent intellectually, and he had a cruel streak in him. One day he crept up behind me and hissed, "You're not reading." Then he whacked me on the hand with the whip he carried. As painful as it was physically, what hurt the most—and still seems intolerable—was the rabbi's degrading, self-indulgent abuse of power.

I loathed going to his school from the first day until the day I was finally bar mitzvahed. Much of my contempt centered on the detestable and noxious man, but I also resented being told what to do and what not to do—by anyone, but especially by Rabbi Borenstein. My most intense ire came from his requiring me to memorize words that had absolutely no meaning for me and then forcing me to recite them as if they did. Something deep inside me rejected this foul combination of cant, rigidity, and claims of absolute truth.

I resolved to suffer my fate by stubbornly remaining clueless. I refused to study, so I never learned anything. In retrospect, by defiantly staying ignorant, I only compounded my conviction that the classes were meaningless.

For a long time, I also employed a kind of guerrilla harassment, doing whatever I could to distract the rabbi from our lessons. I knew he was proud of Max Baer, the Jewish boxer who was World Heavyweight Champion in 1934, so one time I said, "Let's talk about Max Baer."

Off he went, telling us everything he knew about Baer. "Did you know Max Baer is Jewish? Did you know that he wears a Star of David on his trunks?"

To goad him I asked (using the degrading Yiddish word for "female gentile"), "Did you know Max Baer married a *shiksa?*"

Rabbi Borenstein snorted, returned to his desk, and left us alone for the rest of the afternoon.

After more than four years of simmering resentment, my rebellion finally boiled over. It was the stink of the classroom that did it. Of course, any swarm of fidgeting boys jammed into a room with no windows or air-conditioning on a hot August afternoon would stink up a place. But I was used to that kind of stink. I stank that way myself.

One day I found the stench so nauseating and suffocating that I couldn't take it anymore. A boy who worked in the candy store next door agreed to make me a stink bomb for a small fee. I slipped it into the classroom and triggered it without being seen. The exquisite odor—somewhere between rotten eggs and a ripe outhouse—filled the room. We ran out to escape, and the rabbi had to close the school for quite a while. My friends were elated, and I felt I had regained some of my freedom.

My boyish defiance of the rabbi continued through the climax of my religious education, my bar mitzvah in December 1939. My conduct contrasted sharply with Buddy's star turn five years earlier. As usual, he had performed perfectly, gracefully reciting the Torah in fluent Hebrew, precociously addressing the congregation, impressing the dignified gathering of notables, and thereby completely meeting our grandmother's demanding expectations.

I, on the other hand, barely scraped through my ordeal and despised every minute of it. I garbled the strange words in a dull, rote singsong. It must have been clear to everyone that I had no idea what the words meant. My speech was so bad, I'm sure it embarrassed the rabbi. It was a wild affair, because I had stacked the upstairs section with a bunch of kids from my gang, and they threw things and heckled me while I struggled.

We'd celebrated my brother in an elegant downtown hotel with a monumental reception, a lavish banquet, and an orchestra. We couldn't imagine how my father afforded it. He barely had enough money for the mortgage. After friends and family showered Buddy with the customary checks and cash, my father took him aside and said, "There are so many people here, your money might not be safe. Let me take care of it." Buddy never saw his gifts again. He assumed my father used them to pay for his party.

My performance didn't deserve much celebration, and I was glad to have an inexpensive reception at home. But I made sure to hold on to my cash gifts. I used some of the money to buy a bunch of balloons. A couple of weeks later I got my gang to help me blow them up and sell them on street corners to revelers on New Year's Eve. I made a handsome profit that night and enjoyed my first taste of free enterprise. I also enjoyed being free at last from Rabbi Borenstein.

WE MOVED AWAY FROM Queen Street when I was sixteen, a year or so after my parents' argument. My grandparents had died, and my father couldn't wait to unload his mother's holdings, including the dilapidated Trinity houses.

I had learned on Queen Street that I wanted to live free: free to make my own choices; free from being dominated, as my father had been by my grandmother; free from a boss like Henry Trainer, who would first jerk you around and then throw you away; free from arbitrary and abusive authority figures like Rabbi Borenstein who would attack your dignity to make themselves feel important; free from self-righteous talk and arrogant dogma; and free from the many terrors of life that haunted my father.

My passions for fun, freedom, and liberating wealth—to secure my mother's comfort—grew into permanent elements of my essential character. They existed more as boyish dreams. But I have no doubt now that these central parts of my identity took root in me in the home where I was born.

On the other hand, I left Queen Street with major parts of my adult self totally unformed. I had no sense of who I was. Having shrugged off Philadelphia's schools, I took years to begin to know my mind and how to use it for pleasure and purpose. I also had no experience with Freud's two cornerstones of humanness: work and love. It took me a long time in places far from South Philly to learn fully how to work. And years later when I found my first love, a magic carpet flew me to places I had never imagined and then threw me off, leaving me confused and disoriented.

THREE

The Chance

In the summer of 1942, the Nazis were terrorizing Europe and rolling into Russia. America had entered the war and agreed to create a joint chain of command with Britain to defeat the Germans, but it wouldn't be until November that Allied forces would invade North Africa in an attempt to outflank the German army. Largely unknown to the world, in January of that year, Adolf Hitler had finalized his "Final Solution" to exterminate Jews from the planet. On July 22, the German army began to deport hundreds of thousands of Jews from occupied Poland's Warsaw ghetto to the Treblinka concentration camp just northeast of the city, where prisoners were forced to cut wood to feed the burning of bodies in the crematorium.

As I started high school that fall, the leader of a bunch of pro-German kids at Central High had been spewing his anti-Semitism all over school like a poison gas. He had targeted me, ragging on me for weeks, belching the age-old stinkpot of slurs at me: Hymie, Yid, kike.

As I walked into the school's front hall one morning, I saw this wannabe Brownshirt pinning up a poster stamped with a spattering of blood-red swastikas. It celebrated Hitler's policy of killing people with deformations and mental disabilities.

As soon as he spied me, he tried to excite a knot of students by taunting me with the Nazi brag that eliminating such "inferior" persons would ensure they wouldn't produce "inferior" children. We didn't yet know for sure that the Nazis were murdering Jews en masse, but even

I, at fourteen, knew that Hitler's idea of racial hygiene was meant for Jews too.

Surprising us both, I busted that boy right on the nose, shouting, "Do you want to kill Jews too?" Nazi-red blood, the color of his damned swastikas, spurted from his nose. He slunk away, wiping his face with his shirtsleeve, muttering to himself. He never bothered me again.

I've often wondered what was going on inside me that made me hit that thug. I certainly didn't attack him out of some carefully reasoned political convictions. I didn't think deep thoughts about much of anything then, and my notions of Hitler had been shaped more by Charlie Chaplin's hilarious character Adenoid Hynkel, the "Great Dictator," than by reading *Mein Kampf*. Until that day, my only protests against Hitler had been the stream of artful schoolboy cartoons I drew of him.

Throughout my boyhood, I hardly considered hitting anyone. But when I bloodied the Hitler-lover's nose that morning, it felt right. It still does. I hit him out of some emerging instinct I didn't recognize or even think about. Though it would take the next five years, that day I unwittingly began my rite of passage to adulthood.

COMING OF AGE IS inherently mysterious. For me this transformation was a period especially rife with confusion, ignorance, and avoidance. Some cherished memories about that period, though they seemed clear and true for years, proved mistaken. Other memories, though accurate, capture only the surface of episodes I didn't understand at the time. Still others are incomplete, often because I wasn't paying attention. Many of the cute stories I later told about those years were a tangle of confusion and self-delusion covering up the central fact that I desperately wanted to become a man.

For a while I had my cousin Hilly as a mentor to help me sort out my teen years. He was about to be commissioned as a naval officer. His erect, commanding way of carrying himself fired my admiration. I envisioned him in his dress whites saluting, crisply barking orders, and effortlessly capturing the attention of a bevy of patriotic beauties. Still in the grips of my own boyish ambition, I yearned for his calm confidence and self-possession even though I had no idea what these qualities were or what to call them.

Three years before I punched that aspiring Nazi at Central High, Hilly and I had listened together to CBS's broadcast of Hitler's declaration of war against Poland. The Reichstag's cheers in the background chilled me, but Hilly didn't flinch, even though the invasion was personal for him, since his mother's family had come from Poland. He had believed for a long time that Hitler meant to conquer the world and that we would have to go to war to stop him.

During the Dunkirk evacuation of 1940—where 350,000 British, French, and Belgian forces were miraculously rescued from the beaches and harbor of Dunkirk, France, despite being cut off and surrounded by Hitler's army, an episode that essentially saved the Allied war effort— we tuned in to Edward R. Murrow on the radio every night. I thought it was all over for England, but when ordinary English citizens helped sealift their troops to safety, Hilly saw their efforts as a lesson to us Americans. He warned that we needed to rally like the Brits and to prepare immediately for the coming war by building up our dangerously inadequate navy and our expanding army—which at that time was only slightly larger than Bulgaria's.

Hilly and I were in Arden when we learned about the attack on Pearl Harbor from the special bulletin that interrupted our regular program that Sunday evening, December 7, 1941. We somberly put on our coats and went for a long walk on the empty paths of the village. We didn't say much, but walking with him reassured me. Hilly, already a mature young man, seemed mentally and temperamentally prepared for the conflict he had long projected as necessary and inevitable. My boyish imagination couldn't begin to conjure up what the war would bring or what it would mean for me, but I clearly remember believing that things would never be the same.

Four months after that night, Hilly went to war. The Navy deployed him as a gunnery officer on a battle-tested destroyer, first in the

Mediterranean and then protecting supply ships on the dicey Murmansk run to the Soviet Union. I wanted to follow Hilly into the fight, but I was only fifteen.

Buddy, my exemplar of constancy, character, and brains, also enlisted, in late 1942. The army drilled him and his unit throughout 1943 to harden them for combat in the coming invasion. When he joined, I became even more frustrated with my adolescence, because it kept me from going to war too.

⚓

AS MY GRADUATION FROM high school loomed, I chafed at still being too young to enlist. Although the Selective Service had lowered the draft age to eighteen in late 1942, I wouldn't reach eighteen until December 1944, a year and a half away. I wanted to do my part right then.

The news of the war enveloped us all with a reassuring red, white, and blue haze on the one hand and with glimpses of distressing reality on the other. The newsreels celebrated our wins and minimized our casualties, and it was easy to see that our side was, in fact, beginning to turn the tide in both Europe and the Pacific. But ghastly recounts of the Marines' bloody hell on Guadalcanal and the murderous screw-ups by the American army brass in North Africa trickled back to Philly along with returning casualties. It seemed to me that our winning the war was by no means certain.

My unconscious drive to prove my manhood also heated my passion to join the fight. The testosterone that was putting hair on my chest and making me want to chase girls was also generating natural aggressions in me. I probably wouldn't have known where to direct these angers in peacetime, but the war provided ready enemies: the Nazis and the Japanese. Everyone I knew felt the same fury and used the same angry words. I believed my hate was fundamentally justified. All this aggravated my itch to enlist.

I first tried to join the Marines Corps in early 1943. Though I was sixteen, I figured I could somehow sneak into the corps, since they had sent a high school friend of mine to the Pacific only a few months after he had enlisted. I wanted to be a Marine because I believed they were the toughest fighting men. Picturing war through a scrim of boyish romance and naïveté, I dreamed of fighting with the same ferocity and guts they showed on Guadalcanal, our first big win against the Japanese after six bloody, brutal months of fighting on what the novelist James Jones would later call a "pestilential hellhole" of an island. I had no idea how gruesome real-life combat had been there. In any case, all my efforts were for naught. The corps turned me down because I couldn't see well enough.

Then I got lucky. I heard about a program the army had created to train high-grade technicians. The Army Specialized Training Program deployed two hundred thousand soldiers to colleges and universities all over the country to take accelerated courses mostly in science and math. The army also invited qualified seventeen-year-olds to join the program as reservists. These recruits wouldn't begin their full military training until after their eighteenth birthday, but they would jump-start their college studies right away. I leapt at the chance.

On April 2, 1943, most of us seniors at Central High gathered to take an army exam in the same genteel assembly hall where we had listened to FDR's radio address rallying the nation on the day after Pearl Harbor. I learned later that almost a quarter of a million high school seniors took the same test that day, an impressive expression of the army's mix of meritocratic convictions and raw wartime pragmatism.

Because my grades had been mediocre throughout my schooling, no one believed I could pass the test. My dad was especially skeptical. But I was bullish. Despite my sluggishness in my classes over the years, I couldn't see why I wouldn't ace the exam. It was designed not to assess what we knew, like most school exams I had taken, but to find out how well we thought. In particular the army wanted to test our ability to learn and to reason through a problem. I found the test surprisingly easy.

A month later I received the official letter from an army general, certifying that I had passed and that I could enter the program with my parents' permission after my seventeenth birthday. Everyone was amazed; my father was astonished. I savored the moment. I was going to get my uniform at last.

DURING THE FIRST WEEK of 1944, just as I was about to enter the program, my brother was ordered to ship out to England. I went with my mother and Janice to New York City to say our good-byes.

Sending Buddy off to war that day filled me with unnerving and undigested feelings. Since I had never visited New York City, its scale and otherworldly bustle astounded, bewildered, and excited me. I was understandably daunted and dumbfounded by the lavish dazzle of the big city. I can see now how the difference between Buddy's maturity and my lack of it must have also unsettled me, even if I didn't know why at the time.

The four of us decided to go to a movie, probably because we found big talk too hard and didn't have enough small talk to fill the hours before Buddy had to report. We picked Hitchcock's fraught drama *Lifeboat*, a movie about a clutch of civilian survivors of a U-boat attack, struggling against the Atlantic and each other to stay alive. A mother drowns herself after losing her baby. The passengers almost die from dehydration. They have to amputate the gangrenous leg of one man. Another is killed by a treacherous German officer whom they club to death and throw overboard. Looking back, I find it astonishing that we watched this grim saga only hours before my brother would board a troop ship we knew would be threatened by German submarines throughout its crossing.

We had one last meal with Buddy, and as usual, my mother warmed those of us at our table with her quiet cheer and optimism. I worried most about her, but she was a toughie and didn't show whatever she was feeling when we left my brother at his assembly point near the docks.

That evening I sat on the night train back to Philly, trying with little success to gather my thoughts. Although Buddy and I had different tastes and temperaments, I had relied on him throughout my boyhood as the most reassuring presence in my life. That night I lay awake, worried that I would never see my brother again—and wondering if I was going to get the chance to follow him into the war.

FOUR

Enlisted

I was sworn into the army on January 10, 1944, less than three weeks after my seventeenth birthday. I was no longer a boy, but my sense of self was still a work very much in progress. During my first year in the army, I unconsciously tried to fill in some empty spaces. I took a middle name that I hoped would signal a special brand of manliness. I obsessed about my uniform, hungry for it to certify me as a real soldier. And I struggled to reconcile my idea of a fighting man with the army's puzzling insistence that I was smart. What I mostly remember from that time is wanting to kill Nazis. I didn't think much about the Japanese. The idea of getting killed, or the horrors of war, never even occurred to me. I hadn't yet learned that I wasn't immortal.

When I arrived at the Fort Dix induction center, a sergeant told me and two hundred other recruits to write our full names on the first of a seemingly endless stream of forms we had to complete. I scrawled "Alan" in the box that asked for my middle name, even though I didn't have one. I did this without much thought. I wanted to be an officer, and "Major S. Alan Weiss" sounded manly and elegant.

I have comfortably remained Stanley Alan Weiss. I like it. It still fits me somehow. From time to time when friends learned about my weird presumption and asked why I chose Alan, I told them I named myself after Alan Ladd.

"Why him?" they would probe.

I'd smile and say, "Shane! Shane! Come back!"—a reference, I realize, that is lost on most people under the age of seventy, my children and grandchildren included.

My cryptic answer came more from reflex than from thought, but it always seemed to ring true for my friends and me over the decades. The film *Shane* subliminally echoed the story of the war we were fighting in early '44, and we all carried this masterpiece of a morality play in our heads as part of our quip-ready cultural vocabulary. Shane, a gifted gunfighter, shakes off his reluctance to fight and stops a murderous land baron from grabbing the land and homes of ordinary, peace-loving American homesteaders. Joey, the youngster in the movie, worships Ladd's Shane as a strong, modest, handsome, and triumphant fighter, an ideal hero for a boy his age and presumably for me at seventeen as well.

But recently I realized *Shane* couldn't have inspired me to write "Alan" on my enlistment form. The film wasn't released until 1953, about nine years after I entered the army. So maybe I picked Ladd simply because he was so popular.

Then too, perhaps I was drawn to Ladd for another, more personal reason. The characters he played in *Lucky Jordan* and *China*, two clunkers released in the years just before my induction, were more than tough guys. Each flaunted the rules. Each lived and thrived outside the lines. Yet in the end they performed heroically, one foiling Nazi spies and the other destroying a Japanese division. These cardboard characters played by Alan Ladd somehow reinforced my sense that "playing the angles" might be part of being a man.

This was important to me because I had been learning to play the angles, to advance my own interests through well-thought-out schemes, in the months before I entered the army. I had wanted to help my mother financially, so I found a job at a fuel storage plant. We loaded highly inflammable high-octane gas. Not many guys wanted to do such dangerous work, so I was paid very well.

But after a while, I wanted to make some extra money on the side, so I organized a game of craps. I knew guys who wanted a break from our hairy work and who were happy to bet their pay. I was the House, so I didn't play. But the House always wins, in my case from a cut of each game. Now I was making some pretty good money in two ways, one straight and the other with an angle. This worked fine until I got caught, got fired, and lost both sources of the money my mother needed.

I quickly came up with another scheme: I took a job at the Mary Jane Shoe Store. Next I found a second job at the Railway Express, a precursor to FedEx. Then I got a third job at the post office across the street. Every morning I punched in first at the Railway Express amid a bustling crowd of coworkers. No one noticed when I slipped out to check in at the post office, and no one noticed when I then ducked out to the Mary Jane Shoe Store to work a few hours. At the end of the day, I'd circle back and stealthily check out my other two jobs. I was making a lot of money at this multi-nontasking.

One afternoon, moments after I had returned to the Railway Express, I felt a tap on my shoulder. "Hey, kid, do you work here?" the badge thundered.

"Yes, sir," I claimed.

"Walk over and show me where." When I took him to the most plausible place I could find, he asked the workers there, "Have any of you ever seen this guy around here?"

They all shrugged and looked away.

The badge took me to the door, gave me a brawler's shove, and yelled, "Get the hell out of here and never come back!"

After I had been in the army for three or four months, I got a letter from Railway Express that said: "We are so proud of you. You worked for us, and now you're serving in our country's Armed Forces. Please find enclosed, as a token of our gratitude and pride, a check for $200." I knew nothing about irony, but that didn't keep me from laughing all the way to the bank.

When I think now about my scheming, it sometimes mortifies me that I was so willing to be dishonest, bordering on criminal, to make money. But back in 1944, with my mother so constantly on my mind, I was willing to do whatever it took to provide for my family. I probably would do it all over again.

In addition to the money I was bringing in, I suspect that I liked playing the angles for another reason. I felt it took nerve to pull off these schemes. I was daring to do what my father had been too weak even to try.

⁂

AFTER MY INDUCTION AT Fort Dix, the army sent me to Lehigh University in Bethlehem, Pennsylvania, but they didn't issue me a uniform. When they gave me a weekend pass a few weeks later, I felt I couldn't go back to my neighborhood in civilian clothes.

For decades, when friends asked why I'd been so anxious to join the army, I told them I wanted to impress girls with a uniform. Though I'm not sure if this is the actual reason, the wisecrack always produced a knowing chuckle of recognition from my chums.

There was a hard kernel of truth in this patter. I had a growth spurt when I was sixteen. I was tall, skinny, and had broad shoulders, so I looked older. I was afraid that if I didn't have a uniform, girls who didn't know I was only sixteen would think the draft board had classified me as 4-F, which was army code for "not acceptable for service in the Armed Forces" due to physical, mental, or moral reasons. To be branded as 4-F was a terrifying stigma in those days. I worried that girls might gossip and giggle about me, imagining that some hidden, humiliating disability, such as flat feet or a hernia, was keeping me from passing my physical. I dreaded most that they might even suspect me of dodging the draft. (Years later, I was amused to learn that the term "4-F" originated during the Civil War, when the army rejected recruits who couldn't tear open gunpowder packages because they didn't have their four front teeth!)

It all seems ironic now. The burst of growth that made me physically more manly and more passionate to serve also made me feel more vulnerable to girls snickering that I was not willing or fit to go to war. I had told a swarm of girls in Philly for months that I had enlisted, so now, about to go home from Lehigh for my first leave, I had to come up with some khakis to show I really was in the army.

In the days before my first weekend pass, I scoured Bethlehem for an Army-Navy store and finally found what I thought was a proper uniform: a shirt, pants, a tie, and what we sometimes called an "overseas cap." I wore it on the train back home, feeling secure at last and looking forward to strutting my stuff to the girls and showing my mother she had two sons in the army.

You can see me sporting my "uniform" in a photo taken with her that weekend. We are standing in our neighborhood park, posing in an unwitting caricature of the army's "parade rest" that I would learn later in basic training. I'm leaning over her, sheltering her head with mine, holding her close with my right arm, just as a strong son and a fighting man should do.

My khakis at first glance seem sufficient to certify that I am enlisted, but a closer look reveals I'm not a soldier. My pants lack a GI crease; they're not even pressed. I'm wearing hopelessly scuffed civilian shoes. I have no brass or insignia. The camera catches me at a piercingly poignant moment: I want my clothes to show I'm a man, but instead they reveal I'm still a clueless boy playing dress-up.

I HADN'T REALLY CONSIDERED the fact that the army had admitted me into the program because they genuinely thought I could learn quickly and well. Once I was at Lehigh, the implications of their high estimation of my abilities and their ambitious expectations of me slapped me in the face. I found myself in classes with fifteen or so fellow students, all of whom struck me as brilliant. We were expected to cram the equivalent of eighteen months of college into about nine months of accelerated classes in physics, math, history, and English, taught by the university's regular civilian faculty.

I had always thought I was more clever than intelligent, and the kind of "clever" I aspired to include a kind of strength, like street smarts. But in my mind, "smart" smacked of weakness. I believed smart guys weren't fighters. They were sissies who wore bow ties, like the kid at Central High who said, "Egad! The teacher split an infinitive."

One source of my confusion came from a belief widely held in South Philadelphia as I was growing up: that Jews couldn't fight. Our entire community shared the unstated belief that Jews were supposed to be scholars and intellectuals, not fighters. The street reality we boys experienced mostly confirmed this adage. The Irish fought. So did the Italians and the blacks. But most Jewish guys in our neighborhood had no taste for a fight. Moreover, Jewish mothers incessantly taught their sons not to fight. In one of the earliest Queen Street stories in my memory, a mother calls down the stairs: "Hymie, what are you doing down there?"

"Fucking, Mama."

"That's a good boy. Don't fight."

Of course, the fact that all the Jewish men in our neighborhood had gone to war contradicted the notion that Jews can't fight. Somehow I failed to notice that some of these warriors, like Hilly and Buddy, were also smart.

The army confused me further by keeping me in technical courses I consistently flunked. I was in over my head in my math and physics classes from the start, so it made no sense to me when they sent me to Virginia Polytechnic Institute in 1944 to study differential equations and advanced physics. Still only seventeen, I was too full of myself to recognize the pettiness of my case and the absurdity of my whining about it in the middle of a war.

Later that year, my confusion turned into bitter anger at the army's keeping me in the kiddie reserve. The war was getting up close and personal for me.

In October 1944, kamikaze planes were attacking Hilly's destroyer, the USS *Bush*, in the Battle of Leyte Gulf—one of the largest naval battles in history, a part of our fight to retake the Philippines.

That winter, Buddy and many of my boyhood idols from Queen Street came under fire in the Battle of the Bulge. Attempting to split the Allied armies on the Western Front, Hitler launched a sneak attack through the dense forests of the Ardennes region of Belgium, Luxembourg, and France. Caught by surprise, American GIs fought frantic battles to repel the German offensive. As snow fell and temperatures plunged, many soldiers froze to death. In the end, General George S. Patton proved his tactical brilliance and burnished his reputation by driving the Germans back—but not before America suffered 100,000 casualties, the costliest battle in the history of the US Army. Of course, back at home, I didn't know the details, but I saw photos Buddy and others sent home of dead German soldiers. I felt it was a joke for me to march around the parade ground, study German history in English, and sit in another science class beyond my understanding while my friends and family were in combat. I wanted to get into the war more than ever.

But for all my heartfelt champing at the bit, I was one of the lucky ones. The army desperately needed fighting men, so they transferred almost all the men eighteen and older immediately into the regular forces. Thousands, including some guys I knew at Virginia Polytechnic, were sent quickly to the front, ill-trained for combat, and were killed. But watching them go, I couldn't wait for my eighteenth birthday.

It came at last, and soon after, the army ordered me to Fort Knox to begin my training as a real soldier.

FOR ANY SOLDIER WHO has ever trained at Fort Knox, there is a question that will immediately elicit a pained expression followed by some seriously unpleasant memories: "What can you tell me about the hills of pain?"

There were three of them, affectionately known as Agony, Misery, and Defeat. Over the years, Defeat Hill has also been known as Heartbreak Hill. During my time there, our basic training unit would begin our morning at daybreak by hiking up Agony Hill on the way to the weapons-training ranges. Even with our bodies rested and fresh, this climb was challenging enough, tramping on rough gravel, up a gradual grade, perhaps a mile long.

The much more intense torment came in the late afternoon when we had to trudge up Misery Hill to get back to our barracks and dinner.

This second hill rose so steeply that we seemed to be marching into it as much as up it. We carried a full pack, a steel helmet, a rifle, and our fatigue from the day's field drill. Some days, to push us to the breaking point, our sergeants ordered us to climb in double time. The army used Fort Knox's Misery Hill as a critical hurdle in our rite of passage toward manhood and into the fighting army. Marching up that hill, I began growing into a man.

Many of us got up the hill by anesthetizing ourselves in a Zen-like trance and stolidly following the rhythm of the man in front of us. Others drew on their fiercest will to fight off the stress, uncertain with each step whether they could continue to force their bodies to stay in line, but forever proud once they met this gut-wrenching challenge.

A few couldn't cut it and collapsed on the side of the road. The platoon sergeant would stand over them, shout at them, berate them, and humiliate them by maligning their manhood in front of everyone until they were finally moved by enough adrenaline and hate to struggle to their feet and stumble up the hill, marked forever with a scar of shame and self-doubt.

I was lucky. My spirit didn't need to spur my body—just the opposite. My body lifted my physical and inner self up Misery Hill with ease, and it took over as I faced the other rough tests of basic training too—including, later, Defeat Hill. I unconsciously developed the endurance to hike twenty-five miles with forty pounds of field gear and still smile. I relished the rigorous training they gave us. I liked the realistic combat exercises in which I slithered under barbed wire, my rifle at the ready, live fire whistling closely over my head. My body made me good at these drills.

My confidence helped me get along well with the guys I met in the barracks. The army was segregated then, but otherwise my unit included all kinds of fellows from all over the US with all sorts of accents and ways of thinking. For example, I had never met anyone from the South until then. Just as in the war movies of the time, we had to learn to live with one another, however strange we might seem to one another.

There were a few Jewish recruits in our unit, and we drew some anti-Semitic insults from some kids who had never met a Jew. One Jewish guy reflexively got into a fight whenever he heard such slurs, but I thought better of it.

I realized some kids were never meant to be in the army and needed help. If I saw someone struggling on one of our long marches, I'd pick up his gun and carry it for him. If someone was falling behind, I'd grab his pack and lug it until he could catch his breath. Although that might sound like bragging, it was the kind of thing we learned to do for one another. But one kid needed more help than anyone could give. One day our unit was scheduled to begin the exercise where we crawled under barbed wire as live machine gun rounds streaked over our heads. Before we headed out to the range, this kid was extremely agitated. He seemed terrified. He told me he wasn't going to make it. I told the range sergeant that I worried the kid might get hysterical under fire and get hurt, but the sergeant waved me away. The kid went anyway. And just as I feared, halfway down the course, the kid panicked, picked up his head, and got killed instantly. I will never forget that moment as long as I live. It was a stark reminder that I was no longer just playing "soldier." I was being trained to participate in a war that could kill me in an instant. Suddenly, I wasn't feeling so immortal after all.

WHEN I WAS WELL into my basic training, our master sergeant took notice of me. Apparently he saw something in me—perhaps I impressed him with the way I marched and did the field exercises and helped the other guys. He hung around our unit, keeping his eye on me and pushing me. Then he asked me to lead the platoon when we marched.

I had loved leading my gang around on Queen Street, but this was even more fun. I was an apprentice leader without a stripe, moving a platoon smartly through drills up and down the company street and on the way to classes. I loved leading thirty-odd uniformed men as they marched in time to my beat.

"Sound off!" I would shout.

"One, two," they sang back.

I learned to bark commands with the deep timbre of a drill sergeant, ordering, "Column right, *march*!" I still relish the echo of each trooper's right boot hitting the turn ("hut, hut") in the strictest rhythm ("hut, hut"). The sergeant gave me an opportunity to grow as a leader, and I took it.

The sergeant was one of the toughest men I've ever known. He was a big, burly Italian American, probably ten or fifteen years older than me. He had grown up in hard times in New Jersey—in Hoboken, I think—and had battled through the Depression on his own. He fought in North Africa at Kasserine Pass, which is remembered as the first major battle defeat suffered by the United States in the war, and came away as much a casualty of our generals' incompetence as of the guile of General Erwin Rommel, Germany's legendary Desert Fox. The sergeant's battered leg kept him out of any further combat.

When our unit moved on to special armor training, he accelerated my promotions to private first class, corporal, and sergeant, making sure I earned every one of them. He adopted me as his mentee, and I adopted him as my role model, the personification of the kind of strong, fearless man I wanted to be. His confidence in me confirmed and reinforced my confidence in myself.

The sergeant also made me a trainer in the armor school, where I taught troops how to drive half-tracks, a hybrid vehicle with wheels in front and tracks in back that promised high traction and maneuverability. These vehicles were so light and vulnerable that we called them "convertible coffins." Their only virtue was that if you were in the infantry, you didn't have to walk.

I also taught the trainees how to fire eighty-millimeter mortars from the back of the half-tracks. I was always considerate, and the men liked me. But I was a tough, demanding instructor, even though I was still only eighteen. I wouldn't let anyone goof off. If I really had a problem with a goldbrick, I would tell my mentor, the sergeant, and he would teach me how to make the guy measure up. I learned from the sergeant that requiring the troops to train well could save their lives in combat, and I didn't want to disappoint him.

We came to a fork in the road in the spring of 1945. He wanted me to become an officer, but I didn't. He and I dug in, our positions fixed, and our arguments became increasingly heated. When I pointed out that he wasn't an officer, he said, "That's right, and I'll never be one. But you're officer material." He pushed me so hard, I finally agreed begrudgingly to take the qualifying test for officer candidate school, just to get him off my back.

I'm sure I could have passed the test. The qualifying score for officer's school was lower than the score I had already made to get into the Army Specialized Training Program at seventeen. But I didn't want to pass, and I didn't. When the sergeant learned I'd failed, he was furious with me. He accused me of deliberately blowing it. He was so angry, I thought he was going to take a swing at me. I was too young to fathom why the dream the sergeant had for me meant so much to him, but I can see now I destroyed it, and turned his hope into a fury.

In the summer of '45, it was unclear how long the war in the Pacific would continue. I yearned to be part of the invasion of Japan as a sergeant. I believed then and now that noncoms, the noncommissioned officers, were more important in combat than commissioned officers. I also feared that if I were to become a second lieutenant, the war would be over by the time I had been fully trained. Moreover, I believed (probably wrongly) that to become an officer I would've had to commit to several more years of service, and I wanted to go home as soon as I had done my duty. My father was gravely ill. While I was visiting on emergency leave, my mother told me he wouldn't last a year.

By August, my buddies and I sensed that our training had been intensifying for some weeks. The army was clearly readying us to ship out to the Pacific. The reports about the bloody battle for Okinawa over two and a half months had, as Samuel Johnson might have put it, "concentrated our minds wonderfully."

The barracks were full of gossip that the Japanese had murdered American prisoners in especially gruesome ways, and we knew the invasion of Japan would be no picnic. Even an eighteen-year-old sergeant could project the costs in American lives to conquer the Japanese homeland. The war now seemed even closer, even more personal.

Then everything changed.

One day in early August, I sat with a couple of guys in the barracks and puzzled over the *Louisville Courier-Journal*'s story that an American plane had "dropped one bomb" on some Japanese city I couldn't pronounce and "destroyed" it. We understood how our B-29 long-range bombers had firebombed Tokyo with devastating results. But we were mystified to read, in words the *Courier-Journal* took directly from the Truman administration's press release, that this "atomic bomb" harnessed "the basic power of the universe" and loosed the "force from which the sun draws its power." What the hell did all that mean? We scratched our heads about this "greatest achievement of organized science in history."

I tried to make sense of the subsequent stories about Einstein and $E=mc^2$, but had no more success than I'd had in my physics classes. What mattered most to us was whether this would shorten the war and whether we would still need to risk our lives invading Japan. When we learned about the second atomic bomb three days later, we could see that the war was ending. Imagine our relief a week later, on August 15, when Japan surrendered.

Years later, revisionist historians argued that the Japanese would have surrendered without our using the bomb or invading their homeland. They believe we used the A-bomb not so much to save American troops lives but as a first step into the Cold War with the Soviets.

In the 1970s I became a close friend of the leading exponent of this revisionist view, Gar Alperovitz, a brilliant political economist and historian who earned his PhD at Cambridge and was both a founding fellow of the Harvard Institute of Politics and a longtime professor at the University of Maryland, College Park. We're only nine years apart in age, but we're of different generations, so we have understandably looked at this issue through different lenses. I was eighteen years old, fiercely trained and poised to be a part of the force that would invade Japan, when we bombed Hiroshima and Nagasaki. Gar was nine.

Nonetheless, I believe the samurai military who then controlled Japan never would have surrendered, and I believe an invasion of Japan would have been a bloodbath for everyone. I believe Emperor Hirohito ordered the military to surrender only because of the A-bomb. I believe President Harry Truman's decision to use atomic bombs saved hundreds of thousands of Japanese and American lives, probably including my own. I realize my beliefs are not based on academic findings. They are existential, a product of my direct experience and the feelings I had as my fellow soldiers and I waited in our barracks for our invasion orders.

Either way, I believed then, and I believe now, that the atomic bomb almost certainly saved our lives.

I LEFT THE ARMY on August 16, 1946, one year and a day after the Japanese surrendered and about two and a half years after I joined. I will always be proud I served. All these years, I have kept my helmet liner behind my desk, so I can look at my sergeant's stripes on its front and listen for the echoes of counting cadence in the mornings at Knox.

For a long time, while I was happy not to have been put in harm's way, I paradoxically felt my only important regret about my army service was not getting into combat. It was about foolish pride as much as anything—I never wanted to be part of a conversation among combat veterans where I was asked what I had done in the war, only to reply that I never saw action. Now I'm not so sure. My brother, Buddy, and his good friend Kenny Kahn, who became my brother-in-law, wouldn't say much about their wartime experiences. My friend Monte Pearson's wounds spoke for him.

Monte was the best athlete in the neighborhood, and it came as little surprise when he qualified easily to be a paratrooper in the legendary 82nd Airborne Division. He was part of the Allied invasion force that parachuted into Normandy on D-Day in June 1944 and survived. But three months later, his athletic grace was mangled during Operation Market Garden, when Allied paratroopers attempted to land in the Netherlands and capture strategic bridges along the Rhine as part of a larger effort to surrounded Germany's industrial heart, the Ruhr, and end the war by Christmas. It was the largest airborne operation in history, but it met fierce German resistance. As recounted in *A Bridge Too Far*, a popular book and movie later made about the battle, Allied troops sustained heavy casualties and were forced to retreat. Even those who survived—including Monte, who suffered injuries all over his body—were never the same.

We all knew guys like Monte. My closest friend and Kenny's younger brother, Lloyd Kahn, saw a buddy of his blown to bits by a grenade right before his eyes. It left him with a permanently shattered psyche, what we refer to today as post-traumatic stress disorder. But we didn't have a name for it then, and men like Lloyd were too proud to seek help for it. He eventually died much too young.

The kamikazes finally got Hilly's destroyer too, in April 1945. After three suicide planes broke his ship in half, Hilly spent two and a half days with a dozen or so survivors on a raft, taking turns in the water to keep it afloat. One sailor nicknamed Ski selflessly stayed in the water so the wounded wouldn't have to take a turn. But the night before their rescue, 'Ski couldn't hold on any longer, and he slipped off into the dark of the Pacific, never to be found. Hilly, haunted by the loss of his friend, still weeps when he thinks about it.

There is no question that I would have fought if called upon. But I've come to realize that I was lucky in being a little too young to be sent into battle.

Instead, I came home from the army marvelously fit. My body had filled out. Even so, my most important growth wasn't physical; it was internal. My self-confidence and sense of manliness had grown without any conscious efforts. I entered the army as a boy and came home as a young man—still with much to learn, but a young man nonetheless.

FIVE

Learning the Advantages
of Partnership

M y father died on September 30, 1946, six weeks after I returned home. The high blood pressure that had stalked him for so long finally triggered a cerebral hemorrhage that killed him in his fifty-first year. My mother stayed by his side until he slipped off into death, his body and his will to live too weakened to fight.

My mother was a model of strength and composure when we came out of his hospital room. She took me in her arms to console me even though she had just been widowed. Then she sat me down and took my father's wedding ring out of her dress pocket. She showed me the engraving inside: "Always." It was the first time I had seen the inscription.

Her bridal dreams proved prescient. My mother never dated another man. For the rest of her life she remained satisfied with the fullness of her years with her Walter, and she lavished her love on the family she and my father had made together.

I was infuriated but not surprised to discover my father left my mother with no savings or income. He had burdened the family's finances with one last indulgence, using the cash he made from selling his mother's houses on Queen Street to buy an upscale home in Wynnefield, an afflu-ent, largely Jewish suburban neighborhood northwest of the city. Fol-lowing his lifelong habit, he chose flash and show over fiscal prudence or taking care of my mother. Somehow she had managed to keep up a proper front, but it was time for me to step up and support her.

I got a job right away with my mother's cousin, Rubin, who wanted to expand his scrap iron business by buying and selling military surplus. In 1946 the federal government needed to dispose of $30 to $40 billion worth of materials left over from the war, and after years of scarcity on the home front, consumers were hot to buy almost anything. The government gave preference to veterans like me: the right to buy any surplus item simply by matching the bid of any nonveteran.

Rubin saw he could milk this lucrative market by playing an angle. He told me the items for which he had a ready buyer. I would match the bids and buy the items. He would resell them for a profit. He was making a fortune, and he paid me $100 a week, almost $60,000 a year in today's money—a lot more than my army pay and enough to take care of my mother. As with my money-making schemes from before the war, I sometimes wonder now about the ethics of our business and how this must sound today.

Even though I still had no great enthusiasm for school, I wanted to go to college while I worked. I expected to enroll at the University of Pennsylvania, the school from which my father, brother, and sister Janice, as well as Hilly and Kenny Kahn, had graduated. I assumed the university would give me credit for the courses I had passed in the army, and I would use my GI Bill benefits to pay my tuition.

When the dean of admissions refused to accredit my army classes and told me I would have to start over, I exploded at him. I resented his presumption in dismissing what I had earned in the army while he was sitting in his civvies smoking his pipe throughout the war. I resented his professorial bow tie and tweeds and the condescension of one more smart guy who wouldn't fight. I resented his protecting the university's unstated Jewish quota by making it hard for me to matriculate. I despised the academic sophistry that barely covered his anti-Semitism.

I told him to shove his university up his ass.

I was not surprised a day or so later when I received a card with a black border, like a funeral notice, telling me that I was not admitted into the university.

I enrolled at the Pennsylvania Military College, now Widener University, which happily gave me credit for my courses at Lehigh and Virginia Polytechnic. I settled into a daily rhythm, including afternoons working with cousin Rube on our next buys. My classes were so easy that they neither taxed me nor hooked me. I remained a virgin in the garden of ideas.

BY THE SPRING OF '47 I had learned enough about the war surplus business that I felt I could start my own business if I had the right partner. I discovered one in Stanley Kessler, who had earned his veteran's preference the hard way: as a crack fighter pilot, flying a full rotation of combat missions against the Japanese. Stanley was the brother-in-law of a close friend. My very first real business partner and I would go on to flourish largely because we trusted and could depend on each other.

We formed a company, made our own deals, and played our own angles. The government had surpluses of every imaginable product— tools, electronics, aspirin, typewriters, transformers, paper cartons— and offered them all for a fraction of their value. Kessler scoured the depots within a couple of hundred miles of Philly for items he thought we could sell.

I took Kessler's annotated lists to potential customers, made the sales before we bought an item, and asked our buyers to pay us up front so we could use the cash to pay the government. Once in a while we took a risk and bought an item before we had a customer lined up. One time we couldn't resist buying twenty tons of rope for almost nothing—certainly more than enough to hang ourselves, as it turned out. Buddy came home one day to find a mountain of rope blocking the front of his garage, where it had been delivered. We never found a paying customer, and it took several weeks to find a guy in the venetian blind business who reluctantly agreed to take it off our hands.

We had no working capital, so we sometimes got creative. Occasionally, we paid with a check we knew we couldn't cover at our bank, confident it would take weeks before the snail-like government bureaucracy would cash it. We quickly delivered the surplus item to our customer, insisted that he pay us on delivery, and immediately deposited his payment to cover our original check. Our angle was the ancient art of check kiting. We did quite well.

But we weren't doing well enough for me. I had an idea about how to make even more money by playing an even sharper angle.

The government disposed of many of its surplus items as scrap metal. Two firms dominated the scrap metal business in Philadelphia. I met the owner of one when I sold him scrap surplus machinery. I met the top executive of the other through his daughter, Margie, whom I was dating. Both men liked me, and I made a deal with each. I asked them to tell me how much they would pay for a particular parcel of scrap metal I knew the government wanted to sell. If the highest bid from a nonveteran was lower, I would use my veteran's preference to match it and buy it. We would split the difference. They always got a lower price; we always got a handsome cut.

I am sure my brother, who always did business with scrupulous rectitude, would have labeled my scheme "sharp," like my grandmother's edgy real estate dealings. Nevertheless, Kessler and I made *mucho dinero* in a short amount of time. By the end of 1947, I had amassed the equivalent of almost $1 million in today's money, enough to take care of my mother and then some. I was twenty-one years old.

The burgeoning patterns I followed in these early ventures became ingrained habits over the years. They reinforced my conviction that I didn't want to work for someone else, something I had learned on my first job when I was twelve years old. I made two dollars a day working in the storage room of a fur store on Wednesday afternoons and Saturdays. I liked the pay, and I did a good job. But one day the owner fired me. I asked him if I had done anything wrong. He said, "No, but my son is twelve now, so he can do this work."

I still feel the bite of his unfairness, and I resolved then that I would never put myself at the mercy of such arbitrary authority again—just ask Rabbi Borenstein. Later, the army reinforced my resistance to hierarchical control by telling me what to do. I haven't had a boss since my mother's cousin reaped practically all of the profits while I served as his shill.

Working with Stanley Kessler fostered another pattern I still follow: it taught me the advantages of having a partner. Again and again I profited financially and personally when I had a strong colleague. As was true with most of my subsequent partners, Kessler's and my individual strengths meshed well. He brought attention to detail and operational skills to our enterprise, while I built networks of clients and negotiated deals.

The enterprise Stanley and I created was lean—just the two of us. I didn't want to work for or with a bureaucracy any more than for a boss. Ever since, I've never worked with more than one or two degrees of separation from where we make what we sell.

The deal I made with the two scrap metal sellers foreshadowed the attributes I would need in business: the knack for detecting an unnoticed opportunity; the ability to win the trust of critical stakeholders; the facility to negotiate and close a deal; the nerve to crank up the stakes; the chutzpah to play the angles; the audacity to seize the moment; and the speed, agility, and decisiveness to act on my instincts.

During these years I also developed a strong opinion about the role that luck plays in life. I don't believe people make luck. I think that certain people are born lucky and certain people are not, and that's just the way it is. I think I was born lucky—both physically and mentally able to take advantage of opportunity wherever it strikes. But even if you're lucky, luck doesn't stay with you every minute. You have to know what to do with it when it comes. You have to be very disciplined and focused and tenacious. I didn't date the daughter of the scrap metal executive as part of a business scheme. I dated her because she was fun and witty and pretty and because I was twenty-one years old. Fortune unexpectedly smiled on me when Margie took me to her home one evening and introduced me to her father. It smiled again when he liked me. I could have left it at that. But I decided to turn that luck into an opportunity.

By the spring of 1948, my older siblings had found love. Janice married Kenny Kahn, and Buddy married Janice's best friend. Hilly wed right after the war too. I had no interest in such domesticity. I was still trying to grow up.

SIX

First Love

As usual on Sunday afternoons, I was playing football in the street in front of my mother's Wynnefield home. It was early September 1948. I was taunting the other guys with inane chatter when I saw her. I knew at once that she was not like any girl I had met. She had the most extraordinary dark hair I'd ever seen. She was graced with classically beautiful lips and nose. Her skirt and sweater perfectly fit her and the occasion, and they revealed an exquisite, understated taste.

Her carriage distinguished her from other women I'd watched. She held herself with casual confidence, shoulders back a bit, chin up a bit, at once erect, relaxed, and poised, suggesting self-possession and inner strength. She watched us with the studied remove of a curious anthropologist, surveying our tribal ways with a twinkle of detached good humor.

I was transfixed.

She looked at me and I stared back. Most girls I knew, when they first sensed themselves being observed, looked away, whispered to their girlfriends, and waited to feign surprise at the guy's next move. This woman did none of that. Completely comfortable with herself, she greeted me with an easy smile. I went over to her with no clue that I was walking through a door into another life.

She told me that her name was Barbara and she had just begun her sophomore year at Bryn Mawr. One of my friends had invited her to watch our game, so she had strolled over from the other side of City

Line Avenue to observe us firsthand. She had never seen guys play pickup football in the street. I had never met a girl from Bryn Mawr.

We both wanted to get to know each other better. She suggested we go to the zoo. It had never occurred to me to visit this pride of my native city—the first zoo in the nation, the first zoo to feed flamingos carrot juice to keep them pink. On our first date together, Barbara took me by the hand, led me away from my familiar path, and began what would be two years of tutoring me about the exotic. Her zest for the unconventional excited me.

I took her to some places that were new to her as well. I showed her my old neighborhood. We ate spaghetti at Palumbo's, where my father had his state senate campaign dinner thirty years before. We danced there to the King of Swing, Louis Prima, and listened to songs sung by the actor and tenor Mario Lanza, who had grown up nearby. We drank the restaurant's best Chianti.

Though only eighteen, Barbara had dated enough spoiled boys from Scarsdale and the Main Line to know what she didn't want. She was tired of collegiate clichés of reverse snobbery: cartoon-festooned corduroys, porkpie hats, and jalopies. She was fed up with the poking and insinuations of their clumsy fingers.

But she was curious about me. She liked that I had made my own money from scratch. She liked my blue convertible, because I had bought it with my own earnings. We spent a lot of time in my car getting to know each other. We discovered, among other things, that we held a powerful sexual attraction for each other.

Totally absorbed in each other, we spent all the time we could together. I gave up playing football with the guys. I stopped running around with my old neighborhood buddy, Al Himmelfarb, and I never invited him to get a date and join Barbara and me. His rough edges reminded me of the ordinary life I wanted to leave behind. He begrudged my preference for her smooth elegance and promising possibilities, and he complained I was going "high hat" toward him and the old gang.

In spite of profound differences in wealth, taste, experiences, ambitions, and habits of mind, Barbara and my family easily embraced each other without a twitch of resentment from them or a hint of condescension from her. She and my mother shared a natural graciousness and felt completely at ease with each other. Barbara was especially sweet to my sixteen-year-old sister, Flora, who was starstruck by her.

Barbara's every aspect aroused me. Like Gatsby's Daisy, she exuded an air of breathless intensity. I had never known anyone with such fierce energy. Her vitality was infectious. Her effortless elegance hinted at a wealthy upbringing and an awareness of the world I didn't have. She took for granted that she could go to places and do things that, to me, had been inconceivable.

One October weekend we drove to Arden. We strolled through the village and feasted our eyes on the reds and golds of fall. The summer people were gone, and we had the town to ourselves. The silence shut out the world and drew us closer together. We wordlessly retraced the path Hilly and I had taken in December 1941. We then strolled over to Hilly's home, nestled in for the evening, and became lovers.

We settled in for the weekend and opened our innermost selves to each other. She talked about her hunger to understand the meaning not only of her life but also of life itself. She described her pain when Bryn Mawr's academics scoffed at her search. She told me that her father's wealth didn't satisfy her and in fact drove her to find a larger purpose.

I listened to her, fascinated. I didn't understand everything she was saying, and I lacked the words to tell her how much she moved me. But I whispered as best I could to her that I wanted to learn from her, to hitch myself to her and go along for the ride.

⚜

WEEKS LATER, BARBARA AND I traveled to her home in Scarsdale, New York, because she wanted me to meet her father. Louis Marx was born in Brooklyn of Jewish immigrants from Berlin, and he'd spoken only German until he was six. His background was similar to my father's, but unlike my father, he was strong, aggressive, and financially successful.

Marx had quickly driven himself to the top of the country's toy industry and dominated it for a generation as "America's Toy King." His company would go on to be the largest toy company in the world in the 1950s, a success so great that he would appear on the cover of *Time* magazine in December 1955 with Santa Claus. For decades he created waves of new toys—tin trains, yo-yos, and his first big winner, Zippo the Climbing Monkey—that tickled children's fancy, anticipated their tastes, and teased dollars out of their parents' pockets. He discovered how to produce toys cheaply like Ford had made Model Ts, earning the accolade "the Henry Ford of the toy industry." He had a genius for branding, promoting, and pricing, and (unlike Ford) for earning the loyalty of his workers. He had the knack and nerve to knock off competitors' designs and tweak them just enough to elude paying royalties. He became a millionaire—a "toycoon," so to speak—before he was thirty and had amassed a fortune by the time I met him.

Arriving for the weekend, we ran up the steps of her father's mansion and passed under a Greek Revival portico, an echo of the White House. We stepped through the front door into a space large and regal enough for a formal ball. Barbara took me into the stately sitting room with its mirrored bar, where her father liked to play with a few of his many dogs and entertain his guests in front of the huge fireplace.

We opened the French doors onto a terrace and then toured the estate's sprawling grounds. We visited the tulip garden Prince Bernhard of the Netherlands, a friend, had given her father. We inspected Marx's stable of horses. We checked out the indoor and outdoor swimming pools and the maze of tennis, paddleball, and croquet courts.

Marx's palace both dazzled and puzzled me. On the one hand, Barbara had brought me to a magical and wondrous place. Even though I didn't know that the portico's columns were Ionic or that the floors were herringbone parquet, my untrained eye appreciated the exquisite taste that pervaded every detail of the mansion.

On the other hand, I didn't know what to make of the opulence. While part of me wanted all that luxury and more, another part of me distrusted its scale. Each element was striking, but the whole of it seemed excessive, a brag. Moreover, Barbara's disdain of her father's wealth gave me pause. She didn't feel at home in her father's mansion because it symbolized his suffocating power, which she was struggling to escape.

I should have understood her feelings when I met Louis Marx. He was built like a bowling ball and was just as round, hard, bald, and relentless. He had some of my father's charm, but I would learn later that he used it more to draw attention to himself than to amuse others or to have fun.

Marx welcomed me energetically, even though he must have resented me from the first moment. It didn't help that in order to look me over, he had to look several inches upward. What he saw surely galled him. I was wearing the same clothes I wore to sell scrap metals. I talked like Stanley Kowalski, the hard-edged character Marlon Brando played in Tennessee Williams' play *A Streetcar Named Desire*. I knew nothing about manners suitable for an English country house.

He, on the other hand, had spent years of effort and millions of dollars to mask his street origins. He had cloaked himself with all the taste money could buy. He had concealed the last traces of his Brooklyn dialect. He had turned Episcopalian to veil his Jewishness. And now, in spite of all his efforts, I stood before him in his own sacred parlor, his prized daughter on my arm, reminding him of his own rough youth, like something sticky and foul he couldn't scrape off his boot.

It surely made everything worse for Marx when he sensed how enamored Barbara and I were of each other. Like her younger siblings, who would go to Princeton, Vassar, and Stanford, she embodied his hopes of a successor generation whose taste and cultivation would obscure his coarse beginnings. He must have seethed inside when he imagined her running her fingers through my thatch of black hair, among other things.

But he showed no hint of hostility. Instead he invited me to a feast of games. We started with croquet. Louis Jr., Barbara's brother, took me and two other houseguests to the court with its elegant English iron wickets and manicured grass lawn. The players were as exotic to me as the game.

Prince Aschwin of Lippe-Biesterfeld, an accomplished sinologist who lived on one of Marx's properties and would one day go on to be curator of the Metropolitan Museum of Art in New York, chatted with me amicably, trying to make me feel welcome. I had no idea that a sinologist was a person who studied China largely through its art, language, and literature, until he enlightened me. He talked on about the war years, which he had to spend in Morocco because he, like his brother, Bernhard—the prince consort to the queen of the Netherlands—had been a Nazi in the 1930s. I had never met a Nazi, even a former one. He played a courtly and winning game with the self-possession and incision of Sun Tzu. I liked him.

David Schine, the handsome heir to a movie theater and hotel fortune, had majored in high hauteur at Harvard. Dressed by Brooks Brothers in immaculate white linen trousers, he minced like a peacock past me and onto the lawn without a word or even a toss of his head. He played a militant, arrogant game with the same ruthlessness he and the infamous attorney Roy Cohn, his very close friend, would use to attack the United States Army in the McCarthy hearings in 1954. I didn't like him.

I had never seen croquet played, and I didn't know whether to hold the long, clumsy mallet with one hand or two. I found it awkward to swing it between my legs without endangering myself, even though the others were deftly doing so. But when I swung it to the side with one hand, the ball would squiggle off pitifully. All the wickets proved decidedly sticky for me. Aschwin averted his eyes, Schine preened, and Louis Jr. snickered under his breath. I tried not to show my embarrassment.

I felt even more uncomfortable that evening when we gathered in the grand dining room with its sumptuous chandelier and glittering spread of silver at each place. I was never taught the niceties required at such a formal affair: when to stand up, sit down, or pull out a chair for a lady. I didn't know what hand to use for what fork for what course.

My unease grew when, after dinner, Marx invited me to read aloud some of the works of the celebrated American poet Louis Untermeyer, who just happened to be seated at the other end of the table. I had never read much poetry, let alone the work of a prominent poet out loud to him in a room of other literati, but I couldn't refuse. I stumbled through the poem about as well as I had performed at my bar mitzvah. I remember pronouncing "biped" as "bipped," rhyming with "tripped."

Untermeyer went on to discuss different types of poetry, leading Marx to ask me what I thought of "whimsy." I said I thought he was quite an important poet. Famous for his quick wit and puns, Untermeyer glanced at the ceiling and mercifully left my faux pas hanging in the air without comment. Marx—the Spider who had said to Stanley, the Fly, "Come into my dining room"—had cagily revealed my ignorance to his daughter without lifting a pinkie.

The next afternoon proved even more disastrous. Barbara told me her father wanted me to play tennis, and she convinced me that the game would go smoothly if I teamed with her brother in a doubles match. Marx invited a gallery of notables to sit in the shade with their gin and tonics and watch me wiggle with Olympic clumsiness. Since I was pretty good at baseball, I swung my racket like a bat and kept hitting the ball out of the park. The spectators tittered, partly in derision, partly to cover their embarrassment for me.

I thought, *It can't get any worse.*

Then it got worse. Before dinner Marx gathered us on the patio for his favorite game, a vocabulary test. He gave each of us a multiple choice list of increasingly difficult words and asked us to identify their definitions. He scored our answers and read the results out loud. He got a hundred, of course. Aschwin Lippe, with his doctorate, got ninety-eight. I remember Schine and Barbara scored in the nineties. When Marx cleared his throat to command the group's full attention, I winced at what was coming. He winked at me and then trumpeted for all to hear: "And Stanley . . . ahh . . . Stanley. You got . . . twelve." He then stared hard at Barbara, his eyes saying, *So, is this the kind of guy you want?* All at once I felt the heat of his hate toward me.

I suddenly realized his hospitality over the weekend had been a sham. He had been too shrewd to show his hostility openly, because he knew any overt opposition to me would only rile his headstrong daughter and drive her into my arms. His feast of games had really been designed to embarrass me so completely that I would slink back to Philadelphia. He wanted to show Barbara how stupid and bumbling I was so she would stop wasting her time with me and move on—and he wanted to accomplish it all without having said an unkind word to or about me.

EVENTUALLY, I CONCLUDED THAT Marx was not happy with himself, even with all his wealth and prominence. Like many other small-minded, self-made men, he was haunted by a gnawing insecurity that made him grasp for visible, bankable confirmations of his success. He collected celebrities whose friendship advertised his importance—an acclaimed poet here; a pair of princes there; Hank Greenberg, the baseball star, as his best man. He acquired addresses whose elegance broadcast that he had "made it"—his own suite at the Waldorf Towers, a reserved center table downstairs at the 21 Club in New York, and of course, his regal Scarsdale estate with its majestic mansion.

His memory of poverty hounded him. He lived in a constant fury of competitions over almost everything, all designed to show he was the winner, triumphantly positioned at the front of the line. Barbara told me that Marx and his friend Bernard Gimbel (as in Gimbels and Macy's) had a running competition over their children's merits. She said her father was so competitive that he pushed his children to compete with him and each other. He made them learn words he had memorized, including ridiculous ones like "triskaidekaphobia" (the fear of the number 13) and "nocturnal enuresis" (bedwetting) that almost no one else would know. He habitually challenged his guests to compete by taking vocabulary tests, just as he had us do on the patio that weekend. Of course, he knew that he and his children had an edge.

Lurking behind Marx's need to be at the front of the line was his thirst for power and the appearance of it. He wanted to command a room and project authority. His stash of financial and executive power didn't satisfy him. So he ingratiated himself to a galaxy of generals who had commanded our country's massive military power in the war—Marshall, Bradley, Eisenhower, LeMay. He entertained them in his home, named his four youngest sons after them, helped ease some of them into postwar corporate jobs, and basked in their reflected reputations, thereby magnifying his own aura of power.

Even so, he wanted more. Later, in the 1950s, Marx put his own face on his company's toy statue of Napoleon—another roundish, short man who couldn't get enough power and glory. Irony clearly was not one of the tools he kept in his arsenal.

After dinner that Saturday night, Barbara and I stole out into the evening's shadows and made love by the tennis court. But it wasn't enough. I wanted to get revenge on Marx more directly. I wanted to set off another stink bomb, so I decided to knock the little Toy King out of the toy business. In early 1949, I met a guy who told me he knew how to make a wind-up doll that could jump a rope. He said that he'd pitched Gimbels and Macy's, and that they loved the idea. I relished the irony of beating Marx with a toy reminiscent of his Zippo the Climbing Monkey, which shimmied up a string when you pulled it and shimmied down when you stopped. I formed a company, gave it a name the size of my ambition—Toy Corporation of America (Toycoa, like the Aluminum Company of America's Alcoa)—and bet $10,000, a big chunk of my cash, on my venture in vengeance.

Unfortunately, when the doll tried to jump, the rope hit her on the head, and she, like me, fell on her face. No irony there.

Nevertheless, that spring Barbara and I continued to defy her father with our love. We stole into his suite in the Waldorf Towers, danced to Eddy Duchin downstairs in the Westwood Room, and drank wine much finer than what could be found in Palumbo's cellar. And we found the suite's beds more lush than even the most hospitable bushes in Scarsdale.

One day near the end of spring 1949, Barbara told me she'd decided to go to Paris for her junior year. Bryn Mawr depressed her and had failed to help her find her life's meaning and purpose. She hoped the City of Light and the Sorbonne would inspire her.

I was heart-stricken and feared I would lose her, so I decided at once to follow her. I sold my business to my partner, Stanley Kessler, and cashed in my car and everything else I owned. I made sure my mother had what she needed. Then I bet everything I had left on my love for Barbara.

When my mother and brother waved good-bye to me at the dock in New York that morning in August, they saw Barbara's father and sister seeing her off, over at the *Queen Elizabeth*'s first-class gangplank. I hadn't told her I was going to Paris, so Louis Marx didn't know I was sailing on her ship—any more than I had known what he'd been up to that weekend in Scarsdale.

SEVEN

"Imagine Sisyphus Happy"

I found Barbara on the upper deck as we were sailing past the Statue of Liberty. Surprised and delighted, she urged me to move from my tourist-class berth to her posh cabin, where we spent most of the voyage.

Barbara especially welcomed my help when we docked. Louis Marx, always the master of the nuanced gesture, had bestowed on his daughter a new, bright-red Chevrolet convertible, but he hadn't considered how she would get it to Paris. She barely knew how to drive, and France's roads were still damaged from the war. I loved the irony of sitting behind the wheel and driving Marx's daughter in his gift all the way to Paree.

The Paris we entered in the late summer of 1949 was beset with the worst drought in forty years, the largest swarm of tourists since the war, and horrendous traffic jams. Half the shops were shut because of the Parisians' usual August vacation. I had to scramble to find a place to live and ended up renting a grungy room in an inexpensive hotel on a narrow street behind the Ritz.

Barbara became a boarder in the lovely home of the Merciers, a distinguished and erudite family related to a cardinal, a Belgian hero of World War I. They lived four miles west of the city, in Neuilly, a leafy suburb graced with gardens, broad avenues, the Bois de Boulogne, and occasionally, the Duke and Duchess of Windsor. Despite her upscale address, Barbara spent most of her time with me at my place.

It was quickly obvious to Barbara that her Sorbonne professors wouldn't help her in her quest for life's meaning any more than Bryn

Mawr's teachers had. She stopped going to class and spent much of her time reading on her own, mainly the French existentialists, who were all the rage. She found she couldn't stand them. She couldn't reconcile her innate sense of hope with the existentialists' pessimism and embrace of the absurd.

We began my studies by trying to improve my vocabulary. She gave me a thick manual, *English Vocabulary Builder*, compiled by Johnson O'Connor. All the eleven hundred words I was to learn were meaty and would be useful to any thoughtful adult. Each listing included a brief essay on the nuances of the word's meaning and a discussion of its common misuses. I still have that copy at my home in London.

Barbara suggested I begin my reading program with Plato's *Republic*, which was heavy going for me. I loved the idea of challenging my mind by reading the great books and then talking with her about them. She was already steeped in Western philosophy, and I was still in kindergarten. Many of the philosophers she suggested bored me. She urged me to join her in a fling with Nietzsche, but I gave short shrift to him and his idea of the superman.

I got no more kick out of Sartre than Barbara had, but I loved Camus. I worked hard to understand *The Stranger*, because I somehow identified with Meursault—the hero, the outsider—without knowing why. My favorite of Camus's works was *The Myth of Sisyphus*, about the mortal whom the gods had condemned to endlessly roll a rock up to a mountaintop, only to have it roll back down every single time. I was moved by Sisyphus's plight at the foot of the mountain; I was taken by his "struggle . . . toward the heights." And I agreed with Camus's last line: "One must imagine Sisyphus happy."

I made independent efforts, in parallel with Barbara's coaching, to improve myself. I watched polished diners out of the corner of my eye to learn how to use a fork in my left hand and other table niceties. I tried to improve the way I spoke, appointing myself as an amateur Professor Higgins. I was probably the only American in history who has ever gone to France to learn English.

Inspired by Barbara's understated taste, I stole away to London to get outfitted in proper English clothes by a proper English tailor. I came back in my own soft wools and hushed hues, classic suits, and cashmere sweaters. I looked like a young Edward R. Murrow, wearing his calm self-assurance as well as his famous belted trench coat.

That fall we drove west in the convertible with its top down. We stopped at the medieval Chartres Cathedral, home of the revered tunic said to be worn by the Virgin Mary at the birth of Christ, where Barbara gave me a glittering tutorial. We drove on to the breathtaking island abbey Mont-Saint-Michel, where she introduced me to its history. In Normandy, I wandered alone on the beach, through the shell-pocked German bunkers and among the debris strewn about: broken rifles, rusted shell casings and canisters, girders twisted by our direct hits. Barbara had been only thirteen on D-Day; she had little to teach me there.

For Christmas we went to Bad Gastein, a ski resort near Salzburg, Austria. Neither of us knew how to ski, but we sort of tried. We stumbled and bumbled, fell on our butts, rolled in the snow, and threw snowballs at each other. We laughed at ourselves. It didn't matter. We didn't really go there to ski. We were both gripped with the unmistakable conviction that we were profoundly and completely in love with each other.

⁂

FOR ALL MY CERTAINTY about our love on that holiday, I should have seen that it could not hold. Things were beginning to fall apart. I was already dealing with a pair of personal problems that could unsettle our relationship, but I didn't discuss them with Barbara. She was wrestling with a couple of her own, but I didn't learn about them until many years later.

My foremost problem was that I was running out of money. Of course, I needed cash for practical reasons: to live on, to take us where we wanted to go, and to buy books and Pernod. But I also sensed that losing my financial independence might undercut our relationship emotionally, because it bolstered my sense of self-worth and earned Barbara's admiration.

I tried a series of deals to make some money, and one venture paid off for a while. Since the French needed hard currency, they permitted foreigners with American dollars to buy French automobiles. I bought them one at a time and then sold them on the black market for a tidy profit.

None of my other schemes worked. The most cockamamie idea came from Al Himmelfarb, my friend from Philadelphia. He claimed he could hook me up with a Lebanese prince who would help us smuggle gold out of Lebanon. Al wanted me to go to Beirut to close the deal. I was turned down twice for a visa, though, probably because on my application I volunteered the information that I was Jewish. If it weren't for that fortuitous mistake, I probably would have wound up in jail—or dead.

Later Al talked me into working with him to start a business shipping a special French cheese to Philadelphia. We flopped because he failed to get the right importation permits and had no idea how we would get the cheese to buyers.

My last try was partnering with some Frenchmen to sell eggs in Germany, certainly a hungry market at the time. But we didn't find a way to protect the eggs on the train, and they were all cracked by the time they arrived in Munich. With such lame entrepreneurial efforts, my wallet was getting pretty thin by spring 1950.

Another threat to my romance with Barbara was that I felt insecure when I had to mingle in her world. I had felt reasonably self-confident throughout most of my boyhood and increasingly so after the army. And when it was just the two of us, I felt quite secure. But I felt ill at ease in her social and intellectual circles. Her friends lived another life. They spoke several languages. They vacationed as a set at their exclusive haunts. I never felt I was a part of what they had.

Barbara, without intending to, added to my unease on these occasions. She seemed to enjoy showing me off to her friends as her play toy from some strange other world. I knew I was there only as her guest, clearly out of place without her patronage.

One evening, a knot of French and English gentlemen were chatting about their shoot the previous weekend in the country. They asked me if I hunted. I told them that back home we hunted rats. I explained that we waited for them at the sewer, hit them with a stick, and kept score. They glanced at one another while sipping from their cocktails. Finally one of them laughed uncertainly and said, "Oh, that's a funny story." Then they resumed their insular conversation, leaving me stranded.

Barbara was struggling with her own conflicts. She kept them to herself, even though they directly threatened our relationship even more than mine did. One came from her frustration about her efforts to discover her life's meaning. It's clear now that she was in the early stages of a personal, intellectual quest of remarkable scope and depth, one that would eventually consume her as her life's work. Her questions already reached way outside most traditional philosophical inquiries, and the more she pored in vain over the texts of Western wisdom, the more her frustration grew.

Even if I'd had an idea of the scale of her ambitions or of how important and intense her search was becoming, I couldn't have helped her. For all her generous coaching, for all my reading, and for all our delights in discussing ideas, I was still a rookie, and I often had a hard time understanding what the hell she was talking about. It's obvious now that as close as we were as lovers, we were quite separate in the way our minds worked.

Reading her memoir twenty-five years later, I learned about her other internal conflict. One rainy day in November 1949, when she was feeling especially alienated and lonely in her search for life's meaning, she met an American artist in a Left Bank café. She quickly embraced Earl as her soul mate and fell in love "for the first time." She exuberantly told Madame Mercier that evening, "I have met the man I'm going to marry."

I had no idea Barbara was involved with two men at the same time. She was as loving and fervent as ever, both in word and in deed, at Bad Gastein, a few weeks after she had met Earl, and then on into the beautiful Parisian spring.

In late May, however, things began to fall apart. We learned Madame Mercier had written to tell Louis Marx that Barbara was about to marry a man who lacked proper standing. Barbara's father and brother were flying to Paris to save her, and they were bringing along General Emmett "Rosie" O'Donnell Jr., an old friend of Marx's who had led the United States Air Force's firebombing of Tokyo.

I don't know whether Madame Mercier meant me or Earl, but I wasn't yet aware of another suitor. Barbara and I decided to elope. I learned that we could get married quickly and simply in Basel, Switzerland. Early one morning, we set out to drive to a Swiss magistrate. The seven-hour trip gave us a lot of time to think.

As I was pulling out of a gas station on the edge of Basel, I realized I couldn't go through with it. I made a U-turn, heading back toward Paris. I told Barbara that getting married was a ridiculous idea because she was going back to school the next fall and because, as much as I'd tried, I didn't understand what she was after or even what she was saying most of the time. Plus, I was almost out of money and didn't have a way to provide her with what she was used to.

We drove back to Paris, and that was the end of it. But Louis Marx had to have the last say.

Marx insisted I meet him and his muscle in front of his hotel, the Ritz. He directed me to join them in the back of his Rolls-Royce limousine, a perfect place for him to exercise his total control. It was sumptuous enough to intimidate; it guaranteed completely privacy; and since it was speeding down the boulevards, I couldn't get out.

He first loosed his son and General O'Donnell on me, presumably to soften me up. O'Donnell threatened to ask his old friend, five-star General Dwight Eisenhower, to get me called back into the army if I didn't shape up. Perhaps he felt his own four stars were not daunting enough. Then Louis Jr., with the consummate grace of a red-faced, pompous Princeton sophomore, offered something like "Who in the hell do you think you are, coming over here on the sly and thinking we wouldn't find out?"

The ride was decidedly unpleasant, but their words were wasted. While the Marx Brothers were mau-mauing me in the limo, Barbara was packing, readying herself to be whisked away to a posh hotel on the Riviera.

Marx failed to see I was already broken. When they finally ran out of breath, they unceremoniously dumped me behind the Ritz, like a sack of something smelly.

I found some solace with Bill Basnight, an American friend who had recently moved in with me. For months I had enjoyed the uncomplicated company of this nice, regular guy as a respite from Barbara's pompous set. He was a leftover from the war. Like so many veterans in Paris, he was barely living off his GI Bill. He wanted to write for the *New York Herald Tribune* and for the literary magazines that were cropping up at the time. We had fun together. We shared a friend, a Boston blueblood with lots of big tattoos whom we repeatedly had to keep from joining the French Foreign Legion.

Both of us were pretty down and out by July. We were broke and without prospects. Neither of us knew what to do. I had a couple more months of prepaid rent on my place and an ample store of Pernod. I suggested that we flip a coin to see who would go home and who would get to "jump in the Seine"—that is, get the room and the booze. The coin toss sent me home.

<hr />

I LEFT PARIS CONFUSED, depressed, and incapable of making any sense of my two years with Barbara. But I can see now that she and her father had transformed my life in both good and painful ways.

They fired my imagination about the possibilities of an extraordinary life. Whatever latent capacity for personal development I possessed before I met Barbara might well have remained inert if she hadn't stirred me to reach beyond my aimless games in Wynnefield. She triggered an explosion of appetite to define and pursue my own direction. Her intellectual inquisitiveness and drive hooked me, stretched me, and set me on my own path of self-discovery. She introduced me to worlds that were totally apart from anything I had known, worlds I fiercely wanted to be a part of from then on.

But the price was years of inner torment. My madness came from my feelings for her and the life she personified.

I worried, as Gatsby had wondered about Daisy, whether I had any "real right to touch her hand." For years I drove myself to my limits to prove that I did have that right. Barbara remained a painful reminder of both my lost love and my self-doubt, until I came to the point at which I could build an adult sense of my own strengths, based on my own real accomplishments.

Louis Marx's public cruelty toward me inflicted psychic wounds that still make me wince. But what bothered me most was the impotence I felt when he turned his full force on me face-to-face.

The ghost of Henry J. Trainer lurked in the messy emotional innards of these episodes. My father's impotence when his political boss bullied him haunted me and made me resolve never to be weak like him. My memories of Marx's abuse of his power drove me for years to build the strengths my father lacked.

EIGHT

The Spy Who Taught Me

I sailed for home on July 28, 1950, on Cunard's *Caronia*, broke and broken. I was traveling tourist class, but my London tailor's art ensured no one would stop me when I walked into the elegant cabin-class lounge in search of a drink.

I noticed a man at the bar, drawing a strikingly vivid sketch of a 1941 Lincoln Continental convertible in all its glory. Fascinated, I sat down next to him and asked him about his meticulous doodle. He told me that his name was Guy and he was a British diplomat about to become the second secretary in the UK embassy in Washington.

I had no idea what such an officer did, but the title sounded impressive and important. We fell into a voyage of conversations, both of us drinking away every evening. He introduced me to gin and tonics.

Guy struck me as the epitome of an Englishman gentleman. In his late thirties, he was handsome and self-assured. He dressed with a mix of the rakish and the regal, just as I imagined a sophisticated Cambridge-educated diplomat would on an Atlantic crossing. I was charmed by his accent, which conjured up images of Cambridge evenings filled with wit and vintage port.

I was amazed and impressed by the range and depth of his erudition. He was a virtuoso conversationalist, seemingly able to talk about anything: politics, books, music, travel. He served up a stream of stridently anti-American gossip. He pressed me to read Paul Bowles's gloomy existential novel, *The Sheltering Sky*. He celebrated Beethoven in detail. He had holidayed in Tangier in French Morocco and loved its libertarianism.

I was in awe when he laced his tales with what "Winston" had told him about this and that. He invited me to his stateroom to see a book the great man had given him. He dug it out of his locker, where he kept his most prized books and documents. Sure enough, it said something like, "To Guy, in agreement with his views, Winston S. Churchill."

After several rounds of gin and tonics one night, we went to the men's room to pee. I was totally surprised when he reached over and tried to kiss me. I remember my first impression was that his face was scratchy. As usual, he hadn't shaved.

I wasn't homophobic, but the prospect seemed decisively unattractive to me. When I made it clear that there was no way we were going to have sex, he seemed not to mind.

He found lots of other guys on the ship to pick up, and every night, in addition to our usual rations of gin and his usual tour of the horizon, he would tell me about his conquests of the day, mostly to make fun of them. He wanted to tell me how so-and-so would squeal at some point in a certain way, but I would cut him off. It just was not my taste. It finally dawned on me what liberties he had liked to take in Morocco and why he had touted *The Sheltering Sky*, with Bowles's overtones of homosexuality.

Guy and I liked each other's company, and by the time we arrived in New York, we had become friends. His shipboard friendship helped me in some important ways. For one, he gave me some direction. When I confided I wasn't certain what I was going to do next, he told me I should become a diplomat. He suggested I go to Georgetown University's School of Foreign Service. He promised we could have fun together in Washington.

For another, Guy was the first in a series of masters of the spoken word in my adult life who would spellbind me with their verbal dexterity. Like my father, he loved to perform and could captivate a room or a table without a text. Of course, Guy took this art to another level, well beyond Johnson O'Connor's vocabulary builder or Barbara's tutorials.

Guy's charm also served as balm to my grief over losing Barbara. It felt good to be liked, and the good times we had together distracted me a bit from my pain. So did the gin.

I ARRIVED IN PHILADELPHIA without a dime. When my taxi pulled up in front of the paint store in my neighborhood, I had to call out to Kenny Kahn, my brother-in-law, to pay the driver.

I came home emotionally bankrupt as well. I felt disoriented. My two years with Barbara had distanced me from my Philadelphia roots, yet I lacked confidence in the new self I had been trying on for her. I felt like Camus's Meursault, a stranger in both cultures.

Al Himmelfarb piled on. He took my English clothes and airy speech as personal affronts. He railed at me in plain Philadelphia street talk, saying something like "You son of a bitch. You think you're too good for us now."

I couldn't simply revert to my pre-Barbara self. This loss of my old identity added to my despair. I fell into a deep depression. I couldn't get Barbara Marx out of my head.

I became so screwed up one night that I thought I was going to die. I was coming home on the train from New York, where I had been visiting Hilly. I was terrorized by the feeling that "they" were after me. I didn't know who "they" were or what to do. I felt trapped inside the passenger car and needed to escape. I panicked and wanted to jump off the back of the train to end the riot in my head. I managed to stay in my seat but continued to suffer, and when I got home, I hid under the bed.

I talked to my mother about my terrors. She consoled me, but not enough to relieve my pain. She also noticed my new taste for gin and suggested lovingly that I needed to be "a good boy." I listened, but not enough to cut down.

One clear imperative floated around in my frenzy about Barbara: I needed to go back to college immediately. It would be the first step in winning her back. My brother knew I needed a car to find a school, so he bought me a new black Chevrolet for $300. No greater love has a man than he who cleans out his bank account to give his brother a fresh start. I suspect Buddy didn't tell his wife until much later.

I needed to find a school by early September to get on the GI Bill, and it was already mid-August. When someone told me that the University of Chicago offered accelerated courses, I drove nonstop to apply. I asked them how long it would take me to graduate. Whatever time they told me, it was too long. I drove nonstop back home.

Then I remembered Guy had mentioned Georgetown University. The dean of admissions could not have been more hospitable. He said the university would give me credit for all the courses I had taken in the army and at the Pennsylvania Military College, and I could finish my degree in less than two years. I had the impression Georgetown, which seemed to be standing the University of Pennsylvania's anti-Semitic quota system on its head, loved to admit Jews. I wondered if the Jesuits hoped to convert them.

I enrolled in the fall of 1950. Georgetown and I fit perfectly. I was finally ready to learn. Barbara's tutoring and Guy's discourses had inspired me. I no longer worried that bookish guys were sissies. A lot of veterans brought their battle scars to class along with their academic ambitions. I took advantage of three of Georgetown's most gifted teachers, who helped me grow in different and important ways.

I learned from Jules David, a distinguished historian of American diplomacy, that I was smart—not in all ways, but at least in those that would matter to me over the years. A dozen or so of us studied advanced American history with him in a classroom so intimate, he could work side by side with us on the puzzles he posed. I discovered I was quite good in this open play of ideas in a small group. I found I could get the gist of others' views, weave them with my perspectives, and make my own fresh points.

In this way I discovered what has proved to be my most useful intelligence: using my own brain to pick others' in order to find the best answer that otherwise would have gone unseen. I also found my most natural voice—conversational, one better used at a table than in a hall.

Father Frank Fadner, an expert on Russian history, and later dean of the School of Foreign Service, reinforced my instinct that I should not be afraid of stating my convictions to those in authority. In contrast with Jules David's open discussions, Fadner taught by lecture. For our final test he posed a set of true-false questions, which I found easy to answer, except for one. He listed seven or eight leaders of the Soviet revolution, most of whom were Jewish, beginning with Trotsky. He then asked whether it was true or false that the Jews were responsible for the communist revolution and all its horrors.

I liked Fadner and his course, but I was appalled that he could have posed such a loaded question. So I wrote, "False! Or if true, I resign from this class." I fully expected him to think, *Here's one more Jewish smart-ass.* Instead, he gave me a 100 on the test and told me he loved my response.

Carroll Quigley, my most charismatic and influential teacher at Georgetown, drilled me on how to think. Everyone wanted to take his course on the development of civilizations. He taught it with blue fire. A wiry Bostonian, Quigley was tough with everybody in all kinds of ways, and it was hard to get him upset.

Every class with Quigley was nose-to-nose intellectual combat. He taught us to think with discipline and to reason in chains of logic: ergo *this*, ergo *that*. "Think, Stanley, think!" he would goad me. "Think it through." When he died years later, I wasn't surprised to see in his obituary that many Georgetown alumni considered his "the most influential course in their undergraduate careers."

Quigley also encouraged me to reach into my subconscious to draw on thoughts and feelings my conscious self had not yet processed. I still do this. I learned that when I face a murky problem, it helps for me to write down everything I think might be related to the matter—not only everything I know, but also everything I half know, or feel, or barely sense, or have on the tip of my tongue or on the edge of my consciousness. After a few days, new thoughts and fresh clarity will spring up, and I will typically find a way to resolve the problem. Barbara had *introduced* me to thinking, but Quigley taught me *how* to think.

MY GEORGETOWN PROFESSORS HELPED me develop my mind and self in ways that served me well later on, but I was still gripped by my neurotic preoccupation with Barbara, and so I remained deeply depressed. She added to my confusion and grief when she showed up unannounced to see me at my mother's house in Wynnefield on my twenty-fourth birthday, December 21, 1950, the day before she turned twenty-one. She wanted to tell me she was getting married that spring to a man named Earl. This was the first time I had heard of him, and she told me nothing about her history with him in Paris.

In spite of her wedding plans, she wanted for us to be together one last time. We had dinner, and I drove her back to Bryn Mawr. Then we had sex. We didn't make love. We just had very unsatisfactory sex. We had lost even our most elemental connection.

Back at Georgetown, Guy helped me escape my pain. He kept in touch with witty notes on the embassy's gold-embossed stationery, usually lampooning General Douglas MacArthur, whom he loathed. I still have the original copies of a few of the letters and notes he left for me, usually folded into fourths or eighths and wedged into my mailbox or slipped under the door. One of them, dated December 31, is a handwritten note that Guy titled "Weeks Celebrated in U.S.A" with the caveat "Incomplete List," added in parentheses just below the title. It lists twenty-seven fictitious "weeks" observed in the U.S.—from "National Honey for Breakfast Week" to "Posture Week" to "Leave Us Alone Week"—each of which joked about things we laughed about then during our many discussions together, almost always over a glass or two.

I loved going to dinner with him every two or three weeks, just the two of us. I enjoyed the buzz he created with my friends at school—this dashing British envoy who picked me up in his swank 1941 Lincoln Continental convertible with its prestigious diplomatic plates. We sped like madmen up and down Washington's broad avenues, daring the police to stop us so Guy could flaunt his immunity.

Guy always had in his possession a bottle of bourbon, and I liked

THE SPY WHO TAUGHT ME

Weeks Celebrated in U.S.A.
(Incomplete List)
Kim from G.B.
31·12

National Honey for Breakfast Week
"   Bible Week
"   Crochet Week
"   Peanut Week
"   Daughters Week
"   Frozen Food Week
"   Americanism Week
"   Wildlife Restoration Week
"   Large Size Week
         Coin Machine Week
?   Brotherhood Week
         Save Your Vision Week
         Goodwill to Canada Week
         Baby Week
         Watch Inspection Time Week
         Hobby Week
         Newspaper Boy Week
         Sweater Week
         Table Tennis Week
         Wine Week
         Perfect Shipping Month Week
         Posture Week
         Trimmed Dress Week
         Felt Hat Day Week
         Poetry Day in Pennsylvania Week
(+)   Leave us Alone Week
($+)   Save the Horse Week (includes Mule

Dear Stanley
pl. get in touch
(if you wish to).
Office or Ext. 4117,
Other side of this
paper is not
interesting!
Guy

drinking with him. The last night I saw him, we went to the movies to see Irene Dunne play Queen Victoria in *The Mudlark*. We were sitting in the back row, passing the bourbon back and forth, when Guy dropped the bottle. It rattled and banged all the way down the slope of the floor and finally broke, provoking everyone to clear out of the theatre.

As we headed out, Guy suggested we go to his place, a basement apartment in the beautiful home of one of his colleagues. There he found more bourbon and put on Beethoven. I thought he was about to make another pass, so I told him, "No monkey business."

He said he understood and began to read out loud some of Paul Bowles's prose from *The Sheltering Sky*.

Guy's host, Kim Philby, a strikingly handsome man, came in and sat down to chat. He also liked bourbon. Guy had already told me his friend was a spy, a key officer in the embassy's intelligence operations. I was too impressed and too naïve to appreciate this indiscretion. The two of them proceeded to swap speculations about which notables in their crowd and around town were homosexual. I was so starstruck, I didn't consider the oddity of their conversation.

Guy and I spent a lot of nights like that together without worries. We had fun—pointless fun, fun for fun's sake—just as I had as a boy with my gang on Queen Street.

IT WAS JUST A few weeks later and I, trying to get my mind off Barbara, went to see the movie that changed my life.

Years later, I actually got to know John Huston a little, through a mutual friend in San Francisco. I told him that *The Treasure of the Sierra Madre* had changed everything for me—that I'd seen it without knowing a thing about it, and that within a week I had given up everything I had in my life, left school, packed my car, and driven more than 1,500 miles to Mexico to become a treasure hunter. I'm certain he had heard hundreds of people over the years tell him that he had changed their lives, but I doubt there were very many stories quite like mine.

Huston didn't believe it at first, but then he did and was genuinely flattered. I didn't realize at the time that the character who lured me to Mexico with the promise of finding treasure in the mountains—of proving that I wasn't my father, Walter Weiss—was *his* father, Walter Huston, who starred in that film.

When the spring semester was over, I drove home to Philadelphia, and told my mother that I had made a decision to move to Mexico. I left a week later. But before I did, on Thursday, June 7, 1951, I unfolded the *Philadelphia Bulletin* to see how the Phillies were doing, and I was startled to see a screaming front-page story about my friend Guy Burgess. It said he and Donald Maclean, a senior diplomat who had been posted with Burgess at the British embassy in Washington, were suspected of being Soviet spies. The British government believed they were on the run and had launched a massive manhunt to find them.

I learned later that Guy had abandoned his vintage Lincoln Continental at a local Washington garage and had left his prized book autographed by Churchill at a friend's place in New York.

Kim Philby turned out to be a third man in the operation, which history would remember as the highest-profile and most costly conspiracy of the Cold War. When the British finally flushed him out a decade later, he fled, like Burgess and Maclean, to Russia, where the three lived the rest of their lives in exile.

I later read that Guy had an especially bad time of it in Moscow. Early on, a street gang beat him up and knocked out his teeth. The Soviets frowned on homosexuals and took away his privileges. He slid further into alcoholism and died a lonely death in 1963, pining for his homeland.

On that bright June afternoon twelve years earlier, it was time for me to leave my birthplace too. I tossed the *Bulletin* into the backseat of my Chevy, said my last good-byes to my mother, and headed southwest toward Mexico. I found a new home and a much brighter future there than Guy found in Russia.

NINE

Catching the Bug in Mexico

D uring my first weeks in Mexico, I depended on the kindness of strangers. I stayed with a Mexican family who nursed me and comforted me as I wrestled with both dysentery and my devils. They were the first in a long line of Mexicans who helped me at critical moments over the years in my adopted homeland.

My professors also supported me in important ways, both practical and therapeutic. I needed my GI Bill to feed me and to finance my prospecting, and I wanted to make sure I could sign up to earn my credits at Georgetown from Mexico City College, so I fought through my irrational fears of falling through the earth enough to matriculate as soon as I arrived.

Most of my professors in Mexico City had been drummed out of their jobs as suspected communists by the University of California, then in the grips of the Red Scare. I was not at all political, so I found this funny at first. But when I met with each of them to sketch out my plans, I liked them and they liked me, and it bothered me that they'd been run out of their country because of their political beliefs.

My dreams of hunting for treasure gave my teachers a vicarious thrill. They understood why I wanted to skip their classes to go prospecting. They told me that as long as I passed the final exam, I would get credit for my courses. They smiled when I confided my scheme to raise cash for my venture by selling the expensive textbooks the GI Bill provided. They seemed to admire my drive to get something tangible done, my grit in taking risks, and my itch to bet on a big win. Our conversations helped pull me out of my doldrums, and their respect for me and enthusiasm for my plans reinforced my resolve. I wanted to get going.

At the end of the summer term, I passed my exams with reassuringly high grades. I needed only a term or two to finish my degree. I was set to go back to Washington, but I decided to stay, out of instinct more than reflection. From the moment I had met the old-timer at the Hotel Ritz and gone out on my first adventures, the romance of prospecting had hooked me. I loved its whiff of danger, its dash of humor, its rugged terrain, and its exotic natives. I would have to face the painful and intimate consequences of my choice twenty years later. But that fall, I was only twenty-five years old, and I had caught the bug.

⁂

ONE NIGHT AFTER I'D been in Mexico for a while, a strikingly beautiful brunette, born Harriet Elizabeth Dingeldein and now going by Bette Ford, beckoned me to squeeze in next to her at her boyfriend's table at a popular Cuernavaca bar. Her boyfriend, a movie producer, was so busy indulging his ego by noisily regaling his friends with his Hollywood wit, he hardly noticed me.

I focused my attention instead on his girlfriend. She radiated an alluring, reckless energy, but she held her petite body comfortably erect, barely moving. She turned her eyes on mine, and I could tell she was trying to read me and to attune herself to me. Her easy smile sparkled, pulled me in close, and flashed an appetite for engagement and risk. All this made sense when she told me she fought bulls.

Bette came to bullfighting on a hard-luck path. She grew up in western Pennsylvania in McKeesport, a tough town known for manufacturing iron pipes. Her mother and father left her to be raised by relatives. After high school, she hurried alone on a one-way ticket to New York City to become famous as a model and actress. With her beauty and pluck, she flourished. Somewhere along the way, she'd lost her fiancé in a motorcycle accident. Then, while on a modeling shoot in Bogotá,

Colombia, she saw her first bullfight one afternoon. She began studying with some of the best teachers of the art and quickly became Mexico's leading woman matador. I had never met anyone remotely like her. She saw in my fascination a fellow traveler, one who was eager to listen to the stories she had to tell. A few nights later, we became lovers.

Just a wisp of a girl at ninety pounds, Bette fought and killed hundreds of bulls in her career, often ten times her size. She believed bullfighting was a drama, not a sport, and she was fascinated by its violence and "spiritual engagement . . . with power and death." She relished dueling with the bulls, and was drawn to the fight because she knew they could kill her. They almost did. After one fight, she invited me into her dressing room while she was getting a massage. I saw up close the nicks and bruises on her body, fresh from the near misses.

One afternoon she invited me into the ring so I could feel what it was like to fight. "Fighting cattle," used to train rookies, were brought in. "These are just old cows," Bette said to reassure me. They may have been old, but they had horns; they could hurt me, and they clearly wanted to. Bette showed me how to use a cape to wave them off. I tried a few passes, but they kept coming right at me every time I moved. They scared the hell out of me. I stayed just long enough so she wouldn't think I was a total coward, and then used the cape to wave good-bye to them.

Bette and I were a lot alike. We both loved to take risks. We both were starting from scratch in a foreign land, betting on ourselves to win our fortune in wild ventures beyond our grandest imagination as kids back in Pennsylvania. She was one of my favorite people from those early years in Mexico. She roused me from my stubborn depression, and our nights in Cuernavaca pumped me up to press on in my search for riches.

TEN

Getting Screwed, Getting Serious

After several months of trying to hit pay dirt, and several weeks of being tricked by locals who told me the slate we were mining was high-grade ore, I had repeatedly struck out. I had learned to recognize amethyst and slate, two minerals of dubious value, but otherwise I had learned almost nothing about geology. Like Curtin, the good-natured greenhorn in *The Treasure of the Sierra Madre*, I still didn't "know what gold looks like in the ground"—or manganese either. And once more I was nearly broke.

Al Himmelfarb, who had shortened his surname to Himfar, and I had been in touch since I had first arrived in Mexico. He had been one of my closest friends in Philadelphia, and I had good memories of our times together as young veterans after the war. His anger at my post-Parisian pretensions appeared to have faded by the time he visited me at Georgetown. While Al didn't have any luck that weekend convincing me to leave Washington, he had more luck with Nelson Kusner, someone I knew from Central High, and they had gone to Mexico to pursue Al's dream of striking it rich.

Al invited me to join them in San Luis Potosí, a city north of Mexico City that was the center of a lot of mining activity, where they had been spending time. I welcomed the chance to work with an old pal I could trust. Al seemed to know the prospects in that area almost as well as the locals did. As it turned out, he offered me a deal that seemed a lot surer than prospecting and a lot safer than his earlier scheme of smuggling gold out of Lebanon.

The five Sanchez brothers—each more loony than the next—mostly liked to drink and fight, but they dominated manganese mining in western Mexico. Al learned that they had a large stockpile of ore at Mazatlán, a port on the Mexican west coast. They had planned to ship the ore to Japan, only to find out too late that transporting across the Pacific would be too expensive. They were stuck.

Al knew the American market for manganese was hot. It was needed to produce steel for the Korean War. Any amount you bought in Mexico, you could sell in the United States for a higher price, almost risk-free. He bought the Sanchez *hermanos*' entire hoard and shipped it northeast by rail to the city of Matamoros, directly across from its sister city of Brownsville, Texas. To cash in, he needed to get the ore over the bridge, across the river, and onto American trains.

Al asked me to spend the summer in Brownsville to make sure the ore got onto a US train. I didn't mind that he wanted me to do the shit work. He promised me one-third of all the profits once I finished the job. This seemed a sweet offer, so I thanked him for his generosity and sealed the deal with a handshake, as old friends do.

I earned every cent. My inexperience made everything harder. Every morning at dawn, I crossed the bridge to Matamoros to line up Mexican workers to move the manganese. Only after weeks of bumbling did I learn these arrangements should have been done by a brokerage agent.

The cost of getting across the bridge every day, a quarter each way, cut into my dwindling cash. Then one day I heard the guy in front of me say, "*El Capitán—ándale,*" and the gatekeeper hurried him through without paying. I had picked up enough Spanish to know *ándale* meant something like "get a move on." Although I didn't know why these words produced such a magical result, I too said, "*El Capitán—ándale,*" when I got to the gate, and was waved through without having to pay. This worked for weeks until the gatekeeper asked one day, "*El Capitán* who?" I had no idea. I was stuck and had to pay up. Later I learned that the same brokerage agent, El Capitán, who was supposed to help me recruit workers, was also supposed to pay the gatekeeper.

By mid-August I finished moving the last of the manganese ore over the border. I went to San Luis to celebrate with Al and to get paid. I looked for him at all of his usual haunts, but he had disappeared. I found Nelson, though, and was stunned when he told me that Al had gone to New York City. Al owed me about $50,000, which is over $400,000 in today's money. I drove in a fury to New York to track him down.

I found Al in a fancy hotel, in a posh suite overlooking the city. I was not happy. I told him that he should have told me he was leaving and then paid me before he left.

He wrote me a check for $2,500.

This enraged me even more. I told him he owed me twenty times that amount and reminded him that he had given his word.

He looked at me coldly and said, "So, what can you do about it?"

I wanted to throw him out of the window. I was so enraged and hurt, I actually thought I might do it.

Al's double-dealing reminded me of an eerily similar episode in *The Treasure of the Sierra Madre*. A rogue contractor hires the two down-and-out greenhorns, Dobbs and his nicer friend, Curtin, to do some hard labor. He promises to pay them well when the job is done, stiffs them with a pittance, and disappears. They find him, living high on the money he owes them. When he tries to duck them with more promises, they beat him to a pulp and leave him on the barroom floor.

But I knew I wasn't really going to beat up Al or toss him out the window. And I had no legal recourse. He had me. I couldn't do anything—at least, not then.

To my amazement, without missing a beat or showing a bit of contrition, Al began spieling me a new, even grander scheme. He told me he'd met four guys who were building a manganese processing plant in San Luis Potosí, and they wanted him to join them in starting a new company, the Industrial Development Corporation. They'd own half the business, and if I teamed with him, he and I would own the other half. We'd make a legal contract to assure I'd get my share of the profits.

I seethed inside while he spun yet another chapter of his old familiar tale about our finding great wealth together in some faraway place. As he waxed on, I paid no attention to his promises of riches. When he finally finished his pitch, I agreed to join up with him—not to make money, as he assumed, but to wait quietly for a chance to get even.

Al's deceit had triggered my rage. I had never visited the dark depths of vengeance before, and I didn't feel comfortable there. I thought I knew him. He had lived across the street back home. I liked his mother and sister. I had not forgotten the good times we had as buddies in Philadelphia.

I still wanted to believe I had originally read Al right, so I wondered whether he had turned. I thought maybe the money had infected him. Howard, the old-timer in *Sierra Madre*, warned about what gold does to men's souls: "You lose your sense of values, and your character changes entirely." Then too, I thought Al's malice might have come from a lingering resentment of my leaving him behind when I went "high hat" in Paris with Barbara.

Looking back, I can see that the hottest core of my rage at Al came from my anger at myself. I had been half-crazy for two years now, all because I hadn't been strong enough to keep Barbara or stand up to her father. And now I was even more furious at myself, because I had been so naïve, ignorant, and soft that I had repeatedly let myself be played for a chump—by villagers, by a drunk, and even by an old buddy. I needed to get even with Al to show that I had not inherited my father's softness and that I would not live the rest of my life like a patsy as he did.

⸎

THE PARTNERS AL SCRAPED up for his new scheme could have starred in *The Three Stooges*, except there were four of them—two Americans and two Irishmen. Every one of them ran around with his hands in another partner's pocket.

This motley crew had made their money in retail merchandising. They knew nothing about manganese or Mexico. Although they had no idea how to design or run a manganese processing plant, Al expected it to be the first building block of our Industrial Development Corporation.

We celebrated its grand opening in the fall of 1952. All of us partners gathered together in front of the plant's heavy machinery in San Luis Potosí for a photo of the historic event. You can see there a mix of grimaces, stares, and smirks frozen on our faces. The only smile in the group beams from the happy Irish countenance of William O'Dwyer, the US ambassador to Mexico, who had come to bless our American enterprise and to crow about jobs we were creating.

Everyone is decked out in a suit and tie except me. I'm wearing dusty boots and work clothes. I've rolled up my sleeves. That made sense, because Al's second building block of our business was for me to find the manganese ore for the plant to process. Once again Al wanted me to do the shit work. Ironically, Al's dumping this hard labor onto my back turned into a transforming opportunity for me.

I finally began to learn about manganese.

It is no accident that the word "manganese" comes from *mangania*, the Greek word for magic, because it is as close to magical as anything that comes out of the ground gets. Manganese is used in everything, from agriculture to zinc, *including* the kitchen sink. It takes on many forms, from low-grade umber ores containing 12 percent manganese to 99.9 percent metal. It is, as I would write years later in my book *Manganese: The Other Uses*, "a source of manganese or oxygen—or both; of sulfate in glass manufacture; of iron in the production of manganese bronze. It is used for its effect in speckled brick and for its beauty as a gemstone. It is used in feed, food, fertilizer, fungicides, facebricks, frits, flux, fragrances, flavors, foundries, ferrites, fluorescent tubes, fine chemicals, ferric leaching, and ferroalloys"—and that's just the list of its uses that begin with the letter f.

Officially, it is element number 25 on the periodic table of elements, which you might or might not have learned about in eighth-grade science class. According to the *Essentials of Mineral Geology*, it is the twelfth most abundant element in the earth's crust, and the fourth most widely consumed metal after iron, aluminum, and copper. More than three hundred different minerals contain manganese, of which about a dozen are important. Its essential use is in the manufacture of steel, including stainless steel.

By definition, steel is a combination of iron, carbon, and other elements known as ferroalloys, the principal of which is ferromanganese. For every ton of steel, about 2 percent is made up of these ferroalloys—but that 2 percent is the difference between the steel used in a paper clip and the steel used to make the girders of huge bridges and giant skyscrapers. Because manganese forms a high-melting sulfide when heated to high temperatures, it prevents the formation of a liquid sulfide at the boundaries between the grains, making the steel stronger and more pliable. In other words, if manganese were a person, it would be the one friend in the group who goes all out a hundred different ways to do things for the others, while also strengthening the bonds between everybody else in the group. It's also the strong, silent type with just enough darkness and just enough shine to steal every girl. It's that kind of mineral. No wonder I like it.

For the next ten months, I worked as the company's ore buyer. I looked for working mines that were already producing high-grade ore I could buy, and I got to know the owners of the mines. I made friends with them, and step by step I built a network of small producers of manganese.

Although I fed the company a steady stream of ore from my hand-built supply chain, troubles at the processing plant constantly threatened the future of the company from the beginning. Shortly after our grand opening, the workers went on strike for more than a month because the Four Stooges weren't paying them. Labor disputes in Mexico could get out of hand, and people could get killed. I recruited a couple of gunmen, *pistoleros*, to show themselves around the plant. Everyone quieted down, and the workers eventually went back to their jobs once the partners began paying them.

We gradually realized our problems with the plant were more fundamental. The four partners had built an essentially ill-conceived factory, using a design that was fatally flawed.

The only reason to build this type of processing plant would be to upgrade manganese ore so we could sell it in a still-hot market to the steel industry, our ultimate customer. A plant could upgrade the ore in two ways. It could enrich lower-grade ore by mixing it with higher-grade material until it met a customer's specification. Or it could use a flotation method, in which low-grade ore is ground into a near powder and placed in a tank of water. Manganese, which is heavier than impurities, drops to the bottom and is then captured and made into nodules ready for market.

Our plant couldn't do either of these processes. If we had manganese of a high enough grade, we didn't need the plant. If we didn't, the plant couldn't produce what we needed to make money. My partners gradually discovered this when they couldn't sell what we were making.

The Industrial Development Corporation had a pretentious title, but any metallurgist, or anyone else who knew much about the industry, would have taken one look at what we were doing and had the laugh of his life.

By March 1953, we faced a crisis. We either had to raise more money to refit the plant or go bankrupt. It was clear that whoever would try to raise fresh cash needed to own the remaining assets of the company. This meant that one of the two sets of partners, either the Four Stooges or Al and me, would have to give up their holdings to the other. For weeks the tension built between the other guys and Al. He counted on me to help him deadlock any vote, until he could wear the other guys down.

One morning the fight came to a head. The four partners pressed for a vote. I was convinced they didn't know how to make the plant work even if they got more money, but I didn't care. I was tired of all the arguments. I was tired of Al. I was tired of being tangled up in a broken business. And most important, I saw my opportunity to get even with Al.

I broke the tie and voted with the Stooges.

Al hadn't seen my move coming. He was astonished and enraged. He took me into the next room and stomped and yelled at me. I thought he was going to try to hit me. Part of me hoped he would. I was bigger and fitter. It would have felt good to beat him to pulp and leave him on the floor like the cheater in *Sierra Madre*. But I knew I had already hurt him more than I could with my fists.

"How could you do this to me?" he howled.

"So, what can you do about it?" I answered.

We never spoke again.

ELEVEN

Manganeso Mexicano

By the spring of 1953, I had spent most of the first year failing at prospecting and most of the next getting screwed by Himfar. Then Industrial Development Corporation went bankrupt, and I walked away with almost no money in my pocket. Plus, my GI Bill had run out. Obviously, the right time to start a business of my own. I called it Maganeso Mexicano.

My plan was to buy and sell high-grade manganese ore. I wouldn't need a plant to process ore. I wouldn't have workers to pay, so I would have small operating expenses. I started my company with three intangible but precious assets I scraped together from the abandoned bones of the failed processing company: a supply chain of manganese producers to buy from, customers to sell to, and someone to help me do the work.

Of the more than a dozen miners I had found during the previous year, a few were quite tiny operations in which the kids and wife helped out. Some were medium-scale entrepreneurs who worked a local mine or two. A couple were larger-than-life men who dominated the mining in a region. I learned which miners I could depend on, and they came to trust me to keep my word and to deal with them fairly.

To strengthen and expand my network, I must have visited seventy or eighty mines, open pits, shallow shafts, and deep shafts. Sometimes the locals would dig a hole in the ground like you would dig a well, leaving outcroppings that signaled a body of ore in the mine. I learned to detect manganese by its coloration and its feel—and by "learned,"

I mean that I learned from all the people around me, who showed me what to do.

One person who taught me a lot about manganese was Al Rodriguez, a geologist from Paradise, California. Al taught me to look for high-grade ore when I saw a colony of ants, because they fed off some of the elements in manganese. I learned to recognize the presence of the rock from its brittle composition and its light gray color, which was used—in its manganese dioxide form—for ink cave paintings more than twenty thousand years ago. I learned to identify the metallic taste of manganese in water affected by the mineral. I developed a sense about which mines would be real winners and which ones would not—largely because I developed a strong sense of which people I could count on and which ones I couldn't trust.

After my unhappy experience at the Japanese mine, I always had an independent assayer verify my judgment, and if I hadn't dealt with the analyst before, I stood by and watched to make sure he wouldn't screw me.

This supply chain became the first key part of my new business.

I also had customers who would buy the ore. A small set of international mineral companies dominated the world market after the war, mostly led by a clutch of European-based Jews who had been scarred by the Holocaust. Two of the biggest of these firms fielded seasoned, savvy managers in Mexico.

Kurt Reinsberg headed the Associated Metals and Minerals Corporation. He was a German Jew, born in Belgium and raised in Cologne, where he learned about the Nazis up close. He began working in international trading as a teenager in Amsterdam. He took the Nazis at their word and escaped to New York in 1937 with only a batch of Leica cameras as his primary stake. He immediately got a job with Associated Metals, rose quickly in the company, and handled big deals in Mexico even before the war. He was backed by a bright Mexican playboy, Max Zozaya.

Walter Burger led the Continental Ore Corporation. He was backed up by a man named Ernst Kaiser, who had spent the war hiding from the Nazis in Holland.

Reinsberg and Burger had deep knowledge of minerals (Reinsberg, for example, was the king of zinc) and of how to market it. They all spoke several languages fluently. I was fascinated when Burger switched from German to French to English without missing a beat in his speech. Their narrow escapes from the Holocaust made them realists about the darkest side of humans, which in turn made them wise, wily, and hard.

The bankrupt Industrial Development Corporation had disappointed these ready customers, first by failing for a year to supply the kind of ore they wanted and then by going belly up. They didn't have anyone on their teams willing to go into the field, but they still needed high-grade manganese. Fortunately, and most important for my start-up, they already knew they could depend on me to supply them. I had shown them for months that I would deliver what I promised. All I needed was someone to help me do the work.

Enter Ninay Gonthier. Ninay had played an important role in the Industrial Development Corporation, running our office in San Luis Potosí and keeping her head while all the Stooges were losing theirs. She knew the players in San Luis who counted, and everyone liked her. We had worked closely together, and we trusted each other. She knew how to get things done. When the company went bankrupt, I asked her to help me run my new business.

A few years older than I, Ninay was short, stocky, masculine-looking, and not very pretty. She had never married and lived with her parents. Her family had deep but obscure French roots. I seldom saw Ninay's father, an elderly retired French tailor with some mysterious claims to high fashion and royal clients before the war. But her mother certainly enhanced our company's status in town. She had taught English for years in San Luis and was so highly regarded that many prominent people came to her for advice.

The Gonthiers' elegant Spanish colonial home sat on one side of the town's central plaza, facing the commanding baroque cathedral. Perhaps 150 years old, the house had an aura of old money and faded standing. Like most of the fine homes in San Luis, its high-ceilinged rooms were built around a patio. Some were filled with splendid antique furniture that was rarely seen and never used. It was a strange place. Little dogs ran around freely. A flock of parrots chatted away with each other and tried to talk with me. You could have made a Tennessee Williams movie in the Gonthier house.

We set up our company's offices there, a few desks and chairs in three small rooms that faced the plaza. Ninay used one room to meet with miners who brought samples of their ore to a door that opened onto the street.

These were hard times. I had no cash reserve and spent most of my money on the business. My primary customer, Associated Metals, advanced enough money for me to buy ore. When I collected about fifty tons, I would sell the lot and make a modest profit. I lived from hand to mouth and sometimes wound up flat broke.

Fortunately, Ninay and her mother fed me and let me stay in their home for a while. I met a friendly French medical student with a nice little apartment who let me sleep on the floor. I spent most of my time in the field anyway.

To keep going, I had to scrounge for cash in almost any way I could, which sometimes caused me to make decisions I wouldn't necessarily make today. For instance, I began to buy and sell pre-Columbian artifacts stolen from ancient ruins east of San Luis. This trade resembled my manganese business. Mexican grave robbers found me and offered artifacts they had dug up. Sometimes these thieves tried to cheat me with fakes that looked pre-Columbian. I always took the items to an expert who would tell me their real value. Then I sold the authentic artifacts for a profit to a wealthy collector, a dentist named Leon who was drummed out of the University of Pennsylvania for being a communist. Something of a star in his field—one of the pioneers of root canal therapy—he was the president of Mexico's dentist and became a friend.

Looking back, I'm conflicted when I think about the fact that by buying antiquities, I also encouraged grave robbers. I fully realize the ethical shortcomings involved and how this reflects on my younger self. On one hand, I sympathize with those who believe such artifacts belong in the ground. On the other, it was precisely those kinds of transactions that have helped us know and learn more about long-gone cultures since the beginning of time.

One major difference was that mining manganese was legal; dealing in treasures robbed from graves was not. Another big difference was that my markup for the artifacts was much higher. This stream of cash fed me and kept my nascent manganese company from failing.

Along the way I fell in love with pre-Columbian art. I became especially attached to a pair of genderless figures, one about fifteen inches tall, the other about eight inches tall. I've kept them in a place of honor in my home all these years. I've often thought about this couple, buried in a tomb somewhere, living intimately in the netherworld together for hundreds and hundreds of years. When they are positioned the way we think they were in the grave, you get the impression they are quietly chatting. I couldn't imagine one without the other. Over the years, I've had my own serious conversations with these figures, especially the smaller one. I've talked with them about my troubles and frustrations.

While I built my business, I also read. In December 1953 I wrote my sister Janice: *Intellectually I keep reading and reading and reading, and it's taken the form of a bug—an infection from which I hope never to recover. Who would have ever thought it?*

I found the quiet evenings in San Luis ideal for my studies. While working in the dirt and dust of the dark, close passages of a mine, I cheered myself by concentrating on the two things I wanted that night after work: a good book and three fingers of tequila.

Ninay lent me serious novels. I read Maugham, Hemingway, and Fitzgerald. I continued to read the works of the early philosophers. A close friend, a bookish Spanish woman with the non-Spanish name of Irma Dickenson, liked to delve into these thinkers too. She gave me a lot of her books, and we would discuss what we had read. At her suggestion, I took another crack at Nietzsche. I tried to talk with her about Orwell and communistic philosophy, but the only subject she would discuss at length was Catholicism. The Spanish Civil War was still fresh in the minds of Spanish families, most of them pro-Franco.

I needed a quiet spot to read and drink. The only place I could find was the local whorehouse in San Luis. So I made a deal with the madam that didn't include the pretty girls. Most nights, when I wasn't in the field, I walked to the plain adobe building on the outskirts of town, settled into a booth, drank tequila, and read for three or four hours. For two years, this was my near-nightly ritual—the gringo who came to the whorehouse to read.

For all my reading, I would never have found in Fitzgerald or Saint Augustine the crucial lessons I was learning in the field as I built my business. My work was sometimes physically dangerous and required me to take chances, so I made certain rules to remind myself to avoid taking crazy risks.

My most basic directive was Rule One: Don't die. It seems silly to say it that way, but that rule was always very much in my mind. If I was dead, I couldn't succeed.

Rule Two was a corollary of this: Never go down a mine shaft first. To get to the ore, I usually had to climb down ramshackle ladders, sometimes a hundred feet down. Small, thin people had built these ladders, usually out of whatever string and sticks of wood were available. They were always rickety, so I couldn't take safety for granted, especially on my first trip down. I always asked one of the miners to go first. He might give me a dirty look, but I insisted. We never had an accident.

Rule Three was also a corollary to the first: Never get into a fight. My reluctance to fight became firmer as I realized you could not win a fight in Mexico. If you lost, it's likely you were hurt. If you won, the brother of the guy you beat up would come after you and kill you.

I usually could keep Rule Three in my back pocket, because I rarely faced such dustups. Most Mexicans I met liked me, and I liked them. I was the only American ever to visit many of the villages and mining areas where I did business. I was the only gringo who had gone down with them into the depths and darkness of the mines, the only one who stayed with them when cracking sounds in the walls of ore made us wonder what might happen next. I was probably the only American they knew who dealt with them straight up and fairly. I lived easily and naturally among them.

I learned their language in everyday ways, at their tables and as we worked the mines together. Every time I opened my mouth in Mexico City, my urbane Mexican friends laughed, because the Spanish I'd learned in the hills made me sound like a bumpkin.

The Mexicans I dealt with at the mines and in the villages embraced me. They called me *El Gringo Mojado*, the American Wetback. They found it funny that I had crossed the Rio Grande, which they called the Rio Bravo, in the opposite direction from all the Mexicans who went to the States to find work. These were the years when the administration of President Dwight Eisenhower created a program to bring Mexican workers across the border to work the harvest, especially in California and Texas; often they were treated badly and then trucked back when it was over. I took it as a badge of honor that my new friends used the two most contemptuous pejoratives Mexicans and Americans threw at each other to make this joke of a name for me, a gift of great affection.

By early 1954 I could see some modest and growing success. Most important to me, Manganeso Mexicano was my own, and it was real. I wasn't playing angles with war surplus. I wasn't chasing one of Al Himfar's fantasies.

TWELVE

Montaña de Manganeso

I had just come out of a café where I had stopped for coffee and was standing on a street corner when he spoke to me. "*Buenos dias*, Señor Stanley," he said. "I am Genaro Mendoza."

I had driven that morning about two hours north from San Luis to Charcas, a town of about ten thousand and the center of one of Mexico's historic mining regions. Silver had been mined there since the sixteenth century. For years the American Smelting and Refining Corporation processed zinc and copper in a huge plant nearby. I didn't have a supplier of manganese there, and I was looking for one to add to my network.

Lots of people knew I was the only gringo running around in that part of Mexico buying manganese. I sensed, however, that Genaro Mendoza knew more about me than my name and had already sized me up somehow. By then I had bought and sold ore from lots of owners of small mines. A person earns his reputation in the hills either as a son of a bitch or as someone who is decent and does what he says he will do. I had done all I could to establish myself as the latter.

Mendoza and I eased into a nice conversation about this and that. I think he wanted me to have a chance to take my first reading of him. I liked what I saw: a quietly confident, self-possessed man in his early forties.

I also liked what I heard. He spoke with a powerful but unpretentious intelligence without an ounce of bullshit.

Most of all, I liked what I sensed about him as a person. His dignity impressed me. By the way he spoke to me, I could tell he assumed I was rich.

But I was taken aback when he told me that a mine had been built to dig into a mountain a half a century before and had been abandoned for years. The ore was just sitting there, ripe for picking.

How could this man, who seemed to be such a good bet, try this shabby old dodge that locals had by now pitched me dozens of times.

I wanted to trust him, but I didn't want to be played for a sucker again. I said, "I'll tell you what we'll do, Señor Mendoza. You drive me to this mine. If there really is a mountain of manganese, you and I will become partners. But if there's nothing there, I'm not going to pay you a peso." Of course, what he didn't know was that one peso was about all I had to my name.

WE DROVE FOR ABOUT an hour over rugged terrain. The rough trail was better suited for a pickup truck than for Mendoza's car. He told me about himself as we drove. He loved to talk, and I loved listening. He had worked for the American Smelting and Refining Corporation plant in Charcas, known as AS&R. Townspeople who spoke English called it the American Stealing and Robbing Corporation. Mendoza learned a lot about smelting and mining there, but they didn't treat him very well. Then he worked for the same company in Chicago and learned English. They didn't treat him very well there either.

He told me he had saved enough money to start several businesses in Charcas. He owned a taxi company. He had a gas station—an outlet of Amex, the country's oil company. He ran the town's Pepsi-Cola franchise. Both were concessions from the Institutional Revolutionary Party—the Partido Revolucionario Institucional, or PRI—which had dominated Mexican politics for a generation and which he ran locally. He told me about his wife and how much she meant to him.

Mendoza finally pulled up near a huge mound amid the sprawling remains of what had once been a large mine. Scraps of deserted super-structures lay about: weather-beaten stockpiles of random mining stuff, scattered fragments of fallen jerry-rigged ladders. The mine's deep shafts hadn't been touched for years.

As soon as we entered the open pit, I smelled manganese. I chopped around with my miner's hammer and I kept coming up with high-grade ore.

He told me the de Léon family owned the mine. I had no idea who this family was, but he knew their history in detail. José de Léon, a fervent Catholic, had assassinated Mexico's anticlerical president, Álvaro Obregón, in the late 1920s and had been quickly executed. This left a bit of a cloud hanging over the family.

Mendoza explained that José's brother owned the rights to the mine but hadn't done anything with it. He said the brother, a drunk, came to Charcas to get away from his wife and drink the day away in a bar. Mendoza was certain we could make a deal with him.

We needed one more thing: enough money to get the mine running again. There was only one person in the world that I could turn to: former ambassador Bill O'Dwyer.

⌁

THINGS HAD NOT GONE well for O'Dwyer, with whom I had become friendly, since first meeting him in San Luis in the summer of 1952 at the opening of the Industrial Development Corporation's ill-fated processing plant. President Truman had sent him to Mexico to cool the political heat the Democrats were feeling from O'Dwyer's alleged ties with organized crime when he was mayor of New York City following the war. After Eisenhower's election in 1953, however, O'Dwyer lost his ambassadorship and its political cover, and the IRS was still pursuing him for taxes he hadn't paid. Little surprise that he stayed in Mexico, nursing his scars, and joined a law firm in a role that required little heavy lifting.

His wife, Sloan Simpson, the former First Lady of New York City, divorced him shortly thereafter. She was a beautiful former model who was twenty-five years his junior and had helped him sparkle in Mexico's flashy social set. She had moxie, too. Whenever O'Dwyer had needed a favor, he had sent her to meet with the president of Mexico, who couldn't resist her. But now she was gone. His friends had mostly deserted him. He lived alone in the penthouse at the Prince Hotel in Mexico City.

After he lost his job, I visited him whenever I was in town. I liked this hearty, handsome Irishman and his booming musical voice. He was the quintessential Irish storyteller, always ready with the perfect tale, poem, scripture, or toast for the occasion. He would greet me with a bear hug and open enthusiasm. I was flattered that he enjoyed my company. O'Dwyer was about my father's age. He wanted me to call him "General" in reference to his war service, not "Mayor" or "Mr. Ambassador." He always called me "Kid."

I loved hearing O'Dwyer tell about his exploits as mayor and his adventures in Italy during the war. Unlike Louis Marx, who used his bevy of generals as his own private audience, I was delighted to sit for hours *listening* to my friend the general, one more in a string of gifted talkers whom I admired. My father told jokes. Guy Burgess was wickedly witty. Mendoza talked about life. And General O'Dwyer spun tales full of color and inside dope, always punctuated with a kicker punch line and a boom of infectious laughter.

Everyone had accused him of stealing while he was mayor. But the only thing he stole from that I knew about was the embassy's liquor cabinet. The two of us drank a lot of its Irish whiskey while he talked and I listened.

When I arrived from San Luis that early spring day in 1954, he greeted me with his usual warmth. After a glass or two of Jameson's, I told him about the mountain of manganese and explained we couldn't get going without a stake.

"How much do you need, Kid?" he asked.

"Ten thousand dollars," I said.

I had picked this amount out of nowhere. I figured this amount would buy us some start-up equipment and give us enough to pay the workers until we could produce our first railroad car of ore.

He immediately wrote me a check for ten grand. I asked him if he wanted to be a partner, but he waved me off. I told him I would pay him back. "All right, Kid," he said. "If you make it, you can give me back the money. But if you don't, forget it."

That afternoon I hurried back to San Luis and signed a contract with Mendoza, formalizing our partnership. We called it the *Montaña de Manganeso*, the mountain of manganese. We then signed an agreement with Señor de Léon, who was happy to authorize our operating his property in return for a small fee, what we called "de Léon's drinking money." I went to bed late that night with a much different future stretching out before me than had existed when I got up early that morning.

⟋⟋⟍

I HAD TAKEN MY first readings of Genaro Mendoza's character by instinct and by listening to him. Now I took a deeper reading of him by watching how he dealt with the townspeople of San Luis Potosí. I saw how much they admired his integrity, his character, and his fearlessness.

Mendoza knew how to pull people together. He hired hardworking indigenous Mexicans from villages around Charcas. They trusted him and wanted to work for him. He had earned their trust as the *cacique*, the head man in charge of the entire area. Although the PRI had invited him to go into government in Mexico City and make some "big-shot money," he preferred to stay in Charcas. He wanted to help the townspeople. He spoke the language of their everyday life, and they saw how wise and fair he was. They came to him for advice, for help, for his blessing when they wanted to marry.

They also knew how tough he could be. The biggest bullies in town, two brothers, were scared shitless of him, because they knew if they ran amok, he would shoot them.

As Mendoza and I set about to reopen the mine, we discovered how well we worked together. I brought the money, a ready customer, and a knack for promoting the business. He brought a loyal and ready work-force, and he knew everything about how to work a large mine.

At first the men carried the ore up the ladders in bags on their backs. After a while we used burros to lift the bags by pulleys. We loaded the ore into trucks and drove it to the train station in Charcas. I had already sold it.

As the spring wore on, our business was taking off. The Montaña de Manganeso had more treasure than we could mine, and Associated Metals wanted to buy more ore than we could ship. I also sensed I could grow Manganeso Mexicano and my network of suppliers even further if I had help.

To take the next step, I needed someone with two strengths—some-one who could get things done operationally and who was tough enough to back me up physically.

Many of the places where I worked were essentially lawless. I had loved watching Bogie and his buddies fight off the banditos who tried to steal their gold in *Sierra Madre*. But I had learned that it was one thing to get excited about gunplay sitting in an air-conditioned theater in Georgetown munching popcorn, and quite another to travel alone on a dark Mexican road.

One morning around two o'clock, on the way back to San Luis with Manuel, a friend, I lost control of my car as we came around a curve, and I swerved to avoid hitting some burros in the road. We rolled two or three times and landed upside down in a gully about fifty feet deep. We could have been—and probably should have been—dead. When we finally came to a rest, I had a bump on my head. I looked around and realized Manuel was in the backseat. I got out and said, "Manuel, *estas muerto?* Are you dead?"

No answer.

"*Estas muerto?*"

Then came a quiet response: "No."

The irony was that Manuel was always telling me he was going to kill himself. One day, when I was sick with infectious hepatitis, my doctor told me above all else not to get upset. Around the same time, Manuel told me that he was going to shoot himself. So I suggested that if he really intended to go through with it, he should go down to the basement so the sound wouldn't upset me. He never went down to the basement.

Miraculously, neither of us were really hurt, but we were still in danger. Banditos infested the area. To make sure they knew we were armed, Manuel and I took turns firing our pistols until daylight, when we caught a ride into town. By the time we got back to the car, banditos had stripped it, like jackals cleaning a horse's carcass. If we hadn't warded them off with our pistols, I'm sure they would have killed us and *then* taken the car apart.

Another time, I was checking out a possible new source of ore in the south with two local indigenous Mexicans to serve as guides. My car had no problem crossing a little creek going to the town, but on our return a couple of days later, the water had risen. I decided to chance it and got stuck in the middle. While we were sitting there, trying to figure out what to do, a truck pulled up. It was filled with Mexican farm workers coming back home from Texas. I asked them to give me a hand.

The stoned and drunk braceros saw the Texas license plates on my borrowed car, and they broke into a discussion about whether or not to kill me. Texans were notorious for treating immigrant workers badly, and Texas Rangers had been killing the workers' cows to stem the spread of hoof-and-mouth disease. My two guides fled, leaving me to my fate.

Luckily there was one sober man in the truck, the workers' leader. I told him that I was not from Texas but from far north—very, very far north. He cooled his men down and got them to pull me out of the creek. He refused to take money for helping and wished me a safe journey.

The absence of dependable law enforcement in the villages and the backcountry of Mexico made doing business so dangerous that some of my friends had to improvise their own protection. One time a feud between local Catholics and some newly arrived Protestants became so violent, it threatened the manganese properties of the Baron of Kellie-Auchterlonie, a Scottish aristocrat, in a little town south of Veracruz. The baron had gone to all the right schools and knew how to properly dress for the hunt. A bit of Swedish blood gave him fair skin and a shock of blond hair. He was a tough guy who knew how to take care of himself. He pressured the government to send in a squad of soldiers. He then paid their sergeant to warn both sides that he would shoot the first ones to start any more trouble. The fighting stopped.

Two other friends ran a thriving gold mine for years in Guerrero, the ill-fated site of my first prospecting adventure, which was perhaps the wildest and most dangerous place in Mexico. One time they caught thieves trying to steal gold from the company's safe. They took them outside, told them to run, and then had their gunmen shoot them.

At the end of *The Treasure of the Sierra Madre*, the villagers see that three banditos have stolen the prospectors' burros and equipment, so they catch them and shoot them. The movie was set in 1920. Lawlessness and rough justice in parts of Mexico hadn't changed much thirty-four years later.

I needed a smart, effective doer to help me run and grow my field operation—someone who was also strong and gutsy, someone I could trust to cover my back. I remembered playing baseball with such a man, and I returned to Philadelphia to recruit him.

THIRTEEN

Frank Senkowsky

I watched Frank Senkowsky step up to bat on a Sunday in late May 1954. It felt good to be back in Arden, playing ball with my friends and visiting with my family after three years in Mexico.

I had spent some time with Frank and his wife, Florence, who taught school with Harriet, my brother's wife, when the four of them came to see me at Georgetown before I left for Mexico. We had loafed together on a lazy afternoon like this one. I didn't know much about him, but I liked his mix of modesty, warmth, and fun.

Although he was always the tallest and strongest man in a group, he never flaunted his size. He didn't have to. He was muscular, and the relaxed way he moved spoke for itself. He had something about him, like Robert Mitchum: the quiet toughness, the chiseled face, the fearless look in his eyes.

I didn't yet know about Frank's true grit. He had joined the US Air Force simply because he wanted to help get rid of the Nazis. He got his licks in, serving as a gunner on B-17s and bombing German war plants on twenty-one combat missions. He was shot down twice. I learned later that when his .50-caliber machine gun broke while on a mission, he had the nerve and dexterity to fix it in flight and resume shooting, all while wearing a bulky electric suit and with the cold air blowing into his face. He had grace under fire.

The son of a blacksmith, he had learned mechanics in his father's garage. Westinghouse had taught him how to weld, burn steel, and fabricate huge cooling tanks for war transports with only a blueprint, one helper, and a crane. He knew how to build or fix almost anything. He had that good old Yankee (in his case, Polish-American) ingenuity.

Frank didn't know any more about me than I knew about him, and he didn't know anything about Mexico, mining, or manganese, but when I told him what I was doing and asked him to come and help me, he eagerly agreed.

We left for Mexico a few days later. That spring was full of promise. My three years of work had toughened me, and Frank's presence bolstered my confidence. I felt my business was about to blossom.

⚬⚮⚬

FRANK FIT IN NATURALLY from the start. He and Ninay Gonthier quickly developed a friendship. She taught him how Manganeso Mexicano worked. He and Mendoza grew as close as brothers. I introduced Frank to our suppliers. Everybody liked him and his big affable grin. He earned their trust right away.

Frank was also a fast learner. To accelerate learning Spanish, he moved in with a family of Mexicans who spoke no English. Mendoza helped him by gently correcting his mistakes. Before long, he could conduct business in Spanish.

In just a few months Frank mastered the critical skills of our manganese operations in the field. He could recognize the different kinds of ore. He learned what grade of manganese each mine produced. He became expert at blending, the art of mixing various grades of ore to match the specific needs of a customer.

Frank became especially adept at tracking shipments from our suppliers to our buyers in El Paso, Texas. He logged the number of every railroad car we used to ship ore and tracked each to make sure it got to Juárez, just before the border crossing. He made friends with the chiefs of all the important train stations en route. He always brought along a fresh bottle of tequila to help them remember to watch over our shipments and send the bills of lading right away so he could double-check our books.

By Thanksgiving, I realized Frank performed these field operations far better than I ever would. His ability to deliver critical results was more than expertise and skill. It was rooted in his character. He wanted every job done on time, and he wanted it done just so. It was a matter of honor. In all my life I never met a more consummate doer than Frank Senkowsky.

He and I worked closely together for about a year to stockpile enough manganese in El Paso for our first shipment to Associated Minerals, which continued to advance us money to buy ore and to mine the Montaña de Manganeso. Until we made our first big sale, we wouldn't have much cash to live on—or for Ninay to pay our bills.

Sometimes we cut it pretty close. Frank's wife, Florence, joined us that fall. The three of us plus their dog shared one tiny room in the Tuna Courts, a seedy little tourist camp outside of San Luis. After living there for a couple of weeks, we decided to drive to Chihuahua, five hundred miles north, to see one of our suppliers. But when we took our suitcases out to the car early one the morning, the police stopped us and waved their guns in our faces. They had slashed our tires to make sure we couldn't skip out in the night. Ninay hadn't paid the bill.

We gnashed our teeth for a while and then broke out laughing. We stayed in the room until her check came and cleared.

As Frank and I built our growing stockpile of ore that year, our lifelong friendship took root. We rode around together in an old pickup truck, visiting our suppliers, checking in with Mendoza, and looking for new mines to expand our network. Sometimes we would struggle to get up hills on muddy dirt roads. I would gun the truck to get as far up as I could, and Frank would put a rock behind the back tire so the truck wouldn't slide back down.

We had fun together. We played dominoes in the evenings. Frank always beat me. We drank gin or tequila, not to get drunk, but just because we enjoyed it. One day Frank, Florence, and I were tooling down a rough trail in the open country outside Durango, where we had been buying ore. I was driving an old Mercedes Frank had scrounged up. All at once, a bunch of costumed guys on horses were chasing us, keeping up on both sides of the car, shouting something I couldn't understand.

I quickly realized that I had spoiled the morning's expensive shoot of a scene in a film, a Western called *White Feather*. My oblivious dash

between the US cavalry and a party of Cheyenne warriors had infuriated the film's director. But the cast, especially Robert Wagner and
Jeffrey Hunter, thought our escapade was hilarious. They welcomed us
and introduced us to the other stars, Hugh O'Brian and Debra Paget.
They arranged for me to play an Indian in the next shoot, and I got
paid as an extra for a couple weeks. Wagner would go on to be one of
Hollywood's biggest stars.

In the hundreds of hours Frank and I spent on the road that year,
the two of us had lots of time to get to know each other. Every week
or so we drove my DeSoto twelve hundred miles from San Luis to El
Paso to check out our stockpile of ore. We took turns, one of us at the
wheel, the other sometimes sleeping in the backseat. Usually we passed
the hours talking, mostly about ourselves. Unlike most men our age,
we revealed our most intimate feelings, held nothing back, and thereby
became closer and closer friends.

The cash we made from our first big sale of manganese in the spring
of 1955 put us in business. It didn't make us flush, but it gave us enough
working capital to grow.

Since we could sell all the ore we could ship, we focused on expanding our supply of manganese. We stepped up our production at Mendoza's mountain. We also discovered another rich source nearby. We
followed a tip to a prospect where we found the classic telltale sign:
ants. When Mendoza's men dug down fifteen or twenty feet, we found
a rich deposit of very high-grade ore.

Their digging exposed an opening a few inches wide, but we couldn't
tell what was below. I began to chop into it. Mendoza warned me I
could fall into an underground cavern and get hurt, but I kept on banging away with my miner's hammer until I opened up the hole enough
to see what was below: the cache I had been hoping for.

I climbed down a ladder into an unimaginably beautiful chamber,
perhaps fifteen feet high and thirty feet across. Its walls were made
of opulent blue-black manganese configurations, a gallery of exquisite
sculptures. We had found a magic place no human had seen.

We called our new mine La Abundancia, meaning "abundance." It
didn't have enormous tonnage, but it was high grade, and we made a

lot of money with it. We eventually mined it all until there was nothing left, except one especially lovely piece of naturally sculpted manganese. To this day, I keep that piece in my London home to remind me of the sumptuous treasure trove of its origin.

While we cranked up our two mines, Frank scouted for new suppliers. We fronted money for some so they could expand and send us more ore. In one case we reached too far, buying ore from José "Two Gun" Plancencia, a big-time manganese supplier and one of the few Mexicans I knew who had blue eyes.

When we first met Two Gun to seal the deal, Frank gave him a customary *abrazo*, a bear hug greeting that originated to let two men peaceably assure themselves the other was not armed. We thought it was hilarious when three pistols popped out of Two Gun's clothes— one more than advertised. That should have told us right away that something was fishy.

Two Gun asked us to finance some equipment at his mine so he could increase his shipments, and we agreed. But after a while, he stopped sending us ore. I wrote him and insisted that he send our equipment back, but he stubbornly stiffed us. Finally, I told our Mexican attorney to go see him. The attorney threw up his hands and said, "Are you crazy?" Only then did I learn that Plancencia was widely feared as a killer. Even the cops were afraid to go after him. In retrospect, that experience added another general rule to my growing list: Never go into business with a guy known as "Two Gun."

Our trouble with Two Gun was an exception. Frank found more reliable suppliers, including several in the northern state of Chihuahua. He moved there with Florence, opened an office. Our manganese business boomed.

✧✧

ONE DAY KURT REINSBERG told me he knew how we could make a lot of money together in the mercury business. Associated Metals had a contract with Mitsui, a Japanese company, to buy all the mercury we could supply. Reinsberg wanted us to go into the field and build a network of producers as we had with manganese. We would equip them, buy their quicksilver, and bring it to Tampico, where Associated would act as the middleman, shipping it to Japan and selling it. He knew that we had little working capital and didn't want to go into debt to get started, so he said he would advance us the cash to set up and run our supply chain.

Reinsberg suggested a couple of angles we could play to sweeten the deal for us both. First, we could exploit an edge on freight rates. The Mexican government had one set of rates for minerals, including *mercurio*, when shipped by the ton. But for historical reasons, Mexico demanded much lower rates for mercury shipped by the flask. Colonial Spaniards had called the mercury they used to leach gold *azogue*, not *mercurio*, and had transported it in seventy-six-pound flasks, the amount one man could carry. Reinsberg explained that we would ship only flasks of *azogue*.

He also explained that we could exploit a wrinkle in the Japanese import duties. They were very high for pure mercury, but there was practically no duty on mercury less than 99.9 percent pure. Reinsberg wanted us to buy pure mercury and then put dirt in it to make it impure. Frank was an expert at complex blending of manganese and had worked with mercury at Westinghouse. It was a breeze for him to contaminate what we shipped, so we could avoid the higher tariff rates.

Reinsberg clinched the deal when he promised we would evenly divide the profits we made together. We had become close friends, and we trusted each other. I would tell him our true costs. He would tell me his real selling price to the Japanese. We would split the difference down the middle, 50–50.

So I went into the mercury business. Cinnabar, the ore from which mercury came, could be found all over Mexico. It melts at low temperatures, so small producers could use quite primitive techniques to easily smelt mercury. They would burn the ore over a small open fire, capture the fumes in a pipe about three inches wide and several feet long, run the end of pipe through buckets of water to cool the vapor, collect the pure quicksilver in drips, and then sell it to us.

Soon our mercury and manganese businesses were booming. Before long, practically every manganese producer in Mexico sold ore to us, and in a few years we became the country's largest exporter. At the same time, we were making even more money selling mercury to Reinsberg.

I was growing stronger too. My self-confidence ripened. I was working for myself, freely and independently. I had earned the trust of two older men, Genaro and Frank, both of whom were strong and good. I no longer feared falling or failing. I hadn't collapsed into the hallucinated abyss of my nightmares. On the contrary, I had uncovered a dazzling treasure house of aesthetic and financial abundance in real life.

FOURTEEN

The Angel of Independence

I wanted to use my sales of manganese in mid-1955 to pursue my dreams of independence, family, and good times. I moved my mother to Mexico City and put her up at the Hotel Genève, a place with some historical elegance where I knew she would be comfortable.

She liked the people there, and before long she knew everyone. To me she resembled Mary Worth, a much-beloved comic strip character of the time—a gentle, gracious widow with an aura of kindness. She was pretty and always had a smile. People loved her and asked her for advice, just as they had on Queen Street. After about a year at the hotel, she found a lovely apartment, her own quiet place where she settled down and lived happily and financially secure for the rest of her life.

About the same time, I moved to Mexico City as well, in large part for business reasons. Our business had grown enough that each of us needed to focus on what each did best. Frank did everything in the field better than I, so he took over those responsibilities, moving around the country, buying mercury and manganese, and making sure we delivered what we promised to our customers. Mendoza stayed behind, making sure the Montaña de Manganeso and La Abundancia continued to produce. We needed a professional to manage our finances, so I persuaded my brother Buddy, a certified accountant, to bring his family to Mexico and join us.

I moved to Mexico City to do what I knew best—negotiate deals, manage relationships with our major customers. For a while I stayed at the Ritz Hotel, where a lot of mineral dealers hung out. I commandeered a low cocktail table in the lobby of the hotel and ran my business there until I found an office. Ironically, this was the same place I had begun my journey into mining four years before.

I moved to Mexico City for personal reasons too. I had been banging around the backcountry since arriving in Mexico, chasing tips, climbing down into mines, sleeping wherever I could on the road, and ducking banditos and braceros. Now I wanted a place of my own with my own bed, a place grand enough to signal my progress, a place to enjoy my freedom and independence.

I found a fantastic triplex on the tenth floor of a fine apartment building overlooking the center of the city. The living room had a window that looked down the grandest avenue in Mexico City, Paseo de la Reforma. I could see El Ángel, the commanding monument of the Angel of Independence that commemorates Mexico's liberation from Spain in 1810.

The air over the city was so transparent then that I could see Popocatépetl and Iztaccíhuatl a few miles away. Popa and Ixta, as they are popularly known, are two snowcapped volcanoes so majestic, they inspired an Aztec legend, *Los Novios*, about two star-crossed lovers destined to sleep close to each other forever. My new home and its magnificent view certainly trumped the one-room apartment I'd shared with the Senkowskys and their dog at the Tuna Courts.

I also moved to Mexico City to have fun. It wasn't hard to find. I had Max Zozaya to help get me started. I had worked with Max, Reinsberg's assistant at Associated Minerals, and we had become pals. Max knew everybody. He was handsome and likable. He loved women, and women loved him. He had married into an artistically connected family. Through him I met a galaxy of talented, beautiful women at the heart of Mexico's explosive art world, each with a backstory that boggled my mind.

Max introduced me to Lupe Rivera, daughter of the master muralist Diego Rivera, one of the most famous Mexican artists of all time. As a teenager in the 1940s, Lupe had lived with her father and stepmother, the equally iconic Mexican painter Frida Kahlo, who met Rivera when

Anna and Benjamin Weiss,
my grandparents.

Walter and Anne Weiss,
my parents, on Queen Street.

My father (top row, third from left) at the restaurant Polumbo's for a meeting with Henry J. Trainer and the Third Ward Republicans.

My mother as a young woman. She inspired my ambition from the very beginning.

My mother, Anne, with a young Janice (eight), Flora (two), and me (six) in 1933.

The children of Arden at a birthday party in 1939. As usual, I seated myself among the ladies. My sister Janice and I are in the front on the far right.

Buddy and I enjoyed a carefree summer in 1940 or 1941, oblivious to the turbulent events that would shape our future on the horizon.

My graduation from Central High School in Philadelphia, where I wasn't much for reading or writing.

My sister Janice (nineteen), and me (seventeen), with Janice's future husband, Kenny Kahn, in 1944.

On furlough at seventeen to see my mother, wearing my Army uniform. You can tell it's self-styled from the nonexistent crease in my pants.

Enlisted at last but too young to fight. When the Nazis saw this photo, they surrendered.

On leave in 1945.

Here I am in 1949 with my brother-in-law Kenny Kahn as I boarded the
ship to follow Barbara Marx to Paris. I was the only American in history
who went to France to learn English.

My mother loved to visit me in Mexico. She adored the Mexican art and people.

Industrial Development Corporation in Mexico in the mid-1950s. BELOW: With some of my partners.

One of many nights filled with fun in 1960s Acapulco. On the left, our friend Sergio Orlando and his wife; on the far right, me and the beautiful Lisa.

Frank Senkowsky having some fun of his own in 1955.

Lisa and I married on May 23, 1958, in San Francisco.

My wife, Lisa, racing on the slopes in Zurs, Austria. I don't remember if she won the race that day, but she certainly captured my heart. She was a breathtaking skier.

On the set of *The Hired Hand* in 1970.

LEFT: Hans Popper poses with a reluctant Turi, Lisa's beloved dachshund pup.
RIGHT: Gretl Popper with Lori Christina as a toddler.

Lisa and me amid the ruins in Mexico.

ABOVE: Hans Popper was my father-in-law, mentor, and ally. The self-described *ordentlicher Mann*. RIGHT: Lisa and her mother Gretl share a sweet moment.

Lisa's cousins Dr. Robert Popper (right) and Torben Lenzberg (left), who famously quipped, "When it comes to Lisa, vacation is her vocation."

Lisa, Lori Christina, and Anthony—my greatest treasure.

Lori Christina and Anthony.

she was an art student seeking his advice in the 1920s. In 1929, when Diego was forty-two and Frida was twenty-two, they wed—only to divorce, remarry, and divorce again.

Lupe invited me to lunch to meet her mother—Rivera's first wife, Olga, to whom he was married when his affair with Kahlo began. Their home, an elegant Spanish colonial, stood near the house where, in 1940, a Stalinist assassin had murdered Trotsky with an ice axe.

We feasted on delicious Mexican food Lupe's mother had prepared. With cool fans blowing around us, I ate voraciously. I was bowled over when Lupe gave me three of her father's drawings. They still hang in our home in London. I was entranced when they pointed to Rivera's extraordinary portrait of Lupe's mother hanging above the dining table. Then I was dumbstruck when they invited me to buy it. Diego himself was visiting Russia, but they said I could buy it for only $15,000.

I explained that I was just starting my business and living hand to mouth. I still wish I could have bought that masterpiece. Today, it hangs in a museum in Mexico City, as it should—an original master-work from a true genius.

After I moved to the city, Lupe introduced me to Annette Nancarrow, a painter and model. Annette was strikingly good-looking, twenty years older than I, and (as best as I can remember) between her third and fourth husbands. The country's three preeminent muralists—Rivera, José Clemente Orozco, and David Alfaro Siqueiros—had painted her. Her friend, the French diarist Anaïs Nin, captured her sensuality in a character based on her in *Seduction of the Minotaur*. Annette knew everyone in Mexico's fast-living artistic circle. She took me with her into its center, a swirl of fiestas and parties.

Max also introduced me to a group of fun-loving guys our age who called themselves "the Millionaires Club." Miguel Alemán, Mexico's president until 1952, had made their fathers wealthy by giving each a lucrative chunk of Mexican commerce. Melchor Perusquia's father got the Chrysler agency in Mexico and a wedge of Acapulco real estate to develop. Emilio Azcárraga's father got control of Televicentro, Mexico's television network.

These scions of Alemán's friends liked to gather at Focolare, *the* hot spot at the time—a very nice restaurant just off Reforma, not far from my place. They liked Max, and through him I became a part of them.

Some of us played poker in the penthouse home of my upstairs neighbor, Luis de Llano, Televicentro's leading television producer. I had dabbled in some casual poker on Fridays in the army, but the game at Luis's was for real. I didn't have much money, so I knew I had to get really good to compete. I bought a book, *How to Play Poker*, studied it; and began honing my skills.

I developed some special strengths that gave me an edge. For one, I learned to memorize the sequence of the cards as they turned. This required a clear head, so I didn't drink while playing.

I also learned to keep the other players off balance. Those who always bluff and those who never do could be recognized and gamed. But the most dangerous opponent is the one who plays so unconventionally, you can't tell what he is really doing. Sometimes I would throw away winning hands to confuse the table. I would play crazily until I saw their eyes glaze over. Then I would attack.

I noticed too that luck came and went in waves, as in life. When I sensed the cards weren't coming, I learned to discipline myself to drop out early. This was hard, because I liked to play. But when luck returned, I drove the table.

We would play three times a week, well into the early morning. We used cash, and a guy could win or lose several hundred dollars—several thousand in today's money. I was quite careful to keep my poker money separate from my other funds.

Luis, our host, was a good poker player. Emilio Azcárraga, however, played with the wild abandon of a man who was full of himself and whose father was very rich. We called him *El Tigre*, the tiger. He would try big and obvious bluffs. He would also try to pull an inside straight, like losers do. The stakes were more than I could afford, but my poker stockpile of cash grew because I almost always won Emilio's money. I should have called him *La Paloma*, the pigeon.

Since the risks of losing to Emilio were low, I always wanted to raise the stakes. I developed a habit. Whatever stakes other players wanted, I wanted them higher. This table of friends didn't seem to mind. But a few years later, when I tried to raise the stakes with more serious players, my compulsion got me into some choppy waters.

One night over poker, Luis de Llano and I decided to stage Mexico's first musical comedy. I would coproduce it along with two of our other poker regulars. Emilio would bring his family's clout and help me finance it. Rene Anselmo, another producer at Televicentro, would bring his professional expertise and the entrepreneurial talents that would later make him extraordinarily wealthy in the international communications business. Luis, a pioneer in Mexican television and one the most creative minds at Televicentro, would direct. We bought the Spanish-language rights to one of Broadway's hottest shows, *The Boy Friend*, which was then propelling a teenage Julie Andrews into stardom. It was going to be the first comedy of its kind in Mexico. We called it *Los Novios*, which loosely means "an engaged couple," a nod to the two legendary volcanoes/lovers overlooking the city. We wanted to attract any remnant Aztecs who might like musicals. The show was set in the 1920s, featuring dances like the Charleston, something that Mexico hadn't experienced. I knew the people would love it.

Everything went great at first. Luis and his talented girlfriend translated the libretto. He cast the show. I got to meet the chorus girls. We reserved the perfect theater. We got all the right permissions from everybody. The local *New York Times* correspondent, Paul Kennedy, heard we were about to make musical comedy history in Mexico and wanted to write about it.

We were dumbfounded a few days before opening night when the mayor of Mexico City intervened and declared we couldn't charge more than four pesos a ticket, or 32 cents US. We pled our case, telling him we would lose money even if we filled the house every night. He shrugged and said, "*El pueblo*, the people, can't afford your prices."

We said, "If they can't afford four pesos, why don't we give away the balcony for free and soak the rich?"

He wouldn't buy that, either. We opened anyway, and it was a great hit. We sold out the place every night at four pesos a seat, but had to close when all the money I wanted to put into it ran out.

We produced one more Broadway hit, *The Bells Are Ringing*. This time the mayor let us charge what we wanted, and we did better.

My good times also took me to some dark corners of Mexico City. I liked to go to El Paseo, a tiny restaurant in the center of the city where I could drink at a piano bar and listen to Bill Shelburne, an expat, play the American songbook. Late one Friday night after quite a bit of Gershwin and Johnnie Walker Red, I drove the wrong way down a dark street and accidentally banged into a guy on a motorbike, leaving him unconscious on the pavement.

I had been told that if you kill somebody in an auto accident in Mexico, it would cost you about $340 to settle everything. But if you injure someone with your car, they keep you in jail until they figure out how badly the guy's hurt. I called for help and stayed with him. When the police came, they threw me in jail.

They put me in a holding pen along with a couple dozen of Friday night's other street sweepings. It was crowded, filthy, and dark, and it stank of sweat, vomit, and piss. Anything could happen. Nobody was watching, and nobody would care. As the only gringo in the cage, I was on my own. I quickly understood why everyone arrested in Mexico wanted to be put in a penitentiary—because there, at least the guards would watch the prisoners. Here it was every man for himself.

A group of boozy men over on one side of the pen kept eyeing me and nodding their heads, murmuring (as best I could tell) about what they wanted to do to me. At first I thought I would hit one of them to preemptively show the rest of them not to mess with me. Then I realized there were too many of them. Besides, I wasn't exactly Joe Louis. Instead I moved to a corner where I could sit with my back against a wall, did my best to chase Johnnie Walker out of my head, and somehow got through the night.

After a lineup the next morning, the police let me meet with Frank and my brother. They said the motorcyclist was hardly hurt. I told them to get our lawyer to pay whatever it took to get me the hell out of there as quickly as he could. It cost me about $10,000—some $75,000 in today's money. It was worth it—I didn't want to deal with Saturday night's drunks, who I assumed would be an even larger and meaner crowd.

SHORTLY AFTER I MOVED to Mexico City, I began dating a woman named Mary Ann. For two years, from 1955 to 1957, we had a torrid affair. She was very pretty, bright, witty, sexy—and a lot of trouble.

Mary Ann moved in the same circles Max and I enjoyed. She was a girl around town with a not-so-good reputation. I didn't care. I wanted to be with her the first time I saw her. Her lush blond hair and stunning good looks drew me to her.

She made it easy for me to get close. She had an infectious love of life that made her fun to be with.

Mary Ann had had a hard childhood and hadn't had enough money to pursue her ambitions. She dreamed of being an artist, maybe a writer. She had a lot of natural talent, and we looked into an art school in San Miguel de Allende, a town north of Mexico City that was full of expat artists. Her intelligence and sympathetic ear made her a good listener too. We confided in each other intimately, and I felt truly understood.

Mary Ann was the first woman I enjoyed being with as much as Barbara. After a year of dating, I invited her to move in with me. We grew more and more serious. She wanted to get married. We even got a blood test. But I hesitated.

It troubled me when the easy charm that made her so likable would explode in flashes of fury that made no sense. Some nights she got really wild, out of control, even screaming in public.

Most troubling, I didn't quite trust her. I didn't want to believe my friends who told me she was promiscuous. She never flirted with guys when we were out together. But eventually I heard stories so specific and vivid that I feared the rumors were true. I became jealous and suspicious. We began fighting a lot, about nothing and everything.

Everybody was worried I was going to end up marrying her. Buddy,

Florence, and Frank thought she was bad news. My gentle mother, who almost never offered me advice, became so disturbed that she made her own inquiries about Mary Ann's behavior, reported her findings to me like a detective, and quizzed me about my intentions.

A visit with Genaro Mendoza in November 1957 helped clear my head. One night he and I sat by the railroad tracks in Charcas, trying to catch a glimpse of Sputnik 2. He was fascinated that the Russians had put Laika, a little terrier, into orbit. His love-hate for Americans made him simultaneously disappointed that the Soviets had beaten us into space and delighted that they had stuck their finger in America's eye.

Trillions of stars twinkled above us, yet it seemed we could see each one. Genaro pointed out the different constellations and treated me first to a lesson in astronomy. He then offered me a lesson about life as well.

He talked about how tiny we mere mortals are in the immensity of the universe and how brief our lives are in the infinity of time. He confided to me that what mattered most in life was family. He said the only way we can continue to create human good beyond our brief lives is through our children. He told me it was time for me to settle down, marry, and have children.

I returned to Mexico City knowing I needed a fresh start. One night in early December, I told Mary Ann to leave. She screamed, raged, and took her last two best shots at hurting me. First she told me she had been having sex with women, a taunt she hoped would crush my male ego. Then she put her cigarette out on my chest, packed up, and left.

Later that day, a woman from San Francisco called. She said mutual friends had suggested we get together while she was in Mexico City, and she proposed we meet for a drink the next evening. Her name was Lisa Popper.

FIFTEEN

Falling in Love with the Poppers

T he next evening, December 9, 1957—a few weeks before my thirty-first birthday—I went to the Prince Hotel to meet Lisa Popper. Her father was waiting for me at the entrance. I had never heard of Hans Popper, but I liked what I saw: a fit, nice-looking, well-tailored, composed gentleman old enough to be my father. He was strong and friendly, and his handshake immediately put me at ease.

He invited me to sit with him on his balcony and asked me about myself. He was a good listener. I sensed he might have looked into my background already and knew a lot of the answers to the questions he asked me. That didn't bother me. I liked his taking an interest in me.

He talked with me as if I were his peer, though I could tell he played at a much higher level. He said he had an iron ore mine in Canada. We chatted about men in our field. He told me that he had once worked in Dallas for Jake Feldman, one of the country's biggest scrap dealers.

An hour or more passed, and he hadn't mentioned what was keeping Lisa. I didn't mind. I was enjoying the conversation. He asked what I thought of the Eisenhower administration. I told him I supported Ike's sending the 101st Airborne into Little Rock to enforce the Supreme Court decision in *Brown v. Board of Education* on the desegregation of schools and usher nine black teenagers into the all-white Central High School. I was generally unpolitical, though, and didn't have many thoughtful answers to his questions.

Strangely, my naïveté neither bothered him nor embarrassed me.

His graciousness made me feel comfortable. I was especially taken by the way his mind worked and by his forceful intellect.

I sensed Hans was vetting me. Perhaps he wanted to make sure his only daughter wouldn't end up with the wrong guy. I learned later that Popper was meticulous and cautious about everything, so maybe his careful quizzing of me was reflexive.

Next, Lisa's mother came out to meet me. Gretl Popper made me feel welcome in her own way. I was drawn to her, a pretty gentlewoman, a model of Viennese dignity and grace. Her smiling blue eyes radiated a love of life. She shared Hans's openness, but was more intuitive than intellectual. I liked her directness. She wasn't there to interview me; she was taking her own good look.

When Lisa finally appeared, it was too late for just drinks, so we went to dinner. Neither of us was in the mood to start something serious. Lisa, who had cosmopolitan tastes, hadn't come to Mexico to look for an American, and I still felt bruised by Mary Ann. And anyway, we only had time to go out a couple of evenings before I had to go to New York. But falling in love is one of life's most intriguing mysteries.

Lisa stayed fixed in my mind while I was in New York. She wrote me right away: "Shouldn't I leave it to you to make the advance?" Then she showered me with reports of what she had been doing since I left and the good times she was having in the social swirl of Acapulco. The sparkling details reminded me of the combination of playfulness, intellectual curiosity, and fierce intelligence that I already liked about her, and her letter made me want to know her better. I was impressed by her vitality and her appetite for uncomplicated fun.

She told me about the Poppers' visits with the Mexican cultural elite. Luis Barragán, Mexico's greatest architect—who years later would become only the second recipient of the Pritzker Architecture Prize, that industry's highest award—invited them to dinner, where they talked "ART, ART, ART." Siqueiros, the renowned Stalinist muralist, and his wife also entertained the Poppers. Lisa told him she especially loved his painting of the back of a nude woman. He replied that such curves had inspired the original design of the guitar.

Her letters sparkled with such particulars, revealing her taste, her eye for detail, and her ear for the music of conversation. I was impressed with her easy confidence as she mingled with these luminaries. Even more, I liked that she focused, like her father, on their art and on them as persons, not on their celebrity.

Lisa's taste for the exotic also fired my imagination. I had never heard of Chinese pomegranates. She thought they were "pure heaven." She wrote that her evening dress was "made from an Indian sari" and was backless to the waist. I had never seen a sari, so I focused on imagining her bare back.

I couldn't get Lisa Popper out of my mind, and I didn't want to. In New York, I went to the opening of the film *The Bridge on the River Kwai*, but even its drama and dynamite couldn't distract me. I remembered Lisa's auburn hair . . . her dazzling smile . . .

Finally, at two o'clock one morning, I couldn't resist any longer. I had to call her. The operator at the Prince Hotel didn't know which of the Popper rooms was hers. I just picked one, hoping and gambling I wouldn't wake up a grumpy Hans Popper. When Lisa answered, I told her I wanted to see her. She wasn't grumpy at all.

I had a gut-wrenching fear of flying at the time, so I went by train to San Antonio, then drove nonstop for twelve hours to Acapulco, where the Poppers were staying for the holidays, and promptly fell asleep late on New Year's Eve. When I awoke, Hans resumed the conversation we'd had when we first met.

I learned that his values, taste, and intellect had been shaped in Vienna, where he had lived until he and his family had fled the Nazis in 1938. A learned and ardent social democrat, he wanted to know what I thought about the evolutionary and humanistic socialism that had flourished in the Europe of his youth. Like most Americans, I had never heard of it.

He asked me if I knew about Karl Kraus, his most important intellectual hero, a fearless Viennese satirist who had won young Popper's heart and mind by relentlessly torching the city's corrupt elite. I hadn't, so he gently suggested I might delve into him sometime.

Hans also wondered if I had read Erich Fromm's *Escape from Freedom* or his *The Art of Loving*. I hadn't, but I told him I understood he lived in Cuernavaca. Neither of us could have imagined how big a role Fromm, one of the world's most prominent and influential psychoanalysts, would play in our future lives.

Unlike Louis Marx, Popper wasn't trying to humiliate me by exposing my ignorance. His queries were solicitous gestures of respect and regard, investments in mentoring a young man he liked. He wanted to help me grow.

I loved the idea that the Poppers were Middle Europeans. I hadn't read Schnitzler, studied Freud, or listened to Mahler, but I knew that Jewish intellectuals, musicians, and artists in Vienna had helped make that city one of the world's most vibrant centers of ideas and aesthetics. When I listened to Hans Popper, I could feel their aura, and I wanted to soak in it.

As the Poppers prepared to return home shortly after New Year's, Hans surprised me with a couple of unusual tokens of his trust. For one, he asked me to carry an important pre-Columbian artifact out of Mexico. It was illegal, but he knew I crossed the border often and without any trouble. He was both asking me for a favor and promising me a visit to their home in San Francisco when I delivered the piece. Then they gave Lisa permission to spend a few more days in Mexico. It was very flattering to think that, as now seemed clear, all three Poppers had feelings for me.

Lisa and I spent most of a week together, getting to know each other. We fell in love, suddenly, simultaneously, and forever. We didn't think about it. We didn't consider it. We didn't decide to do it. One mysterious moment both of us simply knew we were in love.

I was attracted to her presence and beauty. She effortlessly lit up any room she entered. She had traveled throughout Europe since she was fourteen, and she had excited the imaginations of viscounts, French actors, and champion skiers. I could understand why an entire tennis team had pursued her, all of them at once.

Lisa's intelligence also attracted me. She had a bright, engaged, and

polished mind. She was precociously self-assured. I admired her exquisite visual and musical tastes. She had been born with them. Hans had
honed them. While attending Sarah Lawrence College, just fifteen miles
north of Manhattan, she had refined them to suit herself. She told me
she'd once had an argument at her parents' dinner party with the wife of
a San Francisco music critic about Yehudi Menuhin's encores in Carnegie Hall—to give or not to give?—which I knew nothing about. She was
so feisty that her parents almost asked her to leave the table. I relished
her spirited independence.

We both found pleasure in the company of bright, energetic friends
and liked our fun spiked with music and games. It mattered to me that
Lisa shared my taste for good times.

The fiery core of my feelings for Lisa was my love for her as a woman.
Soon after the Poppers had left us alone, I took her to Cuernavaca. After
dinner we strolled down an ancient stone path in the sweet of the evening. I kissed her and wanted more. So did she.

⁂

I WAS FALLING IN love with Lisa, but I was also falling in love with her
parents. The rich, elegant life they personified fired my ambitions and
inspired me to grow. I wanted more of Gretl. I knew I could depend on
her to level with me. I felt she would always be in my corner, like my
own mother was.

I was especially drawn to Hans. He had built his wealth by himself
and made sure Gretl and Lisa were financially secure. He had the business muscle and daring to operate on a global scale. His success freed
him to live as he wanted and to pursue art, music, travel, and the world
of ideas. I admired him and wanted to learn from him.

Hans's respect and affection for me reinforced my sense of worth.
I sensed he wanted me to be the son he'd never had. This strong, good
man's embrace deepened the way I saw myself so I could fall truly and
naturally in love with Lisa.

On her flight home from Mexico, Lisa wrote me about her dreams for our life together, when we should have children, where we might live—New York or Europe—how she wanted to show me the places in Paris that ran in her blood. She abruptly canceled her plans to ski in Europe at the height of the season to spend time with me.

I hurried to San Francisco. We were serious about each other and didn't want to wait. We had seen each other about ten times, exchanged a couple dozen letters, and made a few long-distance phone calls. We felt our love was certain and, only three months after we met, told our families we wanted to marry.

Our parents were elated. My mother wrote me, "There's just a singing in my heart." She said she wanted "to feel that Dad up in heaven is sharing our happiness." She knew the wonders of married love. She adored Lisa after their first meeting.

Gretl showed her delight by coaching me about the fine points of pleasing Lisa. She loved conspiring with me about an engagement ring. She slipped me the name of her jeweler in New York, a family friend, who knew Lisa's tastes. When Lisa was under the weather, Gretl suggested that I send flowers and offered to pay for them. She even gave me a friend's address where I could write her covertly about such matters.

Hans offered some fatherly advice too. He suggested I surprise Lisa by learning French, which she spoke fluently. He thought this would make "a lifelong impression on her." I found a first-class teacher, studied an hour a day, and painstakingly read a French newspaper using a dictionary. But I gave it up. My teacher, an alluring young woman, made it clear she wanted to give me more than French lessons. Fortunately, I hadn't told Hans I had started.

Most important, both Poppers made me feel like I was part of the family. They began signing their letters to me "Mabo" and "Babbo," the names they had reserved just for each other and Lisa. Hans wrote me that he had been thinking "about my children (I hope you permit the plural)." I wrote Lisa, "I never thought I could love a man." I was now happily engaged to marry all three Poppers.

I was also smitten by their beautiful residence in San Francisco. The Poppers enjoyed performing music at home. Hans regularly played the violin there with his friends in a string quartet. Their beautiful grand piano stood in the parlor.

Hans took me on a tour of the house, a visual version of our conversations. His aesthetic sensibilities pervaded every aspect of the Popper home. He told me an old friend, a German designer, had fashioned their distinctive modern furniture.

He walked me up the stairway so he could tell me about the marvelous paintings on its wall. Each had its own story. He had selected his wonderful artworks one by one on his frequent travels to Europe after the war.

I was struck by how many layers of personal connection Hans had with his art. He showed me an especially stunning work by Gordon Onslow Ford, who I learned had been a member of the surrealist group in prewar Paris. Like Hans, Ford moved to San Francisco after the war, and they became friends. They shared a passion for Mexican pre-Columbian art. They both studied Asian thought and sought serenity in the study of Zen. Hans showed me how Ford's studies of Buddhism had influenced the painting.

He ushered me into a gorgeous custom-built gallery where he kept his most precious treasures, a dazzling array of Asian ceramics and bronzes. He had painstakingly assembled this collection, one of the two or three most important of its kind.

The size and beauty of their home made it the perfect place to celebrate our engagement, and the Poppers threw us a grand party. A hundred or so of their friends and family welcomed me as warmly as Hans and Gretl had.

Lisa told me the guests thought I had an aura of mystery about me. They were intrigued that I spoke English with a strange British-Mexican accent. They had heard I had made some wealth in the mountains of Mexico, but none of them knew anything about manganese. They laughed when I told them that my mother was equally mystified about what I did—that when anybody asked, "What in the world is Stanley doing in Mexico?" she'd reply, "I think he's selling magazines."

Perhaps the Poppers' guests were impressed by the *San Francisco Chronicle*'s report on our engagement, which stated that I was "a graduate of Georgetown University's Foreign Service School and the Ecole de Sciences Politiques in Paris." It sounded good to me, and it seemed to have rung true to the Poppers.

⁊⁊

LISA AND I MARRIED on May 23, 1958, and immediately left for Europe. Hans gave us the honeymoon trip as a wedding gift. He also gave us detailed advice about our travel plans. He gently counseled me to stay at Hampshire House, his favorite hotel in New York, in his favorite suite with its magnificent view of Central Park South.

Our trip had its ups and downs. Since I didn't fly well, I felt I needed to get drunk just to get on the airplane to New York. My young bride had the terrible experience of flying across the country with her grossly drunken groom. After a couple of years, I shook my phobia about flying.

I had no problem at sea. We sailed on America's pride, the SS *Independence*, a posh postwar ocean liner that attracted the glitterati. I didn't have to sneak into first class this time.

One morning I bumped into former president Harry Truman while he was on one of his early morning constitutionals. He was much smaller in person than I had expected, but had every bit of the energy for which he was famous. I had come to admire the man in December 1950, when the president's daughter, Margaret, had sung at a public event and a snarky music critic for the *Washington Post* had written that she "cannot sing very well" and "has not improved." The next day, President Truman fired off a letter to the detractor that read, "Some day I hope to meet you. When that happens you'll need a new nose, a lot of beefsteak for black eyes, and perhaps a supporter below!" From that day forward, he became a model for the kind of plainspoken toughness I've wanted from presidents ever since.

Encountering President Truman on his walk, I introduced myself and told him about Mexico, and we fell into a conversation. He looked me in the eye and laughed and nodded knowingly when I told him how Bill O'Dwyer had sent his bewitching wife to get whatever he wanted from the president of Mexico. Truman was fascinated by volcanoes, and we reminisced about the two beautiful ones outside Mexico City. He told me he was getting off at Nice, because he wanted to see his friend Charles de Gaulle. This was vintage Harry Truman: accessible, down to earth, blunt, a real person. He made it easy for a young American to chat with his former president. He made me feel good about myself and about our country that bright morning. He was the first president of the United States I had ever met. I didn't imagine at the time that when Truman dropped the nuclear bomb, he had probably saved my life.

Lisa knew what she wanted on our honeymoon. She had her heart set on an Alfa Romeo to sport through Italy and France. She wanted to show her new husband some of her favorite places: a beloved room in the Louvre, a special hotel suite in Rome, Harry's Bar in Venice. She also wanted to introduce me to her old boyfriends in Paris. And the ones in Venice. And those in Rome. Fortunately, we had two months.

We spent the last part of our honeymoon on a twenty-eight-foot ketch, sailing around the Cyclades, a cluster of idyllic Greek islands in the Aegean Sea. In the mornings we swam and then loafed on pristine beaches. In the afternoons we wandered through the narrow walkways of ancient villages with their gleaming whitewashed stone houses. In the evenings we dined and danced quietly at harborside tavernas.

In midsummer, the wild Meltemi winds kicked up monumental waves in the Cyclades. Fortunately, we had a captain and a sailor to handle the boat, but the riotous waves made us seasick. One morning when we were both in the grips of our worst nausea, she asked me to get her some medicine.

I told her, "Go get it yourself."

She said, "Well, I guess the honeymoon is over." We tried to laugh.

After the sea calmed, we were recovering on deck when we saw an armada steaming past us, headed east. We were astonished to see what seemed to be the entire US Sixth Fleet: aircraft carriers, cruisers, and squadrons of destroyers—altogether dozens of warships and swarms of airplanes. We had never seen anything so formidable. We couldn't imagine what was going on.

A cable from Hans awaited us in Mykonos: "Please stay on the boat and go immediately to North Africa. Suggest Morocco or Tunisia."

I found a newspaper, in Greek, but I could tell from a huge map on the front page that US Marines were landing in Lebanon. A guy at the front desk told me that the pro-Western king of Iraq had been assassinated in a military coup. The premier's body had been dragged through the streets of Baghdad. Repercussions were rippling throughout the Middle East, and Lebanon was on the verge of civil war. Eisenhower had sent troops to protect its government. Although the Lebanese welcomed our soldiers with flowers, no one knew where violence would break out next.

Lisa and I ignored the advice and made our way back through an unperturbed Athens to our ship in Naples. I was amazed and moved that Hans Popper's love and cunning had reached halfway around the world to warn his "children" of the dangers he feared.

SIXTEEN

The Mysteries of Marriage

B ack in the Western Hemisphere, we returned to some delightful news about two of our wedding guests. Roger Boas was a close friend of Lisa's from San Francisco. Nancy Lee Magid had been a year ahead of Lisa at Sarah Lawrence College and became such a good friend that she was one of the bridesmaids at our wedding. Nancy had also gotten to know Hans and Gretl well during her junior year, which she spent abroad in Paris at the same time the Poppers lived there. When Nancy traveled out from New York for our wedding, she stayed with Charlotte and Siggy (Marshall) Kempner, who were Francophiles and close friends of the Poppers, at their beautiful house near the Presidio. On Nancy's first night in San Francisco, Lisa set her up with Roger and they hit it off right away. While dancing at the wedding, Siggy told Nancy that he thought she was going to marry Roger. And he was right—Roger and Nancy married six weeks later, and settled down together in San Francisco.

Meanwhile, it took some doing to transport Lisa and all her possessions to Mexico City. The Poppers flexed their muscles and made every effort to ease her move. Gretl asked her lawyer to find out how to get Lisa's belongings through customs duty-free. Hans made sure her furs and jewelry would be insured according to Mexican rules.

Hans took especially heroic precautions with Lisa's dachshund puppy. He phoned the president of Western Airlines to make sure they would accept the dog and guarantee her safe passage to Mexico City.

When I was waiting to pick her up, Mexican airport officials told me no one was permitted to make such princess-like arrangements for a dog. They were amazed when Hans's magic delivered Lisa's puppy into my hands. So was I.

The Poppers and I completed Lisa and her dachshund's move to my tenth-floor apartment by late September 1958. But Lisa faced one more bureaucratic tangle before we could settle in securely. She had been born in Vienna and had become an American citizen as a child. In those days, a naturalized citizen could lose her citizenship if she resided outside the United States for a long period. The issue hadn't arisen on her many trips abroad or even when she spent a year in France as a student. Now, we faced a mirthless official in the American embassy.

I asked the woman behind the desk whether declaring my wife to be a Mexican resident would jeopardize her citizenship.

"That's the rule," she said, scrutinizing our papers through her thick, steel-rimmed glasses. Then she added, without giving me a glance, "Are you a veteran of the Spanish-American War?"

"No," I said. I was not even thirty-two years old. Teddy Roosevelt's Rough Riders had defeated the Spanish in Cuba in 1898.

"World War I?"

"No."

"World War II?"

"Yeah."

"Well, if she's married to a veteran of the Spanish-American War or World War I or World War II, she has no time limits."

She stamped our papers without looking up and waved to the next person in line. Marching up Misery Hill at Fort Knox had been worth something after all.

⁂

OVER THE NEXT FEW years we enjoyed spending time with a set of spirited individuals and couples our age. The Italian ambassador to Mexico would spend half of the year with his wife, the other half with his girlfriend. He eventually became the ambassador to Egypt and invited us to visit. Sergio Orlando, a handsome young Italian, headed the Mexican operations of the typewriter company Olivetti. The two Davidoff brothers, Jacques and Leon, somehow made their way through the war from their home in Danzig and built a fortune in Mexico in textiles. Dr. Edmundo Flores was a well-connected Mexican agricultural economist in the government.

Lisa, with her fluent French, polished Italian, and recently mastered Spanish, moved naturally and gracefully among this international set. She was more European than American, and she had cultivated her Continental tastes during years of travel. One couple after another fell in love with her and introduced us to their friends.

We all took turns throwing lively parties, and sometimes dressing up in costume for the hell of it. We always had lots of good food, irreverent banter, and poker and gin rummy. There would be lots of empty bottles on the floor the next morning.

We often gathered at Jacques Davidoff's sumptuous home with its manicured lawns, constant perfume of flowers, and elegant pool lit for swimming at night. Jacques, a passionate poker player and an avid playboy, loved to have fun and knew lots of others who did too. He had Hollywood connections: an aging Cary Grant came to one party, and the athletic Charlton Heston once took a break from filming *Major Dundee* in southern Mexico to swing by.

Soon after Lisa arrived, we moved up to the penthouse of our building overlooking the Paseo de la Reforma. It had a balcony and more room. Lisa graced it with her exquisite taste. We built an open-air terrace on the roof, which gave us a panoramic view.

After a year or two, Lisa decided to throw a big party. I got to see her genius as a hostess in full play, an extraordinary talent that I've marveled at now for more than fifty years. She selected a roster of our most lively and compatible international friends. She knew if we jammed fifty guests into our space, the squeeze would add sizzle to the room. She attended to the myriad details and logistics with Hans's perfectionism and Gretl's impeccable taste.

I contributed the music. The afternoon of the party I happened upon a bedraggled band of Jamaican musicians standing on a downtown street corner with their steel drums and saxophones, looking downtrodden. They told me the manager at their last gig had stiffed them, and they couldn't get home. I told them I would pay their way back to Kingston if they would play at our party.

They made musical magic that night. Calypso's distinctive syncopation loosened hips and inhibitions. Everyone danced—in the living room, on the balcony, up on the terrace under the stars. We set up a limbo bar, and Lisa, a terrific dancer, showed us how to wiggle under it.

Lisa's big party set a pattern. We've had this kind of fun throughout our life together, in many places and with different sets of similarly bright and convivial friends.

Art was the vibrant center of Mexico's culture at the time. Its painters were the pride of the Mexican people. We made friends with some of Mexico's most rambunctious artists. Through her parents, Lisa had already met Siqueiros and the iconoclastic painter and sculptor Mathias Goeritz. We got to know and purchased paintings from José Luis Cuevas, Pedro Friedeberg, and Chucho Reyes. I introduced my bride to my audacious friend Leonora Carrington, the surrealist painter and muse of the muralists. To be in the middle of those conversations was like sitting between Bill Buckley and Ken Galbraith years later when they argued about liberalism versus conservatism.

One time, in 1959, we attended a local art opening and met the brilliant sculptor Alexander Calder and his wife. We invited them to our house for lunch one afternoon. For the longest time, the sculptor sat and listened to our conversation without saying a single word. So I brought over a bottle of tequila and asked if I could pour him a drink. He graciously accepted one, then another, then another. Before too long, he wouldn't stop telling stories, which concerned his wife, since he was leaving our house to do an interview. But it turned out to be an unforgettable afternoon, and to thank us, Calder gave us a small painting he had made. We still have it in our house in London.

Through our artist friends, we met a writer who would become one of our closest friends in Mexico. Carlos Fuentes was already a national treasure when we got to know him, one of the great Mexican writers of the 1950s and '60s, who would go on to earn a reputation as one of the greatest Spanish-speaking artists ever and likely the best Mexican novelist of the twentieth century. One of the best conversationalists and storytellers I had ever met, Carlos—who also later served as Mexico's ambassador to France in the 1970s—was urbane and sophisticated in a way that only Latin men can be, with an ability to make you feel as though you were the only person in the room. Impeccably dressed and perfectly mannered, he was a delight at any dinner party, particularly when he came with his wife, the stunning Mexican actress Rita Macedo, with whom he had a rocky relationship until their divorce in the early seventies. The four of us had a lot of fun nights together. Through Carlos, Lisa and I also got to know the equally legendary writer, poet, and diplomat Octavio Paz, who always wanted to know what we thought of world events before sharing with us his remarkably informed opinions. Eventually, Carlos married the beautiful and noteworthy journalist Silvia Lemus de Fuentes, who hit it off with both Lisa and me. Silvia and Carlos remained two of our closest companions in Mexico and, later, London. Silvia still is.

Often we invited our writer and artist friends to our home for quiet dinners too. We usually entertained only one or two couples at a time so we could have an intimate conversation. This also avoided fights. Mexico's artistic community was rife with raging egos and volatile temperaments, and torn by ferocious political and artistic quarrels. Cuevas's home had once been machine-gunned in a feud about art.

One night the revered Mexican painter Rufino Tamayo and his wife, Olga, came to dinner. Next to the three celebrated Mexican muralists, he was the country's crown jewel. Tamayo and his wife couldn't have been more gracious. Once we sat down for dinner, he began to draw on his napkin. He drew throughout the meal. I assumed he was making the sketch as a gift for Lisa. Instead, at the end of the evening, he wrapped the napkin carefully, put it in his pocket without a word about it, and said good night.

Our artistic friends delighted us both, but in different ways. Although Lisa didn't paint or sculpt, these artists embraced her as a peer. They sensed she had the taste and the soul of an artist. This was especially so with Luis Barragán, the gifted architect. Luis was about the age of Hans Popper. Tall, elegant, and impeccably dressed, he had the quiet self-assurance of a wealthy colonial landowner. While most of our artist friends were militant and fiery, Barragán's temperament and art were distinctively serene.

Luis said his work drew on the art of seeing, and he believed Lisa had such a discerning eye. They discovered they were simpatico both aesthetically and personally. She saw him once a week for years, and he became her most intimate friend in Mexico.

As for me, although I never developed a truly refined artistic taste, I certainly discovered that I liked being with people who had taste.

❧

LISA AND I ALSO shared an interest in Mexico's rich pre-Columbian culture. I took her to the wondrous Mayan and Toltec ruins across central and southeastern Mexico—from tall pyramids to exquisitely decorated temples and palaces that stood as the most inspiring creations of the greatest and most formidable civilizations of ancient North and South America. We visited Palenque, an abandoned Mayan city state in the far south of Mexico. We explored the haunting remnants of temples and tombs, and pondered the macabre sculptures of snakes and skulls that ringed these ghastly sacrificial sites.

Lisa enjoyed our trips as touristic adventures. In fact, she loved the life of a tourist so much, we named her dachshund puppy Turi.

But I felt a connection with the region's archaeology and art deeper than that of a tourist. I had learned about pre-Columbian artifacts not just to deal them illegally, but also because I was interested in what they revealed about the land and people with whom I had become linked. I felt intimately connected with some of these ancient relics, as I had with my pair of genderless figures who chatted with me.

I struck up a similar "friendship" with Tlaloc, the Aztecs' rain god, sitting at the entrance of the National Museum of Anthropology. He was formidable, twenty-three feet high and 168 tons heavy. His savage fangs and googly eyes made him look ferocious. For some curious reason, I came to believe that Tlaloc and I had become close friends.

After the Aztecs faded away, the statue of the rain god fell on its backside in a dry creek bed near Coatlinchan, a small town east of Mexico City. He rested peacefully there until 1964, when the National Museum of Anthropology wanted to move him to guard the entrance to its new exhibition halls. Villagers in his hometown rallied around him, opposed his relocation, and tried to physically block the move until the government bribed them with a package of public works for the town.

The movers strapped my new friend onto a specially built monster transporter. They paraded him through the center of Mexico City before irreverent throngs who were more interested in partying than worship. After they stood him up in front of the museum, I went to see him. I could tell he felt homesick, angry, and humiliated.

That night it began to rain. Though it was the dry season, it rained torrents—for days, it seemed. No one could remember such a deluge. It rained so hard and so long that Beatrice Trueblood, a friend of mine who had helped design the museum and arrange the rain god's relocation, became a bit unnerved.

I drove out to the museum again to have a quiet conversation with Tlaloc. "You made your point," I said. "Let it go."

He did.

◦⊙◦

I KNOW, OF COURSE, that my friendship with Tlaloc makes no sense. But whatever else it might have been, my connection with the rain god was emblematic of the deep, visceral relationship I had developed with Mexico over the years. I had tramped through the country's mountains and crawled on my knees in its dark underworld. I had studied William

H. Prescott's *History of the Conquest of Mexico*. I had mingled with all kinds of Mexicans with all kinds of tribal roots. I continued, on my own, to deepen my connection with Mexico.

I learned a lot about Mexican politics through our friend Dr. Edmundo Flores Fernández who invited me to join an informal club of left-wing Mexican intellectuals. Flores had a PhD from the University of Wisconsin, spoke perfect English, and loved the lively interplay of ideas. When he served as Mexico's ambassador to Cuba years later, President Fidel Castro came to his apartment in the evenings to talk and drink.

Our little group met once a week at Sanborns restaurant in the House of Tiles, a sixteenth-century baroque palace bejeweled on three sides with precious blue and white tiles. Zapatista soldiers had gathered there during their revolution half a century earlier.

Flores's friends were mostly lefty ideologues. They talked a lot about land reform, which was also his passion and expertise. General Zapata would have loved it. They also railed against the gringos, especially American businesses that exploited Mexico's treasures.

Their politics had a distinctive Mexican heat. It was florid, fiery, and full of historical resentments. I liked to hear them argue. But when anyone railed on about the need for violence or belched a whiff of Stalinism, I tuned out. I had read Orwell's accounts of what the communists had done to their own in the Spanish Civil War. I wasn't political, but I was no ignoramus.

I felt most intimately connected with Mexicans when I visited Genaro Mendoza and his townspeople in Charcas. He asked me in the mid-1960s to help him erect a school there, hire a teacher, and build a road so the kids could get to it more easily. Frank Senkowsky and I were happy to pitch in.

At the school's opening, I saw a strange-looking map in one of the classrooms. Its Mexico contained most of California, Texas, Arizona, and New Mexico, all areas that the United States had conquered, swiped, or bought.

"This isn't a real map of Mexico," I told the teacher. "This is part of the United States."

"No!" she replied. "You stole it from us!"

"No, I didn't steal it from you," I said. "But be patient. You'll get it all back in another fifty years or so."

Except for one year in San Francisco, Lisa and I remained in Mexico City throughout the 1960s. Our daughter, Lori Christina, and son, Anthony, were born there.

After the children were born, we moved into a larger home in a lovely residential area northwest of the city and began to enjoy the special joys that came with being a parent. I took Lori Christina to her horseback riding lessons and, every so often, even rode myself. From time to time, we visited a friend who had a hacienda in the countryside, where there were horses to ride and bulls (and aspiring bullfighters) to watch in the fields. In the true spirit of the Mexican countryside, the kids sometimes slept three to a bed.

In the evenings before dinner, I also loved playing baseball with Anthony in the wide avenue in front of our house. There was so little traffic, we didn't need to use trash barrels, like my dad did on Queen Street, to stop cars from interrupting our game. I liked to throw my son a big fat one, just like my dad had pitched to me. Mendoza had been right about the importance of family.

Aside from our perspectives on our adopted homeland, Lisa and I had different views in one other important regard: work. Although she had little interest in working, I was as excited as ever about my business. Fortunately, I now had a new ally and coach in Hans Popper.

SEVENTEEN

Hans and My Grinding Mill

N elson Kusner found me on April 28, 1960, at the American British Cowdray Hospital in Mexico City, where our daughter, Lori Christina, had just been born. Though I hadn't seen much of Nelson since our early misadventures in Mexico with Al Himfar and the Four Stooges, he and I went back a long time. I'd sat in front of him in our geometry class at Central High School in Philadelphia.

That lovely spring afternoon, Nelson and I walked around and around the hospital's quiet courtyard as he spelled out his idea that we should go into business together. I listened carefully. He was intelligent. He knew the manganese business. And he had an interesting idea.

He told me he had been selling manganese to makers of facebrick. They made bricks of different colors by mixing manganese that had been ground into a talcum-like powder into the clay. Nelson had already built a small network of American customers, mostly in the southeastern United States. He'd been getting the ground ore he needed from a plant in Brownsville, Texas.

Nelson wanted us to form a company together that would control the critical parts of this business in one independent enterprise. We would build our own processing plant in El Paso, on the southwestern border of Texas, because it was cheaper to ship west from there and was the same cost to ship east. We would buy manganese from my existing supply chain in Mexico, grind it in El Paso, and then sell it.

Every month or two since my marriage, I wrote Hans a summary of my business activities and asked for his advice. We both relished our exchanges, not just for the practical payoffs of putting our heads together, but also for the familial intimacy we shared.

Hans was naturally cautious. As a boy in Vienna he had been taught the old German saying *Make sure you have lots of legs to stand on.* He constantly urged me to look for ways to diversify my mix of businesses and warned me, from his office in San Francisco, "Don't put all your eggs in one basket."

Hans and I had been looking for opportunities beyond buying and selling mercury and unprocessed manganese. Our primary customers for manganese ore, businesses in the US steel industry, had become a shaky market. A steelworkers' strike in 1959—which won steelworkers a small wage increase and continued control over the work rules—had devastated the industry, and its American buyers had learned to prefer, for the very first time, imported steel. We also wanted to hedge the growing uncertainties of Mexico's political and business climate, so we were interested in prospects in other countries. Kusner's proposition neatly fit, on all counts, what Hans and I had in mind.

Nelson and I agreed that I would provide the start-up money. He wanted to own a piece, so we settled on 10 percent for him. We both liked the idea of his becoming sales manager. We named the company American Minerals. On the day your first child is born, you believe anything you try will work.

Hans loaned me the cash for the start-up. I told him we could build the plant for $100,000 or so and have it running by mid-December. By late June I found a site for the plant in El Paso. I recruited a Mr. McCarthy to build it, and spent two hectic days with him to get him on track. I asked my brother to keep an eye on him. I gave Hans a list of details for his lawyer to put in the formal contract with Nelson. It took me a little more than six days to complete all this scrambling. On July 1, Lisa and I left for Europe to enjoy two months of fun.

The start-up turned out to be a lot harder than I imagined. I assumed everything would fall in place, and everything did fall—just not in place. Hans stepped in again and again to help me get American

Minerals going. He wanted me to succeed, and without his aid, I never would have.

Hans had already mastered every aspect of the mining and metals business. He started as an apprentice in 1924 in Europe's oldest iron and steel mill, where his uncle was president. When the Poppers arrived in New York in the late 1930s, Hans found work with two American steel companies that needed his expertise. In the summer of 1941, President Roosevelt's office asked him to serve on a presidential advisory board to help write wartime regulations on raw materials for the US steel industry.

Hans wanted to work for himself, so in 1945 he started the Western Steel and Metals Corporation in San Francisco. After the war he became a major supplier of iron ore to the recovering Japanese steel industry. His deep technical knowledge helped him spot other opportunities around the world that were hidden in plain sight. He had the entrepreneurial drive to seize those opportunities and make money.

In one case, while on vacation in Denmark in the summer of 1950, Hans discovered a couple of Danish World War I destroyers languishing in a stagnant backwater. He knew that the high nickel content of their forty-year-old armor steel plate made them especially valuable. He bought them, chartered Liberty ships to pick them up, and sold them as scrap for triple what he had paid.

Hans also knew firsthand how to build every element of a minerals processing plant. In 1951, he and a partner operated an iron ore mine on an unpopulated island off British Columbia, called Texada. They built a huge installation, including roads, a dock, a mine facility, housing for the workers, and several crushing mills, each substantially larger than the one we needed for American Minerals.

My absence from the start-up in El Paso that summer created a vacuum that inevitably drew Hans into the mess. Since we'd first met, Hans had showered me with the goodness of his heart. He continued to do so for years. But now, for the first time, I also saw in action the extraordinary strength of my father-in-law's character.

Hans ran everything in his business and in his personal life with Teutonic exactitude. Only two weeks after Lisa and I sailed for Paris, he wrote me that he was appalled by the "sloppiness and looseness" of my hastily assembled team. He had quickly learned what I should have already known: McCarthy wasn't an engineer. The last project he had run had been a total flop. He couldn't even estimate the cost of a concrete slab accurately. Hans also believed Nelson Kusner, though a talented salesman, was "utterly incapable" of building a plant.

In London, I received another letter, complaining that McCarthy and Kusner hadn't taken even the "most primitive steps," such as getting a building permit or an easement, without which we might have been unable even to access our site because it wasn't on a street. "It is impossible to tie up all the loose ends unless I move to El Paso," Hans wrote, "and in that case, I would kick out McCarthy, Kusner, and everybody else, and do the job myself."

My father-in-law's frequent reports about these troubles in El Paso somehow didn't register with me. Lisa and I were leisurely touring from one pleasure spot to another. When I wrote back to Hans, I waxed poetic about the magic of the Mediterranean Sea:

> Our stay in Capri is lovely. Our villa is high up, looking directly over the Faraglioni, the three mysterious rock formations in the foaming sea below. From our terrace we can see the village, which takes a different dress with each new reflection of sun or moon.

Meanwhile, over the course of the summer, Hans fumed at McCarthy's and Kusner's lack of progress. He knew precisely what equipment we needed, so he grew increasingly impatient with their dithering about what drying kiln and which dust collector they should buy. He couldn't stand their "yakking on and on and on" about almost everything.

Since Hans approached any task methodically, he was most frustrated that McCarthy and Kusner couldn't even provide him with a basic plan, a layout of the plant they were trying to build. After two months of pressing them for such a design, he lost his patience and called in his own top professional to produce the plan.

Then Hans Popper loosed the fateful blow of his terrible swift sword. He chewed out McCarthy and told him plainly that he didn't know how to do his job. But that was nothing compared with how he lambasted Nelson Kusner. He told Kusner in a blunt letter that he was "disappointed" in him "in many ways." He said Kusner shouldn't let his "fantasy or temperament run away with" him, and warned him that if he continued "boasting" about everything and trying to "jockey for position" for personal advantage, he would "lose out in the end."

Hans's frustrations boiled over and inflicted some collateral damage. He summoned my brother to San Francisco, stood him at attention, and lectured him. He called the El Paso team a bunch of amateurs. He berated my brother for being "stupid" because he had agreed to a deal Hans called "dumb." Buddy came away convinced forever that Hans Popper was a son of a bitch.

This added to my brother's growing disillusionment with his life in Mexico. He was already feeling harassed by the Mexican government on tax matters. One afternoon on the way home from work, a swarm of left-wing Mexican demonstrators stopped his car and shook it. He told me later that he had muttered to himself, "God, get me out of here, and I'll get the hell out of this country." He soon took his family back to the United States.

Hans deservedly threw a punch at me, too. He wrote me while Lisa and I were still playing on the Mediterranean: "I should be almost angry with you. You should have realized that it is hardly possible to get this project started without a great deal of effort. You should have either postponed your trip or delayed the project." He added gently, "Needless to say, I am glad to do my part." He pulled his punch a bit, but I still felt it, even after I returned home and went to work. The truth was, he took out his anger on Nelson and Buddy, but the only person to blame was me.

I labored for the next two years to get American Minerals up and running, without making much progress. I hired three managers, none of whom could get the job done. The first glimmer of profitability in 1961 turned out to be a mirage, a delusion of my bumbling bookkeeper. I was suffering under my own delusion: I thought I could run a business in Texas without being there.

I FINALLY REALIZED I had to play my ace. On July 4, 1962, Frank Senkowsky flew to El Paso and I told him, "This is your plant now." Frank moved his family and took direct charge of the day-to-day operation. He quickly discovered that the books were still baloney. Although I had been told we were breaking even, we were $100,000 in the hole. The plant seemed to be humming along with three shifts of twenty-three workers, but they had no idea what manganese was or what they were doing. Frank did the right thing and shut the plant down until we could come up with a solid plan.

My father-in-law saved me again by playing his own ace, in the form of a Canadian tracker with sparkling blue eyes, one real and one made of glass. Clarence Major sometimes made his living as a guide for hunters in the Yukon wilderness. He had run a gold ore plant similar to our operation and had served as the kingpin in other mining operations for Hans. Popper knew Major could make almost anything work, so he flew him to El Paso to fix our crippled plant.

Major didn't say much. He liked to live on his own out in the bush, free from human sounds. He never talked about what he knew or what he could do. Like Howard, the old-timer in *The Treasure of the Sierra Madre*, he was full of humanity, ancient wisdom, and seasoned practicality.

Major reconfigured the plant according to his own design. He brought in his own construction team and personally directed them. He moved into a trailer on the plant's grounds so he could hear the machines turn. He could tell whether the grinding mills were working right just by listening.

Clarence Major and Frank Senkowsky were both consummate mechanics and men of action. They loved working together, and they finally got our operation going. It cost more than twice as much and took more than twice as long than I had originally told Hans.

For all our troubles at the plant, we had one thing right from the beginning: Nelson Kusner proved to be a very gifted salesman. He flew to market in his own single-engine plane. He hopped on his Italian motorcycle, so small you could almost put it in a suitcase, and roared up to the door of his customers, looking like the kind of wild, friendly guy you would want to do business with. He could mimic the hometown accent of any prospect. He did a Southern drawl as sweet as sorghum syrup that convinced brick makers in Athens, Georgia, and Holly Springs, Mississippi, he had grown up in the next county over. His command of the manganese business and his unforgettable personality built us a base of loyal buyers.

Luck helped us too. When American Minerals started, we shipped our product like our competitors did: in hundred-pound paper bags that the buyer had to tear open, one by one, to use. Handling ground manganese this way was dirty, costly, and labor intensive, both for the buyer and for us.

By chance I met Bud Coleman, an ingenious Californian who had conceptualized a revolutionary new way of transporting and utilizing ground ore. He called it the FLO-BIN: a four-foot-square steel box that would hold two tons of ground ore, filled tidily through a hole on the top. We shipped racks of them by rail or truck. Our customers put the box on a stand and neatly fed a measured amount of ore directly into the brick mixture through a dispenser on the bottom. They sent the empty bins back to us, and we used them over and over again.

The FLO-BINs gave American Minerals a decisive edge in the market, and we pressed our advantage. We designed the equipment needed to handle the boxes in each brick plant and installed it at our own expense. Our customers guaranteed in exchange that they would buy only from us. With this mix of new packaging technology and old-fashioned moxie, we soon ran most of our competitors out of the game.

By mid-1963, American Minerals began to prosper. We expanded. We ground manganese from sources other than just Mexico, such as US government stockpiles. Later we bought plants in southern Illinois, southwestern New Mexico, and Philadelphia. For the next twenty-five years, American Minerals remained the stable, profitable core of whatever mix of businesses I pursued.

I started American Minerals in my mid-thirties, when I was still not very reflective. It should have been clearer to me then that I was a lousy operational manager. Though I lacked self-awareness about many things at the time, I did take away one clear conviction from my struggle to get the El Paso plant going: I learned that any start-up worth trying would likely take at least twice as long and cost at least twice as much as planned. This rule of thumb has stayed with me. I know not to expect instant results, and I know the importance of patience, tenacity, and will.

Oh, yes, and it's also helpful to have a rich father-in-law.

EIGHTEEN

Hans and Gretl

H ans and I liked the hedge American Minerals gave me against the whims of the steel market and Mexico's increasingly cloudy politics, so I looked for other opportunities to diversify. I found one in the early 1960s.

We were selling manganese to the Campos brothers, two bright, young Mexican engineers. They needed our ore to make flux, the key material used in welding machines because it could join two pieces of steel and leave a smooth seam. The older brother, Francisco, learned a new formula for making this flux from, interestingly, a metallurgical institution in Kiev, Ukraine. I knew the Campos hermanos were onto something good.

When the brothers told me they wanted to build a plant near Mexico City, I suggested we become partners. Selling flux that we made with our own manganese, like selling ground manganese to brick producers, made us less dependent on the steel industry. Mexican nationalism also worked in our favor. Once we built our plant, the Mexican government closed the border to any imports, including products that were better and cheaper than ours but offered by foreign companies.

We dominated the Mexican flux business. We built another plant to make equipment for welders, such as helmets and welding guns. In 1964 we built a flux plant in Brazil. The flux production business remained obscure to most laymen, but we made a lot of money in it throughout the sixties.

Hans Popper's counsel about the importance of having a mix of businesses proved wiser than I could have imagined. I learned this painfully.

The mercury deal I had made with Kurt Reinsberg of Associated Metals had been working wonderfully since the late fifties. Associated Metals continued to front us the money to buy mercury from our network of mostly small suppliers all over Mexico. We continued to contaminate it enough to avoid the high Japanese tariffs on pure mercury. We kept on shipping it to Associated, which then sold it to Mitsui, a huge Japanese company. We showed Associated our costs, just as we had agreed, and they showed us their contract, listing their selling price. We continued to split the profits fifty-fifty. Kurt and I liked each other's company and had drawn close personally. We enjoyed a great partnership rooted in mutual trust and secured by the oodles of money we were making together.

By 1960, Continental Ore, Associated Metals' competitor, saw what we were doing, smelled a winner, and was dying to get into the mercury business. The head of Continental's Mexican operation, Walter Burger, had also become a good friend. He kept pitching to me, but I told him that we had a contract with Associated and a deal was a deal. I soon found out that not everyone operated that way.

In late April 1961, Walter invited me to his office and showed me two versions of the Associated Metals contract with Matsui. One was a copy a former employee of Associated in Tokyo had shown him. The other was a copy of the one Associated had given me. "This is what your friends are selling for," Walter said, "and this is what they say they are selling for."

I was shocked by what I saw. The Tokyo version charged Matsui a much higher figure than the one Reinsberg had shown me.

I was enraged. Associated Metals had stolen several million dollars from our pockets. But what hurt and angered me more than losing the money was that my friend, Kurt Reinsberg, had been cheating me for years. Once again I had been tricked by someone I had trusted. I wanted revenge.

I dreamed up a wacky scheme to force Associated to cough up the stolen money. First I bought an active mercury mine. Then I told Frank to hide enough flasks of the mercury we were buying for Associated until we had the equivalent of what they owed us. I intended to hold this cache as hostage until Associated paid us the amount we had been cheated. In the meantime, I hoped the mine would mask my dodge by making it appear we were producing the mercury there.

Frank told me this was a really bad idea. He pointed out that it would be obvious to anyone that our little mine couldn't possibly produce the huge amount of mercury we were storing there. He feared that would get us into trouble. He wanted me to go to Reinsberg and make a deal. But I wanted revenge.

I thought the sweetest vengeance would be to persuade the Japanese to buy mercury directly from us and cut Associated out of the deal altogether. I decided to go to Tokyo and make my case directly. Surely the Matsui brass would switch to us once I showed them the proof of Associated's cheating.

I went to Hans. He told me that the Japanese wouldn't care that Associated had cheated me. They would wine and dine me, but in the end, I wouldn't be able to get them to buy mercury from me, since they were satisfied working with the company they were already doing business with. I listened, but I didn't hear. I had to learn for myself, and I took off for Tokyo.

Matsui behaved precisely as Hans predicted. The first night they took me to an exquisite dinner club where beautiful, traditional geishas pampered me with subtle dances, embroidered kimonos, and of course, quite properly, no offers of sex. When I came to the office the next day, the executives greeted me with much bowing, quiet murmurs, and courtly hospitality. That night they took me to dinner again. I sensed that they were treating me with special courtesy simply because I was Hans's son-in-law.

I finally told the Matsui executives I hadn't come to Tokyo to go to nightclubs. I showed them how Associated had been cheating me and pitched them to buy from me directly. They said they were really sorry for me, but it wasn't their concern. They had no interest in changing suppliers. Associated was keeping to the terms of their contract, so Matsui was satisfied.

On the way home I digested Hans's sober advice, now confirmed by Matsui's polite shrugs. My rage at Reinsberg hadn't cooled, but I realized that hijacking Associated's mercury was as harebrained as my trip to Tokyo and a lot more dangerous. We had bought the mercury with money Associated had advanced to us. They owned it. If I continued to press the point, Frank would be the fall guy. They could have him arrested and thrown into a Mexican jail.

Once again Hans helped me out of a predicament I had created. He asked Lou Glicksberg, his crack lawyer and most trusted confidant, to get me out of the corner I had painted myself into. Glicksberg knew the legal innards of the mining and minerals business and had negotiated with most of the leading attorneys who served it. Most important for me, Lou had worked with Associated Metal's top lawyer.

Glicksberg pointed out the obvious: the Associated Metals and Mining Corporation, an enormous company, had a huge legal war chest. He warned that if I sued them, I would sit in court for years while they drained me. To make it worse, our mercury contamination scam would surely come out in a trial and damage our company's standing.

I realized I had no choice but to make a deal. I left Lou laboring at the negotiating table, and Lisa and I left for a tour of Switzerland. The best he could get for me was just a pittance of cash. I cabled Hans from the Hotel Splendide Royal in Lugano: "Settled Associated. Still have my suspenders, if not my pants."

I remained bitter toward Reinsberg. Our friendship never recovered. My anger at myself eventually faded, in part because I learned from the episode and changed. I got even harder. I resolved once again never to let anyone play me—especially not even a friend—and no one ever has.

⚜

MY FATHER-IN-LAW COACHED ME in a multitude of business arts beyond assessing investment prospects. He could have compiled a handbook and called it *Hans's Bits of Wisdom*. Early on, I asked him for advice about the foreign ore markets, which he knew and where I was a rookie. He said money is made or lost on changes in the international market, so it was necessary to "smell" the market by being continuously in the selling game. Here was a rare instance where Hans valued intuition as well as brains. Smell the market—I loved the idea.

Later I told Hans about a problem I was having with some partners who wanted to help close a deal with our customer. He was clear: "The negotiations must be in *one* hand: yours." This counsel didn't surprise me, given his taste for control. But it also made practical sense to me, and it reinforced one of the instincts that made me a damned good negotiator over the years.

Hans Popper gave me more than his coaching. He often backed me with cash, either as a joint investment or as a loan I paid back. He also used his standing and influence when I needed them. I wanted to sell manganese to Mitsubishi, but I didn't know anyone there. Hans volunteered to help. He had worked with the company's senior executives for years, and he promptly wrote them a letter that got me in the door.

He helped in another case by smoothing out a problem I had at Kaiser Steel, a major customer for my bulk manganese ore. My day-to-day dealings depended on a middle manager who loved to jerk me around, sometimes to help a buddy of his who was my competitor, other times just for the hell of it. Hans knew Kaiser's top brass as a peer, and he knew how Kaiser worked. He told me which buttons to push, and pushed one or two himself on my behalf. My nemesis never knew what hit him.

Remarkably, Hans never made using his clout or his cash to help me conditional on my taking his advice. He always offered his views while showing complete respect for my own. In the early sixties, as I was still getting to know him, he persistently threw cold water on a major deal I was hot to make. His unrelenting counsel that I take a harder line in my negotiations began to wear thin. I felt he wanted me to play my hand as if I had all his aces in it.

I wrote him, "Remember, I do not negotiate while having Hans Popper's money or income as a base of security."

His reply took my breath away: "Actually I have been backing your firm with money strictly for the reason that I wanted you to have the benefit of negotiating in an independent manner and without the feeling that you are financially pressed. If you now let this influence your considerations, you are throwing away the purpose for which we advanced you all this money."

I had never known or even imagined such a mix of love, generosity, and force in any man. Hans was mentoring me, helping me with his clout, and putting his fortune squarely behind me. Yet he wasn't doing this to dominate or direct me. He wanted to liberate me, launch me, and let me set my own course. It felt wonderful.

I spent a lot of time in Hans's dignified suite at One Montgomery Street in the center of San Francisco's financial district. His team made me feel welcome. I became especially close friends with two of them: T, a nice younger guy, a dutiful family man who did whatever Hans told him to do in the practical, day-to-day work of the office, and L, a dignified, wily older lawyer who was close to Hans. Both were gentlemen.

One spring day as I entered Hans's office, it sounded like a bar fight was in full cry. When I opened the door to the conference room, I found my two friends in a raging argument. T was furiously chasing L around the big table, shouting something like "I'm not going to take the fall. You told me everything was legal."

It was a little bit funny. They both wore dark business suits, starched white shirts, and classic silk ties. I was afraid T might catch L. He could have easily taken him down, and someone could have been hurt. I broke up the brawl, settled them down, and went out to look for Hans, to find out what had caused my two friends almost to come to blows.

I didn't like what I learned. Hans and L had been playing close to the edge on taxes. They had set up a company in Panama to finesse the huge profits Hans's main company had been making. Hans had partners whose lawyers agreed with L that the arrangement was completely legitimate. But now the IRS was sniffing around. T feared he would be the patsy, even though he was straight as an arrow and would never have done anything he thought was illegal.

Hans felt vulnerable too. He might have been—I don't know for sure. It was frightening. I've always believed that once the tax people go after you, they really go after you. In the worst case, Hans could have gone to jail.

He asked me to help him. I told him I would do whatever was needed. It took weeks to get the job done, and only Hans ever knew what I finally did. When I was finished, my father-in-law was no longer at risk.

I understand why someone might be tempted to commit grand larceny. At least the stakes could be worth the risk. But I always felt a distaste for petty larceny, where the possible penalties overwhelmed the piddling payoffs. Whatever angles I played from time to time, I always played it absolutely straight on taxes. The payoff simply wasn't worth the potential reward. The IRS could really hurt you.

I was amazed that someone as smart and usually careful as Hans would do something so stupid. I couldn't understand why he'd risked everything he had—wealth, friends, family, standing, freedom—to chase some small potatoes in his taxes.

I'm sure Hans was grateful for my help, especially since it pulled him out of jeopardy and could have put me in it, but he never said so. He never hinted that he was embarrassed by what he had done. He certainly never suggested he had done anything ethically wrong. All he said was that what he had done had been dumb, because getting out of the hole he had dug for himself wasted so much time and energy.

I had put Hans on a pedestal. Now I saw he wasn't perfect, but I didn't love him any less.

THE POPPERS' EMBRACE REINFORCED my growing self-confidence. Now in my mid-thirties, I felt at ease mixing in their crowd, and I'm certain Gretl found me a delight at her dinner parties. Most of the time.

The Poppers hosted a dinner party in their home one evening to honor their old and treasured friends, Jake Feldman and his wife. Hans had worked for Feldman in Dallas before moving to San Francisco and starting Western Steel and Metals. Feldman had built one of the largest scrap iron companies in the country and was a highly respected civic leader in Texas.

The Feldmans had known and admired Lisa since she was a young girl. Now the Poppers wanted them to get to know her husband and see why they were so proud of me. Hans had tried to help me a year earlier when I had wanted to compete for some business with Feldman's company. It hadn't worked out, so I'm sure he hoped the evening would give Feldman a chance to see me at my best.

It didn't go well. A couple of days after the dinner, Gretl wrote me a heart-wrenching letter in her touching Viennese English, sharing her "impressions" of me that evening:

> I love you and you know that. With every meeting I get to know you better and to love you more. I get to know your few little weaknesses and your many nice sides . . .
>
> If you had been able to judge yourself, you would have been surprised. There was sitting a handsome, suntanned man of no distinction who repeated everything he said three times, who for some reason brought up the name of Stanley Marcus at least four times without knowing or saying anything about that man. Even the things that handsome, suntanned man said about business sounded empty. He complained that Jake was not in his office when he visited, as if Jake was compelled to be there. There was no charm, no diplomacy, no greater intelligence present.
>
> And all that because of that ridiculous scotch drinking.
>
> If an intelligent, refined person knows he has a dinner party where one expects a sophisticated conversation, then he should take only one drink. You knew you would have dinner with the Feldmans, but you were not strong enough to resist.
>
> You are very dear to me. I am very proud of you. (I am proud, *basta*!)

Gretl wasn't embarrassed by me; she was embarrassed for me. She wasn't scolding me. She wanted me to look at my screw-up as a learning opportunity.

I still don't know why I showed up drunk at Gretl's dinner party. Maybe I just wanted another drink. I do know, however, that over the years Gretl offered me extraordinary love to draw on as I made my way. What amazing grace.

NINETEEN

New Partners, New Opportunities

I n the early 1960s I began to hunt for adventures beyond El Paso and the Sierra Madre. I wanted to do business at a higher level, with greater range, and on a bigger scale. Hans and I had different views about this. He wanted total command of the critical elements of his enterprise. He'd had only one major partner, and he bitterly regretted it. His resentment and distrust of this man haunted our discussions about the series of partnerships I'd tried. As a honing steel sharpens a knife, his relentless skepticism throughout helped me learn more about partnering and find out more about myself.

By this point, I had come to believe about partnership what Andrew Carnegie had once said about teamwork: it is "the ability to work together toward a common vision . . . the fuel that allows common people to attain uncommon results."

It was certainly true of my first partner, the old fighter pilot Stanley Kessler, who helped me expand our war surplus business after the war to make the first money I ever made. It was true of the working relationship that Frank Senkowsky and Genaro Mendoza brought to our collaboration in Mexico, with each taking responsibility for the part of the business that matched up to our individual talents. Even from the partners who had screwed me out of my share of the profits, Al Himfar and Kurt Reinsberg, I learned that partnership could have its strengths—though my experience with those double-dealers also taught me that no matter how much you trust somebody, you should always work to verify he's doing what he says he's doing.

But for all the success I had experienced in my partnerships up to that point, these were just a warm-up act for what was to follow.

During the sixties, I partnered with three men whose skill and friendship helped me move beyond Mexico and achieve success around the globe. Ralph Feuerring, a Swedish American, was born in Berlin to a wealthy family and had come to MIT by way of Jerusalem. Ara Oztemel, a Turkish Armenian American, was born in Istanbul to an architect's family and had come to Boston's Northeastern University by way of Cairo. Henry Leir, a German American, was born in Silesia to a hard-pressed family and had come to New York by way of Luxembourg.

All three came to America touched by holocaust or genocide. Ralph arrived in New York in March 1941 when it still wasn't clear whether Sweden could retain its neutrality or keep its Jews safe. While in the US Army, he fought the Nazis in Europe and the Japanese in the Pacific. Ara grew up in one of the few surviving Armenian families in Turkey. Leir left Bonn for Luxembourg in 1933 when Hitler became chancellor. He left Europe for America when the Germans invaded Poland in 1939. The first Jews the Nazis took to Auschwitz came from his hometown. The Nazis murdered them all.

All three knew metals and minerals. Ralph followed his family's tradition by studying metallurgy at MIT. Ara started a chrome plating company while going to college. Like Hans Popper, Leir went to work as a teen in a storied Middle-European steel company and soon mastered the business. All three were gifted dealmakers, traders at heart, independent middlemen. They dealt across borders, defied corporate forms, and succeeded handsomely.

I had a different kind of relationships with each man as a result of their different ages. Ralph was five years older than me, like my brother, Buddy. Ara and I were born the same year. Leir, meanwhile, was my father's age. What's more, each wanted something different from me, and I wanted something different from each of them.

Ralph Feuerring came to Mexico to find me in 1956 on Nelson Kusner's recommendation. He wanted to buy my manganese ore. He had been buying ore in India, shipping it through the 120-mile Suez Canal between the Mediterranean and the Red Sea, and selling it in the United States. When President Nasser of Egypt nationalized the canal in 1956, however, the shipping costs from India became prohibitive. Over the next few years, I sold him manganese, and we did some other deals.

Ralph and I developed a friendship with many of the qualities a good partnership requires: trust, respect, and compatible strengths. It was Ralph who connected me with Ara Oztemel, with whom he had been doing business, in 1959.

Ara needed cash for the fledgling trading company he had formed to do deals with the Soviets. With the Cold War approaching its height, trade between Western nations and the Soviet Union was at a standstill. Ralph had sent Ara to me, thinking I might be interested. Ara touted a motley mix of prospects, mostly commodities and products he hoped to import, including Soviet-made scooters that were Vespa knockoffs. Ara's breezy style rankled my father-in-law, and his tendency to make vague, over-the-top pitches offended Hans's sense of propriety. He dismissed Ara's proposal with his most withering term of contempt: *schmus*, German for "nonsense."

I didn't bet on Ara's scooters, but I began to spend time with him. He looked like a Buddha—bald and round—but had none of the holy man's asceticism or taste for meditation. He was a fantastic dancer and athlete in spite of his girth. He had played jazz clarinet and saxophone for a living for a couple of years as a young man and still had the chops to sit in with professionals at a party or a club. He could hold his liquor and loved to chase fun, adventure, and money, all bundled together. So did I. I found him fascinating, larger than life.

In early 1961, Ara came to me again. Once more he needed a large amount of cash to make a deal with the Soviets to import their chrome ore to the United States. The deal was ripe to make. The US needed metallurgical-grade chrome to make stainless steel but had no domestic source. Moreover, Ara said he had an angle. He somehow had developed a personal connection with Anastas Mikoyan, an Old Bolshevik who is remembered by history as the sole Soviet politician to hold a senior position at the center of power under Soviet leaders Vladimir Lenin, Joseph Stalin, Nikita Khrushchev, and Leonid Brezhnev—a span of six decades. Mikoyan wanted to promote trade with the West and had a natural tie to Ara: he was Armenian.

I liked the boldness and scale of Ara's proposition. I liked its dash and dare. It smelled of the exotic and the outlandish. I loved the irony of buying a mineral critical to equip America's military—in the heat of the Cold War—from the Soviet Union. But where was I going to find the $50 million Ara needed to pull it off?

Enter Henry Leir.

⁓

I HAD MET LEIR the previous year in San Luis Potosí. He had come specifically to find me, and I was deeply flattered. He was a legend in the international metals and minerals industry. He had built a thriving minerals trading company in Luxembourg in the 1930s, befriending the royal family and helping that country rebuild its economy. I didn't know it at the time, but in 1937 Leir wrote a utopian novel in which he imagined internationally minded industrialists engineering enormous public works projects for peaceful and humane purposes. Throughout his lifetime he had learned several languages, cultivated a taste for poetry and other arts, and used his wealth to help scholars, the sick, and children in need.

After he came to New York to escape the Nazis, Leir started the Continental Ore Corporation, became a major player in the world markets, and made a fortune.

Leir liked to recruit bright young men, teach them about his business, and back them with his money and clout. They always did very well, and Leir profited from this stable of talents as they made their own wealth. My friend Walter Burger, his top hand in Mexico, had tipped him about me. He came to my office in San Luis Potosí in the spring of 1960 and opened by saying he had heard good things about me. He was then very direct about what he wanted: to "marry me."

Taking this offer of partnership in stride, I replied that he knew a great deal more about minerals and commodities than I did, but I knew something about love. "Frankly," I said, "I'd rather be your sweetheart than be your wife."

Thus we began an elaborate six-month square dance. It was part negotiation, part his efforts at seduction, and part my struggle to figure out what I wanted. All the while Hans Popper whispered warnings in my ear about the dangers of partnering—with anyone.

Some of my wants were clear and definite. I wanted to expand my business reach beyond Mexico. I wanted to make bigger deals than I had so far. I wanted to deal in commodities beyond my manganese trade.

My other wants floated into vague boyish exuberance. I wanted to mingle with other dealmakers in exotic places. I wanted to be a bigger deal myself. I told Hans I wanted to be a "roving ambassador," whatever that meant.

Leir shrewdly played to what he sensed I wanted most—to be his partner, to rove freely, and to make deals in our names. He invited me to meet with him in one of his stylish offices in Lausanne, Switzerland, for a series of intimate talks that fall. He suggested we create a new corporation with an investment fund we would jointly underwrite, fifty-fifty. I could headquarter my operations in his London office or could work out of the United States if I preferred. I could use Continental's resources and make deals throughout the world on his and my behalf. We would split whatever profits we made. Then he invited me to his London and Luxembourg offices to assess the promise of such a role for myself.

I was pleased when Hans first told me he couldn't help being impressed by Leir's cleverness and generosity. But then he tore Leir's offer apart, piece by piece. Hans doubted that Leir would throw business from his Continental Ore Corporation to our new company. Why would he want to give me half the profits? Since any winners would come from my work, why would I want to split the profits with Leir?

However, I believed Leir's assurances that Continental would help our new company prosper. After having been cheated twice by good friends and once by a group of villagers who told me that slate was manganese, I thought I had learned to know a commitment when I heard one. I wanted to join with Leir for two personal reasons that ran counter to my father-in-law's instincts: First of all, I believed that working with a strong partner would multiply my reach and effectiveness. I didn't tell anyone my other reason: My ego made me hungry to introduce myself as the partner of Henry J. Leir.

Leir and I called our company Stanley A. Weiss & Company, Ltd. I set up an office in San Francisco in 1964. Leir treated me with unfailing courtesy and never threatened my independence. But Hans had been right on one point: Continental didn't send any promising prospects to the partnership. I didn't either. I piddled around with it and focused my energies on other opportunities. It finally fizzled away to nothing. We closed it after two years.

But from the start, Leir was always in the back of my mind. A year after our first meeting, when Ara Oztemel said he needed $50 million to buy chrome ore from the Soviets, I reached out to Henry Leir. He agreed to put up the money.

Ara and I went to the New York offices of Amtorg, the Soviet trading company, and closed the deal on Friday, June 2, 1961. We flew to Moscow to finish the formalities. That weekend, President Kennedy and Secretary Khrushchev met for their one and only meeting at their famous summit in Vienna, which Kennedy would later refer to as "the worst day of my life." Years later, a 2008 opinion piece in the *New York Times* would recall:

> Despite his eloquence, Kennedy was no match as a sparring partner, and offered only token resistance as Khrushchev lectured him on the hypocrisy of American foreign policy, cautioned America against supporting "old, moribund, reactionary regimes" and asserted that the United States, which had valiantly risen against the British, now stood "against other peoples following its suit."

Kennedy recognized later that the Soviet premier had "beat the hell out of" him. It beat the hell out of Ara and me too: By the time we arrived in Moscow, US–Soviet relations had fallen into a freeze that was both deep and dangerous. What had been *da* on Friday in New York was *nyet* on Monday in Moscow.

Ara, like Buddha, said we should be patient and wait. Since we were there, he said, we might as well enjoy ourselves, something we both knew how to do. What surprised me most as we did so were the contradictions between what I found around me and in the heads of those I met, and what I had expected to find.

The Soviets assigned a beautiful young woman, a dancer, to look after me. Her mother was Ukrainian; her father, from the Belgian Congo. She took me around Moscow. I had never seen anything like Russia's unique architectural mix of golden domes, helmeted cupolas, and Stalinist squat. As she showed me the city, she sang sweet songs about the wonders of communism and the happiness it brought to everyone, but her ideological tastes made no sense to me. She celebrated Mao's communism, even though she had never been to China. And she criticized the communism she lived in every day, because she thought Khrushchev was a revisionist.

She proudly took me to the recently created Lumumba University, named for Congo's prime minister who had been killed a few months before by some combination of Belgians, Congolese rivals, and the CIA. She introduced me to some of the African students the Soviets were training there. I expected to be hit with blasts of Marxism and anti-Americanism. Instead, to her embarrassment, the students jumped all over me to help them get to the United States.

The gap between Soviet doctrine and experience was very real, and it awakened me to the realities of life in the Soviet Union. Back in my hotel room, I tried an experiment to see whether the room was bugged. I said out loud, "God, I wish I had more soap." A minute later there came a knock on my door. The valet was standing there with more soap.

I visited Leningrad too, flying there on a Russian plane. As we boarded, all the passengers were greeted by a woman who kept saying,

"Good luck." Given the spotty safety record of Soviet planes, this gesture proved to be a lot more alarming than comforting.

I then flew home by way of Brussels and, boarding my afternoon flight to New York, spied Jason Robards, tipping his hat good-bye to Lauren Bacall, soon to be his wife. I didn't know who he was at the time, but I knew who she was: she had been married to Humphrey Bogart, the man who changed my life.

Coincidentally, Robards and I wound up seated next to each other. Although we had never met, we kept glancing at each other as if we might have. Then it dawned on us both that we were seeing ourselves in the mirror: he looked like me, and I looked like him. Since we were both well on the way to getting drunk, neither of us was all that clear-eyed.

Robards said, "Why don't we entertain the people on the plane?"

I asked how we could do that.

He said, "Well, we really look alike, so people will think you are me."

I said, "But I don't have your voice."

He waved me off. "It doesn't matter."

We took turns. He recited poetry. I pretended. Everyone had a hilarious time. We finally collapsed in our seats laughing and proceeded to put the final touches on our drunken escapade. We became friends. I read a few years later that Bacall divorced Robards because of his drinking. I knew then that I was lucky: Lisa just constantly complained about mine.

After a few months, the Soviets rewarded Ara's patience by ratifying the deal he and I had thought we'd already made. By then Ara and Ralph Feuerring had formed SATRA, the Soviet–American Trading Corporation, and the Soviets granted them the exclusive authority to bring Soviet chrome ore into the United States.

Both Ara and Ralph were skilled at buying and selling minerals internationally, and they made a lot of money together. But after a while, Ralph became concerned that barter deals, even those as hot as Soviet chrome, might cool. He wanted me to join SATRA as an equal partner and anchor the company with the physical assets of American Minerals and my flux business.

While back in Mexico in November 1963, I was coming out of

Sanborns—where we used to go in the mornings, and where the left-wing Mexican intellectuals used to go to complain how terrible the United States was—when the news came that President John F. Kennedy had been murdered by a lone gunman in Dallas. I was beyond sad; I felt traumatized. It was the first time during the 1960s—but not the last—when I remember the news hitting me as a kind of wake-up call and leaving me to wonder, *What has happened to America?*

⁓

IN 1965, I JOINED Ara and Ralph in the Soviet–American Trading Corporation. Each of us brought independent value to the company: Ara brought his Soviet connection; Ralph brought a German steel plant, an English company that imported minerals from Eastern Europe, and an appetite for tight financial management; I brought the heft of American Minerals.

My mill in El Paso and my flux plants in Mexico and Brazil made up at least a third of the value of SATRA, and the venture was working, enduring, and real. By the end of the 1960s, as the *New York Times* would later recall in Ara's 1998 obituary, "as much as 80 percent of the trade between the US and the Soviet Union was handled by his SATRA trading company, Dunn's [Financial] Review reported in a 1975 profile"; and at one point, Ara became "one of only two American businessmen the Soviets allowed to have private homes in Moscow." The other was industrialist Armand Hammer, who, the *New York Times* recalled, was "a bitter rival once accused by Mr. Oztemel of seeking an interview with him just so he could gather intelligence to make his own chrome ore deal." History has given a number of people credit for reigniting trade between the US and the Soviet Union, but make no mistake: Ara Oztemel was its true pioneer. And with Henry Leir, I was proud to have played a role.

Ara and I liked and trusted each other, and we made money. In 1965, the SATRA partnership seemed perfect. But then I learned that in addition to profits and trust, an enduring partnership requires that differing business temperaments and personalities mesh compatibly. Ralph and

Ara couldn't have been more different in their personal styles. Ara lived large, plunging into London's posh gambling houses and splurging on whatever gave him pleasure. Ralph was a modest, contained man, conservative about everything.

After three years, Ralph became uncomfortable with the enormous risks Ara was taking. Ara was importing Russian hydrofoils and already dreaming that Soviet cabin cruisers would be the next hot winners. Partnering with him was like riding a roller coaster. Ralph didn't want to bet the company on making a billion dollars one day at the risk of going broke the next. I didn't either.

I had other differences with Ara as well. I was spending more time in New York, because I liked working at the center of the action and doing my part. But Ara preferred that I stay in Mexico, not because he disliked me, but because he wanted to partner more in name than in practice. It wasn't the money or his ego that made him this way. He just loved to go it alone. He was a loner at heart—ironically, like Hans Popper, his opposite in almost every other way.

Our differences came to a head over a movie. One 1967 day in Saint-Tropez, where Lisa and I had gone for fun, I bumped into Raoul Lévy, a famous French film director who had a string of hits starring Brigitte Bardot, whom he had discovered and made one of the best-known sex symbols of the 1950s and 1960s.

Lévy tipped me that the Russians had made an extraordinary film version of *War and Peace*. Based on the classic novel of the same name by Russian giant Leo Tolstoy about the history of the French invasion of Russia—one of the most important works of world literature—the Soviet version, Lévy said, was cinematically grander and far more authentically Russian than the "Americanized" version starring Audrey Hepburn and Henry Fonda, which had been nominated for four Academy Awards in 1956. He suggested that we get the rights to show it in the States.

Although Ara and I were close friends, he normally didn't want me to get too mixed up in his business with the Soviets. But in this case, he liked my idea. SATRA brought the film into the United States, and Ara made a deal with theater magnate Walter Reade's distribution company to show it in their theaters as they had been doing with other foreign films. So far, so good.

But then Ara and I fell into an irreconcilable disagreement about dubbing. I had studied all eight hours of the film. It entranced me, and much of its power for me came from hearing the actors speak their native tongue. I felt we needed, above all, to protect its soul, the beautiful Russian language it featured, by using subtitles. Ara insisted that Americans would want to hear it in English. Walter Reade, who had dubbed other foreign films, sided with Ara, so he won.

I decided we should split.

War and Peace premiered in New York with all the ruffles and flourishes Reade could drum up. It had won awards all over the world, including an Oscar in the US for best foreign film. But leading American critics lampooned the dubbing, calling it "disastrous," "madness," and the ruin of "any merit" the film "may have had." It flopped in the United States commercially.

My fight with Ara about dubbing *War and Peace* didn't cause me to leave our partnership. It just triggered my departure. Down deep, I wanted someone who would work with me as a full partner, someone for whom partnering was personal as well as business, someone who would respect, for example, my passion for the beauty of a film's language.

Even though I wanted to forget the *War and Peace* experience, after the episode was over I made a point of thanking Raoul Lévy for bringing the film to our attention. One of the most important French directors of all time, and a world-class playboy, Lévy had a lot of women friends, but he ended up with the wrong one: arguing outside the door of one mistress, who told him to leave her alone, he ended up with a shotgun blast in the stomach, killing him instantly. The death was ruled a suicide. To this day, there are many fans of Lévy's work who aren't so sure.

⚬⚭⚬

I BROKE WITH ARA, but we parted as friends. Fortunately, I still had the right partner in Ralph Feuerring. We formed a new company out of the thriving physical businesses we had brought to SATRA in 1968. We called it Ralstan, a fusion of our first names. Ara kept the rich chrome business with the Soviets but paid us a part of his profits on it for the next few years. His pioneering trade between the Soviets and the West made Cold War history. He prospered and continued to live to the fullest until his death in 1998.

Ralph and I settled into a comfortable and profitable partnership that lasted the rest of his life, over forty years. He ran the company, crunching the numbers and making sure we continued to thrive. He seemed not to mind what I did or didn't do.

Ralph had attributes and talents I admired and aspired to. He had earned the kind of sparkling college degree I wanted. He spoke Hebrew, German, Swedish, French, Italian, and English. I got around okay in Spanish and was still working on how to accent my English. He had studied Spinoza and Plato. I had dabbled in them. It took decades for me to try to write, but even back then he was a brilliant writer and could have been a great journalist. Like my father, he had a natural gift for uninhibited, extemporaneous, and funny speeches. I never have been able to speak easily or well to a group.

In many ways Ralph and I were opposites. He played everything straight. I instinctively looked for an angle. He was unself-conscious and self-assured. I was still wrestling with my insecurities. He was naturally modest. I wasn't yet sure how to present myself. He was smallish and wore little glasses. I wasn't and didn't. He was meticulous. I knew I should be, but didn't have the taste for it. He was serious about everything. I liked to have fun.

I wanted to make sure our different tastes wouldn't cause problems in our partnership. I liked a good hotel and a first-class seat. Ralph, though wealthy, was frugal. He would fly at night on a one-stop flight just to save a few bucks. So I suggested we take the same salary, add up what each of us had spent on travel at the end of the year, and give him the difference. That way neither of us had to worry about what I spent. It worked.

So did our partnership. I believed that partners who lived differently could still work together compatibly. Good ones can find ways to bridge differences. Ralph and I drew on the trust, respect, and braid of independent strengths we had built over the years.

Partnering with Henry J. Leir, for all its glory, had been too cold. Partnering with Ara, for all its adventure, had been too hot. But partnering with Ralph was just right.

TWENTY

Ah, San Francisco

O ne hot Friday afternoon in the early 1960s, Herb Caen handed me a basketball and dared me to dribble past him across an invisible line into Enrico's Sidewalk Café. Herb was Mr. San Francisco. Everyone in the Bay Area started the day by reading his column in the *Chronicle* over breakfast. Those favored with a mention would sparkle around town for weeks. Every Christmas he gave his friends a holiday kiss by naming them in a tour de force of extended doggerel ("He's nice . . . Stanley Weiss"). Herb knew everyone in San Francisco, and the glitterati who came to town wanted to meet him.

Herb's columns captured the essence of the city. He served up rich nuggets from everyday life he gathered while walking around the neighborhoods. He punctuated his offerings with a staccato of three dots to make sure even a lazy reader could get each of his playful word twists and savor all of his cracks.

He dished gossip with a racy flip. He once told about going to the Condor Club, the world's first public topless bar, with Marshall (*The Medium Is the Massage*) McLuhan and Tom (*The Kandy-Kolored Tangerine-Flake Streamline Baby*) Wolfe. He reported that when McLuhan tried to make a lame joke about what he had seen, the cerebral philosopher of communications "tittered at his own remark."

Herb reminded his readers that standing up for one's convictions was in San Francisco's DNA, and he crusaded for his causes with bite. He had seen murderers hung when he was a kid reporter on the police beat, and he found capital punishment "dark and dreadful." Since it was supposed to deter crime, he suggested that Caryl Chessman—the so-called Red-Light Bandit convicted of being a thief and sexual predator, whose death sentence in 1960 had become a worldwide cause célèbre—be "gassed in the middle of Union Square at high noon."

Sometimes Herb painted a heartbreaking Edward Hopper scene with just a few deft words: "Tough, tired old faces on Market St. . . . who've known too many winters. The lonely men, lost under their hat brims, sit in the still darkness of small hotel lobbies, staring at nothing."

Sometimes he simply sang a love song to his beloved San Francisco: "A lone white sail fluttering home at dusk past the amber lights of the bridge that only a dreamer could have built . . . and then, the moon rising fast out of the far-off East to beam whitely down on the hills and valley and restless waters of the tiny city that has no boundaries . . . San Francisco. Ah, San Francisco."

Enrico's, where Herb and I had been drinking that afternoon, sat in the heart of North Beach, a neighborhood he especially loved. "The place to be on a hot day," he tipped his readers. In recent years this once-quiet, mostly Italian community, where Joe DiMaggio had polished his swing as a boy, had become hot every day in a new way. It now had a vitality and in-your-face irreverence that matched Herb's own.

The Beat writers settled there in the 1950s and lifted their middle fingers to traditional American culture and literary forms. They delighted in offending the tender sensibilities of the San Francisco police. The cops found obscenity everywhere. They arrested the bookseller who sold Allen Ginsberg's poem, *Howl*, on obscenity charges. They closed down Michael McClure's play, *The Beard*, an ode to seduction and attraction. Herb labeled these artistic rebels "beatniks," a name he coined partly out of puzzlement, partly out of local pride.

In the sixties, a fresh wave of firebrands was raising hell in the neighborhood. A cocktail of cowboys, hookers, car parkers, prizefighters, and after-opera socialites gathered at Enrico's late at night to feel the buzz and hear some edgy jazz. Lenny Bruce and Mort Sahl, who would become known as two of the pioneers of shock comedy, with their strong overtones of social commentary, were getting started at the hungry i, a nightclub in a nearby basement.

Herb loved games, and that Friday afternoon he'd spontaneously invented a North Beach version of a Harlem Globetrotters dribbling contest for the two of us. The point of the game was to try to dribble past the other. Dribbling is, of course, a refined art, a product of countless hours of practice. We took turns going at each other, drawing on whatever unskilled athleticism we could muster, laughing and talking trash all the time. Our Stoli-fueled dribbling was as improvised as Herb's game.

Herb kept himself trim and fit, and he moved pretty well. But I was ten years younger and in great shape. I put some smooth moves on him and repeatedly waltzed across his invisible line, all the way to Enrico's bar and into a wondrous friendship.

Herb played games just to have fun with friends. So did I. We had a hilarious time with his basketball that afternoon. Neither of us worked up a real sweat. He saw I didn't need to beat him to feel good about myself. He saw I had no point to make, except to have a good time with someone I liked. He sensed I was comfortable with him and myself.

Herb loved my beating him. He put his arm around my shoulder, flashed his beaming, effervescent smile, and wordlessly welcomed me to his crowd and his San Francisco. How I ended up in his company is one of my favorite memories.

*

DURING THE 1960S, I spent a lot of time in San Francisco. I did business there with American Minerals' customers. For a time, I ran my partnership with Henry Leir in an office there. Lisa and I moved there for a year or so when our son, Anthony, was born. I loved it. How could I not love the spirit of the old forty-niners, who had left their homes and bet everything on finding treasure in a faraway place?

Roger and Nancy Boas, who had met at our wedding and lived in the city, were our close friends in San Francisco and our frequent companions for this exciting new stage in our lives. I loved the city for the same reasons so many others did at the time: its energy, its freshness, its creativity. I loved its hot music, rowdy ideas, riotous comedy, tolerance, and insistent drive for change.

More than anything, I loved San Francisco because I found a trove of new friends there, and I was ripe for new friendships. The feeling that I didn't belong at parties like Barbara's in Paris was gone. I had become more self-knowing and more self-assured. I had developed and sharpened my views on a range of matters. I had read Orwell and Maugham. I had crossed swords with Mexico City's political intellectuals over breakfast. I had listened to the cream of Mexico's artists. I had mined the treasure of Hans Popper's wisdom. I had developed my own convictions about Russian movies and pre-Columbian artifacts. I felt I could be comfortable with anybody, anywhere, because I was finally comfortable with myself.

My friends and I made Trader Vic's our headquarters. The restaurateur Victor "The Trader" Bergeron had begun his career with a small saloon in Oakland, moved to Cuba to hone his bartending skills and knowledge of rum, and then passed through Hawaii before returning to San Francisco, where he invented the mai tai. In Trader Vic's he had created an exotic Polynesian restaurant out of an old forsaken garage off a side street in lower Nob Hill. You had to walk down an alley to find its entrance. Two massive humanoid tiki carvings stood guard, expressionless, mysterious. They gave no hint of the magic we found inside.

When you walked into Trader Vic's, you entered another world—an opulent, idyllic South Seas paradise, replete with luxurious plants, shrunken heads, and woven bamboo chairs. Bergeron offered a colorful menu with outlandish dish names, such as Bongo Bongo Soup and Tama Tama Balls. His cuisine was part Cantonese, part Malaysian, and altogether sumptuous. Lisa and I dined there often.

Whenever I could, I joined eight or so of San Francisco's most vibrant and talented wits, who met for lunch once a week at the restaurant. I had some of the best times of my life at that table with these friends. Jack Vietor, a magazine publisher and heir to the General Foods fortune—he liked to say he was Jack Benny's boss, because Benny was Jell-O's pitchman—started the custom.

Jack and I swapped stories about Mexico. He told me that he had been in Cuernavaca on December 7, 1941, when Mexico joined the war. That night he looked out his hotel window and saw a crowd running around in the plaza, waving machetes and shouting, "*Vamos a matar los gringos!*" ("Let's kill the Americans!") He hid under his bed until the hotel owner assured him that the crowd had cooled down once they learned Mexico had declared war against Germany, not the United States.

Max Gutierrez, the tough, gracious ex-Marine who served as the Trader Vic's maître d', always reserved a special table in the most sacred part of the restaurant for us. The group included a pair of accomplished novelists, a couple of the country's most innovative advertising talents, a hilarious ventriloquist who practiced proctology during the day, and San Francisco's two most beloved columnists. All of them were free spirits who were making their mark professionally on their own contrarian terms. They were gifted, funny conversationalists, full of ideas and convictions.

While still a kid, Barnaby Conrad fought bulls in Spain, calling himself *El Niño de California*—the "California Kid." He almost lost his life when a bull gored him in his leg. His novel, *Matador,* became a *New York Times* best seller when he was thirty. A few years later Ernest Hemingway picked a fight with him for horning in on his bull-fighting turf.

Barnaby and I fell into a natural friendship. We both knew what it was like to face death in a Mexican bull ring. He had killed bulls there. I had waved a cape at some cows and run like hell.

Barnaby lived life to the fullest. His El Matador reigned for years as the hottest nightspot in town, a must-stop for every visiting celebrity. He played smooth jazz on the piano and guitar. His charcoal drawings hung in the National Portrait Gallery. He continued to write, both fiction and nonfiction.

Herb Gold was the most prolific writer in the group. He published his first poetry at seventeen and went on to write a steady stream of acclaimed novels and nonfiction. About the time we met, his novel *Fathers* was hot and the *New York Times* was paying him top dollar for his features.

Gold had come to San Francisco in 1960 to do a play with the Actor's Workshop—and stayed. The beatniks were morphing into hippies then, and he was the only guy at the Trader Vic's table connected with either group. He had gone to school with Allen Ginsberg, the Beat poet, and he moved into the beatnik colony, where rent was cheap. One night he invited Ginsberg to join us for drinks at Trader Vic's. I found him to be smart and funny, even if I didn't really understand a word he had to say.

One story I'll never forget about Ginsberg is about a time not long after that first meeting, when Gold invited him to join most of the Trader Vic's crew at a ski resort where we had gone together for a long weekend. Ginsberg showed up about two hours late, having trudged through snow to find the place where we were staying. It likely didn't bother him, because whatever substance he had ingested or inhaled made it clear that he wasn't feeling any pain. He ended up staying for about fifteen minutes before deciding it wasn't his scene. For about an hour after he left, we had a discussion about sending a search party out for him, fearing that he might pass out somewhere in the snow, leading to headlines that the author of "Howl" had died from frostbite after a bunch of San Francisco transplants had sent him out into the cold.

Beatnik stories aside, Gold covered the hippies' big happening, the Human Be-In, for *Playboy* in 1967 and caught their fever. He wore a striking beard, dressed in denim, and looked like a studly rabbi. He was never without a long cigarette holder and smoked almost constantly, especially when he drank. He had dark, penetrating eyes, kept himself in good shape, and attracted women like a magnet.

Gold and I both liked pizza, so we'd have some together and chat. He knew all kinds of things I didn't. He had hitchhiked across the country as a kid. He had studied philosophy at Columbia. He had spent a lot of time in Haiti and became an expert on Haitian art; he introduced

Lisa and me to its primitive beauty. He taught creative writing at San Quentin State Prison and played tennis with murderers and bank robbers once a month. He told me he was impressed that they always made honest line calls.

Walter Landor was an advertising genius who invented the art of visual branding. He built a pioneering industrial design business based on his conviction that "products are made in the factory, but brands are created in the mind." He is the man who gave the world the iconic logos of Coca-Cola and General Electric, Levi Strauss and Marlboro, Fujifilm and 3M. His personality was as vivid and unforgettable as his logos. Born in Munich, he blended European urbanity with San Franciscan ginger. He looked a bit like Walt Disney only handsomer, with more hair, a fuller face, and a better mustache. He trained in art and design in London.

Walter converted an old ferry, the *Kalmath,* into an office and design center. He docked it at Pier 5, the heart of the city's waterfront, so it couldn't be missed. During the day he did business there, and at night he threw magic parties on its deck. He donned a gold-braided captain's hat, tilted it at an angle, and welcomed Lisa, me, and his other friends to unforgettable evenings.

After we got to know each other, Walter called me once a year to ask me what he should do with his money. This puzzled me. We never talked about such matters otherwise. I never suggested that I had any such expertise, so I never knew how serious he was. Each time I would make something up. It amazed me when he told me my tips always paid off. It felt good to be called "brilliant" once a year.

Howard Gossage was the quintessential adman, the original West Coast version of Don Draper, the iconic character from the fantastic television show *Mad Men.* Known as the "Socrates of San Francisco," he loathed traditional advertising and raged like a freebooter against browbeating customers with billboards and "multibillion-dollar sledgehammers." He not only created a firm that flourished; he also defined a radically different approach to advertising, by inventing interactive ads. He courted customers by directly engaging them in his clients' world and problems. He promoted Qantas Airlines by offering a live kangaroo to the winner of a contest to name a new international flight. He created an international paper airplane design competition to promote the magazine *Scientific American*. He also wrote some of the first ads in history that advocated environmental conservation, and coined the term "Friends of the Earth Day," which was eventually shortened to just Earth Day.

Howard worked and played with passion. Like Landor, he decided to do both in one offbeat location. He bought an old firehouse from the city and turned it into an office and a place to party. At the end of his workday he loved to gather a rich mix of talented friends, which included everyone from author John Steinbeck to my old inspiration, John Huston. He would laugh with them over cocktails and invite them to dance to his favorite mariachi band. His given middle name was "Luck." How could I not love him?

Dr. Gerry Feigen, one of Gossage's closest buddies, was a psychiatrist turned proctologist. He did ventriloquism for fun and threw his voice better than Edgar Bergen. He was a gas. He developed an elaborate backstory for "Becky," his own version of "Charlie McCarthy." He said she had been married seven times because she was so oversexed that four of her husbands died, two divorced her, and the last one couldn't keep up.

I admired Gerry. He had a social conscience. He and "Becky" spent a lot of time in hospitals with troubled children. He took special pride in the fact that he didn't rely on scripts as Bergen did.

The sharpest wits in our group were the *San Francisco Chronicle*'s two premier columnists, Herb Caen and Art Hoppe. Herb's humor at the table, like his column, came in snaps, crackles, and pops: puns, plays on words, turning phrases on their head. He had a genius for quick repartee. No matter what anyone said, he would come back and top it with the speed of a bullet.

Art's humor had a different tone and tempo. He told funny stories, like those of his friends and fellow high-profile humorists, the *International Herald Tribune*'s Art Buchwald and Russell Baker of the *New York Times*. A lot of them were comic moments he captured from the campaigns he covered. Others were satirical fables that made you laugh and made a point about politicians who deserved a kick in the ass.

Art brought a relaxed, amiable, Quaker-like temperament to our lunches. He took in all the banter with a great big smile, cocked his head a bit to the side, and laughed from his belly at the others' jokes and lines. He was a lovely man who loved his family. Unlike Herb Caen, he had no taste for jet-setting. He'd rather sit on his porch with his wife and watch the lights twinkle over the Bay in the evening.

Art was at peace with himself, but he was not at peace with the world or our country. He thought we were living "through the most critical moments in the history of the human race." He worried about nuclear war, opposed racial injustice, and joined in a peace march against the draft, which he believed was an assault on individual freedom. He had started as a liberal, became disgusted with both parties, and turned into a libertarian with George Orwell's *1984* as his bible. He was part of the turbulent, defiant politics of San Francisco in the sixties—as was the entire group at Trader Vic's.

Politics dominated our conversations. Howard Gossage and Gerry Feigen brought a swarm of heated convictions about all kinds of causes. Gerry raged against French president Charles de Gaulle's decision to test a nuke in the Pacific. Howard railed against the US government's plans to dam the Grand Canyon and stormed against the *New York Times*'s effort to start a western edition. The distinctive way Howard made his points was part of his charm and his force. We all loved his unusual stutter. He always hammered his arguments home with what his friend Tom Wolfe called a "wild, cosmic laugh" that "came in waves, from far back in his throat, like echoes from Lane 27 of a bowling alley." I can still hear him.

This group of World War II veterans agonized about the Vietnam War and what it was doing to our country. Herb Caen, who had served as an Air Force officer in Europe, rehearsed his screeds against it for his column. Art Hoppe, who had served in the Navy in the Pacific, called it "monstrous butchery." He once lamented with an angry, broken heart, "I now root against my own country."

Howard and Gerry told us about a new radical magazine they were helping get off the ground, called *Ramparts*. They hoped its fearless muckraking, such as its exposures of the CIA's illicit activities, would dramatize the case against the war. (The magazine would, in fact, go on to do much more than that, inspiring a generation of journalists and influencing everything from *60 Minutes* to *Rolling Stone* to *The Pentagon Papers*.) Howard's genius was helping to make it a political force, but Gerry worried that unless it got some fresh financial backers, it was going to crash.

I'd never thought much about politics. Hans Popper had stirred my curiosity a bit. Now my friends' heady discussions made me think seriously for the first time about political matters. Although I didn't agree with everything they said, listening to them began to pique my interest.

More than anything else, I loved lunching with my friends at Trader Vic's because of the easy, good-hearted fun we had together. We liked wordplay and wisecracks, not to show up or show off, but just for the hell of it. We didn't judge each other. We didn't compete or throw elbows. We liked spontaneity. We liked to make and take dares as an accelerant to fire up our good times. We all shared the same appetite for the city's special love of life.

At the time I never thought much about why these men welcomed me warmly and wholeheartedly to their table. I threw in a quip or two, but I was minor league as a wit. I had little to contribute to the political conversations. I mostly just listened. They knew I had made some money and that I had married into the Popper family, but none of that mattered. I made no effort to win their friendship. It came naturally.

❦

MY TWO MOST INTIMATE friends in San Francisco, however, were not part of the group at Trader Vic's. I met Harry Hunt at the Black and

White Ball in the spring of 1958. He made his way across the crowded dance floor and introduced himself to Lisa and me. He told me later that we had caught his attention because we stood out from the usual dowdy group of opera lovers and socialites. I could have said the same about him. He was tall and strikingly handsome, and he had a gorgeous date on his arm.

Harry Shelby Hunt had been born into a wealthy and influential family near Pebble Beach, a place of breathtaking beauty on the coast, just south of San Francisco. He learned to cowboy on his father's ranch. We're about the same age, and he joined the Marines at about the same time I wanted to. They shipped him to the Pacific, and he wound up in Shanghai just as the Japanese surrendered. Like a lot of veterans, he drifted over to Paris after the war.

Harry dressed impeccably, had Waspy good looks, and kept himself as fit as a gunnery sergeant. He was very eligible. He moved in San Francisco's most select circles with unassuming ease. He was invited to everything that mattered socially. He also mingled with the city's hippies.

After we got to know each other a bit, Lisa suggested that Harry join us for a week of skiing at Sugar Bowl, a small ski resort in the Sierras, near Lake Tahoe. Harry and I were equally clueless about how to ski, but we both thought it must not be hard to do since others seemed to glide down the slopes so smoothly.

On our third day, the two of us decided we were ready to tackle the Silver Belt run. It went down a steep, narrow gully filled with rocks. At the top you had to drop down in a steep chute. At the bottom you had to make a sharp right turn or you would fall about forty feet, like going off the side of a building. As rookies, we had no idea that elite skiers annually came from all over the world to compete in the Silver Belt Downhill, just because it was so challenging.

Harry took one look and told me it would be suicidal to tackle it. But without thinking, I said, "Oh, come on. Let's give it a try," and took off. Harry hesitated for a moment and came after me. We laughed all the way down. I stumbled at the bottom and crashed in a cloud of snow.

Harry came tumbling down soon after and landed on his ass on the other side of the gully.

We sat there for a while, cackling like schoolboys. I don't know where my spontaneous, crazy impulse had come from. My shout to Harry as I took off was more an invitation than a dare. We could have killed ourselves. Instead, we became friends for life. I loved Harry's zest for living and could tell he knew who he was and was at peace with himself.

His mechanical skills amazed me. One day he decided he wanted to build the best motorcycle you could have, so he did. Then he decided to race it, and he did. Motorcycle racing consumed him for a while, until he almost killed himself in a race. I had no more appetite to race motorcycles than I had to fight bulls.

Like Hans Popper, Harry relished modern paintings and ancient Chinese porcelains. Lisa and I admired his taste. I knew I would never acquire his refined discrimination.

I loved jazz, but Harry was passionate about it. He introduced me to San Francisco's best jazz clubs and musicians. He became pals with the legendary Miles Davis, one of the coolest trumpet and flügelhorn players ever and one of the most influential musicians of the twentieth century. He met Davis through the girlfriend they shared.

I helped Harry get through some hard times, but he helped me too. One night after a movie, I got drunk—really drunk—in downtown San Francisco. I climbed on top of a parked car. I was in danger of getting arrested, falling off and hurting myself, or staying there in a loud, wobbly, slobbering stupor for all to see. Harry gently talked me down and took me home.

Decades later, he visited Lisa and me in Switzerland. He saw that I was drinking much too much vodka and sensed I had been doing so for a long time. I was in denial about my drinking. He sent me a simple note saying: "Go easy on the potato juice." Only a friend as close and loving as Harry could hold up a mirror to me and get me to look at myself.

Harry was a person who always seemed to attract the most interesting and fascinating people. One of those people was the actor and writer Peter Coyote, a countercultural icon in the city who became a friend. After working in radical and experimental street theater in San Francisco for a decade, Peter was "discovered" in a Sam Shepard play and would go on to be one of the most accomplished actors of his age—working in more than 120 films, with directors ranging from Steven Spielberg to Roman Polanski, while lending his distinct speaking voice to narrate more than one hundred projects, including Ken Burns documentaries, the Winter Olympics, and iconic television ads for Apple.

✍

MY OTHER BEST FRIEND in San Francisco was Bernard Petrie, whose father—described in the *New York Times* as "a pawnbroker's son who made a fortune in ladies' apparel back when women didn't mind being called ladies"—had amassed one of the country's great fortunes as a retailer and investor. The two of them had a rocky relationship, so his dad sent him to Culver Military Academy and West Point. Bernard then excelled at Michigan Law and edited its review.

He came to San Francisco to practice law. With all his wealth, brains, and standing, Bernard could choose to do just about anything he wanted.

Bernard liked to socialize, and everyone wanted his company. But he chose to move only in certain quiet circles, attending the San Francisco Symphony and Walter Landor's fun evenings on his boat. He dabbled in the theater, playing Lincoln in a production at the Actor's Workshop. It was a great casting move: he had Lincoln's gaunt face, sharp nose, hollow cheeks, soulful eyes, and quiet dignity. He was equally fickle about his work and chose to represent only those clients who interested him. One bizarre case made him famous in town as an ace defense attorney: A woman accused her husband, an army captain, of attempted murder. She claimed he had tried to blow her up by mailing her a bomb from Vietnam. It had exploded en route without hurting anyone. Bernard not only got the captain off, but also got the couple to reconcile.

Bernard's choices made him complicated. He lived with great self-discipline, never letting his emotions rule. He held himself closely, so what you saw at first was all that you could get. He always stood erect, like a West Point cadet at parade rest, in a way that gave no hint that he had a whiplike backhand and lightning agility on the tennis court. At a gathering, he stood at the side of the room by himself, making no effort to engage. Yet if someone came over to chat, he was warm, gracious, and a great conversationalist.

Somehow Bernard and I fell in together. Our friendship moved him to make exceptions to his usual choices. He lived ascetically, perhaps because of the shadow his alcoholic father cast. He didn't drink, smoke, gamble, or enjoy food, and he didn't mingle much with those who did— except for me. He didn't like to travel, but he came to Mexico to visit Lisa and me. He brought his lovable quirks along, though, including his own water. He also brought the strict moral code he lived by, absolutely straight down the line. When Lisa asked him to carry some things back to the States, he scrutinized each to make sure none was illegal. Bernard was a guy who would never cross the street on a yellow light. He wasn't a rule breaker.

Our friendship blossomed in our conversations. Both of us were good listeners. He was interested in any book I had read. He had a first-rate intellect and was one of the most thoughtful persons I've ever known, but he wasn't an intellectual, like Hans Popper, caught up with political philosophers and journals. Neither was I, but we discussed history and politics. He was Republican and conservative but moderated over the years as his party moved further to the right.

In 1966 the two of us traveled to Brazil and then to Punta del Este, a lush, peaceful resort on the coast of Uruguay. We strolled on the pristine beaches of white sand in the evenings and opened up to each other. I think this was the first time Bernard had talked with anyone so intimately about his life. There we were, two men, both about forty years old, each now with an intimate amigo to whom he could tell everything. I knew I could trust him. I had 100 percent confidence in him. I never met anyone with more integrity than Bernard Petrie.

OF COURSE, ANOTHER REASON I loved San Francisco is because the Poppers lived there. They spoiled Lisa and me. They took us to the symphony and the opera. Gretl whipped up dinner parties for us as often as possible, and they gave us the run of their grand manor, which seemed like a second home, a wellspring of good times and unlimited familial love.

Hans and Gretl adored their grandchildren and embraced them with great delight. Lori Christina was old enough for them to shower her with concerts, ballet, and piano lessons. When she was eight, she snuggled up next to her beloved grandfather and read out loud *The Hobbit* and *The Lord of the Rings* to him. Together they answered the riddles posed by the slimy little character named Gollum. Hans loved riddles, and he loved Lori. Even now I can see some of his distinctive essence in the ways she thinks and composes herself.

Hans invited me to join him when he puzzled over weightier riddles. He regularly welcomed an array of gifted scholars, mostly from the University of California at Berkeley, to his home for informal seminars on international politics. I knew they were more learned than I, and I assumed they were smarter. But once in a while, I would think a point through for myself and offer an opinion. They listened with respect, without any hint of condescension.

We celebrated every Christmas Eve with the Poppers. They invited their closest friends, mostly Middle-European Jews who shared their taste and history. The guests included Lisa's dear cousin Dr. Robert Popper and his wife, Marcia, and sometimes Torben Lenzberg, her wonderful, fun-loving Danish cousin, joined us. Altogether, twenty to thirty usually came for dinner.

Before we sat down, we gathered in the Poppers' spacious living room, which Gretl decked out and lit for the holidays. A majestic Christmas tree, magnificently decorated, stood in the corner and dominated the room, a Viennese custom the Poppers had brought to their new home. Marcia Popper and I liked to stand in front of the tree and chuckle together. She had grown up in Milwaukee in a Jewish family like mine, with Russian roots and similar remove from Christmas Eves and trees.

One of my great joys then was to see Lisa back in her native environment. San Francisco had been Lisa's primary home. She was still very much a part of the city's social scene, and she had a distinct grace everybody loved. She threw her parties with her own panache. One in particular proved her genius as an impresario of good times.

We had recently gone to see the great Russian conductor, composer, and pianist Sergei Prokofiev's ballet *Romeo and Juliet*—with its legendary "Dance of the Nights"—performed by the visiting Royal Ballet and arranged by its celebrated choreographer, Sir Kenneth MacMillan. I've never been that taken with ballet, but somehow the performance seized us both. Of course, Shakespeare's story breaks your heart, no matter how it's told. I had never heard Prokofiev's musical genius, which moved me and caught me by surprise. The spectacle of the dancers' brilliantly colored costumes and their animal energy captured my imagination.

Lisa had some connection with the production's brass, perhaps through Hans. Once the curtain fell, we hurried backstage, where she impulsively invited all the stars to the Poppers' home for a party. They came, some still in their costumes. The Actor's Workshop had also just finished performing, so I called Bernard Petrie and invited him to bring the cast to our bash. They showed up, some also wearing their trappings. I rang up Harry and my Trader Vic's lunch bunch too. When the party was at full blast, we must have had seventy guests.

We had music: someone just sat down at the piano and began to play. We had wine: Harry and I raided Hans's cellar. And we had action: Katharine Ross, who had been studying at the Actor's Workshop and hadn't yet broken out as a star in *The Graduate* or *Butch Cassidy and the Sundance Kid*, showed up. Her ravishing beauty turned everyone's head when she arrived. She was between her first and second husbands, and both Bernard and Herb Gold had been chasing her. Neither had any luck that evening.

We danced, drank, and cavorted until dawn. God knows where Lisa's parents were that night. They didn't mind. As I said, they spoiled us.

I connected with San Francisco deeply. My natural values, tastes, ways of thinking, and sense of humor ripened there—confirmed, reinforced, and crystallized by my friends. I never left my heart in San Francisco. San Francisco remains in my heart.

TWENTY-ONE

At Odds

In the February before our wedding, Lisa wrote me from Sun Valley, Idaho, about her love of skiing: "If for once you feel all toes and fingers, have a patch of blue above you, snow which loves you, and make a turn which feels right—time is gone. It isn't today or yesterday, but a moment all your very own."

I had kidded her about indulging herself in an extended vacation at that posh resort, and she'd pushed back hard. She knew what she wanted and made sure I understood skiing had to be an essential element of our marital deal: "Skiing is as much a part of my life as your mines are a part of yours. I realize one is daily bread and the other pure pleasure, but truthfully that's just the way it is."

She insisted I make two promises before we married: to take her to Paris every spring and to learn to ski. I had never put on a pair of skis. The roll in the snow I had with Barbara at Bad Gastein that Christmas in 1949 certainly didn't count. Skiing was beyond my experience, dreams, or imagination. But a deal's a deal.

In Zurs, in the Arlberg ski region of Austria, I enrolled in what Hans told me was the best ski school in the world. People went to Zurs to learn the Arlberg technique for downhill skiing, which had been developed there between the wars by Hannes Schneider, the inventor of modern ski instruction.

Lisa bought me a stunning ski outfit—pants, jacket, skis, and boots—all in black. When I walked to class with my skis on my shoulder on my first day, I was thirty-one, in great shape, and looked like an athlete. People thought I was an instructor and asked me for directions. They didn't know I was about to begin in the class with a bunch of kids whose average age was six.

While Lisa polished her art in the top class, I started in kindergarten. I first had to put on wide skis, like everyone else, although I was twice as tall. The kids laughed at me. So did the instructor. So did I. I felt like Gulliver surrounded by Lilliputians.

Every day I went to a regular class for four hours and a private lesson for a fifth hour. By the end of the second week, I could sort of ski, but mainly I was making chunkety jumps. I then moved up to more advanced classes. Classes were tough and demanding, but by the end of the month, I could ski—nothing like Lisa, but not bad.

I worked at improving my skiing for years. Most of the skiers we knew studied only with private instructors, as if group classes were beneath them. But I kept going to ski schools for a long time. I felt they were for normal people, like me. I enjoyed the camaraderie, and I liked the guys who ran them.

Just as Lisa had hoped, skiing became part of my life and our marriage. After each Christmas with Hans and Gretl, we skied for about ten days at Vail and Alta, our favorite American resorts in the Rockies. In February and March, we skied for about a month on the more demanding Swiss, Austrian, and French slopes at Davos, Klosters, Zurs, and Val d'Isère.

Skiing had not yet become the mass sport we know today, and ski resorts were the playgrounds of a self-selected community of wealthy, fun-loving socialites who could afford expensive jet travel, posh ski lodges, and the latest equipment. We met just about everyone in this jet set each year at the same time and at the same places, because, like us, they loved to ski.

Most of the same set also convened in Saint-Tropez in the summer, where the sun had a different slant and role, the sports depended less on skill, and clothes dwindled down to a precious few. Brigitte Bardot mingled, showing us up close why the bikini had become so famous on her gorgeous frame. Fred Chandon, the young Frenchman and playboy who was president of Moët & Chandon—the venerable, world-renowned champagne that reached back to the 1740s—lent us his yacht. The fun we had at night on the French Riviera seemed an extension of après-ski at Kloster.

Whatever the season or place, Lisa found herself in her most natural habitat among this set. She already knew many of these people from her Paris days, and this social whirl gave her the kind of carefree life she had cherished as a girl and still yearned for.

I found plenty of friends whom I admired for their talent and accomplishments, not their pedigree, such as the novelists Irwin Shaw (*The Young Lions)* and Larry Collins (*Is Paris Burning?*). One real character I met in Saint-Tropez was Chuck Barris, an American who became famous for hosting *The Gong Show* and creating *The Dating Game* and *The Newlywed Game*, two long-running American game shows. In the years that followed, Chuck had a lot of friends (including US senator Ted Kennedy) visit him in Saint-Tropez, where he eventually lived full-time. Chuck famously wrote an autobiography later in life called *Confessions of a Dangerous Mind,* in which he claimed to have been a hitman for the CIA in the 1960s and '70s; it was turned into a movie directed by and starring George Clooney. In my office, I still have a toy silver phone that Barris gave to me, which rings when you pick up the receiver—useful, he said, for whenever you were on a call you wanted to end and needed to excuse yourself "to get the other line." Some of my friends believe he was in the CIA, and other friends don't. As for me, I don't care.

Saint-Tropez aside, I loved skiing because it required a mix of athleticism and skill that couldn't be bought. Lisa's father had taught her when she was fourteen and always made sure she had the best of instructors, but she had to earn her prowess through her own hard work. She always deflected any praise for her skiing, but down deep, she surely must have had a private pride that fired her and animated her on the slopes.

I loved her daring and her speed, her beauty and her grace. Lisa was never more alive than when skiing, and I was never more in love with her than when I saw her on the slopes.

⁂

ON MARCH 15, 1965, Lisa and I were skiing in Verbier, Switzerland, when I received a phone call from my office in El Paso. My mother had died.

She had lived comfortably in Mexico City since I'd moved her there. She liked to visit our family in the States so she could shower her love on all her children and grandchildren. She was in Los Angeles helping Flora, my pregnant younger sister, ready a room for her coming baby when she had a heart attack. She was sixty-five years old. I wrote in my diary that it was "the saddest day of my life."

I didn't deal with my grief well at all. I didn't know what to do except go back to Philadelphia, where her body had been sent, so I could join my family in mourning her. I assumed Lisa would go with me, but she chose not to. I was too distracted to think much about it at the time.

After I returned home and regained my balance, I realized Lisa had taken quite a while to make her way back to us in Mexico. She had even stopped off in Washington, DC, a town she had never particularly liked.

I became angry, really angry. How could my wife not come with me to honor my beloved mother? How could she not help me deal with my grief? How could she spoil herself at Washington parties while I was in the grips of such sadness? When her own mother died years later, she wrote me that she realized what a mistake she had made by not coming with me to Philadelphia. Now I realize that because Lisa was a pampered kid, an only child with both parents still living, I don't think she really understood what it meant to lose a parent. When she thinks about it now, it strangles her. If she had it to do over again, I have no question that she would have been with me every step of the way.

The mysteries of marriage come in all flavors, some sweet, some not. Lisa and I had been married nearly seven years. We had a really special marriage, a wonderful daughter and a terrific son, a lovely home in Mexico City, the Poppers' grand place in San Francisco, friends we liked in both cities, and all kinds of fun we both enjoyed. Everything seemed fine. But most marriages, even good ones, show wear and tear after a while and can become vulnerable.

Of course I still wanted to be married to Lisa, for life. I always have and always will. But my anger at her self-indulgence when my mother died triggered a change in how I thought and felt about our marriage. I began behaving differently, doing things I hadn't done before.

My unease with my marriage was just one element of a more general turbulence that was going on deep inside me in the sixties. I still don't understand what was happening to me. I was at odds with myself. One part of me was growing stronger, more self-confident, more skilled and comfortable with myself—acquiring loving friends, learning to partner. Another part of me overindulged and got high on aggression.

⁂

I THOUGHT IT WOULD be fun to meet Richard Burton. I had never met him, but I found him in Puerto Vallarta without much trouble in December 1963. Everyone who could read a newspaper knew he was shooting *The Night of the Iguana* with John Huston on the west coast of Mexico. Earlier that year, Burton had fallen deeply in love with the voluptuous actress Elizabeth Taylor on the set of *Cleopatra*. The story was that their first on-screen kiss lasted so long, director Joseph Mankiewicz had to ask them whether he could say "cut." They just kept on kissing, the beginning of what would go on to be called "the most turbulent love story ever told."

It was quite a scandal, since both Burton and Taylor were married to other people at the time—Taylor to husband number four, Eddie Fisher, whom she had stolen from fellow legend Debbie Reynolds, the Hollywood darling who had starred with Gene Kelly in *Singin' in the Rain*. Reynolds had given birth shortly before to a daughter, Carrie Fisher, who would go on to play Princess Leia in the *Star Wars* films. Taylor would later say that betraying Reynolds, who was her friend, would haunt her until the day she died. The affair had given birth to the modern paparazzi, as the world's press and photographers followed them wherever they went. The Vatican didn't help matters, calling their affair "erotic vagrancy" while condemning both of them.

I flew to Puerto Vallarta and found Burton in a small bar one night. He was cooling off from one of his legendary brawls with his lover. Burton and I spent a great evening there, just the two of us, matching one another drink for drink.

Burton told me his father was a heavy drinker who encouraged his son to begin throwing back whiskey at the age of twelve. In his biography years later, Burton would repeat the tale, remembering that at Oxford, he had once consumed a yard of beer in ten seconds, and it was said that he could consume as much as half a gallon of vodka or cognac and still perform flawlessly on stage.

On this night, however, alcohol fueled one story after another from a man who, though one of the world's most famous actors and celebrities, had never forgotten where he came from. Burton was the twelfth of thirteen children born to a coal miner dad and a bartender mom in a small village in South Wales. His mother died when he was two, and the family had to borrow money even to pay for the funeral. I knew that he was a legendary ladies' man, but I had no idea the extent of it until he told me that for the past fifteen years, despite being married, he had bedded a different woman every other night. According to some later reports, this activity would continue for years! It would earn him the title "Hollywood's first sex addict."

Despite the alcohol we were imbibing, Burton had an incredible memory, regaling me with long passages from Shakespeare and various poems with such eloquence that it was easy to see why he was such a magnetic and legendary presence onstage. The Welsh music of his voice washed over me, much like Guy Burgess's British baritone had in Washington more than a decade earlier. I mostly just listened to him into the dark of the night.

I left for Puerto Vallarta while Lisa was enduring the final weeks of a difficult pregnancy with Anthony. It didn't occur to me at the time how self-indulgent, irresponsible, and adolescent I was to duck out of town for a night of drinking with Richard Burton.

But something positive did come from that trip. The night before I went drinking with Richard Burton, I had heard about a card game. Sandy Whitelaw, a British actor, producer, and director who was John Huston's number two, was taking everyone's money playing gin rummy. I asked if I could join, and Sandy, likely sensing another victim, quickly invited me. I proceeded to take back everything he had won plus his own money. It was the start of a lifelong friendship.

In the years that followed, I hit the slopes in Gstaad with Sandy, a terrific athlete who had skied on the British Olympic team at the 1956 Games in Italy. He used to flatter me by saying that I was a better skier than he was. Sandy had a Jewish roommate in college and always joked that he wanted to be Jewish. When we were together, he'd call himself Sandy Whiteberg, "the other Whitelaw." He went on to work on several iconic films, including Bernardo Bertolucci's racy classic *Last Tango in Paris* with Marlon Brando. He spoke so many languages that he became the film industry's go-to person for subtitling foreign films, adding English subtitles to more than one thousand films in his career. He was a terrific guy who lived in Paris until his death in 2015. I miss him.

∽ΣΣ∽

WHILE I WAS IN Puerto Vallarta, I was taken by the beauty of its sweeping bay. The town was still, in the 1960s, mostly untouched. Alfredo Terrazas, a close friend and one of Mexico's most distinguished architects, owned about three miles of its pristine beach. He wanted to develop a magnificent complex there and make it a model of taste and social values. His goal was to build some private homes looking over the bay and set aside some land for the area's poor, all echoing the town's authentic Mexican character. He felt it was important to avoid the commercialism and excesses of Acapulco and Miami Beach.

Terrazas invited me to join him as a partner, invest in his dream, and do something worthwhile together. We might even make some money,

he pointed out. I agreed. Such a deal! Everything went well. He did all
the work and sent me blueprints and drawings. I loved them.

I didn't think much more about it until quite a bit later, when a
man who worked for us called me at home in Mexico City. He seemed
nervous and scared. He said a neighbor, a Mexican who lived in Puerto
Vallarta, was building a house on our land. I told him to tell the guy to
stop, and assumed that would take care of it.

A few weeks later our man, Eduardo, called again to say the guy was
building a second story on the house. I told him to take a bulldozer and
knock it down. He did.

The next day Eduardo reported that our watchman had been arrested
and was sitting in jail. He said the neighbor, a Really Bad Hombre, had
paid off the mayor. I told him to pay the mayor more than the Really
Bad Hombre had paid, and get our man out.

I soon got a call from the mayor, who suggested we meet face-to-face
with the Really Bad Hombre to settle the dispute. When I sat down in
the mayor's office, the first thing I saw was a poster proclaiming that
Puerto Vallarta and Whittier, California, Richard Nixon's hometown,
were sister cities. I had to chuckle. I wondered what Nixon would do to
squelch a squatter in Whittier.

The Really Bad Hombre sitting across the table looked as dangerous
as I had been warned. He was breathtakingly ugly, with the chilling
green eyes of a zombie. He could have played the heavy in any horror
movie or thriller. Our lawyer had been too scared of him to join us.

I was glad Eduardo came along. He was a tough guy. Once, after
being bitten by a snake, he had run three miles to get treated. We both
carried pistols, and I'd brought a troop of armed men to cover our backs.
I still didn't feel safe.

We argued heatedly with the Really Bad Hombre. He pointed to one
legalism: gringos couldn't own land on the water. We countered with
another: I didn't own the land. Terrazas, a Mexican, did. We made no
progress. It became clear that the conflict wouldn't be settled as a matter of law. The Hombre had his own methods.

Eduardo and I resigned ourselves to the Hombre's insistence on building a house on our land. We thought we could live with that and go ahead with our plans on the rest of the beach.

The Really Bad Hombre had one more move. Later he sent in scores of Indian squatters who commandeered the beach and began to build huts. It became clear that there was only way we could have stopped them: a shoot-out. I didn't want to get into a firefight, so we stood down. Terrazas and I got our money back by selling our land to the governor of the state. The squatters disappeared the next day.

I accepted this fate without too much regret. Who wants to die on the beaches of Puerto Vallarta?

WHILE I WAS UNWILLING to take on fearsome real estate developers, my appetite for aggression usually flared up at the card table. As always, I compulsively raised the stakes. I ruthlessly drove the game wherever I wanted, whenever I could. I imposed a rule on my friends that whoever hosted a game had to guarantee the losses of any player we didn't know. My combined willfulness repeatedly pissed off other players, even close friends.

One New Year's Day I flew from San Francisco down to Acapulco and joined a big poker game hosted by Jacques Davidoff, who had become a close friend and who later became a legendary benefactor for cancer research. It was one of those nights when everything went my way. When I was winning like this, I played as if I were in heat. I insisted on raising the stakes and thereby muscled the game.

One guy kept losing big, while I was winning hand after hand. We didn't know each other, but it got personal. When we finished, he told me, "I never want to play with you again. You keep pushing everything."

"It could have gone the other way, but it didn't," I told him. "So it's going to cost you $22,000." That's over $150,000 in today's dollars.

By now the guy was red in the face and said he would have to write a check since he wasn't carrying that much cash. I turned to Jacques and said, "Sure, a check's okay. Jacques will guarantee it."

Jacques shouted that he wasn't going to be responsible. I got angry at him for not sticking to the rule. He got angry at me for putting him on the spot. My churlishness was infuriating everyone.

Even though I accepted his check in the end, the guy became apoplectic. He turned out to be very rich, and he felt I had questioned his integrity. I thought he was going to take a swing at me. He found me later in a nightclub and still wanted to fight. Nothing happened.

Eventually I learned that the price of my aggression at cards could be too high. One night sometime later, I played gin rummy with Davidoff and a bunch of other friends. I kept winning and, as usual, kept upping the stakes.

By four o'clock in the morning, I had won about $40,000 (nearly $300,000 today), mostly from Jacques. He became enraged and complained, "You have this old habit of raising the stakes." Then he stopped speaking to me altogether. I realized I had crossed a line.

I wanted to win, but more for the thrill of winning than for the cash I would pocket. Raising the stakes wasn't about money. I did it to increase the risk, like a tightrope walker who always needs a more audacious stunt. The higher the risk, the greater the thrill of winning. In poker, unless you could bet enough to make the others uncomfortable, you could never bluff. They would shrug and say to themselves, *It doesn't matter if I win or lose.* For me, it needed to matter. Otherwise, what was the point of playing?

But now my insatiable thirst for risky thrills was about to cost me a dear friend. I told Jacques how precious his friendship was to me. I coaxed him to let me play one last time with him, at his house, for whatever stakes he wanted. I promised I wouldn't raise them. That evening I deliberately let him win back half of what he had lost. He felt better. So did I. We liked each other in spite of the fact that I could be a pain in the ass, and we resumed our friendship.

All the years I had gambled at cards, I had loved to win and hated to lose. Now I found I had come to dislike winning as much as losing, if it was going to cost me a friendship. I resolved never to gamble with Jacques again, and I didn't.

But my post-Davidoff resolution didn't keep me from playing poker elsewhere. I spent time in New York City in the late sixties, mostly on business. I regularly hung out at Elaine's in Manhattan, a wonderfully piquant nightclub where visiting movie types, sports and musical celebrities, and fast-lane writers mingled, from Norman Mailer, George Plimpton, and Gay Talese to Yankees great Mickey Mantle and Rolling Stones front man Mick Jagger to film tough guys Clint Eastwood and Kirk Douglas.

The legendary owner, Elaine Kaufman, made me feel at home. We would sit and drink and talk. She was a great conversationalist. She and her regulars knew I was from Mexico, so when they saw me come in, they would all sing out, "Oh, here comes Don Ramon."

After hours, Elaine let Coco Brown, whose father was a big-shot Hollywood producer, host a poker game in a private room. It was illegal, but no one bothered us. One night, we were joined by Ben Gazzara, who played tough guys in movies and on TV and Broadway, where he had originated the role of Brick in Tennessee Williams's ode to Southern family dysfunction, *Cat on a Hot Tin Roof.* The last game simmered down to another duel, this time between Gazzara and me. I knew I had the winning hand, but he kept betting like he had it. I couldn't figure him out. He seemed to be following some movie script in his head instead of facing the reality of his cards. He finally bet $10,000 (almost $70,000 today). I won. He got furious. He couldn't believe it. He refused to pay me and stomped out.

I took out my frustration with Gazzara on Coco Brown. Once again I insisted that the host had to guarantee any new player's losses. Coco refused. We quarreled. My Mexican rules didn't travel well. It was yet another bad night all around.

I later soothed my wounds by getting a drink with a friend whom Lisa and I had met at a party not long before, who was the most famous adman in New York and probably in history: David Ogilvy. He was the "father of advertising," the real-life man in the Hathaway shirt.

We had met in Gstaad. Ogilvy liked me, but he absolutely adored Lisa. We visited him a few times at his château in France. After I got stiffed by Ben Gazzara that night in New York, I remember David saying that poker and alcohol don't always mix. He wasn't the only one who knew that my biggest indulgence in the late sixties was drinking. I had begun to drink hard, and I didn't know why. It wouldn't be the last time that alcohol would play a role in things I'd later regret.

TWENTY-TWO

Destroyed

Hans Popper liked to call himself an *ordentlicher Mann*, an "orderly man." He took pride in his masterful self-control, methodical planning, and decisiveness. But these characteristic strengths, the very heart of his being, began to falter in the summer of 1967.

The only other time I had seen Hans off-kilter was when his mother had died three years earlier. She had worked as a reporter in Vienna and was a real toughie. The family called her "the Enforcer."

After losing his mother, Hans, full of grief, closed himself off and played his violin for hours. After playing through his sorrow, he put it aside and never played it again. He sent Gretl to his mother's funeral. He couldn't bring himself to go.

That July 1967, I had to stay in Mexico, but Lisa and our children joined the Poppers at the family home in Gstaad, Switzerland. She found him disoriented and deeply sad. He hovered over Gretl, professing his love of her over and over while thanking her for all that she had done for him over the years. He asked Lisa to buy some lavish jewelry for her mother's birthday, an unprecedented gesture. All this frenetic attention unnerved Gretl.

Lisa wrote me that the atmosphere at the Poppers' seemed eerie. Hans talked about "retiring from life." She didn't know what he meant or what he was going to do. She wondered if he was going mad.

Lisa's reports made me more anxious for Hans. I was concerned that his poor health was unraveling him. He had suffered three heart attacks.

He had lost a lot of weight. I asked Robert Popper, Lisa's cousin, for his medical opinion. He could offer no diagnosis but was amazed that Hans had lasted as long as he had, commuting so often around the globe at his age.

I also wondered if Hans's strange behavior might be coming from the stress of his business. He was in the middle of a difficult effort to liquidate his holdings. He had told me he might have to go to Japan once this was done. It didn't make sense to me.

Hans called me in early August. He didn't sound like himself. He wanted to meet with me, but my always decisive father-in-law didn't know where or when. He wanted me to buy two tickets, one to San Francisco on Saturday, the other to New York on Sunday. He said he would tell me later which one to cancel. Then this consummate planner said he didn't know where he was going after our meeting.

Hans and I met on August 11 in his favorite hotel, the Hampshire House, in the suite with a commanding view of New York City's Central Park, where Lisa and I had spent our honeymoon night. He told me he was in the grip of a crisis. He confided everything, and what he said destroyed me.

He was leaving Gretl to start a new life.

Over the previous ten years he had fallen in love with W, a Japanese woman. He didn't feel he could live without her. He couldn't stand the elegant dinners, concert halls, and boardrooms of San Francisco any longer. He planned to live with W in Japan in a simple, ascetic way. He hoped to find an inner peace with her there for the rest of his days.

But now, just as he was about to join W, he had become concerned about Gretl. He worried that his leaving might break her. He feared she might not survive the shock. He was scared that she might even hurt herself. He couldn't bring himself to put her in such danger. He didn't know what to do.

Hans's revelations angered and baffled me. I was angry at him for wanting to leave Gretl, a rare and beautiful soul, a woman full of pure love and unlimited generosity. I knew how much what he wanted to do would hurt her. Besides, I believed marriage was forever.

I also couldn't understand why he felt he had to leave. He already had everything he wanted. For years he had visited Japan for months at a time and steeped himself in its art and culture. He had found a way to be with both of the women he loved. Why did he need to change anything?

I kept my feelings to myself. I simply said, "What can I do to help?" I would have done anything for him.

He told me I was his closest friend, the one person on whom he could most depend. He wanted me to go to Gstaad to help and comfort Lisa and Gretl. He handed me a long letter for Lisa, telling her what he was going to do and why. He had already asked his nephew, Robert, to deliver an even longer one to Gretl.

He also gave me a thick document for Gretl, which he called the "Appendix"—a painstaking list of all their assets. The document explained in clear language how she could access them and whom she could ask for help. He asked me to give it to her only when I thought she was ready to look at it. He wanted her to feel free to use the fortune in any way she wanted. It was his proud declaration of her independence.

Hans told me he had always tried to direct and plan every detail of his life, but he now realized how little he could actually control. He was going to a monastery to find himself. It would take weeks and weeks of solitude and quiet. He needed to withdraw from everything and everyone in order to sort things out.

I flew to Gstaad to do what he had asked.

We assumed we wouldn't see Hans for a couple of months, but "weeks and weeks" turned into little more than a weekend. The "monastery" turned out to be the iconic Hotel Imperial in Vienna, built a century before as a palace. Still at war with himself, he had made no progress at sorting things out.

Hans had built the Poppers' home in Gstaad a few years earlier. He made it strong enough to weather Switzerland's worst winter storms. Ceiling beams of beautiful, light wood made the great room inviting, and a grand Steinway made it alive. A soaring circular stairway graced the house's center. Hans gave the house the hopeful name of Chalet el Camino, meaning "the way" or "the path."

He proudly told us at the time that he was constructing this magnificent chalet so he could gather with his family in the Alps he loved so much. But now, in the grip of this awful crisis, I came to understand that wasn't true. I realized he had known even then that he was going to leave Gretl. Hans, who privately called himself "a great schemer," had built the home so she would have a place to live when he joined W in Japan.

But now his return took the air and light out of the place, turning it into a dungeon. He was back, but he wasn't really back. It was clear he still wanted to go to W, but he wouldn't let himself. His paralysis suffocated everyone. Gretl couldn't escape his presence or his anguish or his toxic sense of guilt. Life was unbearable for them. I was afraid that one or both of them might commit suicide.

When Hans had gotten into his tax mess, I knew precisely how to fix it. Now I was stymied. I didn't know what to do. I walked for hours up and down a particular path in Gstaad, trying to think of something that would help.

Finally, it hit me. I thought of the one person who might help the Poppers: Erich Fromm.

BOTH OF THE POPPERS admired Fromm. He and Hans were about the same age. Like the Poppers, he had come to the States to escape the Nazis. The three of them had the same Jewish, Middle-European roots and sensibilities, and they shared the same democratic socialist politics.

During the summer, I had studied Fromm's most famous book, *The Art of Loving*. Published to critical acclaim in 1956, it argued that love—including self-love—was a skill that could be taught and developed. This notion about love was less mystical and more grounded than any I had come across. I had become interested in how the mind causes us to act in ways that affect not only us but also the people we love. I hoped I might learn something that would help me understand Hans's behavior. I can see now that I probably also wanted to better understand my two selves as well. Fromm's special gift for clarity drew me to him.

Fromm now lived and worked in my old Mexico stomping ground of Cuernavaca. Although he wrote prolifically as a humanistic philosopher, he was also a practicing psychiatrist. It wasn't so much the substance of his writings that made me think of him. I mostly thought he could help the Poppers because both of them respected and trusted his authority.

When I suggested seeing Fromm, Hans was reluctant, but he finally agreed and asked me to make the call. I can only imagine what Fromm must have thought when he picked up the phone and heard the voice of someone he didn't know, who was calling out of the blue from Switzerland on behalf of a Hans Popper, whom he had never heard of.

Fromm couldn't have been more gracious. I yammered on for nearly a half hour, feeling awkward and tongue-tied. He heard me out, asking only a couple of questions. It dawned on me that he could have written a book on the art of listening. Finally, perhaps to get me off the phone, he suggested that if Hans would write him a letter, telling his story, he might be able to offer some suggestions, but he wasn't taking any more private patients.

When I relayed Fromm's invitation, Hans marched upstairs and typed away for three hours. He produced at one sitting, without any rewrite, a nine-page cry for help. He asked me to fly to Mexico and deliver it to Fromm personally.

Fromm saw me right away that afternoon at his spacious villa in the country. He cordially ushered me into his study and asked me to wait while he read the letter. Then we talked for an hour and a half, into the early evening. I had never met anyone more perceptive or considerate.

Hans's letter made an enormous impression on Fromm. Hans's personal history and way of thinking fascinated him. The Poppers' case also attracted him as a professional. He told me that to his surprise, and in spite of his earlier intentions, he felt a need to make an exception and meet with them.

Fromm had one crucial reservation. He understood Hans was in agony, but he also believed that Popper wanted to "use" him in a self-serving scheme. He wanted Fromm to use his standing to persuade Gretl to come to peace with Hans's leaving, so that he would be freed of his guilt and could join W without as much pain. Fromm asked me to emphasize to Hans that he would have absolutely nothing to do with such a manipulation.

With that caveat, he was confident that if he worked with Hans for several days, he could help him pick a path and resolve his dreadful dilemma. He thought he could help Gretl too, not by trying to convince her of anything, but by helping her cope.

I hurried to the phone to report the terrific news to Hans. Amazingly, he began to pull back again from the entire prospect.

I was furious. I raised my voice and told him that he would be making the gravest mistake of his life—one that would devastate Gretl, himself, and the rest of us—if he didn't see Fromm. I told him that if he didn't go along with everything Fromm suggested, he should forget my helping him anymore.

During the decade we had known and loved each other, Hans had coached me, financed me, mentored me, helped me avoid mistakes, stiffened my flagging resolve, and given me strong directions. Now our roles were reversed. He agreed to go to Cuernavaca.

Something magical happened during the week Hans and Fromm spent together. Fromm helped him embrace his right to love, to accept his humanity in loving two women at the same time, to stop taking everything so compulsively seriously, and to have more faith in Gretl's strength. When I picked him up after his last session, he was like another person. With his psyche relaxed, Hans felt free to send for W. She joined him in Tuscany in October. They settled in an idyllic hotel, in the Tuscan hills.

After Hans left, Gretl came to Cuernavaca to meet with Fromm for several weeks. He helped her set her own independent course. She developed a plan to invest herself and some of the fortune listed in Hans's Appendix in a school for needy children. She began sensibly by volunteering four hours a day at a Head Start center.

But Hans couldn't leave well enough alone. From the beginning of his troubles, he had insisted that Gretl's happiness—and his own—depended on her learning to live an independent life after decades of deferring to him. Now she had begun freely making her own choices, but he still wanted to meddle in her life from his Tuscan nest.

He tried to recruit me to help him with his schemes. I pushed back. He couldn't understand why Gretl refused to write to him while he was living with W—a level of narcissism that surprised me and made me wonder if I even knew the man Hans was turning into. He thought Gretl was moving too slowly on her big plan for a new school. He wanted me to nudge her, as if I were supervising her project in his stead. I took Gretl's side and told him to leave her alone. Remarkably, he didn't take offense at my assertiveness.

At the end of the year, Hans asked me to meet with him again. He said I was the only person in the world, other than Fromm, whom he trusted enough to advise him on his situation. We met in Bern, Switzerland, where W was recovering from some surgery.

Hans and I then met alone in his hotel suite, which had a view of the formidable Jungfrau, the so-called Top of Europe—the highest summit in the Bernese Alps, soaring more than thirteen thousand feet into the sky. It was also where, fifteen years before, Hans had almost died of a heart attack while climbing.

He told me he wanted to make one last move, a U-turn this time. He had decided to spend what was left of his life with Gretl. With Fromm's help, he'd realized that the freedom he sought from his old life had to come from within himself rather than from W and a new venue. First he would tell W that his Swiss doctor had ordered him to go to a sanatorium in Locarno in late February for two months, alone and closed off from everyone, to recover his health. This was true.

He would then ask W to return home instead of waiting for him alone in Tuscany. He would tell her they would live in Japan once he was well, though the truth was, he had already decided to return to Gretl. He planned to write W later and level with her. In the meantime, I wasn't to tell Lisa or Gretl anything about his lying to W. He knew they wouldn't understand.

Finally, he asked me to tell Gretl that he wanted to return. I insisted that this message had to come directly from him. A few weeks later he wrote her. Out of her own true love she joyously welcomed him back, all with Fromm's blessing.

*

FROMM REMAINED A VALUED friend to the Poppers and to me long after Hans's crisis passed. Each of us had an enduring but different relationship with him. Gretl had someone she could talk to professionally. She drew on Fromm as her trusted advisor for years afterward.

The personal and intellectual affinity Hans and Fromm had found for each other in their first meeting deepened. They swapped reading lists about Zen, pre-Socratic Greek philosophy, and fresh visions of a Marxist future for Europe. Fromm also learned about Hans's encyclopedic knowledge of European logistics, so he asked him to suggest a place to vacation in Locarno, the Swiss town with the nicest climate, with more than two thousand hours of sunshine each year. Hans, who could have been a travel agent, not only sent him to the one hotel located directly on the lake, but also specified the floor, the side of the hotel, and even the particular room to request.

Fromm and his wife visited the Poppers at Chalet el Camino in the spring of 1968. Gretl played Schubert for everyone. Ideas, dreams, and love danced in the great room again.

TWENTY-THREE

Ramparts

Hans Popper and I had drawn closer than ever during his crisis. In January and February 1968, I poured my heart out to him in a flurry of intimate letters about my own struggles. I wrote that my nerves had been "bubbling over" during a recent "bad period." I know now that from time to time over the years, I would feel painfully at odds with myself. Neither my self-indulgences nor the good fun I had at Trader Vic's could distract me.

When this happened, some need to grow in new ways gnawed at me. I usually moved past such a funk with a burst of new efforts to improve myself. In '67 and '68 I took speed-reading classes, practiced yoga, read and studied compulsively, and worked hard to learn to write. I was growing my own views. I pored over the treatises of George Kennan, the diplomat and architect of America's containment policy on the Soviet Union, on America's role in the world. I also read a hilarious satire, *Report from Iron Mountain,* in which a so-called government study group concluded that war is indispensable to a successful, civilized society.

Appalled by the way that I saw whites treating blacks during my travels in Texas and Mississippi, I also became much more interested in race relations in America. I dug into Malcolm X's *Autobiography,* in which the American Muslim minister provided a more racially charged and, in my mind, violent alternative to the Reverend Dr. Martin Luther King's philosophy of nonviolent protest. I read Stokely Carmichael's *Black Power,* which helped animate the Black Panther movement in the

United States and a more radicalized approach to civil rights activism. In fact, I read just about everything I could find about race in America. I realized that, being white, I would never understand the most crucial realities of being black in the United States.

I used my letters to Hans as writing exercises and opportunities to sharpen my thinking. He welcomed them as invitations to debate, one of his favorite indoor sports. My helping him in his crisis had left us sort of equals, and my intellectual growth made our interplay of ideas richer.

We disagreed a lot. We looked at the future from different temperaments and histories. We came from different political cultures and modes of thinking. I brought a breezy, red-white-and-blue optimism to the troubles of the world. I sprinkled my arguments with the lingo of the New Left I was picking up at night in San Francisco. I railed against the country's "rotten society" as only a wild lefty could, echoing those in the movement who were trying to fight the establishment and achieve social goals—from civil rights to the empowerment of women—outside the traditional structures of political parties, labor unions, and activist organizations. I was betting on a "new wave of tough, young American intellectuals" to take on the "reactionary establishment." And "WHO CAN TRUST ANYONE OVER 30!?" I shouted, in caps.

I was forty-one.

Popper remained faithful to his classical Marxian dogma throughout. Revolution required an elite vanguard who would lead a people with common interests, even if those people were unaware of them: Lenin's Russia in 1917. Mao's China in 1951. He saw the youth I was betting on as an "anarchistic, amateurish movement" that lacked intellectual depth and power. He doubted "any pies would come out of these kitchens."

Hans and I had a wonderful time making our points, listening to each other, and being heard. The Viennese waltz of his youth had been worn down by Stalin's tyranny and America's inhospitality to socialism. I could move with a bounce, because I had only begun to think about such matters. We were never happier with each other.

I WAS ALSO STRUGGLING with a dilemma about what to do next in my life. Like my father-in-law, I believed there were more important things to pursue than making more money. I already had made enough to do just about anything I wanted. I felt torn between staying in business and leaving it to write or to promote political change. I sent Hans a "personal financial and psychological balance sheet" to illuminate my choices.

I reviewed my nonbusiness options for him with little optimism. I said I might try to do "serious writing," but even after five years of "self-imposed apprenticeship," I wouldn't have a guarantee of anything "except writer's cramp." I didn't want to enter American politics, because I despised the existing political alternatives. I recognized that I wasn't professionally prepared to go into movies or publishing. I would have to buy my way into such creative ventures with risk money until either it ran out or I hit the lottery.

But then my thoughts turned back to the hottest political monthly in the land, which I had fallen in love with: *Ramparts*, the godchild of my Trader Vic's friend Howard Gossage. I decided that I wanted to buy the magazine—and chase these dreams all at once.

By February 1968, *Ramparts* had taken off. It had become the country's leading and most iconoclastic journalistic voice for the new direction of left-wing politics. As the *New York Times* would observe decades later, it was "the most freewheeling thing on most American newsstands during the second half of the 1960s." Its circulation had exploded sevenfold in just two years. Almost a quarter of a million readers looked forward to its monthly cocktail of rebellion, panache, and clout.

Its editors raised hell about lots of issues, but most of all they, like me, wanted to end the war in Vietnam and to promote racial justice. They did this the old-fashioned way: with classic muckraking.

Ramparts not only printed Black Panther leader Eldridge Cleaver's letters from prison, but also hired him as part of the staff. The magazine not only promoted new leftist voices, but also published the diaries of

Cuban Marxist revolutionary Che Guevara. Some of the generation's best writers and most influential voices on the left—from Seymour Hersh to Susan Sontag to Christopher Hitchens—competed to get into *Ramparts*, where they exposed hidden graft and corruption, such as secret Central Intelligence Agency funding of trusted cultural and student groups. At one point, the CIA was so nervous about *Ramparts* that it spied on the magazine's writers.

Ramparts also invented an irreverent tone and visual identity that set it apart—a style that one of the magazine's young writers, Jann Wenner, would mimic when he left in 1967 with one of *Ramparts*' contributing editors, Ralph Gleason, to start a new magazine dedicated to chronicling the music of the late sixties, which they called *Rolling Stone*. The editors at *Ramparts* wrapped their explosive exposures in outrageous covers that attracted new readers like *Playboy* centerfolds hooked teenage boys. They had kick-started their ascent two years earlier with a startling cover: a full-color photo of a master sergeant in uniform, wearing his combat decorations and Green Beret and saying, "I quit." *Ramparts*' December 1967 cover showed the four editors burning their draft cards. Not my style, but I admired their guts.

They bought full-page ads in the *New York Times* to trumpet coming exposés. As *Time* magazine would observe, *Ramparts*'s reporting at its height presented "a bomb in every issue." This produced a ripple effect. The *Times* covered these revelations as news and then deployed its own investigators to chase the story. *Ramparts* itself became news. Television crews and celebrities swarmed *Ramparts*'s offices, and its editors became stars. In a highly charged encounter in 1967, *Ramparts*'s ace investigator Robert Scheer appeared on *Firing Line*, the conservative television show hosted by the man who would become my neighbor and good friend years later, William F. Buckley. Bill embodied the young generation of conservatives who came of age in the second half of the twentieth century, famously announcing himself in 1951 with a takedown of his leftist professors during his undergraduate years in the book, *God and Man at Yale*. On *Firing Line*, Bill tried to bait Scheer into admitting he was un-American. Scheer countered instead by accusing

Buckley and conservatives like him of being "highly anti-American" for their defense of the indefensible, such as the communist witch hunts in the 1950s led by Senator Joseph McCarthy. Appearances like these made Scheer a star.

Even so, in late 1967, *Ramparts*, for all its heat and effect, was running out of money. The editors had depended from the beginning on the kindness of idealistic millionaires. But when the magazine came out with an evenhanded take on the Six-Day War between Israel and its Arab neighbors, Egypt (then called the United Arab Republic), Jordan, and Syria, fierce Israel supporter and *Ramparts* benefactor Marty Peretz pulled all of his inherited wealth out of the magazine, and the wells ran dry.

Gerry Feigen, my puppeteer proctologist friend from San Francisco and an editor at *Ramparts*, saw me as the next in this line. He wanted me to write the Big Check to save his and Gossage's baby. He introduced me to *Ramparts*'s other editors to close the deal.

I liked the editors right away. I spent some time getting to know Scheer, nearly a year removed from his *Firing Line* appearance. He had broken the magazine's first big story, an exposure of the CIA's secret program to use Michigan State faculty to train South Vietnam's state police. And he had almost defeated an incumbent prowar Democratic congressman in '66.

I especially liked Warren Hinckle, the magazine's twenty-nine-year-old editor and driving force. No one who met Hinckle ever forgot him. The first thing you noticed was the black patch covering his left eye, which had been injured when he was a boy. He wore a Prince Valiant helmet of longish black hair. He dressed to be noticed, flamboyantly, like one of the Beatles costumed for an album cover. He usually held a half-empty glass in his hand.

Hinckle led *Ramparts* with the swagger and audacity of an Irish buccaneer. He pushed stories that bit pompous big shots who could bite back. I loved his fearlessness. We were simpatico from the first of our many nights meeting at Enrico's. He recalled all this in his rollicking memoir, *If You Have a Lemon, Make Lemonade*, saying, "I liked

Stanley because he was as willing and able to talk business in bars and restaurants as in an office. He exhibited a prehensile ability to remain sober through evenings ending at dawn, drinking cognac and discussing money and politics." I liked him for the same reasons.

It helped too that each of us knew right away what the other wanted. Hinckle rightly sensed that I wanted to buy "some meaning" to add to my life. I knew he desperately needed money—my money—to stay afloat. I committed $50,000 from the start to show I was serious. I told him they could keep it even if we couldn't make a deal. But he and his editors wanted the Big Check: half a million dollars. He recalled later: "We sorely needed an angel, and here was one right from central casting—fun loving, lean without a lean look, liberal and libertine, well-tanned, rich, and above all highly desirable in that he desired us."

I told Hans it wasn't good enough just to sit around and talk "about radicalism over countless cups of coffee." I said that I could make good things happen if I owned *Ramparts* and that I thought the magazine was a chance for me "to try my hand at creative expression." Most important, I believed my ownership would give me the "chance to spend a life with young, vital, deeply involved human beings." I wanted to be a part of that "new wave of tough young American intellectuals" I had touted to Hans.

For all these reasons, I set about finding a way to buy *Ramparts*. To do this was, in Feigen's and Hinckle's minds, a simple matter. They thought I should sit down and write the Big Check. The editors would then spend this cash freely, just as they had been doing for years.

I knew this would be like giving blood to a patient who was hemorrhaging at a faster rate than the transfusion. I may have been romantic about *Ramparts* changing my life, but I was absolutely cold-eyed about its financial troubles. The magazine needed both money and a workable business plan that would enable it eventually to carry itself. Seeking to move the magazine to a sound financial footing, I came up with a package of fresh ideas.

I retained a first-class accounting firm to audit the books. The accountants estimated that if circulation grew as projected, *Ramparts* could break even in a year and half. I asked a friend who was a successful newspaper publisher to look at these projections. He assured me they were realistic.

I believed I could raise enough money to keep *Ramparts* alive for the next eighteen months only if its month-to-month operating deficit was cut. I looked for structural ways to reduce its costs. *Ramparts* regularly paid a chunk of money to service a million-dollar short-term debt it had accumulated. I wanted to slash this cost by converting almost all of this debt to stock or long-term obligations. I wanted to reduce *Ramparts*'s taxes by merging it with a profitable corporation that could use the tax loss over the next few years.

I also had some grand schemes for raising new revenue. I speculated that *Ramparts* could sell more advertising, and I wanted to sell it in advance to reduce our near-term deficits—a kind of publisher's check kiting, I suppose. I dreamed of publishing books and starting a book club for *Ramparts*'s readers. I envisioned partnering with Europe's two smartest magazines, *Nouvelle Observateur* and *Der Spiegel*. Together we would create a European *Ramparts* that would compete with the international editions of *Time* and *Newsweek*.

Bubbling over with enthusiasm, I reported all this to Hans Popper. I told him I was thinking about getting a group together to raise $250,000 (about $2 million in today's dollars) to buy controlling interest in *Ramparts*. I invited him to join in and asked for his advice.

He told me he liked *Ramparts*'s efforts to rally opposition against the status quo, but he didn't want to invest in it. He thought the more I succeeded in putting the magazine on a sound business footing, the more vulnerable it would be to commercial influences that would corrupt its integrity.

Hans said if I wanted to be involved in sociopolitical activities, I should get out of business altogether. "One cannot eat his cake and have it too, my boy. Never," he advised me. Above all, he sternly warned, "You must not invest any money in *Ramparts*. It is a bottomless hole, and you will be forced to add more and more."

I sent Hans a crisp list of my terms for a deal. *Ramparts*'s editors would have to agree to my package of cost reductions, so there would be no more than $150,000 of short-term debt, and operational losses would be no greater than $100,000 a year. I would raise the money to cover those losses for the next two years only if I got control of the company. I assured Hans and myself that Hinckle and his crew were unlikely to agree.

Instead, Hinckle nonchalantly smiled at most of my terms. He didn't mind if I wanted to convert *Ramparts*'s short-term debt. It should be easy; most of it was held by the magazine's supporters. My idea of a merger to cut *Ramparts*'s taxes was complicated, but he didn't care because it would be up to me to make it happen.

Hinckle didn't even mind my owning the magazine, because he didn't think I would mess with him and his editors. He wrote in his memoir that I didn't strike him as the kind of guy who would "hang around the office looking at galley proofs." Besides, he had already unseated *Ramparts*'s wealthy founder Edward Keating in an office coup when he got too big for his britches.

Hinckle was willing to agree to just about anything I asked for, as long as I would write the check for half a million dollars, the only thing that really mattered to him. After several more nights at some of the finest watering holes in San Francisco, he actually came to believe I had agreed to do this. He thought that all that was left was "drawing up the papers."

I clearly remember it differently. I never intended to pay $500,000 for *Ramparts*, and I know I never said I would. There is no doubt in my mind that I was determined not to invest more than half that. I wouldn't even have done that much without the package of cost reductions, in which the editors showed little interest.

I thought I stated my numbers so clearly, Hinckle should have understood them. But since he believed the Big Check was the only way to save his darling, he might have blocked out what I said. Or maybe I let him believe what he desperately wanted to believe, because I didn't want to disappoint a guy I really liked and with whom I would have loved to work. Memory can be a phantom.

WHILE DECIDING WHAT TO do, I asked Erich Fromm to meet with the *Ramparts* team at his home for a couple of days—as a crutch, to help me weigh the pros and cons of the deal, to either validate what I was thinking or talk me out of it if he thought it was a bad idea. I decided to bring Hinckle and three of his editors, including Robert Scheer and Gerry Feigen. I asked my very close lawyer friend Bernard Petrie, who was quite austere (not to mention a Bill Buckley conservative), to come along to ride shotgun. Not surprisingly, our trip to Cuernavaca turned into a circus.

In his memoir five years later, Hinckle gave an earthy, blow-by-blow account of our visit with Fromm. He had the brass to spare no one, including himself, in his telling of the fiasco. His version of my own folly rang mostly true, but I felt badly about how hard he beat up Fromm, who was just trying to help me as a favor.

In retrospect, I should have known that the *Ramparts* crew boarded the plane to Mexico City with a jumble of grim apprehensions and assumptions about what was going to happen. On the one hand, Hinckle had apparently led them to believe I had already promised the check. Though this was not true, it should have made everyone happy. Yet they came with a belligerent sense of entitlement and an anxiety that they were there to be tested.

Hinckle and Scheer came late to the plane after, as usual, "dallying in the airport bar." They took offense right away when they discovered that they were seated in tourist class. Hinckle and his editors were renowned for spending extravagantly on elegant hotels, restaurants, and travel. Hinckle recalled this was "the first time I had been in steerage in an airliner since I discovered credit cards." One of the editors worried that "the new owner is trying to tell us something."

When we assembled at Fromm's dining table that Sunday afternoon, he began in a professorial way to describe the roots of his political thinking. He feared that necrophilia, man's love of death, had drawn us into the terrible war in Vietnam we all opposed, and that it could trigger the nuclear holocaust we all feared. He wanted a humane society based on biophilia, the love of a humane life.

Fromm had laid this all in out in 1964 in his *Heart of Man*, bought by millions of readers. I thought the guys from *Ramparts* would welcome his opening remarks as an invitation to a healthy discussion of how to pursue shared values. I couldn't have been more wrong. Instead, they viewed Fromm in the same way Roy Hobbs, Robert Redford's character in the fictional baseball movie *The Natural*, viewed the shrink who was brought in by the team during a losing streak to discuss how "losing is a disease"—rolling his eyes before standing up and walking out of the room as his coach shouted at him to sit down.

According to Hinckle, his crew's fears and resentments toward Fromm and our visit ran rampant from the start. They felt scrutinized even though Fromm was doing all the talking. They thought I wanted the psychiatrist to "poke and plumb" them "to see what neuroses we were made of." They feared I had brought them there to "run some sort of intellectual gauntlet." And they were absolutely right.

The *Ramparts* editors "were itching to get into a scrap" right away, but Hinckle remembered they "bit their tongues and smiled" at first. They were careful to stay on their good behavior in the opening session to avoid offending what Hinckle called "the money," i.e., me. So they listened to Fromm "with the polite restiveness of kids kept in school during recess." I had no idea. I thought things were going just fine.

I didn't even notice the first skirmish. Hinckle recalled that when Fromm offered expensive cigars to the editors at our afternoon break, "each *Ramparts* lout grabbed up two or three." They were delighted to abuse Fromm with their "piggishness."

When we resumed the session after a nap, Hinckle and Scheer couldn't restrain their hostility any longer. They began goading Fromm like two schoolboys. Scheer made Fromm bristle by whining about being dragged to the seminar against his will. Hinckle got under his skin by asking him why he hadn't taken up arms against Hitler, an amazing disrespect toward a man who helped save Jews from the Nazis and who lost family to the Holocaust.

That evening, after Fromm retired, the *Ramparts* crew guzzled his cognac and "indulged in a giant release of guilt and venom" directed mostly at me, Hinckle remembered. Even my old friend Gerry Feigen lashed out. He asked me who I thought I was, "locking us up with this famous old fart who won't let us get a word in edgewise."

The editors intensified their badgering of Fromm the next morning. By lunchtime he finally ran out of patience. He took me to his private study and chewed me out for exploiting our friendship for my own ends. He railed at me for bringing the *Ramparts* gang to his table.

Fromm fingered Scheer as the most offensive of them all. His voice rose as he unloaded on the editor's arrogant and provocative behavior. All at once, he stopped in midcry, looking at something over my shoulder. I turned to see Scheer shuffling out of the bathroom. We both realized he had heard our entire conversation. Fromm turned on me, freshly enraged that I had brought such a despicable sneak into his home.

Our last session erupted like the finale of a fireworks show when the remaining pyrotechnics are fired off in one breathtaking climax. Feigen triggered a fight with Fromm by suggesting they discuss an article by Columbia professor and Polish immigrant Zbigniew Brzezinski, reviled by many for his soft line on Eastern Europeans, his support of the Vietnam War, and his work as the head of policy planning for President Lyndon Johnson's State Department as the war rapidly escalated. The doctor shouted that he would "not have that man's name uttered in my house. He is a monster, a man of the Cold War."

Scheer baited Fromm by accusing him of shutting off open debate like a totalitarian. This set Erich off. He jumped up, pounded on the table, and exploded at Scheer, shouting that the journalist had confirmed his "darkest suspicions" of the "real motives of the parties here" when "I caught you spying on my private professional conversation with Mr. Weiss."

Scheer rose to defend himself in a torrent of profane indignation. He explained that the toilet wouldn't flush. Then he elaborately reenacted how he had rolled up his sleeve, reached in the tank, and pulled up the bulb to make it work. "A guy can't have diarrhea and just walk away, for Chrissakes," he said with exacting exculpatory self-righteousness.

By now Fromm and all the editors were on their feet, shouting. The usually dignified dining room broke into a melee of accusations, shaking fists, and purple faces. A thirty-one-year-old editor offered to belt the sixty-seven-year-old author of *The Art of Love* right in the mouth. Fromm's wife hurried to his side with medicine, mindful of his massive heart attack the previous year.

The blowup did make the *Ramparts* editors finally realize that there would be no Big Check. They failed a test of their own making. Scheer realized that their own impishness had put them "in the soup." Warren, fixated to the end on the wrong number, delivered a classic Hincklesque punch line: "It is not every day half a million dollars goes down the toilet."

I had hoped that owning *Ramparts* would launch me into Popper and Fromm's world of political and social ideas. At the same time, I'd wanted to work and play with Hinckle and his crew. I wanted them to embrace me as a peer. Instead, Hinckle's crew dismissed Fromm as an "old liberal," a relic from the 1950s, who lacked the radical fire of their New Left.

This made no sense substantively. Fromm was a leading voice against the Vietnam War. Just a year before they sat down at his table, he brought the crowd in a packed Madison Square Garden to their feet with a keynote speech demanding that we immediately stop the killing in Vietnam. He had helped found and fund the National Committee for a SANE Nuclear Policy—or SANE, for short—the most militant of the American peace organizations. He had been a major influence on the New Left's primary manifesto, the Port Huron Statement. None of the *Ramparts* editors had anything like Fromm's radical credentials.

It didn't matter. Although the editors couched their hostility toward Fromm in political terms, its primary roots were generational. Rebellion against authority was a major element of the New Left's DNA. The greater the authority, the hotter the rebellion. They attacked Fromm because his age and stature made him exactly the kind of father figure they wanted to fight. Fromm fought back not so much because of political differences, but because he resented their baiting him and their disrespect. I didn't have the standing or skills to bridge the gap that divided the two generations, so their mutual hostility inevitably boiled over onto me.

Though I'd found myself once again in conflict with men I liked and respected, I still didn't like to fight. Ironically, I had brought everyone together in Cuernavaca to evade a quarrel with Hinckle. I didn't want to feud with the editors. I wanted to work with them and have a good time. I certainly didn't want to fight with Fromm. Nonetheless, my efforts to avoid conflict triggered the opposite: a riot that hurt my friends and humiliated me. I should have known better than to invite anti-establishment crusaders to sit face-to-face with the establishment as they perceived it.

Still, I had to count my blessings. At least no one put out their cigarette on my chest.

TWENTY-FOUR

Chicago's Fierce Dogs

Thankfully, Fromm and I had developed a special personal relationship that weathered the *Ramparts* fiasco. We liked each other. I read more of his writings and drew closer to him. He and his wife, Annis, often invited me to dinner in their home in our common adopted home country of Mexico.

I was interested in Fromm's politics. As the calendar turned to 1968, he told me why he opposed the Vietnam War, worried about the nuclear arms race, and was active in a host of left-wing organizations. He had been advising Senator Gene McCarthy in his unlikely campaign for president, which saw the Minnesotan become the first Democrat who sought to unseat an incumbent president from his own party (Lyndon Johnson). Fromm echoed what my friends had been preaching at Trader Vic's: the war in Vietnam was a mistake.

The Fromms were also interested in my studies of yoga. I told them of the wonders of hatha yoga, a discipline of physical exercises and breathing.

For a couple of years, I had been going to yoga class early every morning for two hours of meditation and relaxation. I studied with a seventy-year-old Viennese master teacher who had fought against Spanish dictator Francisco Franco, escaped from a concentration camp, and lost most of his family to the Nazis—the same guy who had lent me his copy of Fromm's *Art of Loving*. With his help, I had almost become a yoga master myself.

The Fromms were intrigued and asked me to give them some lessons.

I brought them mats. We rolled them out in their open, airy main room—the same room where we had gotten into a shouting match with the *Ramparts* editors a few months before. We took off our shoes and lay down. We breathed, relaxed, stretched, and meditated. My friend, the world-renowned psychologist, for all his nimble and agile intellect, wasn't very good at yoga. But none of us cared. As in the art of loving, in yoga you don't compete or keep score.

"IT'S TIME FOR YOU to do something with your life," Erich Fromm told me. We had just finished our yoga session in the Fromms' great room. He came over to me with his neatly rolled mat under his arm, looked me straight in the eye, and issued his directive with a command-ing blend of fatherly authority and affection. He was speaking both to me and for me. He was saying out loud what had been in my heart for at least a year or two.

"So, what should I do with my life?" I asked Fromm.

He didn't hesitate. "You should send six thousand dollars to Gene McCarthy. He's running for president."

The amount puzzled me. "Why not ten thousand or five thousand?"

"No, no, send six thousand," he insisted.

I shrugged. After all, psychoanalysts can be a little peculiar. Maybe six was a lucky number where Fromm grew up.

I couldn't see how sending a check to any presidential candidate, whatever its size, would change my life. I remained apolitical. My breakup with the *Ramparts* crew had only reinforced my naïveté when it came to politics. Nonetheless, I did what Fromm suggested. I respected his wisdom, and I believed you never can tell what might happen.

It turns out that I picked an interesting moment to get involved in politics, as 1968 would prove to be one of the most eventful political years in American history.

At the end of January, shortly after I made my donation to the McCarthy campaign, the North Vietnamese launched a monthlong offensive in the cities and civilian areas of South Vietnam. Broadcast nightly into American living rooms, the so-called Tet Offensive created the real sense that America and its allies were being overrun by the enemy, which only deepened the opposition to the war. In March, with anger and disillusionment over Vietnam riding high, McCarthy nearly upset Johnson in the New Hampshire presidential primary. A week later, New York Senator Robert Kennedy, sensing an opportunity, declared his candidacy, causing a split in the Democratic party among many who were inspired by McCarthy's courage in standing up to Johnson but believed Kennedy to be a stronger candidate. Personally, I was furious. I thought Kennedy was an arrogant little shit and a complete opportunist, who couldn't hold a candle to McCarthy's principled bravery. It wasn't until years later that I really came to appreciate RFK and all he had done to advance the issues of race and poverty in America.

With Kennedy in, the race was thrown wide open on March 31, when Johnson shocked the country by announcing in a nationally televised address that he would not run for reelection. The world hardly had time to absorb Johnson's stunning withdrawal when less than a week later came the tragic news that Martin Luther King Jr. had been assassinated by a white man while standing on a hotel balcony in Memphis, Tennessee. I was deeply saddened by the news, as I had come to believe that King represented America's best hope to solve the racial tensions that were tearing the country apart. Little did we all know that within a few months, we'd be mourning the death of Robert Kennedy too, who died less than twenty-four hours after being shot by a young Palestinian, moments after leaving the stage at the Ambassador Hotel in Los Angeles, where he had claimed victory in the California primary.

With the world seemingly on fire, I could feel myself being pulled to that same sense of greater purpose that had propelled me to seek ownership of *Ramparts*.

My contribution to the McCarthy campaign got me invited to the 1968 Democratic Convention in Chicago. In August, I had planned to go to Thailand from my home in San Francisco to check out a mining project arranged by my cousin, Hilly, but impulsively decided to go to the Windy City first. What I found there amazed me and still fills me with rage. I should have read poet and native son Carl Sandburg's "Chicago" before I got off the plane. He had warned, more than fifty years before Chicago's dictatorial Mayor Richard Daley sicced his police on a bunch of kids, that August, that Chicago was a "brawling" and "brutal" city, "fierce as a dog."

The convention was the most turbulent political gathering of my lifetime—and the most consequential. The decisions the delegates made and the riotous ways they made them rattled the country for decades. They split convulsively over whether we should continue to fight in Vietnam, the central issue of the generation and the one about which I had the strongest convictions.

But I never went to the convention hall, only a cab ride away, not even to watch them make history. Instead, I looked around for fun, as usual. For a while I thought I had found it at the Hilton Hotel, where I was staying and where McCarthy had his headquarters and where many of the delegates were staying—including the man who would win the nomination, who had entered the race only after Johnson withdrew: McCarthy's former colleague from Minnesota in the Senate and the current vice president of the United States, Hubert Humphrey.

I wandered into the Hilton bar, which faced Grant Park in the heart of the city. A brunette at a lively table caught my eye, and we began to talk. She said her name was Barbara Raskin, and she offered me a seat between her husband, Marcus, and his partner, Richard Barnet, who were in town from Washington, DC.

We all felt an instant solidarity even though we were strangers. We spoke a common lefty lingo. We cursed the convention in unison, and I ordered another round of drinks. We felt removed from the events that were happening four miles away. We felt free to indulge our indignation as if the bar were a safe and holy sanctuary. It was no surprise to me years later when I learned that Barbara had gone on to become a famous author.

But the convulsion over Vietnam wasn't limited to the convention hall. Outside our windows, I could see crowds of protesters and battle lines of cops. The Hilton reeked of their tear gas, vomit from its victims, and stink bombs the Yippies had thrown into the hotel just for the hell of it. At about midnight I stepped outside and took a place in front of the entrance, hoping for a breath of fresh air.

I was just standing there, minding my own business, when a policeman walked up to me and told me I couldn't stand there.

"Why not?" I asked.

"Because I say so," he growled.

I got angry. I didn't like being told what to do. After all, as I'd said, I was just standing there.

All of a sudden, I saw a bunch of cops beating up a guy nearby. They were pounding his head and kicking him in the gut with their boots. I got even angrier. It wasn't in my nature to be aggressive. I never saw myself as brave. I still didn't like to fight. But I couldn't just stand there and let the police stomp the guy like that. I ran over, jumped into the fray, and tried to protect him. The cops turned on me, but they mostly had it in for the other guy. They beat on him some more, threw him in the back of a police car, and sped off into the night. I worried about what they were going to do to him once they had him alone.

I ran back into the Hilton bar and told my new friends what I had seen. I told them I was afraid the cops were going to kill him. Marc Raskin said we ought to go to the police station to make sure they didn't. I went with him, Barbara, and Barnet to the jail, where the cops were holding the guy in a cell. We found a group of his friends there, writers for the *Village Voice*, who were also worried for his safety. They told us that the guy was Tom Hayden and that the police and the FBI had targeted him as one of the protest leaders. We stood watch together until he was released on bail just before dawn. Hayden would become known as one of the "Chicago Seven" protesters, who were tried and convicted for conspiracy to incite violence in Chicago. The convictions were eventually overturned, and Hayden went on to greater fame as the husband of actress Jane Fonda, whose brother, Peter, I would come to know well in the next few years.

The next morning, I went upstairs to the fifteenth floor of the Hilton to see the kids who had been working for McCarthy. I had visited them on my first day in Chicago. I loved their energy and optimism. But the convention had rejected their peace plank, and McCarthy was on the verge of defeat. Daley's thuggish cops had stormed into their rooms the night before, rousted them with nightsticks, and beat the hell out of them. The headquarters looked like a hospital emergency ward. The kids lay around the room, their hair matted with dried blood. Here I had been living in Mexico all these years, and I had come back to this. Was this really my country now?

I was disgusted by the whole government machine—the mayor, the police, the presidential candidates. But the person whom I came to despise most during that week was Humphrey, who sat in his hotel room twenty floors above the violence in Grant Park as kids were being pummeled and never said a word—a level of political cowardice I have rarely experienced before or after, which will always, for me, overshadow all the good that Humphrey did in his career.

I flew to Bangkok the next day. I arrived drunk, still choking with anger. My cousin Hilly and I met at a French restaurant to schmooze some Thai army brass who were interested in our venture. At the time, the city was an open playground for our military when they needed a break from the war. Someone had invited a high-ranking American admiral and his son to join us.

Full of fury, I exploded at them and the whole table. I let loose about our country's fighting this damned war in the name of freedom while cops were beating the shit out of idealistic kids at home. I railed against the admiral. What was his son doing in this restaurant anyway? Why wasn't he out there doing something to end the war? I don't remember ever in my whole life blowing up with such rage.

The mining venture turned out to be a complete failure. While the mine was a bust, Hilly and his wife Aileen had a wonderful time in Thailand. A geologist who traveled with us ended up falling in love with a beautiful Thai girl. All in all, it wasn't a complete waste of time.

I've wondered since then what made me so angry. I think it partly came from a sense of impotence. Knowing I couldn't do anything to stop the war or to protect the McCarthy kids against the cops' brutality enraged me. I know too that seeing Daley's thugs violate my most basic idea of America fed my fury.

Now that I had seen politics' dark side in Chicago, I still didn't know what I was going to do with the rest of my life.

TWENTY-FIVE

Everything Changes

H elping Hans get through his marriage crisis changed me. In the crunch, I had given him my best self, and the best part of me grew stronger as a result.

The crisis also changed our relationship. Hans had desperately needed me. He trusted me to do for him what he couldn't do for himself. He praised my sensitivity, cleverness, and maturity. He thanked me again and again. He had peeled back layer after layer of his private self to me.

Working with Hans in his crisis changed my view of him. For most sons, there comes a moment when you realize that your father isn't as perfect as you thought. I had idolized Hans for a decade as a surrogate father, a model of both strength and goodness. Now I saw him in a more realistic light.

His agonizing struggle weakened him. It saddened me to see his drive and self-possession wane. Still, I understood that even a man as strong as Hans could deteriorate physically and emotionally when in the grip of such a trauma. The generous and warm-natured Hans I had enjoyed for years evaporated, and he retreated into a self-serving crouch.

More than anything else, it was his behavior toward W in the final act of this drama that forced me to revise my sense of his character. As planned, Hans wrote her in March 1968 and told her that he would not be joining her. Then he cut her off.

She flooded him with letters and cables, pleading for an explanation. For a while, she wasn't even sure that he was still alive. W wrote me and asked for advice, help, and news. She told me she came from an old and honored samurai family and was now irreparably shamed in the eyes of her mother and friends. She was determined to return to Switzerland to see Hans, to find out for herself his condition and his state of mind.

Once again Hans asked me to serve as his middleman, this time to his heartbroken lover. I cabled W that Hans's condition was so fragile that any further emotional stress would endanger his life. In fact, Hans *was* ill, but not that ill. My lies worked. She promised me she would leave him alone when she visited Europe in June.

W stopped in New York on her way home. Hans asked me to deliver a wad of cash into her hands, and I did. At the end, I served as more than just his go-between; I became his bagman.

Although I loved Hans Popper, I finally saw what I had blocked out. My father-in-law, whom I had idealized for ten years, was actually the most magnificent son of a bitch I had ever met.

HANS DIED THREE YEARS later, in April 1971. I was in London when I learned of his death. I left immediately to catch a plane to San Francisco. On the way to the airport, my cab died in the middle of the highway. I flagged down a driver in the middle of the highway and caught a ride. I was absolutely determined to attend my father-in-law's funeral.

Gretl asked me to give the eulogy, so I went to Hans's study to write. I found a note for me on his desk. I assumed he wanted me to administer his estate. I was dismayed to learn that he had decided not to ask me.

Then I saw a letter crumpled up on the floor near the trash can. It was one I had sent Hans, complaining that Lisa showed little interest in using her talents for anything useful as her mother did in so many ways. I can only imagine his despair when he read it, his dismay that I had the nerve to tell him what he had known for years about his only child.

I wrote my eulogy in the first person plural, speaking for all of us, though I was really speaking for myself. I celebrated Hans's probing mind, his warm nature, his endless drive, his love of life. I said that while he rarely made moral judgments on others' foibles, he was intolerant of those who wasted their potential. I praised him as a consummate teacher who had helped us all grow. I ended with a short meditation on the many things he had spent his life collecting:

> Hans was a collector. But not a collector of dead things. Each object was for him another clue in his search for the beauty and understanding of life. And in his heart of hearts, Hans considered himself an intellectual—in the deepest sense of this word. He was a political being. And he probed ceaselessly in his readings, his correspondence, his discussions—searching for the core of all meanings and all actions. In this scholarly and political sense Hans was by definition a radical—in the finest sense of this word. And Hans was a philanthropist in the most human sense. He gave material things when he considered this useful or important. But he gave always himself. To budding artists and musicians, to political and social movements, to educational experiments, to his family and his friends and strangers on the walk, he gave himself. His was not the philanthropy of the pseudo-anonymous; his were the gifts of his life.

But it was too late for the conversation I wanted most to have. I couldn't talk with Hans about repairing our rupture. We couldn't explain, soften, or take back what we had written. We couldn't relieve our hurt by saying how deeply we loved each other. The cruelest grief comes when we lose a loved one with whom we have an unresolved quarrel. Hans was dead, and at age forty-five I faced the rest of my life without his loving, fatherly counsel.

WITH HANS GONE, GRETL and Lisa now depended on me to act as the head of the family, as I had with my own mother.

My mother-in-law had inherited investments in dozens of companies in several countries on four continents. She now owned diverse commercial real estate in Australia, Los Angeles, and Denver, but Hans hadn't sorted out the winners from the turkeys. His art collection had a market value of over $1.5 million (nearly $9 million today), but she would need the help of an array of experts to sell it. A major chunk of her inheritance remained locked up in a soured partnership, which Hans's primary partner turned bitter rival had kept him from liquidating.

Gretl faced a flurry of daunting and pressing financial questions. A stable of Hans's trusted lawyers, accountants, and financial gurus stood ready to advise her, but they worked slowly, and they didn't always agree. It took them months just to clarify how much ready cash she could depend on for her living expenses. She had full authority to make decisions as the executrix and beneficiary of the will, and she was a strong, sensible, independent woman. But she had no taste for or interest in such matters, and she was still full of grief from the loss of Hans.

Gretl turned to me. For the next couple of years, I worked closely with her to make sure that her financial affairs were in an easily understandable order so she could make her own decisions. I took her to Hans's Swiss bank so she could access the accounts she now owned. Although I had no formal legal authority, I asserted myself on her behalf with Hans's scrum of attorneys and accountants and insisted that they make sense of where she stood in practical terms. I found art dealers like Giuseppe Eskenazi to help her decide what to do with Hans's collection. Eventually I suggested that Bernard Petrie assume the role I had been playing. They both loved this arrangement; it was a perfect fit that lasted until her death years later.

Gretl had an intuitive sense of beauty in color, form, sound, and life itself. She graced a room with old-world charm and new-world vivacity, with a smile for everyone, her blue eyes sparkling like tiny, twinkling stars, all without a whiff of vanity.

And she had her inner beauty, that of the soul and the heart, most evident in her selflessness. She worked at San Francisco's Laguna

Honda, a historic almshouse and asylum turned hospital. The sick, the troubled, and the destitute came there for long-term care when they had nowhere else to go. Gretl insisted on doing menial chores none of the other volunteers would do. She fed and nursed the residents with her own hands.

One day she invited me to join her on her rounds, and I got to see her magic at work. I watched her awaken a fresh sense of dignity in an ailing elderly woman, just by brushing her hair and helping her put on a new dress. She made everyone she touched a richer person.

Helping Gretl helped me heal from my own loss of Hans. It reminded me how I had aided him in his crisis and how closely we had drawn together as a result. The role she asked me to play was the very lead position Hans had withheld from me at the last out of pique. Her trust in me soothed my hurt from his slight. Her confidence in me strengthened my belief in myself. Helping Gretl get settled helped me start on a new phase of my life.

TWENTY-SIX

The Pentagon Papers
and Project Harvest Moon

One spring morning in New York, a year after Hans died, I called Barbara Marx on a whim. I asked her to meet me in the city that evening. I had seen her only two times in the previous twenty years—her surprise visit on my twenty-fourth birthday and the time I bumped into her at a New York literary soiree in the mid-1960s.

In fact, Barbara had reentered my mind by chance. Her sister, Patricia, and her husband, Daniel Ellsberg, had recently come to the Popper home in San Francisco with an old friend of mine, peace activist Stanley Sheinbaum, to ask me to help raise money for Ellsberg's legal defense. Educated at Harvard and Cambridge, Ellsberg was a Marine Corps veteran and former Pentagon military analyst who later had become an antiwar activist. After leaving the Pentagon in 1967, he had taken a position at the Rand Corporation, where he worked on a top-secret report for Defense Secretary Robert McNamara on American decision making in Vietnam from the end of World War II through 1968. The study became known as *The Pentagon Papers*.

In 1969, Ellsberg secretly gave copies of the classified report to the Senate Foreign Relations Committee. Then, frustrated that many of the most damning aspects of the war were being kept hidden, he caused a global uproar in 1971 when he released all seven thousand photocopied pages of the report to the *New York Times* and other newspapers. The study revealed that the Pentagon knew fairly early on that the war couldn't be won, and that the Johnson administration had repeatedly lied about Vietnam to Congress and the American people. Ellsberg was arrested and charged with twelve counts of violating America's Espionage Act of 1917. I wanted to help Ellsberg because I believed he was right about the war and I admired his moral courage. At Sheinbaum's urging, I pitched a list of friends, personally, by letter and phone, and then I wrote my own check.

I had other reasons to help Ellsberg. Louis Marx thought his son-in-law should be jailed for life as a traitor for releasing *The Pentagon Papers*. Marx didn't like Jews, refused to acknowledge his daughter's marriage to one, and insisted on calling Ellsberg "Ellsworth." Having felt Louis's hard malice firsthand, I had fraternal feelings toward Ellsberg. I was pleased two years later when the charges against him were dismissed, in large part due to White House misconduct toward him. I found it ironic that instead of Patricia's husband going to jail, several members of Richard Nixon's White House were convicted instead, which played a role in Nixon's Watergate scandal and resignation a year later.

※

I STILL DON'T UNDERSTAND the whim that moved me to call Barbara. I certainly had no interest in resuming our relationship.

Barbara's reaction to my call surprised me. She recalled in her memoir a few years later that she had felt "profoundly moved to hear" my voice and had been "irresistibly compelled to see what" I was like. If we had met a decade before, I might have felt like that too. But that night, as I waited for her to arrive at the Algonquin Hotel that writer Dorothy Parker and her Round Table had made famous, I felt completely at ease, at peace with Barbara and our history.

As I watched her walk into the lobby, I saw much of the girl I had loved in Paris. She came toward me with the same restless energy. She still held her head up like a ship's carved figurehead, her chin lifted into the wind. She greeted me with the authority and resolve of a mature woman, no longer a girl in search of herself.

We took seats in the corner of a banquette, close yet apart. The Blue Bar was quiet that night, and so were we for a while. Barbara took my hand and held it as if that were her right. She recalled later that we sat there, "speechless," looking "into each other's eyes—nothing ever dies that once was felt deeply."

I remember it differently. Sitting next to her there confirmed that whatever I had felt for her all those years ago had finally burned out in the Mexican sun and the bright mornings of San Francisco. That part of me had grown over anew with my marriage to Lisa.

Barbara sketched in her memoir, *The Hunger of Eve*, a lovely but poignant reminiscence of how we began our conversation. She wrote:

> There he was—elegant, transformed, in a turtleneck sweater, so handsome, drinking champagne.
>
> "What does it feel like?" I asked. "You've achieved everything you wanted—wealth, beauty, high position. Has it been worth it? Does it feel satisfying?"
>
> He shook his head. "No, it's worth nothing. It has no purpose—I have no purpose."

She then proceeded to tell me about herself. Of course, I don't recall her exact words now, but I later found echoes of what she told me about her hopes and passions in her memoir. She said she felt a love for the body of all humankind. She told me she lived in a cosmic time and kept reexperiencing the cosmic birth of the universe. She believed mankind was now on the verge of an evolutionary leap to the next phase of its development, a new birth into a universal species with a universal consciousness.

Barbara had finally found her purpose. She was now traveling across the country to raise a citizens' movement to pursue these historic opportunities. She believed a citizens' space program would help diverse people see what they had in common, lead to world union, and spur the realization of mankind's potential. Her father had given her seed money to start Project Harvest Moon to build a colony in space.

She said she remained frustrated by the fragmentation of knowledge and the myriad points of view that kept humans from seeing their common interests and shared future. She was excited about a process called SYNCON (synergistic convergence), which she believed would enable a group to see how to fuse their individual points of view into a unified sense of wholeness. She told me she was about to go to a conference at Southern Illinois University where the participants would "SYNCON" together and, in such oneness, find an ecstasy like that of birth itself.

Though I admired her enthusiasm and her good intentions, I had no idea what she was talking about.

Since we met that night, Barbara has become a celebrated futurist and has built a following of believers in what she calls "conscious evolution." In 1984, she was even nominated by her followers as a Democratic candidate for vice president of the United States, which led to a speaking role at the Democratic Convention that year—ironically, in San Francisco. I still don't understand what she is trying to do or what she means. I wish her well. I thank her for the memories. Above all, I thank her for lighting my inner fire.

The morning after our encounter at the Algonquin, we began radically different journeys: Barbara flew to Carbondale, Illinois, to promote her vision of humanity's future. I flew to London.

TWENTY-SEVEN

Moving to London

L isa and I had enjoyed our years together in Mexico. We comfortably commuted to San Francisco for family gatherings and dinners at Trader Vic's. It always felt good to come home from the ski resorts and European cities Lisa loved. I could monitor my Mexican business out of the corner of my eye and then fly off to Brazil, Europe, or the States to one of my and Ralph Feuerring's plants.

But by the summer of 1971, I felt it was time for us to move. I wanted to give our children opportunities I wished I'd had as a boy—ones we couldn't find for them in Mexico. We would keep our house, and I would still spend time in Mexico City even though my business had become international and was no longer centered there. But I could afford for us to live almost anywhere.

With tongue in cheek, I gave Lisa two choices: New York or London. I already knew she wouldn't move to New York because of her European tastes. I wanted to go to London. I wanted to live in a country whose traditions, tastes, and values I had always loved. And besides, London was close to Paris.

I had been an Anglophile—and later a Celtophile—since boyhood. As a twelve-year-old, I'd loved watching Robert Taylor, a brash, young American, in the movie *A Yank at Oxford* as he won over his skeptical British classmates and help them beat Cambridge in the spring's big boat race. In my Paris days, I'd gone to London to find a tailor to dress me properly for Barbara. For years my fabricated accent had echoed

Guy Burgess's Cantabrigian English. In some visceral sense, London had already been my home for decades.

Lisa and I found a perfect place to live on Chester Square, just to the southwest of Buckingham Palace. The Duke of Westminster had built this "garden square" in the nineteenth century as part of Belgravia, a fashionable residential district in London. It epitomized the best of Great Britain's taste at the zenith of the empire, and it claimed a number of remarkable British residents through the years, from author Mary Shelley to rocker Mick Jagger to playwright Andrew Lloyd Webber to Queen Wilhelmina of the Netherlands. Our new home, six floors of gleaming white stucco that faced a carefully tended garden, had been designed with typical British understatement.

It was so utterly British, we hardly noticed the large number of Americans—mainly Hollywood actors and producers—who also inhabited Chester Square. The romance of watching BBC's wildly successful 1971 series *Upstairs, Downstairs* on the telly in our own upstairs-downstairs home enchanted us. The ironic mix of the real and the made-up somehow confirmed we were in the perfect place.

OUR CHILDREN HAD FLOURISHED in good schools in Mexico, but were about to graduate to new ones. We had moved to London in large part because we wanted them to go to the very best schools we could find to get them ready for university.

Lori had gone to the French Lycée in Mexico and had no trouble getting into the French Lycée in London. Anthony's case was more complicated.

When Anthony was four, we wanted him to attend Greengates, an elite English school in Mexico City. Since he spoke only French, which he had learned from his nanny, I drilled him in English to get him ready.

"What is your name?" I repeatedly asked.

"My name is Anthony Weiss," he said haltingly.

"How old are you?"

"I am four years old."

I thought we were ready. But when Mr. Coelho, the school's head-master, said, "Hello, what is your name?" Anthony dutifully replied, "I am four years old." Everyone laughed. He got in anyway.

Now, in London, we focused first on Hill House School, founded, owned, and dominated by Stuart Townend, a colorful individualist who liked cigars, women, and Ovaltine, not necessarily in that order. Townend welcomed non-English students. He had been a champion athlete, so Hill House offered a rich mix of sports as well as music and the development of character. I also liked the idea that Prince Charles had gone there.

Early one morning I went to the school's doorstep and waited for Townend to arrive. The "Colonel," as he was always addressed, invited me in for a chat. We swapped stories about the war. I told lots of lies about my army service. He told me a lot of truths about his. He had led an artillery unit that had chased the Germans across France, had been badly hurt in combat, and had served with the troops who opened the gates at Buchenwald—one of the first, largest, and most brutal of the concentration camps on German soil.

Townend could admit anyone he wanted, and he waved Anthony in the door.

Anthony enjoyed Hill House, especially its sports, for a year. But Lisa and I worried he wasn't learning enough. We decided he ought to go to Westminster or Saint Paul's, the two academically elite schools in London.

I charmed my way through the door of Colet Court, the underschool of Saint Paul's, and induced the headmaster's secretary and gatekeeper to get me an appointment with the headmaster. When he asked me why I wanted Anthony to go to his school, I explained I'd always wanted my son to understand the Crimean War. He laughed and offered to arrange an entrance examination. I asked him not to. I explained Anthony would never pass, because, after all, he had just spent a year at Hill House. The headmaster understood, nodded sympathetically, and waived the test.

Anthony struggled at Colet Court and Saint Paul's. He always thought he was in over his head. He felt I had thrown him in with kids who had been able to recite Virgil in Latin before they could walk. I understood. I still resented all those smart-ass guys with their fancy bow ties at Central High. But unlike my father, who let me drift, I insisted that my son take advantage of the opportunities he was given.

Occasionally, I tried to expose Anthony to the wider world by taking him on trips with me. When he was around ten years old, I decided to take a special group of people—including a German baron and his wife, a French prince, and my famous architect friend from Mexico, Alfredo Terrazas—to look at a gold mine prospect owned by a Canadian near Fairbanks, Alaska. Anthony came along. While in Fairbanks, we quickly realized it was like one of those old gold rush mining towns from the days of the prospectors, where the percentage of prostitutes to other people was probably three to one or something like that. The first thing my son did when we returned to London was to tell his mother, "Did you know that the incidence of prostitutes to other people in Fairbanks is three to one?"

I said, "Thanks a lot, Anthony."

All of our efforts to find the right schools in London for our children and to give them unforgettable adventures paid off. Lori Christina graduated from Yale and went on to become a part owner of the Philadelphia Eagles football team, among dozens of other ventures, many of which benefit children and families. Anthony became a mountain climber and got the degree at Georgetown's School of Foreign Service that I never took the time to finish—and then earned a master's at the London School of Economics. He's a business executive and a terrific leader who, I'm told, has the same ability to delegate work to people he trusts as his old man.

SINCE BOYHOOD, I HAD feasted on male camaraderie as a member of a series of virtual men's clubs. I discovered and reinforced essential elements of myself there. I found fun with my gang on Queen Street, tasted politics by arguing with intellectuals in Mexico City, and acquired an ear for repartee by listening to the wits at Trader Vic's. The value of these informal fraternities for me was unspoken, implicit. None had its own building, library, or history. None had a name. None had a list of members. None had an emblem or token signifying membership. As one character declared in the most famous line of dialogue from my favorite movie, *The Treasure of the Sierra Madre*, "We don't need no stinkin' badges."

I saw the gentlemen's clubs of London differently. They were an intrinsic part of the British culture and taste that had drawn me to England. Hundreds of London gentlemen's clubs cropped up in the nineteenth century, each reflecting a distinct and treasured identity, which its members believed they personified and which they protected with strict protocols of exclusivity.

When I arrived in 1971, I wanted to join two clubs whose character I particularly admired. I had become an avid tennis player, and I wanted to belong to the Queen's Club, one of the two best tennis clubs. Friends sponsored me, and I quickly became a member.

I also wanted to join the Garrick Club. Since its founding in 1831, its members had included the cream of British theater, music, and letters: Olivier and Burton, Gilbert and Sullivan, Maugham, and Coward. The most interesting men of English politics and journalism gathered there, and I wanted to mingle with them. I wasn't alone. The Garrick Club had a waiting list of fourteen years.

I asked Harry Evans, the editor of the *Sunday Times*, how to get in. Harry had lived in San Francisco for some months in the late 1950s, and friends of ours had made him feel welcome. Now he returned the favor by befriending me. He sent me a list of all the club's members and told me to mark the ones I knew. I didn't know any of them. Harry took the matter into his own hands. He called the guy who ran Reuters to second me, and they worked some magic together. I became a member two weeks later.

The Garrick Club's members proved even more sparkling than I had imagined. For all their accomplishments as the keepers of England's arts and letters, I discovered that the art they mastered most was the art of conversation. I learned this when I lunched with them at the "long table."

We customarily gathered first in the club's polished bar twenty minutes or so before lunch to chat a bit. At one thirty we promptly moved into the stately Coffee Room, a Georgian triumph, which was lit by a row of tall windows on one side, warmed by rich red walls, and enlivened by a gallery of portraits. It was a perfect place to hear and to be heard.

Members who came alone found a seat at the long, narrow table that commanded the center of the room and seated over twenty. We fell into impromptu conversations with whomever we found across from us, about whatever suited us, playing whatever hand we were dealt. The conversations at the "long table" had a quieter tone, a subtler wit, and a more leisurely pace than the flurry of wisecracks at Trader Vic's. The ability to explore a rich range of ideas and subjects with fluency, civility, and intelligence was a common thread uniting the club's members. Everyone I met there had this gift.

Most of all, I wanted to join the Garrick Club because it was so hard to get into. It reminded me of crawling through a tiny hole into a mine, an act that always somehow made the ore I found there seem more valuable. Yet I had no interest in publicly flashing my prized membership to others like a badge. I kept my point of pride to myself and enjoyed my self-satisfaction privately.

One part of me succeeded in charting a new life course during the year after Hans died. I felt good in London. It gave me a perfect place to play tennis, engage in good conversations, and enjoy the comfort of new friends. But my sense of place and self remained anchored in the United States. And even as I was settling into London, another part of me felt restless and unsatisfied.

TWENTY-EIGHT

Adrift

As I struggled to find a fresh direction, I reached out to Erich Fromm in a series of rambling, overwritten confessional letters. I told him I clearly knew what I didn't want to do: make business the center of my life. But I had only the vaguest notion of what I wanted to do instead. I said I hoped to engage in more "humanistic strivings" and more "selfless involvement," awkward terms that had (and still have) almost no concrete meaning for me.

I told Fromm I felt intellectually inadequate, lacked self-assurance, and continued to be bothered by not having finished college. I confided that I felt adrift and dependent on the good opinion of others. I wrote him that instead of deciding on the direction I wanted to take, I hoped to "satisfy people whose instant love and praise I wanted."

Eventually I became too agitated and impatient to communicate through letters, so I went to see Fromm in Locarno, interrupting his vacation. Full of indecision and angst, I babbled on and on for most of an afternoon. He patiently listened as I wrestled with my hopes and contradictions until all at once he shouted, "Bullshit!"

I realized I had been spouting utter nonsense, wandering all over, under, and around in search of some point. I mumbled some excuse and quickly left, deeply embarrassed.

I reverted to old instincts and again set out to define myself by hooking up with people I admired. By this point Marc Raskin and Dick Barnet, whom I had met that night at Chicago's Conrad Hilton Hotel, had become my new Hinckle and Scheer.

I had become enamored of Raskin and Barnet since our chance meeting in Chicago. I felt our standing watch together in Tom Hayden's jailhouse that riotous August night had given us a sense of solidarity. I had gotten to know them better since then. They had visited Mexico from time to time to visit Fromm and to see me.

Both men impressed me as models of cultural, intellectual, and political achievement. Both were gifted musicians: Raskin, a prodigy on the piano at Juilliard, and Barnet, an accomplished violinist. Both had graduated from elite colleges and law schools: Raskin from Chicago, Barnet summa cum laude from Harvard. Both had worked in centers of power for lions of the establishment in Washington, DC: Barnet for John J. McCloy at the Arms Control and Disarmament Agency, Raskin in the White House, for McGeorge Bundy, National Security Advisor to presidents Kennedy and Johnson.

I liked their gutsiness. They had convictions and acted on them. They wrote and spoke fearlessly. Both men had left their sweet jobs because they opposed the Vietnam War in particular and vanilla liberalism in general. In 1963 they founded the Institute for Policy Studies (IPS) to provide an independent, radical voice. By the time we met at the convention, they had already mobilized some of the country's most articulate left-wing intellectuals on a wide range of policy issues. I wanted to work with them, learn to write and speak like them, and promote the public good like they did.

Marc Raskin seemed to welcome my interest in their work. A year or so before I moved my family to London, he and Barnet had come to visit me in Mexico City. Ivan Illich, a celebrated social thinker, invited a small group of us to dinner at his home in Cuernavaca. This charismatic ex-priest had founded a center there, a kind of open university that attracted radical critics of education and other social policy from all over the world.

Michael Maccoby, a young colleague of Fromm's, had been invited too. Michael had earned a spectacular academic record at Harvard, Oxford, and the University of Chicago. He had trained as a psychoanalyst with Fromm, and they had just finished coauthoring a study of Mexican village life. Maccoby had sympathized with me during my comedy with the *Ramparts* editors, and he joined the Fromms in my yoga classes. I thought we were friends.

I was amazed when Maccoby tried to persuade Raskin and Barnet to get me disinvited from Illich's dinner. Apparently he expected the conversation to be so profound that only a select, highly trained few should participate. He didn't think I could offer anything to the discussion. Perhaps he was right. I just wanted to listen to a table of big-league intellects mix it up, hoping some of their learning would rub off on me.

Raskin said if I wasn't invited, he wouldn't go either. That settled it. We all went together. Illich did most of the talking. Others chimed in. I listened. I loved hearing them talk. We all had a rollicking good time.

Maccoby's effort to exclude me angered me. This was the first case of my directly experiencing what I feared most: exclusion from circles I hoped to enter, simply because I lacked scholarly credentials. I was also angry at myself for repeatedly neglecting my formal education and making myself vulnerable to such snobbery. The Illich episode reminded me why I wanted to work with Raskin and Barnet, and Marc's standing up for me made me think he would be glad to have me join them.

IN THE SUMMER OF 1971, I was straddling the Atlantic. I was eager to acclimate to my new life in London. But I was also determined to find a place at the Institute for Policy Studies in DC. It had been so effective in advocating for principled resistance against both the war in Vietnam and the growing corruption of the Nixon White House that Barnet and Raskin had earned a spot on Richard Nixon's famous "Enemies List." Within four years, the FBI would also have more than seventy informants passing in and out of its doors. I needed advice about how I could join IPS, and it came from an unexpected source.

Just before I had left for London, Michael Maccoby visited me one evening at my home in Mexico City. He was also moving, to Washington to become a Fellow at IPS. He didn't know I was still angry about his efforts to disinvite me from the Illich dinner the previous year, and he had come to offer a *despedida*, an affectionate Mexican custom of saying farewell to a friend. We talked over dinner and into the night. He was still full of himself, but he had also grown in many ways. We were able to patch up our relationship.

Maccoby knew Raskin and Barnet well, and he understood how IPS worked. I hoped he would help me find a way to fit in.

He seemed simpatico with my aches and ambitions, but he didn't think I would be satisfied by trying to define my identity at IPS. A practicing psychoanalyst, he said I needed to understand myself more fundamentally in order to set a new direction. He suggested I undertake psychoanalysis with him to learn what was tearing at me. We agreed we would begin in earnest as soon as possible.

I pressed him to see me as often as he could in Washington that September and October 1971. I worked hard, but I was impatient. Laboring at analysis as if I were mining, I thought that if I just dug harder and faster I would find the mother lode.

I quickly learned that Maccoby and I worked at different tempos. I told him about one dream I had, in which I was playing poker with very large stakes but I didn't understand the rules of the game, and I was too embarrassed to ask what they were. We explored the dream's meaning until I'd had enough. He groused that if I didn't have the patience and determination to try to understand a dream to its core, how could I ever expect to fathom my own identity? He complained I was superficial about getting to know myself.

He said that, unlike me, every Fellow at IPS had a "deep base" in some discipline, such as law, political philosophy, or economics. He had, of course, built his own professional base in psychiatry and anthropology. He said without such a base, I would be seen as—and would in fact be—a dilettante. I accepted this premise. It echoed my sense of intellectual inadequacy.

Maccoby was skeptical that I really wanted to make a significant change in my life. He felt that if I were serious, I would have asked Fromm for help. He pointed out that I hadn't really done anything decisive or drastic in acting on my ambitions. He thought my moving to London was directionless. He told me I was altogether too satisfied with myself and my lifestyle. He was right about all of this, of course.

For all our efforts, Maccoby and I weren't a good fit. Sometimes when struggling to answer a question, I'd catch him smirking. Eventually I ran out of things to say—or things I wanted to say to him. After a few weeks, I told him I had decided to discontinue our formal meetings.

We remained friends, more or less, and he informally counseled me from time to time during the 1970s. He became an internationally respected expert on leadership and went on to coach leaders of major corporations and government agencies all over the world. He also wrote a best seller, *The Gamesman*, along with a bookshelf of studies.

Recently, I happened upon a long-lost file of letters and memos about my work with Maccoby. I asked him to lunch so we could compare our memories of our work together. He couldn't have been more gracious as we reminisced. Finally, he said, "If I knew then what I know now, I could have been a great deal more help."

I thought to myself, *If I had known then what I know now, I might not have needed so much help.*

ↂ

IN SPITE OF MICHAEL Maccoby's skepticism, I still hoped I could find a place at IPS to grow personally. I thought I needed to be physically present at their offices to do this, so I continued to spend a lot of time in Washington. Lisa, understandably, chafed at my absences—here we were, newly resettled in London, and yet I was announcing that I'd be spending more time in Washington. Gretl thought I was using it as "an escape home."

In late October 1971, I began an all-out invasion of IPS. I met with each of the fellows, one at a time, face-to-face. I thought a total immersion—seeing them morning, noon, and night—would win me a place at their table. Instead, the fellows greeted me with resentment and suspicion.

Most of them were intellectuals, proud of their learning and disdainful of someone like me who lacked it. Most of them had never tried to make money and had little regard for those who had. They couldn't believe that this wealthy, well-tailored forty-four-year-old with a backstory about finding treasure in the Mexican mountains really wanted to be a student.

IPS's leaders mostly saw me as a moneyman. Like *Ramparts*, IPS depended on a handful of wealthy backers. Although I had already written a hefty check, they were waiting for me to pay much more before rolling out the welcome mat. But my escapade with *Ramparts* had made me cautious. I was determined not to give a lot more money until I knew I could contribute in a nonmonetary way as well.

IPS's lack of hospitality pushed me into a tizzy of self-doubt. I couldn't understand why the organization didn't welcome me. All my life I had made friends easily. Wherever I had gone, people liked me. After a while I realized that most of the fellows had different tempera-ments and habits from me. They took themselves very seriously. I liked to have fun.

I continued to admire Marc and Dick as intellectual models, but as I got to know them better, our friendship cooled. It bothered me that Marc misunderstood his wife's friendship with me. Barbara welcomed me to Washington with open arms. She had made the Raskin home into a rambunctious salon where her friends could argue and drink into the night. She insisted I join in. The environment suited my tastes.

Unfortunately, her fervor bothered Marc, and I began picking up some bad vibes from him. Barbara confided to me that he was jealous. He thought she had a crush on me. The truth was, she offered me exactly the mix of fun and intellect I had hoped to find in Washington, but that was it. It took Marc a while to realize nothing else was going on.

My view of Dick Barnet also changed after I got to know him up close. He asked if he could use my house in Mexico City to write a book one summer. He worked there on *Global Reach*, a powerful and pioneering study of the influence of multinational corporations, which he coauthored and published in 1974. I very much admired it.

But I didn't very much like what he and his dog did to my house. His dog shat all over the beds, and he left it that way. Barnet finally sort of said he was sorry, but by then it didn't matter. I didn't like being taken advantage of. I didn't have much to do with him after that.

ONE OF THE BEST things to come out of my relationship with Marc Raskin in the early 1970s was a lifelong friendship and business partnership with Sidney Harman, an entrepreneur known around the globe for changing the world of music. Born in Canada and raised in New York, Sidney had invented the world's first integrated hi-fi receiver with his boss, Bernard Kardon, in 1953. They founded Harman Kardon the same year and quickly became known for creating some of the best audio systems in the world.

Marc had suggested that Sidney meet me, and our first conversation happened over a transatlantic phone call. Sidney told me about a plant he was building in Bolivar, Tennessee, which he intended to be a model of progressive business—a place where whites and blacks would be paid the same salary. His partner in the plant ended up going bankrupt, and he asked me if I'd be willing to guarantee his share. It was a risk that could end in total failure, but it appealed to my growing sense of social justice, and I agreed. I'm glad I did. The Bolivar plant was a great success and became a popular case study at business schools around the world. That began a nearly forty-year business partnership between Sidney and me.

In 1976, Sidney accepted an appointment as the Deputy Secretary of Commerce under President Jimmy Carter. Like many businessmen who take government jobs, to avoid the perception of impropriety, he sold his company to Beatrice Foods. They quickly screwed it up. When he returned to the private sector three years later, he asked me, along with three venture capitalists, to join him in repurchasing the business he had sold to Beatrice. He named the new conglomerate Harman International Industries. For me, it turned out to be a good investment: Sidney took the company public in 1986 and made us both a lot of money. But I was hurt that he didn't invite me to join the board of directors. Sidney had such a huge ego and was such a narcissist, it probably didn't even occur to him.

A few years later, he asked me to join him in another venture. I did. It went bankrupt. He later asked me to join the board of Harman International. I didn't really see the point, but Sidney argued that he needed me to be a yes vote. I agreed. By then, we had become close friends, spending a lot of time together and taking roles in the various philanthropic ventures that each of us had started. Then one day in 2006, he abruptly told me that he wanted me off the board. No explanation given. How a friend of nearly forty years could do that, I had no idea. I sold my shares, and we went our separate ways.

Shortly before he died of leukemia in April 2011, Sidney called about having lunch. We got together, and he told me he felt betrayed. In 2006, there had been a call of the board, in which the board members had advocated bringing on a younger chairman. He assumed that I had been one of the people in on the call. He was wrong: I wasn't. In fact, the very first time I had heard about that call was that very moment, from him at lunch that day. It made me sad to think that he'd ended a close, four-decades-long friendship over a misunderstanding that easily could've been clarified. But I have no regrets. Sidney Harman was a terrific friend for a long time and I learned a lot from him. I still get together from time to time with his wonderful wife, Jane Harman, who represented the Palm Springs, California, area for nearly two decades as a member of US Congress and now heads the Wilson Center think tank in Washington.

I STILL WANTED TO be a part of IPS and hung around for most of the seventies. I liked the energy of the place. I loved the fellows' stomach for a fight.

But I dialed down my intensity and tempo and looked for a niche that fit my more casual tastes. I made friends among the fellows who didn't fit IPS's standard academic mold. I felt especially comfortable with doers who acted on their convictions to make things happen.

One such person was Orlando Letelier, who had played a major role in Salvador Allende's socialist government in Chile before General Augusto Pinochet's military coup in 1973. When I met him, he was leading the exiled Chilean opposition to the general's dictatorship from his IPS office. We had good times together. I kidded him once that he didn't seem like a real communist. He smiled and explained he wasn't a communist; he was a democratic socialist. Hans Popper would have enjoyed being with him.

Pinochet's secret police didn't care about such distinctions. One fall morning, their agents assassinated Letelier and an IPS intern with a car bomb in Washington's Sheridan Circle, at the top of a long street called Massachusetts Avenue that houses dozens of different embassies. They murdered them on American soil, only a few blocks from IPS.

Letelier's murder incensed Saul Landau, another fellow and a friend. He wasn't content with just shouting his outrage to fellow believers. He used his skills as an investigative reporter and filmmaker to expose the foul conspiracy of Chile's intelligence officers and hired thugs. Landau pursued the case relentlessly and, alongside a very aggressive FBI, helped convict the killers. In court, it was revealed that Pinochet had ordered the hit, one of thousands of crimes for which he was never brought to justice. To this day, there is a small round memorial to Letelier's memory in Sheridan Circle.

⁂

ALTHOUGH HUNGER HAD PLAGUED parts of the world forever, most people in prosperous countries hardly noticed. I hadn't. But when Bangladesh suffered a ghastly famine during most of 1974, eventually taking more than a million lives, hunger exploded into a major international issue. Edmundo Flores, our old friend the economist from Mexico City, headed an effort by a bloc of developing counties in the UN, known as the Group of 77, to find ways to deal with the problem.

Flores arranged for Lisa and me to be invited to the United Nations World Food Conference in Rome. My invitation as an official participant gave me a sense of standing, but I had no responsibilities, so my role there fit me perfectly. I knew Gretl, with her heartfelt social conscience, would be pleased that we were at such a conference, so I wrote her about what I saw and heard.

My account read like a casual tourist's letter home: a little of this, a little of that. I reported that giant agribusinesses were influencing the UN's efforts to deal with hunger, because they wanted to control foodstuffs for profit. I wrote that, on the other hand, the opposition that I stood with was using the conference to make its case that hunger couldn't be eliminated unless multinational corporations' power was redistributed in underdeveloped countries.

I told Gretl that the star of the conference was Secretary of State Henry Kissinger, whom I considered a war criminal at the time for the role he played in perpetuating the Vietnam War and extending its reach into Laos and Cambodia. I grudgingly found him impressive, and said so in my letter. He had received his Nobel Prize a year earlier and was at the top of his game. On November 5, 1974, he fearlessly declared the bold goal on behalf of the entire world that "within a decade no child will go to bed hungry." It wouldn't be the last time I'd come face-to-face with Mr. Kissinger over the next decade.

I didn't tell Gretl that the conference in Rome turned into a mostly social occasion for us. We had the perfect place to play: the five-star Hassler Hotel, which stood near the Pantheon and had served as the headquarters for the US Army during the war. It offered spectacular views of the city and overlooked the majestic, baroque Spanish Steps, where Audrey Hepburn and Gregory Peck had romped two decades earlier in *Roman Holiday*, the romantic comedy about a reporter and a royal princess who find love. The picture had won Hepburn the Oscar for Best Actress, along with the lifelong devotion of millions of fans like me—not just because she was a graceful and striking talent, but because she dedicated herself to a new cause when her film career wound down, as Special Ambassador to the United Nation Children's Fund. She had never forgotten what it felt like to be a starving child in Holland at the end of World War II, and did everything in her power to bring food, medicine, and clothing to as many poor children as possible.

It had been about three years since I had moved to my London home and started to seek a larger purpose than making money. The conference on hunger offered me a feast of opportunities to work for humane purposes, but none moved me to act.

⚯

I HAD SEVERAL CHANCES in the early seventies to set the new direction for my life. No one in the world was better suited to help me than Erich Fromm. All I had to do was ask. I didn't.

I also could have pursued the education and credentials I had ached for over the years. Maccoby suggested I study at the London School of Economics, founded in 1895 for "the betterment of society," to achieve some betterment for myself, to get the "base" of deep academic knowledge we both believed I needed in order to be taken seriously. I had the means, the motive, and the opportunity. Yet again, I reached into my well-worn bag of excuses and avoidances.

For the first half of the seventies, I did what I wanted. Like an adolescent, I screwed around aimlessly, chasing one whim after another. I might have grown personally if I had worked longer and more seriously at IPS. But after a year or two I backed away from trying to discover myself by imitating role models. My hope to find fulfillment through osmosis faded.

I had not yet realized that some of the skills that came to me naturally and worked for me in business might help me contribute as a citizen. It would take me over a decade to see this clearly and to act on it.

TWENTY-NINE

Wild and Crazy in New Hollywood

I have always loved movies. They do more than just fire my imagination and feed my fantasies. Movies stir me to take action. I've mined them for heroes and stories to shape my identity. *The Treasure of the Sierra Madre* prompted my move to Mexico; I idolized Alan Ladd so much, I filled the empty space in the middle of my name with his; and *A Yank at Oxford* inspired a lifelong love of Great Britain

But I didn't just want to watch movies. I wanted to make them. My experience as a coproducer of Mexico's first musical had whetted my appetite. Filmmaking, like writing, is art. You create it. You put your name on it. It endures. I wasn't ready to write a book, but it seemed making a movie would be easier and more fun than laboring at a desk. It most certainly would offer a bigger chance to mingle with big-bet producers, hell-raising actors, and gorgeous women.

I took my first stab at moviemaking in 1965. In Los Angeles to comfort my younger sister, Flora, after the death of our mother, I looked up an old friend, Larry Turman, an agent turned producer. I had been introduced to Larry by a couple I had gotten to know in Mexico, and then happened upon him during a trip back to LA together a year or so earlier. Larry was glad to hear from me and asked me to read a book he thought would make a great film. It told the story of a young college graduate who doesn't know what he wants to do with his life, is seduced by an older woman, and then runs off with her daughter. Larry hoped I would like the story and join him as a partner in making it into a movie.

When I read the story on the plane back to Mexico City that night, I thought it was terrific. The next morning, I called him and told him I was in. I knew nothing about making movies, but I figured I'd learn. How hard could it be?

Over the next month, I made two trips back to LA to work with Larry, meeting with various people we tried to interest in making the film. Larry told me they had found this young actor from Chicago who might be good in the lead role, a largely unknown method actor who drew notice in a handful of acting credits on and off Broadway and in a few small roles on television and the big screen. His name was Dustin Hoffman.

I thought that everything was going great and that we were on our way.

A little more than a month into our collaboration, Larry called to tell me the astonishing news that he had recruited Mike Nichols to direct the film. Nichols, already known as one of his generation's most brilliant comedians for his work with his equally brilliant writing partner, Elaine May, had won a fistful of Tony awards as a director on Broadway. Nichols was then heating up Hollywood by directing *Who's Afraid of Virginia Woolf?*—a black comedy that earned my old drinking buddy Richard Burton's now-wife, Elizabeth Taylor, her second Academy Award. Speaking haltingly into the phone, Larry told me it would be complicated to set up things with another person now and asked me if I would mind dropping out of the deal.

Of course I minded. But I said, "We have nothing in writing, so you're free to do what you want."

The dark shadow of Al Himfar passed over me. But I had grown up by now and realized that it was just business—a kind of business that I've come to understand is routinely practiced in Hollywood, which gives short shrift to loyalty and is far from the code I've always followed. People always like to rag on scrap metal dealers, but when you shake hands with them, the deal is done. Not so with Hollywood producers. I've been friends with a lot of them, and for all their personality and fame, each one is fundamentally a shit at heart. I haven't met one of them who would hesitate to throw a close friend under a bus if it meant closing a deal.

It wasn't the end of the world for me, but I had no idea at the time that *The Graduate* would go on to gross over a $100 million, earn seven Academy Award nominations, win Nichols an Oscar for best director, and launch Hoffman as one of the best actors of his time. Turman went on to a successful career as a producer.

⁂

A FEW YEARS LATER, Mitch Lifton—a friend I had gotten to know through my pals at Trader Vic's—had earned a reputation directing plays at the Actor's Workshop in San Francisco and wanted to get into the movie business. He sent me stories and scripts in London from time to time, hoping I would like one and front enough money to find someone in the industry who would underwrite it. I thought *The Hired Hand*, a Western he had optioned, might work.

Coco Brown, my poker buddy at Elaine's, joined. His father had made scores of movies, including dozens of Westerns. But I had learned my lesson after the success of *The Graduate*. This time I insisted that the three of us sign a formal agreement to document the details of our partnership.

I sent the book to Henry Fonda—cold—with an old-fashioned letter of introduction using the names of friends who were known to him, including Coco's dad. I had never met Fonda, but he had always struck me as a class act. Besides, it was a Western—and who else, besides John Wayne, would I send it to but the man who had played a gunfighter more times than I could count? He got back to me within a week, saying that he liked it. He felt he was too old for the lead, though. He thought his son, Peter, would be just right for the part.

Young Fonda was hot at the time. Just a year or two earlier, he and countercultural soulmate and actor Dennis Hopper had recently released their psychedelic blockbuster, *Easy Rider*. Universal's bosses never grasped the movie's appeal—from its perpetual drug use to its groundbreaking soundtrack featuring sixties icons Jimi Hendrix, the Byrds, and the Band—but they understood the bottom line: a gross of over $40 million for a film that cost about $400,000. They rewarded each of the two stars $1 million to make whatever movie he wanted next. Peter liked *The Hired Hand* and was ready to ride.

His producer, Bill Hayward, asked me to meet him in New York to work out an agreement. He was not quite thirty years old and loved fun almost as much as I did. We hit it off right away. We quickly agreed on the basics: They needed the rights to the story, which we owned. We needed Fonda's star power and his ability to get Universal to finance and distribute the movie.

The rest of the details about points, percentages, and credits—juicy movie matters—fell into place. My troika got what we wanted: a cut of the net profit and appropriate credits. Peter got artistic control. He was jealous that Hopper had directed *Easy Rider*, so he very much wanted to direct as well as star. The agreement Bill and I reached committed us all to work together to produce "a first-class full-length feature film."

At Hayward's suggestion, I went to Santa Monica to meet Peter. His home commanded a godlike view of the ocean across a vast beach. As I approached the house, I saw a stream of beautiful young women coming in and out. A few almost had clothes on. I spotted Peter inside, sitting in a big hot tub and smoking dope. This was hardly a surprise. The rumor was that all of the drug use seen on-screen in *Easy Rider*, from marijuana to LSD, was real. He invited me to jump in. I did. The girls didn't seem to mind.

Peter told me he loved New Hollywood but hated Old Hollywood. I asked him what he disliked about it. He said something like "They all have mansions in Santa Monica and lots of naked girls running back and forth. And they're always drinking."

I said, "I think I get it. The difference is that the Old Hollywood drinks a lot of booze, but the New Hollywood smokes a lot of dope."

I made it clear to Hayward and Peter that I wanted to actually help produce the movie, and immediately pitched in to scout for a location in Mexico. Candice Bergen, the stunning model turned actress who was the daughter of legendary ventriloquist and comedian Edgar Bergen (whom I knew), had just finished shooting *Soldier Blue* near San Miguel de Allende, a Mexican town I knew very well. I hoped their set might still be there so we could use it and save some money.

Hayward and his girlfriend offered to take the daylong drive with me from Mexico City to San Miguel de Allende to take a look. We set out by car one morning with Humberto Reygosa, who worked for me in the area. It got cold in the high country, so I took extra sweaters, but I brought hardly any money.

Once there, we saw the set had been dismantled. I thought the location might still work. Bill didn't agree. We went to a bar to discuss. After a while, Bill and his girlfriend, who was flying high on amphetamines, said they were going out for a bit. An hour or two later, I wondered where they could be. Reygosa and I walked down to the center of town to find them. No such luck.

I knew the town intimately from my mining days—every bartender, every bar. I entered a favorite one and ordered a whiskey. As I held the glass up to my mouth, it came to me where Bill might be. I told the barman I would be back and asked him to hold my drink for me.

I hurried to the jail. Hayward was a tall, blondish, good-looking guy, so I asked the jailer if he had a big gringo there. He pointed us to the holding cell. We found Bill there, completely naked, fighting a whole bunch of Mexicans who were locked up with him.

They might have killed him. The jailer shrugged again until I gave him some money to move Bill to a solitary cell. I handed him a sweater to cover himself and asked him what had happened. It turns out that Bill and his girlfriend were so horny, they couldn't wait to get to their hotel room and just starting going at it in a somewhat isolated public place in the center of town—where, naturally, people had heard them and complained, leading the police to arrest both of them with their clothes strewn on the ground around them.

I found his girlfriend in the women's prison, also naked, still high from something. She wasn't in good shape. She was locked up with a woman charged with murdering her two children. The rest of my money got her moved to a cell by herself, and I gave her a couple of sweaters.

The police had already taken all the cash the two lovers had, except

Hayward's roll of German marks, which they thought was Monopoly money. We didn't have enough pesos or dollars to bribe the jailers to release them, so Bill and his girlfriend were stuck in jail overnight, albeit safely in their separate solitary cells.

I had to figure out my next move. I asked Reygosa to go to Guanajuato, the state capital, and ask the governor to get my friends out of jail. The next morning, the governor—who had a high regard for me and my business in the area—called the jailer and told him to let Hayward and his girlfriend go.

Having succeeded so brilliantly at not finding a location, I decided to move on to casting, a traditional playground for producers. At the time, my business partner, Ralph Feuerring, and I wanted to sell a steel mill in a little town in Germany. A top corporate executive named Mac was the key to the deal.

We were in a club one night in Cologne, trying to get Mac to come to terms with us, when I remembered that his American girlfriend wanted to be a movie actress. I told him that I was making a film with Peter Fonda, and it had a part that would be great for her. I hoped dangling this sweetener might help us close the deal. Mac got very excited. He found a phone in the back of the joint, called his girl in the States, and shouted, "I can get you a part in a movie!"

A couple of weeks later, Mac offered his private jet to help Fonda, Hayward, and me scout for a location in New Mexico. He brought his girl along to make her pitch. I brought Frank Senkowsky. We had a crazy flight that day. Peter took command even though he was stoned. He pulled off his big cowboy hat, waved it wildly, and screamed directions about where to look. The pilot made all kinds of breakneck dips and dives. We finally found a place to shoot, but flying a Lear Jet at hundreds of miles per hour over the desert is not the best way to look for movie locations. This was one time my fear of flying made some sense.

Once we landed and cleared our heads, we sat down to consider what role Mac's girl should play. Although already of a certain age, she was sure she would be perfect playing the female lead, Fonda's abandoned wife—a richly layered role at the heart of the film. It was Peter's call, so I asked him straight out. He glanced at the actress and then looked down at his boots, a mannerism that reminded me of his father's understated authority. He finally suggested she might play the town gossip, a busybody who was an older woman.

She blew up at Peter, insulted by his slight about her age as well his stomping on her dream. Mac blew up at me. Ralph and I ultimately sold him the steel mill, but my ham-fisted effort at casting made it a lot harder. Hans Popper had always told me I shouldn't mix business with art.

When the shooting moved to Hollywood from location in the curiously named town of Cuba, New Mexico, I wanted to get involved as an actor, just for the hell of it. Peter said I should be a cowboy. I grew a dark beard, found some old boots, and got me a ten-gallon hat and scuffed it up.

My first scene didn't work out very well. I was supposed to walk a horse over to the saloon. The horse didn't like me, and it kept stomping on my foot. I looked like a greenhorn. That's why they cut it.

I did a lot better in my other scene. My role called for me to play poker and drink beer with three other guys in the saloon. I was terrific. I should have been; I had been rehearsing the part for years. The only challenge was that the scene took thirty-five takes to film.

Most of the crew who made *The Hired Hand* preferred pot over booze. The film floated to the theaters in August 1971 on a cloud of weed smoke. It opened to mixed reviews. If you were sober, it seemed slow and boring. *Time* found it "pointless, virtually plotless, and all but motionless." Others liked it a great deal. I told people that if you watched it while stoned, you'd like it—because you'd lose your sense of time, and it wouldn't seem all that bad. Everything would seemed elevated. All the actors certainly were.

The film made it onto network television a few years later in a slightly longer cut than the one that ran in the movies. Surprisingly, it experienced a revival years later, when Robert Redford's brilliant home for independent, the Sundance Channel, released it to DVD. Some people tell me it's now considered a kind of cult Western classic from the early seventies.

Peter Fonda, who had cut his directing teeth on our film, told me years later that it probably would have been a much better film if he hadn't directed it—or at least if he had known then what he found out later about directing.

I hadn't expected to make any money on the film, which was just as well because I didn't. My carefully negotiated deal for a percentage of the net profit meant nothing. Movies' books were kept so they almost never made net profits back then anyway. The only payment I received was the twenty dollars per diem the Actors Guild required I be paid for three days of drinking beer and playing poker on camera at the saloon—which is pretty good work, if you can get it.

What I did want—what was most important to me—was a formal credit, and Bill Hayward made sure I got it. That August I got to see "Executive Producer Stanley A. Weiss" right there in black and white in *Variety*. Bill was a good egg. It made me sad thirty-seven years later to learn that he had taken his own life in the California trailer where he was living, by shooting himself in the heart. I prefer instead to remember him as the young hippie daring enough to make love to his gorgeous girlfriend in the middle of a rough Mexican town—a Hollywood-worthy story if there ever was one.

THE WILDEST AND CRAZIEST fun I had in the 1970s came as an offshoot of the movie world. I loved to play at a hideaway on the west coast of Mexico. I was a guest of Bert Schneider, the producer of smash countercultural movies, including *Easy Rider*, and the man who helped bring the faux-Beatles band the Monkees to television in 1966. We were there with Bert's sidekick, Benny Shapiro, who grew marijuana there; Benny's wife, the stunt double for Jane, Tarzan's mate in the movies; and their beloved parrot, Fuck-Face.

Bert and Benny came down to Mexico City to see me sometime in the early seventies. Bert wanted to bring *Hair*, the hit antiwar musical, to the Mexican stage. They thought I had a lot of influence with the Minister of the Interior, and they hoped I could help them grease the skids. I couldn't. But the three of us became friends. They invited me to come to their haven whenever I wanted.

It was hard to get to. I first had to fly to Puerto Vallarta, where I had spent a night drinking with Richard Burton a decade before. Then I took a boat ride down the coast to Bert's and Benny's place. You could get there only by water.

There was no pier, so a canoe came out to pick you up and leave you on the beach. I found their beach houses nestled in a little fishing village. They had thatched roofs, open-air windows, and a gorgeous view of the Pacific. There were no cars, no streets, no phones, and no *federales*. Benny had paid them off to keep them away from his pot farm.

Bert and Benny had built this remote refuge because they thought they might need to run there after Richard Nixon was elected. I learned later that they had actually used it as a lair, the place where they hid Huey Newton, the political activist and cofounder of the Black Panthers, when he was wanted for murder. Bert and Benny helped Newton elude the FBI and escape to Cuba.

It was also a perfect place to do whatever you wanted. Benny had been well connected in the LA jazz world and had managed Miles Davis, but he was content now with just growing his patch of weed, happy to let the rest of the world go by.

As we lolled about together, I also got to know Bert some. Movies were his family business. His father was president of Columbia Pictures, a mogul of Old Hollywood. Bert personified the power and up-yours panache of New Hollywood. He was a tall, good-looking guy who had been thrown out of Cornell University for too much gambling, too many girls, and too few decent grades. Introduced to each other by Jack Nicholson, Bert and Candy Bergen carried on a torrid affair through the late sixties and early seventies until, famously and finally getting tired of his drawing the attention of every young lady in every room they entered, she left—a breakup that pained him for years. When I met him, he was obsessed with sex, dope, and far-left politics.

I laid back and took it all in. I swam in the Pacific and went scuba diving for my first and only time. Benny's wife loved to cook, so we ate well. Everybody was always high or drinking. I was never one for dope, but I loved to drink.

As I fed my appetite for fun in the early seventies, I always had a hell of a good time. I ran with some friends whose taste for hard-core wild-and-crazy went over the line. They risked self-destruction. For all my shenanigans in Mexico—and in Gstaad, where my life also inter-sected repeatedly with the film world—I faithfully adhered to Rule One from my early mining days: Don't die.

THIRTY

My Gstaad

Hans Popper discovered Gstaad, Switzerland, in 1964, when he traveled there looking to buy vacation property in the region and ran into his old friend Yehudi Menuhin, an American expat considered to be one of the great violinists of his day, who had made Gstaad his home. Menuhin convinced Popper to make the quiet but exclusive community his home, too.

The village fit Hans well. Its refined aesthetic soothed him and fed his contemplative temperament. The beauty of his beloved Alps, which he had climbed and skied as a young man, made him feel at home despite the awful memory of his heart attack on the nearby Jungfrau in his middle age. Hans especially loved the summers, when Menuhin led an annual music festival renowned among elite concertgoers, which continues today. The chalet he built for Gretl remained as a monument of his classic understated taste.

In the years after Hans's death, Gstaad began to attract a wider variety of characters than the quiet set he preferred. He would have enjoyed the company of the few who shared his sensibilities. He would have ignored some who would've seemed too frivolous

He certainly would have been delighted with John Kenneth Galbraith and Bill Buckley, who came to Gstaad for the same reasons Hans had: its charm, its serenity, and its skiing. He would have loved exchanging ideas with these two world-class intellectuals: Galbraith, the distinguished liberal economist from Harvard; and Buckley, the quintessential Yale man and conservative publisher of the *National Review*. Hans would have loved hearing Buckley play a Bach harpsichord concerto and Galbraith tell stories from five decades' worth of service to American presidents, from Roosevelt to Truman to Kennedy to Johnson. He would have admired their intelligence and charm, their prolific writing, and their friendship, loyalty, and respect for each other, which remained strong despite years of combat over diametrically opposed ideas in the theater of public debate. Many didn't know that during the final two months of Ken Galbraith's long life, Bill Buckley traveled from New York to Cambridge, Massachusetts, once a week, every single week, just to speak with him.

I think Hans would have been especially proud of the friendships I had with each of them, and the many nights we talked about the state of the world.

I met Ken while skiing. I was standing at the bottom of a run one day when I saw this towering, thin man coming down the run, barreling toward me in all his six-foot, eight-inch glory. I was sure the moment was going to end in disaster, but he miraculously came to an explosive stop without hurting himself.

I introduced myself and offered him a tip about his skiing. He was open to any suggestion. After I had showed him short skis, he bent his knees and was able to make turns.

I first met Bill Buckley and his wife, Pat, over lunch at the Eagle Club. Our relationship developed through our mutual friendship with Ken Galbraith.

One evening over dinner at the Buckley chalet, Bill asked if I'd be interested in hearing him play a piece from his favorite musician. I followed him to his upstairs loft, where I expected to hear something from Beethoven or Bach—only to be surprised and delighted to hear him launch into a full-scale, full-throated rendition of Elvis Presley's "Heartbreak Hotel."

One of the most intense discussions I remember Bill and Ken ever having was over a classic essay published in the *New York Times* in 1970 by the conservative economist Milton Friedman, which argued that the only social responsibility of business was to maximize its profits for shareholders. Bill, baiting Ken, observed that it was unnecessary for Friedman to write such an article, since it was so obviously plain that the only responsibility corporations had was to make money. Ken replied that he was just happy that Friedman had finally found work, and then channeled every single terrific argument from the anticolonial, environmentally sustainable, globally progressive thinking of the New Left, sprinkled with a few dozen references to about a thousand years of enlightened economic thinking. And from there, they were off for the next four hours, giving each other the business while giving me a master class in global economics.

In so many ways, the two of them both embodied the generation they came out of while also being light-years ahead of their time. Today, I hear the exact same arguments being made by the Left and Right about corporations and globalization, but with such intense vitriol and mistrust. I can't help but think back to Bill Buckley and Ken Galbraith—and how much more we could accomplish when ideological opposites could treat each other with civility.

⚜

HANS WOULD HAVE DOUBTLESS had little interest in the movie stars and other celebrities who flocked to Gstaad in the 1970s. He would have disdained the starstruck groupies. I didn't mix much in this social scene either, but I did find a few good guys I liked to pal around with.

I've had the remarkable and peculiar good fortune of getting to know, among the many European friends I've made through the years, three of the men who played James Bond in the movies—Sean Connery, Roger Moore, and Pierce Brosnan. Two of them, Connery and Moore, were regulars in Gstaad.

Roger Moore was the first Bond I met. I liked him for his good humor and lack of pretension. He told me once, at the zenith of his career, "Ah, I'm just a good piece of British beef."

Roger fell in love with Gstaad after shooting a scene in the Alps for *The Spy Who Loved Me*—the tenth Bond film, Moore's third of seven he filmed, and one of his most successful 007 films of all time. Released in 1977, the film sees Bond trot around the globe investigating the hijacking of two submarines—one Russian, one British—carrying nuclear weapons. Early in the movie, the bad guys chase Bond high into the mountains. He jumps on his skis and, in a spectacular display of downhill virtuosity, gets away from them.

After the film came out, Moore returned frequently to Gstaad. One day I saw him on the top of the mountain, and he waved me over as I arrived at the top of a ski lift. He looked just like Bond, handsome and poised to subdue any kind of evil. He was surrounded by a host of fawning admirers who expected him to take off and replicate his dazzling downhill triumph in the movie.

Unfortunately, there was just one problem: Roger Moore didn't know how to ski. He was stuck there, waiting for his ski instructor. He didn't want to disappoint his fans and didn't know what to do.

I suggested he make a comedy out of his predicament. Plain lousy isn't funny, so I suggested he be totally lousy. Exaggerate. Do a couple of snowplows. They'd think he was kidding. They'd start laughing, get bored, and go away. He did, and they did, and we became friends.

When the Eagle Club, an exclusive ski club built on a mountain overlooking the town, asked Roger and me to join their executive committee and support them in some practical ways—he representing the United Kingdom and me representing the US—we were glad to pitch in. We were happy to work with a Belgian baron, a French marquis, an Italian count, Russian prince Nicholas Romanov (a direct descendant of Czar Nicholas II), and a handful of other friends who had no titles.

Lisa and I often ran into Roger in the South of France. One thing that is not widely known is that he is an extraordinary artist, especially a caricaturist. Over lunch one afternoon, he began to sketch hilarious cartoons on pages of the menu. At the end of the lunch, he gave the drawings to Lisa and me.

A drawing from an impromptu sketching session at the Restaurant de Bacon with Gstaad's James Bond, Roger Moore.

Of course, Roger isn't the only charmer in the Moore family. His son, Geoffrey—an actor, producer, and restauranteur in his own right—is every bit his father's son.

For men of my generation, Sean Connery and Steve McQueen defined what it meant to be a manly man in the 1960s. To me, with all due respect to my other friends, the young Connery—who was extraordinarily handsome and had that great, deep Scottish accent—defines James Bond. Given his iconic stature, you'd almost forgive him for being one-dimensional, but he's anything but. What's most striking when you spend time with Connery is that he has an insatiable curiosity about the world and will talk about everything under the sun—*except* movies, unless you can deftly steer the conversation in that direction.

He follows politics closely and was a leading supporter in recent years of something I've grown deeply opposed to: Scotland's separation from the rest of the United Kingdom.

In fact, there was a period of time when Connery talked so much about it that I couldn't take it anymore and maneuvered the conversation to some of his favorite movie roles—which is a treat, because when he starts talking about the roles he has played, he goes into that character, and becomes that character right in front of your eyes. All of a sudden, you'll have sitting before you the Russian submarine captain from *The Hunt for Red October*, or the old-school Irish cop from *The Untouchables*, or the agent with a license to kill who sings "Underneath the Mango Tree" to get the attention of otherworldly beauty Ursula Andress as she exits the sea in one of history's most famous bikinis, in *Dr. No*. Maybe it's something all actors do, but with Connery, watching it is like having an out-of-body experience.

It's something Pierce Brosnan—whom my wife likes to call "Piercey"—does all the time too. Lisa and I first met him one afternoon when we were at lunch with an acting school classmate of his and a close friend of ours, Lizzie Spender. Lizzie is the wife of Barry Humphries, aka Dame Edna, and the daughter of the great English poet Stephen Spender. She saw Brosnan across the restaurant and waved him over to our table, where we shook hands. The second time we ran into him was in Thailand, at our favorite resort in Phuket. We saw Brosnan on the beach, spent time together, and became friends. He couldn't possibly be nicer or more charming, and like Connery, when he tells stories, he fully goes into character and *becomes* the person he's talking about—although half the time, I don't think he realizes he's doing it. It just happens naturally, which is part of the charm.

The question I get about the Bond actors most often, naturally, is "What do they drink?" Those expecting "a martini, shaken, not stirred" are always disappointed.

Connery gave up whiskey due to a heart condition and likes red wine now, especially merlots from Chile and others he finds during weeklong trips he takes each year to the vineyards in France.

Brosnan and his wife also love wine, leavened with the occasional Irish beer.

And Moore, sadly, has announced to the world that, now in his eighties, he can no longer drink. Type 2 diabetes has forced him to leave martinis and scotch behind. His greatest vice today is Diet Coke, which he sometimes mixes with nonalcoholic beer in a concoction he calls a "Band-Aid"—which, in a cruel twist, can only be stirred, not shaken.

Gstaad was that kind of place. Once, when my friend Herb Caen was visiting from San Francisco, I introduced him to Odile Rubirosa, a gorgeous French actress and model who had been the fifth wife, now widow, of the legendary polo-playing playboy and Dominican diplomat, Porfirio Rubirosa. Internationally known for his sexual prowess, the Dominican was so renowned for a certain part of his anatomy that waiters in Paris named their oversize pepper mills "Rubirosas." Herb immediately began to call her "Big Deal" Rubirosa. At one point, she leaned into him and said, "I was going to fly to Acapulco this morning, but I overslept." He later wrote an article that used that quote to perfectly sum up the people who frequented the Eagle Club.

Before Roger Moore and I joined the executive committee, the US was represented by Budge Patty. A dashing veteran of the US Fifth Army who had participated in the liberation of Paris, Budge moved back to Paris after the war and took up professional tennis. From 1947 through 1958, he won twenty international tournaments in Europe, most memorably in 1950, when he won both the French Open and Wimbledon. He and I became friends in Gstaad, and he asked me to take his place as the US representative when he'd had enough. To my great surprise, about fifteen years ago, and every year since, Budge has given me one of the greatest gifts anybody has ever given me: a top seat to the men's semifinal match at Wimbledon. As a former champion, he receives tickets for every match—but he chooses instead to sit in the Royal Box.

We also got to know Roman Polanski, who is not only a terrific skier and storyteller but is considered one of the truly great global film directors. Polanski survived the Holocaust before conquering Hollywood.

In 1969, he retreated to Gstaad after his wife, Sharon Tate, was brutally murdered by the Manson Family. In 1977, he pleaded guilty to statutory rape in the United States and served a forty-two-day prison sentence before the prosecutor agreed to a plea bargain. When he heard that the judge was going to reject the deal, he escaped to Europe, where he's battled extradition ever since, supported by one European judge after another, who refuse to turn him over. Even though he's angry—he rightly feels like he proclaimed his guilt, apologized, went to jail, and served his time—he is still one of the greatest artists of his time. Not long ago, he screened a picture of his life for a small group of us, and it was just stunning. His next film, *An Officer and a Spy*, will no doubt be an international blockbuster and win many awards.

Two other good friends are Victor Dial, a handsome American expat who hailed from a distinguished North Carolina family, and his companion, the lovely Federica Sessa. Victor's grandfather had served in the US Senate after World War I, and his own father had met a tragic end during World War II. After surviving the infamous Bataan Death March in 1942, when Japanese soldiers in the Philippines forced captured US and Filipino troops to march more than sixty-five treacherous miles to a brutal prison camp, Victor's father was killed by a US airstrike on a Japanese boat carrying some of those same POWs to the Japanese mainland. Victor would run Ford France for more than fifteen years before becoming the marketing and sales guru for Peugeot and helping the car manufacturer move into Eastern Europe after the fall of the Berlin Wall.

ONE OF MY DEAREST friends in Gstaad in the late sixties and seventies was a prominent art dealer based in London named Tommy Grange.

We had met the Granges on a ski holiday a decade before in Zurs. Tommy had gone to all the right schools and fought with valor during World War II as a member of the elite Black Watch Regiment, the infantry battalion of the Royal Regiment of Scotland.

I really liked being with Tommy. There was very little we didn't talk about, except his war. He never spoke about what he had done, let alone brag about it. We liked to discuss classic works of history, and two documentary series in particular: Kenneth Clark's survey of Western culture since the dark ages, *Civilisation*; and Jacob Bronowski's history of the development of the human race, *The Ascent of Man*. I knew very little about such matters, but Tommy knew a lot. He was erudite. He spoke with the voice of Richard Burton, so everything he said seemed true.

I had helped Tommy out of a couple of other jams over the years. One time, I had helped him solve the case of a stolen masterpiece. He had lent an important painting to a countess, the widow of an earl from one of Britain's most prestigious families. She hung it in her chalet in Gstaad and refused to pay for it or return it. He didn't know what to do.

I told him we should just go get it. We marched to her house in the middle of the day, because I didn't want to risk getting shot while breaking in at night. I climbed up to the second floor, wiggled in the window, and took Tommy's painting off the lady's wall. Then I hopped back down and handed it to him. Justice had been served.

Tommy and I had a lot of great times together. He's one of the people I've known in my life whom I've always wished I could have spent a lot more time with—or at least had more years with. He struggled with a lot of demons in his life. In January of 1978 Tommy's wife cabled me to say that he had died. Later, after I learned that he had been dying for some time, I asked her why she hadn't let me know. She never gave me a proper answer.

⁂

THE WILDEST FRIEND I made in Gstaad was born Panagiotis Theodoracopulos, or Taki, who is widely known in Europe today as a far-right conservative writer liberals love to hate. Taki is always provocative and occasionally goes too far. The son of a very wealthy shipowner from Greece, who remembers Nazi officers occupying his house as a boy, Taki was precocious and combative from the start. When he was twelve, he got kicked out of an American prep school for beating up an older schoolmate who had tormented him. He began to play in the international jet set at an early age, backed by the shipping fortune of his father. He played tennis in the Olympics. He won karate tournaments. He's always loved fast cars, sleek yachts, and chasing beautiful women.

On Taki's first night as a member of the Eagle Club, he ambushed the Aga Khan—the imam of a sect of Shia Islam known as Nizari Ismailism—and a British diplomat in the clubhouse at midnight by throwing cream cakes in their faces. His attack triggered a brawl. Although the ambassador knew some judo, Taki easily took him down. The Earl of Warwick was not amused.

When Bill Buckley met Taki, he liked his conservative politics and gave him his first shot at writing by sending him to Vietnam to report for the *National Review*.

For years now, Taki has written "High Life," a weekly column for the British conservative magazine *Spectator*. He fills it mostly with gossip and irreverent commentary, which he writes with color and snap. He has a knack for simultaneously lampooning the vacuous international social scene of which he is a part and puffing up his friends with lines like "My friend Stanley Weiss had a chalet full of people who'd rather read than bullshit." Often he also has the courage to take on things that others won't. When he addresses serious subjects, he does so with a whip-smart intelligence that digs deeply into history and is always a pleasure to read.

Taki takes special satisfaction in calling out the foibles of the Left and political correctness. His columns are meant to be fun and provocative, but his pen has also been sharp enough to hurt. Especially in the early days, he often poisoned his prose with racial, homophobic, and repulsive slurs, which he doesn't do quite as much anymore. About half of the time, you don't know if he's being serious or not. When his friends denounce him, he welcomes their fury, perhaps because he knows they turn to his column first anyway. I know I do.

Taki's mouth has gotten him into worse trouble than his writings. One day he waltzed unchallenged through Heathrow's customs carrying a hidden bag of cocaine. When the passport officer helpfully told him that an envelope was about to drop from his pocket, Taki replied: "If you only knew what was in it." He was thrown into London's worst jail for three months. While there, he wrote a candid, self-aware memoir of his experience, called *Nothing to Declare*, but the fact remains, he is now a convicted criminal.

Once again the Eagle Club was not amused. One grandee tried to get Taki thrown out. Ken Galbraith, who had always disdained the club and didn't even like Taki, wrote the grandees a letter saying that "since half of the membership of the club belongs behind bars, it is unfair to pick on Taki."

I like Taki because he's a helluva lot of fun. Even people who say a lot of bad things about him are the first ones to invite him to the party, because it's impossible to have a dull time with Taki around. He's also a good and fiercely loyal friend.

Through the years, Taki has introduced me to some of his close journalist friends in Gstaad, who then became friends of mine—none better than Arnaud de Borchgrave. Arnaud was the son of a Belgian count and a legendary foreign correspondent for *Newsweek*, who had been injured as a member of the British Navy on the beaches of Normandy during the D-Day invasion in 1944. He went on to fearlessly cover at least eighteen wars in his career. When Taki introduced us, I already knew Arnaud by reputation. Small in stature but immensely brave, he had been wounded in Vietnam and had once lobbed a grenade at a North Vietnamese soldier. People still talked about his courage there. During the years that my politics were shifting from right to left, Arnaud's moved from left to right—which angered his boss at *Newsweek*, Katharine Graham, so much that she fired him. He went on to turn the *Washington Times* into a voice for conservatism in Washington and a darling of Bill Buckley Republicans. Despite our political differences, Arnaud became one of my closest friends.

I also remember a time when Taki invited Margaret Thatcher to Gstaad to speak. It was years after she had stepped down as prime minister. I had met her several times before, but what I remember most about this event is that she wanted to dominate everything. She treated me and everybody near her as if we were children. If you tried to interrupt her, she would shush you and keep talking. At one point, I told her what a terrific prime minster she was but then added, "But you were lucky."

She heard that, and she asked me what I meant.

I said, "Well, you're lucky that you had that war, and more lucky that you won it." Great Britain and Argentina had battled after the junta in Buenos Aires invaded the Falkland Islands, a UK colony, in 1982. I knew that if it hadn't been for the Americans, the UK wouldn't have won.

Needless to say, Thatcher didn't like that comment very much. When it all came out, I think Taki believed I had pulled a "Taki" on him.

When Taki and I first became friends forty years ago, I learned right away that he likes to play the fascist, long before Donald Trump did the same for entertainment value in America. Taki talked on and on in the late sixties about how much he loved the right-wing colonels who had taken over Greece in a coup and then suspended civil rights and tortured thousands of their enemies.

By mid-1974 the colonels were flaming out, so I goaded Taki by counting the ways they had hurt Greece. He didn't like it when I reminded him that they had run the country's economy into the ground and that they were caught flat-footed when the Turks invaded Cyprus. He called me a communist, and continued to do so until the Berlin Wall came down in 1991 and communism collapsed in and around the Soviet Union. Taki screamed, "So where are you going to go now? To Havana?"

I said, "No, I'm going off to Phnom Penh."

He proudly stuck that line into the *Spectator*.

THIRTY-ONE

Gaining Traction

In the mid-1970s, after years of seeking a sense of greater purpose, I finally got down to business. I wrote a book. It took me almost two years and was one of the hardest things I ever did. Writing it changed me, changed my idea of myself, and opened up a host of exciting new possibilities for the rest of my life.

I had wanted to write for years. I knew I would never be able to command a room with the off-the-cuff spoken eloquence of a Guy Burgess, a Bill O'Dwyer, or even a Walter Weiss. I was too afraid of getting tongue-tied and embarrassing myself. I had more confidence in my promise as a writer. I felt I already had some ability, and I believed my tenacity and my capacity for work would help me develop my skills and overcome my self-consciousness.

The final spark was ignited in London by Trevor Tarring, the editor of *Metal Bulletin*, an international publisher of information on the steel-related markets. Trevor was one of those Englishmen who ride a bicycle to work. I liked that. We met for lunch from time to time to talk trade and enjoy each other's company. At one such meal in early 1975, Trevor suggested I write a book on manganese. He told me there was no serious work on its nonmetallurgical uses. He said if I would write such a book, he would publish it.

We sat there and traded ideas for the next couple of hours. He told me later if we had taped our conversation, we would have already had a draft of the book's beginning.

By then I had been in the business for almost twenty-five years. I welcomed the opportunity to write about something I knew, and I plunged in. I wrote to every country's Ministry of Mines, shared my background, explained what I was doing, posed a set of questions, and asked for their help. To my surprise, almost every one of them answered, including competitors and strangers. I had almost two hundred individuals to thank in my book's acknowledgments.

Only India did not respond. When the book was published, the dust jacket said, "Stanley Weiss went to Mexico armed only with a paperback, *How to Look for Minerals and Metals*." I finally heard back from the Indian Minister of Mines, who made no reference to my book, but rather asked how he could find a copy of *How to Look for Minerals and Metals*.

I also wrote to everyone I knew, or knew about, in the manganese business. After a year of hunting and gathering, I faced a mountain of replies. I struggled to make sense out of the jumble of letters, charts, and graphs, all of which had come in different formats and categories of data. In the end, though, I did what I set out to do. *Manganese: The Other Uses* was published in 1977.

I'm proud of this book. Writing it was an enormous breakthrough for me. I had felt insecure intellectually for as long as I could remember. Now I had proven to myself that I had the discipline and the intelligence to do something important and difficult, and do it well.

I dedicated my book to the memory of Hans Popper. I would have loved to hand him a copy and tell him how I felt. Instead, I wrote Erich Fromm, his closest surrogate, and confided, "I don't think I'll ever quite be the same."

⚬⚬⚬

KEN GALBRAITH SEEMED SERIOUS when he told me I should get a doctorate, so I swallowed my amazement. I had recently sent him a copy of my book, fresh off the press. I was surprised and pleased when one of the most widely published thinkers of the past half-century told me, a rookie writer, he liked the way I wrote. Ken had also made it clear over our many chats in Gstaad that he regarded me as smarter and wiser than I had ever thought.

"People like doctors," he said. "Look at Marty Peretz." Marty, a decade after his association with *Ramparts*, had become the publisher of *New Republic*. "He has more influence now simply because he's called Dr. Peretz. You should have a PhD from Harvard like him."

I loved the idea. I said nothing about my not having finished at Georgetown. I asked, "So how would I go about doing this?"

"Oh, that's easy," Ken replied. "I'll go with you to see the dean."

Ken and I flew to Boston a week or two later. When Galbraith had served as the US ambassador to India during the Kennedy administration, a job he did extraordinarily well, he'd ignored the State Department's maze of protocols and dealt personally with President Kennedy. Now my formidable friend put that power to work again, leading me directly to the desk of the dean of admissions at Harvard's graduate school in Cambridge.

He towered over the dean and bluntly pronounced, "I want Stanley Weiss to go into your doctoral program. He's smart. He doesn't need any of the usual prerequisites."

The dean, clearly anxious to accommodate Harvard's superstar, nodded approvingly.

"But you don't understand," I blurted. "I never finished college."

Galbraith hesitated, but only for a moment. "It doesn't matter," he said. "After all, Stanley already knows all those things. Sign him up."

The dean nodded again.

I told them how honored and flattered I felt. Then I asked, "So how long will it take me to get my doctorate?"

"Well, you couldn't do it in less than two years," the dean said.

"But I don't have two years," I said. "Lisa would kill me!" For twenty-five years I had regretted not finishing my undergraduate degree at Georgetown, but now my wife came first.

Galbraith turned to the dean, threw up his hands, and asked, "So what should Stanley do?"

The dean still wanted to please the star professor, so he reached into

Harvard's rich grab bag and pulled out an ingenious suggestion that satisfied both Galbraith and me. "Why don't you become a fellow at the Center for International Affairs?" he said. "Each year they take one international businessman and twenty diplomats as fellows. It's quite prestigious."

"So what would I do there?" I asked.

"You could lecture," he said.

I shuddered.

"Or not, if you don't want to."

I relaxed.

"You really don't have to do anything," he explained.

Now I was excited.

With Galbraith's backing, a recommendation from Erich Fromm, and another nod from the dean, the center quickly invited me to be a fellow for the 1977–78 school year.

Faced with the news that I would be living in Cambridge for the year, Lisa was beside herself with indignation. She had already been unhappy with my many absences in recent years. I invited her to join me at Harvard, which she did, briefly. While Lori Christina was in her final year of boarding school, Lisa wasn't going to leave Anthony and our friends in London to live in some chilly academic village where seminars and lectures passed for good times.

But Lisa also knew how stubborn I could be when I really wanted something. She asked how long I would be gone, and I told her I would be back in six months. I didn't tell her I had already rented a house in Galbraith's neighborhood for the entire school year.

⁂

WHEN I FIRST WALKED across Harvard Yard that September, through which everyone from John Adams to Cole Porter to Susan Sontag had passed as students, everything seemed full of possibilities for me. Everyone seemed welcoming. I felt good. I felt at home. I liked being there. I liked the idea of my being there.

At the same time, I was probably the only fellow on campus who had brought his own personal secretary. Her name was Kathy Ratzburg, and she also transcribed papers for Bill Buckley and Ken Galbraith.

The head of our fellows program at the Center for International Affairs hosted our first gathering at the Faculty Club. I mingled easily among the other fellows, a likable set of diplomats from all over the world. Then I took a seat in a leather chair and began my year of learning by listening to a mind-bending lecture on Japan. The talk entranced me, but then again, *any* discussion in front of the club's great fireplace would have seemed profound to me.

I liked the way the director ran the fellows program. It was a tight ship. No bullshit. No pretensions. I found some of my fellow fellows quite bright, others not so much, and all of them articulate. They were diplomats, after all. They knew how to talk to large groups about almost anything with an ease and confidence I lacked. But they mostly liked to discuss the international conferences and negotiations at the heart of their profession. Not my cup of tea.

I looked around for another way to contribute to the program. I learned that the center took the fellows to Canada every year. I asked the director why they never went to Mexico, our other neighbor. He said they couldn't afford it, so I offered to help. I called my old friend Edmundo Flores, now serving in President López Portillo's cabinet. He arranged for all of us to fly to Mexico City, visit the president, and meet with his cabinet colleagues. I left the fellows in Flores's hands when he showed them the country's ancient ruins, which I had seen long ago. The fellows loved me for their Mexican trip.

The dean of admissions had been right: My fellowship did have a certain prestige at Harvard. Some students at the law school looked me up and asked me to give them an informal seminar. They wanted to hear what I had learned in business. They wanted to discuss how they might succeed professionally and what I thought they might do. Although I didn't have the self-assurance to speak to a crowd, I was at ease sitting around a table with a small bunch and exchanging ideas about their future and their life.

My fellowship also gave me the run of the campus and its many offerings, and I found other classes with gifted professors. But most of my learning that year happened outside of classrooms. Almost everyone I approached welcomed my interest in their work. I picked brains wherever I found them—in a chance meeting at a reception or at the suggestion of one intellectual who would lead me to another. I became skilled at such headhunting, and I pursued it with a prospector's unrelenting drive. It was amazing what I learned at Harvard for the price of lunch.

A swarm of research centers at Harvard and MIT welcomed me as well. Instead of classes, they offered informal seminars and talks from practitioners and scholars. Most of these programs had been created by academic entrepreneurs and were underwritten by patrons who wanted their names on the door. They invited me to receptions, open houses, and dinners, a mix of academic marketing and genuine hospitality.

Among the swirl of topics I sampled, one issue grabbed me most: the dangers of nuclear power. Thirty years earlier, I was convinced that my life had been saved by an atomic bomb. From my El Paso plant, I still sold the manganese dioxide used to create the first step in the production of nuclear weapons. But now, with the Cold War reaching its peak, and the nuclear arms race between the United States and the Soviet Union heating up, I became concerned about the nuclear threat. I worried about nuclear terrorists, the spread of nuclear weapons, accidents at nuclear power plants, and the possibility of a nuclear war between the two superpowers.

I sought out anyone who was working on these problems. I faithfully attended a weekly arms control seminar at Harvard's Program on Science and International Affairs. I drove to MIT one Saturday morning to hear its president, Jerry Wiesner, who had served as President Kennedy's special assistant for science and technology, warn about nuclear proliferation. I went to discussions of the politics of nuclear power at one of Harvard's undergraduate houses. I invited every visiting nuclear specialist to lunch so I could quiz him or her personally.

The more I listened to these experts over the year, the more disillusioned I became. I was aghast at the way most of them thought and talked about nukes. They seemed frozen in a bubble of theory and abstraction. They rambled on about the doctrine of mutual assured destruction (MAD), casually observing that the use of warheads by two opposing sides meant the utter annihilation of both. They predicted the number of casualties from nuclear exchanges with surreal precision. I can still hear them arguing on and on about the dire consequences of our having only 24,000 nuclear weapons when the Soviets had over 25,000. Madness!

These scientists and experts were lost in analyses unconnected to real-world human consequences. I didn't know all that much about the technical details, but I had some idea what a couple of atomic bombs had done to two Japanese cities.

I worked hard throughout my year at Harvard to make the most of the opportunity Ken Galbraith had given me. He kept his eye on me. He welcomed me to his family, his fortieth wedding anniversary, and his Vermont farm. He hooked me up with his favorite colleagues to broaden and deepen my inquiries. We dined from time to time and compared notes about what I was learning. I especially valued his reassurance when I told him I thought the nuclear high priests were morons. He chuckled and said he had been trying to expose their nonsense for decades.

I LEFT HARVARD IN the spring of 1978 a changed man. My appointment as the business fellow at Harvard's Center for International Affairs, along with writing my book, went a long way to heal my complex about not having finished college. This hang-up disappeared altogether, as only time and the accomplishments of one's children can, when Lori Christina graduated from Yale and Anthony from Georgetown's School of Foreign Service, whose board I served on a few years later.

I no longer felt intimidated by articulate intellectuals with more prestigious credentials. For an entire school year, I had repeatedly engaged stellar academics up close. They knew much more about their specialty than I ever would, but I learned they often didn't understand much about practical matters. Most of them were smart, just as I'd expected, but I discovered that frequently the ways they thought didn't help much in making real-world decisions.

Most important, I now saw myself differently. I left Cambridge with a clearer and greater appreciation of my own abilities and the value of my business experience. I realized I could do hard, important work most specialists couldn't do or wouldn't dream of doing. I understood I could deal with everyday problems—and that's just what I intended to do.

THIRTY-TWO

Turning Fifty

I turned fifty in December 1977. Lisa threw two birthday parties for me with her usual grace and care. After the first, in London, she invited twenty-five of my best San Francisco friends to my old stomping ground. She persuaded Max, the maître d' at Trader Vic's, to give her a private room for the evening. She worked directly with Victor Bergeron, Trader Vic himself, to select the menu. She decorated a long, thin table for us, sat me next to her at the head, and placed everyone else in a perfectly selected seat.

More than any other birthday, my fiftieth affected how I thought about my life. Half a century is a long time. It seemed to me that I had been young up until that point, and then all of a sudden, I wasn't young anymore. Life just changed. I continued to do big things and would do so for years to come, but I didn't feel wild and crazy anymore. For the first time in my life, I wondered if this is what contentment felt like. I couldn't help remembering a quote from Victor Hugo that I had once seen on a sign in a small shop in Paris: "Forty is the old age of youth, but fifty is the youth of old age."

At our table at Trader Vic's, witty conversation swept over the table quickly and furiously. My El Matador friend, Barnaby Conrad, and columnist Herb Caen played dueling wits over the room's din. Lisa circulated a T-shirt and colored pens so everyone could autograph it for me. It now resides, along with many other sentimental masterpieces, in our London home.

After dinner, each friend celebrated me in his own way. Michael McClure, the beat poet and playwright, recited a poem for me. Gerry Feigen, the ventriloquist and psychiatrist turned proctologist, brought "Becky" over next to me to chat. She tweaked me hilariously with my own words. A raucous quartet, including Harry Hunt and Bernard Petrie, sang "Manganese," a ditty that columnist Art Hoppe had written for me. Walter Landor, the visual branding pioneer, wrote a special poem titled "The Legend of the Manganese Mime."

The Legend of the Manganese Mime

Stanley Weiss—his life and time—
had the time of his life
with Lisa his Wife,
his Princess Lori,
son Anthony his Glory,
and Gretl the Epoxy of it all.

Stanley, a Mime
who can turn on a dime,
who can ski across bumps
and can take his lumps,
a man of the world
wherever unfurled,
as a peon,
a lord,
on a par
with Giscard,
a Harvard student,
and always a friend.

When you ask Stanley for advice,
you do not have to ask him twice.
He always is extremely nice.
For free!
No fee!
Be it me or be it you—

John Kenneth Galbraith, too.
Be it Carlos, Prince of Spain
working toward the throne in vain.
Be it Anthony or Lori
vying for scholastic glory.
Even Lisa has been rumored
to bend an ear—if properly humored!

And for those who cannot see
the Manganese for the trees,
he becomes a tease:
writes a whole book
where all can look
how Manganese is done
for profit and fun
(and a place in the sun),
as if to say:
"Once a mine is mine,
it's time
for the mime
to move from the self to the sublime."

Regarding his interest in politics
(as hard to get rid of as other ticks),
it bleeds his funds and good ideas,
eases his conscience,
and calms his fears.

But be you honest or dummy,
he will always beat you at Gin Rummy.
He beat the Champ in Vallarta's sun
where Liz and Dick and iguanas looked on . . .
The morning after
his watch was gone.
He was robbed so gently, as were we
while sleeping off his victory.

Then there were films—
gold in Alaska,
land in Vallarta,
and other disasters.

By contrast:
Countless mercurial scoops
with Mexican, Russian, and US groups.
He has done all this with the greatest of ease
like a Manganese mime on a swinging trapeze.

So what NOW,
Manganese Mao?

All roads are open.
You've travelled many.
Your scoring, Stanley,
has been uncanny.
Don't ever change your rare technique.
Whatever you do:
Retain the mystique.

About the future—let me quote
an ancient Chinese sage who wrote,
"To prophesy is tough indeed
if it's the future you wish to read."
This Chinese quote from the Manganese book
is just what I need to get off the hook.

So I'll be glad to predict
Old Stanley's past
by rereading this poem . . .
if someone ask'd!
But if no one asks
Here is my GIFT:

The wistfulness of Chaplain,
The mischievousness of Stan and Laurel,
The pathos of Keaton,
The absurd arrogance of Groucho,
The insane zaniness of Harpo,

Rolled all
together
into one BIG laughing heart
from me
to you.

I settled back in my chair beside my wife and basked in the warmth of my friends' love. The truth is, if you wake up in the morning and you're happy, it doesn't make a damn bit of difference how old you are. And I was happy.

THIRTY-THREE

The Citizens Party

I n January 1979, America was in a bad state. The excitement of down-home Georgia governor Jimmy Carter's election as president three years earlier—and the hope that it would move America past the fissures opened by Richard Nixon's Watergate scandal, the end of the wretched Vietnam War, the fall of Saigon in 1975, and the busing crisis of the seventies—had disappeared. Islamic revolutionaries' overthrow of the Shah in Iran had caused an oil crisis, driving gas shortages and spiking prices in the US and ultimately resulting in another round of mile-long gas lines. In the aftermath of this turmoil, creeping unemployment and inflation would both reach double digits.

The coming months would also bring the Soviet invasion of Afghanistan, the American boycott of the Summer Olympics in Moscow, and the 444-day captivity of fifty-two hostages from the American embassy in Tehran by the followers of Iran's new leader, the Ayatollah Ruhollah Khomeini. That summer of 1979, Carter would deliver a speech to the nation in a cardigan sweater about the malaise he saw at the heart of America's national soul, which only made him look weaker and more pathetic. It would pave the way to the White House for the sunny former actor and tough-talking Republican governor of California, Ronald Reagan, who called America "a shining city on a hill," promised to bring the hostages home from Iran, and urged Americans to believe in themselves and their country again.

Before all that happened, though, on one snowy Saturday night in late January 1979, four friends and I decided over dinner to start a new national political party.

We had gathered that weekend at the O'Hare Hilton in Chicago for another purpose: to promote a project on economic democracy to a group of liberal funders. It was the brainchild of Gar Alperovitz and his fellow economist, Jeff Faux. Gar and Jeff had pitched their project to prospective donors. Now they were having a quiet dinner with me and two other backers, David Hunter and Arch Gillies.

David was the most influential progressive philanthropist of his time. A native Chicagoan and son of a Presbyterian minister father and a social worker mother, he had a footprint that went far beyond his position as director of the Stern Fund, a small liberal foundation in New York founded in the 1930s to advance progressive causes such as voting rights and civil rights. He had mentored a generation of other foundation leaders and brought needed attention and funding to a range of social issues, from protecting women abused by their husbands to environmental sustainability. They followed David's lead and thereby multiplied Stern's investments.

Like a gifted venture capitalist, David found hot young talents and gave them enough start-up money to show that their ideas would work. Then he convened a tailored set of funders, brought the promising social entrepreneurs to their table, and got out of the way.

David and I had grown close during the year I was at Harvard. He sensed I was looking for ways to contribute as a citizen by supporting projects that fit my convictions and taste. He shared my concerns about the dangers of nuclear energy and introduced me to his friends in the progressive funder community. With grants from Stern and contributions from his network, David had helped me create and finance the Nuclear Information and Resource Service (NIRS), which I launched as a vehicle to bring like-minded progressives together in a community while driving action around a series of nuclear-related threats that we both exposed and highlighted.

David Hunter was a social democrat like Hans Popper. He believed the government should promote economic justice and redistribute power and wealth, but with classic American pragmatism. He funded nonideological, innovative, results-driven projects. He was about ten years older than me and ten years younger than Hans would've been. Just as Hans had coached me in business, David mentored me about how to use one's money and energies to do public good and contribute as a citizen.

David had also coached Arch Gillies. When Arch became president of the John Hay Whitney Foundation, David showed him how he might broaden its agenda by investing in inner-city neighborhoods. Always the matchmaker, David introduced Arch and me in 1978, and we immediately began to work happily together.

Arch was a political man, and he was very good at it. He had been president of his class at Choate and vice president of his class at Princeton. In the 1960s, he had worked at the center of the very practical politics of four-time New York governor Nelson Rockefeller's presidential campaigns, and he became an advisor when Rockefeller served as vice president of the United States under President Gerald Ford. Archie ran for Congress on Long Island and for City Council at Large in New York City. For years he managed the powerhouse operation run by Jock Whitney—the newspaper publisher, philanthropist, and former US ambassador—to help elect liberal Republican senators.

I admired Arch enormously. He impressed me as a rare and special breed of politician, full of moral courage and driven by deep, passionate convictions.

At dinner that night at the O'Hare Hilton, Arch's idealism was ablaze, and his political shrewdness was in full play. He told us that we were at a historical moment when a new party was both necessary and possible. He said we needed a new party to pursue Gar and Jeff's vision of economic democracy and to deal with the energy crisis that was endangering our economy, threatening our environment, and entangling us abroad.

He told us the Republicans would oppose what we wanted and the Democrats wouldn't grasp it. The liberal wing of the Republicans that had attracted him as a younger man no longer existed. Neither President Carter nor Massachusetts senator and liberal lion Ted Kennedy could rise to the challenge we were facing. He thought Kennedy had irretrievably forfeited his presidential chances in 1969, when he drove his car off a bridge on the small island of Chappaquiddick off the coast of Massachusetts, leaving the scene of the accident while a young campaign aide named Mary Jo Kopechne drowned inside—a tragedy that had taken Kennedy nine hours to report. We all despaired about Jimmy Carter, who was defining new lows of presidential ineptitude.

Carter's collapse, Kennedy's forfeit, and the Republicans' rightward turn, Arch argued, created a political vacuum that would draw independent voters, as well as staunch Democrats and disaffected Republicans, who, like us, were looking for a new leader to follow. The moment was ripe. But committing to help start a new party was, for me, an unnatural act. Even though elections were literally very serious business for my father, I had never taken politics seriously.

Even as a child, I gave no thought to my dad's pinning Republican candidate Alf Landon's sunflower button on my shirt in the last week of the 1936 campaign. When a local Democratic leader later asked me to replace it with a Roosevelt button, I was unmoved—until he offered me a quarter. At dinner that night my father convinced me to switch back by giving me fifty cents. I was a nine-year-old with great political integrity.

In 1940, as a young teenager, I watched the Republicans nominate Wendell Willkie at the party's convention. I sat with my father and Willkie's other supporters who packed the galleries of Philadelphia's Convention Hall and bombarded the delegates below with shouts of "We want Willkie!" When Willkie won on the sixth ballot by one vote, I jumped up and cheered like I was at a baseball game and the Phillies had just won a championship.

Thereafter I remained a political adolescent, even as an adult. I went to Chicago in 1968 for the Democratic Convention more out of curiosity than for any political purpose. My visit to the 1972 Republican Convention in Miami Beach could have been a bit from *Get Smart*, the TV spoof of James Bond movies. I stayed in a posh hotel where my partner, Ralph Feuerring, had offices. Each morning I went to our business meetings dressed in a Savile Row suit. At midday, I changed into blue jeans, slipped into a limousine, and then got out about two blocks away from a park where the activists gathered. Every day I handed them $5,000—about $28,000 in today's money—some mine, some I had raised from friends. I can't remember what these activists were doing with the money. I'm not sure I knew even then, except in the most general sense that they were trying to stop the war by helping the Democratic nominee for president: George McGovern, the US senator from South Dakota.

In 1976 I ran for delegate to the Democratic Convention—sort of. My friend Ronald Dworkin told me that Democrats Abroad, an organization of Democrats living outside the US, could now send voting delegates to the convention. He suggested I join the group so we could run together. Dworkin—a renowned legal scholar the *Guardian* would later call "the most original and powerful philosopher of law in the English-speaking world"—had earned law degrees at both Harvard and Oxford, clerked for the revered federal judge Learned Hand, earned millions on Wall Street, and then taught law at Yale, New York University, and Oxford. He was famous in ways that I was not, earning a following of students and other admirers.

Nobody knew me except a few friends. My campaign consisted of one mailing. Two volunteers—my wife and my mother-in-law—stuffed envelopes and licked stamps in our London townhouse. My dad, who knew how to get out his vote, would not have been surprised that Dworkin was elected and I wasn't. That was okay with me.

Now, after avoiding active politics for decades, I plunged into one of the most difficult undertakings in American politics: creating a new party. After all these years, it's still a mystery to me why I did it.

I did believe we needed to find new energy sources to avoid the dangers of nuclear reactors. And Arch persuaded me that a new party was necessary, because the two old parties were hopeless. So however clueless I may have been about operational politics, I was serious about this commitment.

I can see now that my decision, in spite of my casualness about politics, was a deeply natural act in one way. I liked starting something of consequence, from scratch, that no one else was doing. I had done it before—and would do it again.

I can also see now that my experiment with electoral politics was one more in a string of efforts to find a way to be a good citizen, to contribute to my country. So this time I took politics seriously, much more than with any of my earlier flings.

After dinner that night in Chicago, we all stood up—me, Gar, Jeff, David, and Arch—shook hands, and went off to bed, full of resolve. It didn't occur to me that we had no candidate, no members, no manager, no war chest, and except for Arch, no substantial electoral political experience.

I gave my all to the this endeavor over the next two years, but often found that I had wandered into an absurd situation I could never have imagined. I felt I had discovered some bizarre tribe whose ways astonished me. I had no idea our biggest problems would be ourselves and our most painful wounds would be self-inflicted. I was an innocent full of good intentions on a dubious romantic quest, who had no idea that the challenges of scale, the calendar, and the common law of American politics virtually doomed our efforts from the beginning. I didn't know anything about ballot access, fund-raising laws, or other exotica of operational politics. I didn't know anything about anything.

⁂

WE BEGAN TO ASSEMBLE, more by instinct than by design, the basic building blocks of a party. We needed a candidate for president—someone whose stature would give our new party instant credibility, who shared our convictions, and who could make our case to the American people.

We had only two men in mind: Barry Commoner and Ralph Nader.

Commoner had the public stature we needed in our candidate. He was a household name, widely respected, and very popular. *Time* had splashed him across its cover in 1970, calling him "the uncommon spokesman for the common man." A Harvard PhD in biology and a professor of environmental science at Washington University in St. Louis, he spoke with the authority of a scientist.

Since the 1950s, Commoner had been warning Americans that polluting our environment endangered us. He warned about the toxicity of the pesticide DDT, about the side effects of petrochemicals, and about radioactive fallout from nuclear weapons tests. I had been delighted with his devastating cases against civilian nuclear reactors in his book *The Poverty of Power*. I had studied it when I was at Harvard. I still have my copy with my meticulous underlining, quadruple exclamation points, and cheerleader's marginal notes.

Arch had been a longtime friend and admirer of Commoner. He knew firsthand that Barry, who had stumped the country, giving dozens of speeches a year, could stir a crowd. *Time* had called him "a professor with a class of millions." To us, it was as if Commoner had been rehearsing for the role we had in mind for decades.

Arch flew to St. Louis to enlist him. Barry declined and offered instead to help recruit Ralph Nader. This was no false modesty. He genuinely believed Nader would be our strongest choice.

Ralph was a public interest lawyer who had come to prominence in the mid-1960s with his book *Unsafe at Any Speed*, an exposé on the safety of American cars that led to the first seat belt laws in America. In 1971, he cofounded the advocacy organization Public Citizen, dedicated to exposing government and corporate corruption that threatened US consumers. Over the next decade, a cadre of young idealists came to Washington to help Nader publish more than a dozen books, on issues ranging from abuse at nursing homes to water pollution to airline safety. By the mid-seventies, he was also seen as one of the leaders of the anti-nuclear movement, founding an organization called the Critical Mass Energy Project to coordinate national opposition to nuclear power. He was principled and passionate but also self-centered and arrogant.

A few weeks after Commoner turned us down, Arch, Barry, and I took Ralph to dinner at a Thai restaurant near the White House and tried to persuade him to be our candidate. Even after all these years I can still hear Ralph's voice careening down Pennsylvania Avenue into that spring evening, full of what he thought was self-knowledge and certitude, as he declared, " I will never run for president!" He would, of course, go on to run for president five times over the next thirty years, most disastrously in 2000, when his quixotic campaign took just enough votes away from Democratic vice president Al Gore to hand the presidency to Republican governor George W. Bush of Texas. Ralph and I were friends, but I haven't spoken to him since then. Sometimes I don't even wear a seat belt.

Hearing that Nader had turned us down, Commoner jumped in as a full partner and our natural leader as if he had been with us from the first. Arch had a campaign strategy that would exploit Barry's natural strengths. We had no illusions that we could win the election in 1980. Our goal was to get at least 5 percent of the vote, which would qualify us for several millions of dollars in federal funds for the 1984 election. We would use it to build an enduring party: the Citizens Party.

To do this, Arch proposed an ingenious "inside-out" game plan. He remembered that, in the 1964 New Hampshire primary, many Republicans had been reluctant to vote for either Arizona's archconservative Senator Barry Goldwater or the recently divorced Rockefeller. This had left a political vacuum filled by a write-in campaign for Henry Cabot Lodge Jr., then the US ambassador to South Vietnam. As the Granite State's 1980 Democratic primary approached, Arch believed lots of voters wouldn't want President Carter or challenger Ted Kennedy, which would create a similar vacuum. He thought Commoner could win more Democrats' votes than anyone expected, because he was such a fascinating candidate and because Democrats would be looking for a fresh face.

Arch also remembered that the segregationist former Alabama governor and presidential candidate George Wallace had taken the base he had built inside three Democratic primaries in 1964, turned it into a new third party, and won five states in 1968. Arch believed Commoner could similarly take the supporters he would win inside the Democratic primaries in 1980, lure them out into our new third party, catch the inevitable wave of free media, and win the 5 percent in November we needed to get federal funding in 1984.

To achieve any sort of credibility, our party also needed members. We pursued a kind of "build it and they will come" approach to recruiting. Over the summer and fall of 1979 we gathered a cadre of supporters from three distinct pools. Some were celebrated figures: well-known local officials, such as civil rights leader Julian Bond, and prominent liberal writers, such as Chicagoan Studs Terkel and Gore Vidal, the archenemy of my pal Bill Buckley. Others were leaders of public interest groups and community organizations, such as the National Welfare Rights Organization and the Gray Panthers. These were David Hunter's natural "family." We also attracted ordinary, hitherto nonpolitical citizens.

By late 1979, Arch and I were feeling pretty good. The basic building blocks of the party—a candidate, a strategy, and members—were coming together.

On October 22, Arch and I met with the others on the party's executive committee, including many new members we had never met, at the Summit Hotel in New York. Arch, who was chairing the meeting, asked the committee to endorse his inside-out plan. He pointed out the emergence of the political vacuum he had projected: Ted Kennedy's prospects had imploded in August when, in an interview with CBS reporter Roger Mudd, he couldn't say why he wanted to be president. Meanwhile, Carter saw his approval rating plunge.

Arch's motion got only two votes: his and mine. We were astonished. We hadn't seen it coming. We hadn't realized that most of the activists and leaders of public interest groups we had recruited had a vision of the party's purpose that was fundamentally different from ours. They didn't want to run a candidate for president. They feared that a presidential campaign in any form would drain resources from their individual organizations' work at the local level. They wanted our party to focus on building a national alliance of such activists. Various publications would later call them "Trickle-Uppers."

Arch and I had followed David Hunter's lead and supported many of these groups. After all, I had founded NIRS so citizens could learn about the dangers of nuclear reactors and take direct action locally. We agreed with them that tactics like marches, sit-ins, and protests could produce important results, and we welcomed a national coalition that would multiply their effects. But it had never occurred to us that anyone would want to start a new party and not run a candidate for president.

We were even more astounded to discover that David Hunter had joined the Trickle-Uppers—many of whom he had recruited—and voted against Arch's strategy. Even Barry Commoner voted no. He wasn't ready to run, and Arch's plan would have required him to commit. Moreover, some of the more suspicious Trickle-Uppers had been whispering that there was a hidden conspiracy—that instead of trying to build a new party, the true goal was to provide Barry with a personal platform on which he would run for office. Commoner's "no" vote was, in part, because he didn't want to feed their paranoia.

Our misreading of the committee that afternoon still puzzles me.

Arch and I effectively forfeited the vote on this most critical strategic question. I knew nothing at the time about the special art of building and counting a vote. I have since learned how crucial it is, especially when stakes are high, to meet personally with every eligible voter, to listen deeply, to try to win the support of each based on shared values and purpose, and to know on whom to count. Arch had known how to do this since he was a teenager. In the years that followed, he mourned that he didn't do so this time.

When we lost the vote, Arch resigned on the spot. He and I held a wake over lunch the next day. He had given up his job at the Whitney Foundation out of conviction that the Citizens Party held promise. Now he gave up the party he had helped conceive, out of frustration more than anger or pride. Although we agreed that the party's hope of winning the necessary 5 percent of the vote in 1980 was now doomed, I told Arch that I was staying.

In early 1980, a year after the five of us had exuberantly decided over dinner to start a new party, only Jeff Faux and I remained active. Gar Alperovitz had moved on to other ventures. David Hunter had moved away from politics. Thankfully, Arch continued to coach Commoner and me, but he too moved to the sidelines.

The feud between those who wanted to run a candidate and those who didn't raged throughout 1980. It intensified other bitter disputes that spread and broke out when we gathered in Nashville in late February for a meeting of our steering committee and the delegates of local chapters from across the country. For two and a half days, all hell broke loose. One of the most rancorous issues was diversity. We could not have seemed more unified in our common purpose to make our party as diverse as the country, but in reality, we weren't. We were attracting about as many women as men, but we were almost entirely white.

Intent on fixing this imbalance, the committee passed a series of increasingly formal resolutions, from strict quotas for state delegations to an aggressive affirmative action plan for the party to a broad new committee tasked with scrutinizing racism in the country. It was as if they believed the party could achieve the results we wanted simply by employing ever stronger language in setting ever bolder goals. Quarrels quickly became ugly and personal: opposing any idea, based on the merits of the idea, brought charges of racism.

Some then accused the committee of acting unilaterally, fearing that covert steps were being taken without their consent to run Barry Commoner for president.

All this exploded in a dramatic and painful climax on the final day of the conference, when the ugliness was focused on Bert deLeeuw, who managed our Washington office. Then in his mid-thirties, Bert, whom I didn't much like, was idealistic and honorable. He had chosen the hard life of a community organizer out of a deep moral commitment, and had worked for over a decade to organize the poorest minorities to fight for themselves. He was aligned with those who were most vehement about both the party's diversity and not running a candidate. It didn't matter. The most divisive individuals in the room singled him out and accused him of subverting the will of the organization and ignoring the committee. He was humiliated.

I never got drawn into their fights or attacked by any faction. But I was sad and disappointed. The Citizens Party, which hardly existed yet, was already collapsing into chaos.

I COULD SEE THE party's divisions would never be resolved. As spring wore on, I turned my focus to nominating Commoner as our candidate and setting the campaign in motion.

Those of us eager for a presidential candidate had outmaneuvered those who didn't, by making our case state by state. In April 1980 I joined a few hundred other delegates in the ballroom of a rundown Cleveland hotel that would close for renovations once we left. The plan was that the convention would offer two nominees for president, and our members would choose a candidate. This was fantasy. Inexperienced politician though I was, even I knew Barry Commoner was the only candidate for anyone to consider.

I thought Commoner had grown politically and gotten tougher during the year we had been working together. I sensed he was tired of being kicked around by some of the party's more abusive members. He had begun throwing a few elbows. In Cleveland, his ambition kicked in. He turned his focus away from the Citizens Party's quarrels and began to concentrate on the daunting task of running for president.

A month later, eight hundred cheering supporters came to a rally for Commoner in LA. Studs Terkel warmed up the crowd with his gutsy street rhetoric. Commoner took it from there. He set everyone on fire with a speech that was more Brooklyn than Harvard. Later we also took in a chunk of money at a fund-raiser at Gore Vidal's home. That night Vidal took Terkel, Commoner, Lisa, and me to dinner at Hollywood's premier deal-making restaurant, Musso & Frank, which literary greats from F. Scott Fitzgerald to Dorothy Parker to Charles Bukowski had made their second home.

We needed a political pro to run the campaign, and we found one in Hollywood. I had been tipped that Bill Zimmerman was a gifted political professional who could do the job. We wanted to sign him up that night, but first we had to make sure he was the right guy.

When Bill sat down with us, I was struck by his confidence. Just thirty-nine years old, he had led the occupation of the University of

Chicago administration building by students protesting the draft and the Vietnam War, and then negotiated the end of the seizure with the school's provost. He then left university teaching to found an organization to reequip a North Vietnam hospital that US bombs had destroyed.

He had also airlifted food to Native Americans at Wounded Knee, South Dakota, who had seized the village as a protest against the US government's mistreatment of the Sioux. When the FBI tried to starve the Native Americans into submission by blockading the delivery of food, Bill rented three light planes, recruited pilots and crew, covertly flew to Wounded Knee, and dropped 1,500 pounds of supplies at dawn.

He agreed with our agenda. He had chosen electoral politics as the primary way to promote change and had faced down California's militant Trickle-Uppers. He had started his own political consulting firm and had run a number of impressive local and statewide campaigns.

Vidal and Commoner quizzed Bill about how he would run the campaign. We knew that if we couldn't get Barry's name on the ballot in enough states, we wouldn't have a presidential campaign. Each state had different requirements, and the two major parties had engineered intricate rules to keep third-party candidates from qualifying. It quickly became clear that Bill knew a lot more than any of us did about how to navigate this maze.

At some point, we came to an unspoken consensus. Commoner spoke for us all: "Bill, come to Washington and run our campaign."

"I have a young son here in California," Bill said. "I'm not going to Washington."

I may have been ignorant about political mechanics, but I knew how to close a deal. I called him that night and asked what it would take to get him to Washington. He took a deep breath and said, "A thousand dollars a week, a round-trip ticket back to LA every weekend, and absolute dictatorial authority over the campaign."

"Great," I said. "When can you come?"

Later I learned that Bill had offered conditions that he thought I couldn't accept, but that weren't so crazy I would be offended. He was amazed when I agreed, and he knew he was "stuck."

ON JUNE 8, BILL ZIMMERMAN moved into my Washington apartment on Connecticut Avenue, a short five-minute drive straight to the White House. The next morning, we stopped by the run-down building off Dupont Circle that was housing our office. It looked low-rent, with a maze of secondhand furniture covered with old typewriters and pizza boxes, and a lonely mimeograph standing in one corner.

I knew Bill's first challenge would be to deal with a lot of hostility. Bert deLeeuw, our national director since April, thought he was managing the campaign well, so he and his team understandably resented this Californian hotshot and his new authority. Their animosity eased when they learned how much Bill shared their political convictions.

Over the next few weeks, Bill interviewed each staffer: "What's your job? What results are you producing? How do you monitor whether you're succeeding?" His manner was reassuring and professional. Bill told me the more he probed, the more appalled he was by what he found. There were no agreed-upon goals. No one knew what the hell they were doing. They were elated if they had arranged a house party of ten supporters in a state of four million. The office was hemorrhaging money, paying staff who were not producing results. When we came home each night, he would laugh hysterically at what he had found, and we would go through a bottle of scotch.

The staff cared more about process than about results. If a decision was made by an individual, not a group, it was automatically wrong. If the group was not equally balanced by gender and race, the decision was automatically wrong. Once Bill applied a results-driven standard to their work, the office was in an uproar.

None of this fazed Bill. Without announcing it, he quietly left party headquarters, left Bert in place, and moved the campaign's critical operations to my home. I'm not sure that Bert and his people ever knew the difference.

Bill sent for the crack team he had used in two massive successful signature drives in California. Since I was funding them, and since we were working in my apartment, he could deploy them wherever he thought best to gather enough signatures to get Commoner on state ballots. On Election Day, Commoner appeared on the ballot in thirty states.

Bill also quickly brought in his go-to guy, twenty-nine-year-old Ken Coplon, to raise money. The two men couldn't have been more different. Yet for years, whenever Bill got involved in a cause, he asked Ken to help. Where Bill was methodical and self-possessed, Ken was outrageous and off the wall. Over the weekend of his twenty-first birthday, in a gesture of class guilt, he had given away his entire inheritance of $21,000 (which would be about $120,000 today) to a bunch of left-wing organizations.

As Ken moved in, we focused on a new political tactic called direct mail, which sought to democratize campaign finances by raising many small contributions by mail and thus reducing the influence of the rich few. Ken personally owned lists of hundreds of thousands of prequalified prospects that were so hot, he made us a profit from our first mailing— and he continued to do so with every mailing throughout the campaign.

But we faced two suffocating realities in 1980 that doomed our hopes of Commoner winning 5 percent of the vote: the independent candidacy of John Anderson and the power of the media to frame the race. I understood the first, but the second still makes my head spin.

Less known and less credentialed than Commoner, Anderson entered the early Republican primaries as a congressman from Illinois with little national reputation even after almost twenty years in the House of Representatives. He earned the media's attention, however, as an articulate contrarian who challenged Republican orthodoxy on issues such as arms control and energy dependence. He appealed to those who rejected the likely candidates in both major parties—the same segment of voters Arch had targeted with his inside-out strategy. When Anderson ran in three early primaries, he exploded onto the public scene, just as Arch had predicted an outsider candidate would. The engines of celebrity-making revved up and made him a national figure. He appeared on *Saturday Night Live* and became the darling of the *Doonesbury* comic strip.

When Anderson realized in April 1980 he couldn't win the Republican nomination, the voters he had excited with his feisty run inside the GOP were waiting outside both parties to join him. On April 22, six months almost to the day after the Citizens Party rejected Arch's inside-out strategy, Anderson announced he would run as an independent. By June, Gallup reported that 24 percent of the electorate would vote for Anderson. His ascendancy left little space for Barry Commoner.

Anderson's surge hurt us the most in our fund-raising. His campaign soaked up the big money we had hoped to get. Heavyweights in LA, like TV producer Norman Lear, my old *Pentagon Papers* friend Stanley Sheinbaum, and even our friend Gore Vidal had begun tapping our prospects in Hollywood for Anderson.

Our inability to raise large contributions through the summer and fall had a devastating effect on our campaign. When I'd recruited Bill, I told him he could rely on having at least $250,000 (more than $770,000 today) to buy media late in the campaign—which wasn't much, but I knew that Bill's ingenuity would multiply its effects. I always keep my promises, but now I couldn't, and it was gut-wrenching for me.

That fall Ken and I played a fund-raising game every day in my apartment. We cold-called prospects, knowing they were long shots. Every time we got a no, I took a shot, and he took a sip, of scotch. By four-thirty or so in the afternoon, we would be totaled.

In the stretch run, we confronted the other suffocating reality of presidential campaigns: the power of the media to define who is running. Barry Commoner's candidacy hardly existed, because TV didn't consider him a "story."

Commoner wanted to avoid the traditional campaign's emphasis on images and symbols. He wanted to focus on substantive issues. He wanted to offer the voters intelligent choices about critical policies and to debate them with other candidates. He had been campaigning for months, but it wasn't working, and he was increasingly irritated with his lack of media coverage. In particular, it plagued him that the stubborn practices of the media deprived the voters of a debate on the central issue of the time—renewable energy—because he knew more about it than any of the other three candidates did.

WITH FIVE OR SO weeks to go before Election Day, the Citizens Party had no money to buy advertising and was generating no news, but Bill had a plan. He called Commoner and me to my apartment and pitched us a radio spot he had dreamed up while driving down the Santa Monica Freeway the previous weekend. It begins with some restaurant noise, the tinkle of a glass, and then a man says, "Bullshit!"

"What?" a shocked woman says.

"Carter, Reagan, and Anderson: It's all bullshit," the man says.

The restaurant noise fades away, and Barry Commoner comes on and says, "Too bad people have to use such strong language, but isn't that how you feel too?" Then he goes on to make the case for the Citizens Party.

I loved it. Barry didn't. It violated his whole idea of a campaign run on the issues. It offended his sense of dignity. Arch Gillies told him it was a terrible idea because it wouldn't make a difference and it would demean him.

Commoner finally agreed to make the ad, provided he wouldn't have to say the repellant word himself. Bill got an actor to say it instead.

Our $700 bought one spot on CBS radio to run right before the national news came on 350 stations across the country. Bill waited for the check to clear before he sent the tape. As he had expected, he got a call right away, telling him, "We can't run this. It uses a word CBS doesn't allow on the air."

"Let's not argue," Bill replied. "Ask your general counsel to read Section 315 of the Federal Communications Act and call me back." He knew that in 1934 Democrats had prohibited networks from censoring political ads in an attempt to keep Republican-owned stations from using their muscle in campaigns.

The ad ran on October 14.

"The result was spectacular," Commoner recalled later. "In two days, the Citizens Party received more news stories and broadcast time than it had received in its entire history." Revered CBS News anchor

Walter Cronkite, the *Today* show, and *Good Morning America* all did pieces. Nearly every major newspaper in the country carried stories.

But Commoner's reaction was more bitter than sweet. The stories were, after all, not about issues. They were about the impudence of saying "bullshit" on the air.

To some, using that term was no big deal. In his op-ed in the *Los Angeles Times*, Lawrence Weschler wrote about his own "unscientific random sample of public sensitivity" about the ad's profanity. He called "at random twenty telephone numbers and asked whoever picked up to fill in the blank: 'The presidential election campaign so far has been mainly . . .' Three people hung up; five used words like 'boring,' 'confusing,' and 'exasperating'; and twelve said 'bullshit.'" But to others, including Commoner, it was a cheap stunt. He complained that the *Detroit Free Press* had not carried a word about his plan to revitalize the auto industry, but it had run a front-page story about the commercial. The irony hurt.

Zimmerman hustled to keep the story alive by holding press conferences that featured a rented bull. Of course, these pranks wore thin, like a joke told too many times, and ultimately had little effect. On Election Day, Barry Commoner got 234,294 votes. John Anderson won 5,720,060, almost 7 percent of the total—enough to qualify for federal funds, just as Arch had hoped to do.

Reagan, meanwhile, trounced Carter, carrying forty-four states and ushering in a new era of conservative leadership. Little did we know that 1978—when we were so convinced that things needed to change—would come to be seen as the apex of worker prosperity in America, particularly among working-class voters, who have seen a slow and steady decline in real wages and standards of living ever since, even while executive pay has gone through the roof.

Although the Citizens Party flopped, I profited in several precious ways. For one, I acquired two treasured friends in Bill and Ken. Our friendships grew in a rich mixture of work and play, part Alamo and part *Animal House*. Ken remembered later, "Oh, Stanley's place. Oh my God, that was so much fun!"

I also learned more about who I wasn't and what I didn't want to do. I learned that I never again wanted to work in electoral politics. In truth, the most important result of my two-year ordeal is that it moved me away from being a lefty surrounded and hounded by commissars and closer to becoming a fiscal conservative.

At home in London preparing for travel. Papers, articles, blue plastic folders, paperclips.

Lori Christina and Lisa like to poke fun at my many obsessions.

This photo with my close Mexican friend, Alfredo Terrazas, and my son Anthony in Alaska is one of my very favorites. We didn't invest in the Alaskan gold mine—despite what Anthony told Lisa about the trip!

Harry Hunt's wife Monika and Bernard Petrie, a man of true integrity and one of my closest friends in San Francisco.

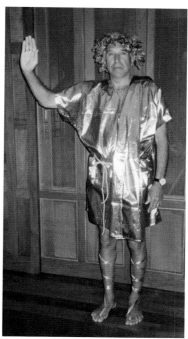

LEFT: While most of the climbers on our Outward Bound trip were in their late twenties, I was in my sixties and my friend John Whitehead was seventy. We climbed for ten days. RIGHT: Showing off my legs as a Roman god at a New Year's Eve costume party at the Amanpuri Hotel in Phuket, Thailand.

Arch Gillies and I founded the Citizens Party in 1979. It was my first and last foray into electoral politics.

The first BENS gala was held in January 1986. We paid tribute to President Eisenhower on the twenty-fifth anniversary of his great farewell address.

When my friend Taki invited Margaret Thatcher to speak at an event in Gstaad, I told her what a terrific prime minster she was but then added, "But you were lucky." She didn't like that very much, and Taki said I had pulled a "Taki" on him.

Former Secretary of Defense Les Aspin joins me at a BENS event.

I am proud that BENS earned the support of leaders like Condoleezza Rice.

I met *Gong Show* host Chuck Barris through Larry Collins, the author of *Is Paris Burning?* I guess I have a knack for attracting spies as friends!

I was honored to have such respected and wonderful people as Lesley Stahl, the night's emcee, and former first lady Jacqueline Onassis at a BENS Eisenhower dinner.

When I wasn't impressing Henry Kissinger with stories about meeting important world leaders in the men's room, I was honored to have him attend a BENS event with Lady Lynn Forester de Rothschild.

My friend and counselor Larry Smith. Larry pushed me and BENS forward in ways I could never have imagined.

I met my close friend Harry Hunt in San Francisco in 1958. Twenty-five years later, he would be one of the first supporters of BENS.

From left to right: Sidney Harman, Brent Scowcroft, Bill Cohen, me, Jane Harman, and General Richard Myers at a BENS event.

Another of our honored BENS supporters is four-star General David Petraeus, the former commander of US Central Command and the commander of US forces in Afghanistan and Iraq.

I traveled to Afghanistan with BENS. It was sort of like when I first joined the Army—I got half of a real uniform.

My grandson Julian shares my taste for adventure and Lisa's love of faraway lands.

Anthony and Lori Christina,
my proudest achievement.

From left to right: Julian, Lori Christina, me, Lisa, and our granddaughter Milena.

My daughter Lori Christina is part owner of the Philadelphia Eagles. Here we are at an Eagles home game.

On our street in London for Thanksgiving with our family. Back row, from left to right: Anthony, his wife Natacha, Lisa, me, Lori Christina's daughter Milena, and Lori Christina. Front: Anthony and Natacha's son Sacha and daughter Tessa.

My partner, my best friend, my wife . . . Lisa. We've treasured over fifty years of marriage together.

For our fortieth wedding
anniversary in 1998
I surprised Lisa with a
party in Venice.

Our fiftieth anniversary
in 2008 was a transatlantic
affair, with celebrations in
Paris and New York.

With my siblings
Janice, Flora, and Buddy
in the 1930s and . . .
a few decades later.

THIRTY-FOUR

Seeing What Wasn't There

I n my last months at Harvard, I discovered an organization that seemed to have great promise: Physicians for Social Responsibility (PSR). Founded in 1961 by a group of scientists dedicated to preventing the spread or use of nuclear weapons, PSR had played a role in the passage of a Limited Nuclear Test Ban Treaty in the early 1960s. I was moved by a powerful film this group of doctors had produced. It showed the medical effects of a nuclear war. We saw doctors quickly running out of supplies and becoming completely overwhelmed as they tried to care for the casualties. The human disaster of a nuclear exchange, which was mostly masked when discussed in the abstract, became inescapably real. The film made it impossible to avoid the scale, consequences, and madness of such a tragedy.

A distinguished radiologist, Dr. Herbert Abrams, then at Harvard, multiplied the film's force. He spoke only about what he knew best, the medical effects of nuclear weapons on human beings. He personified a caring physician's tone and authority that earned trust. It occurred to me that if PSR stuck to speaking as physicians on strictly medical questions, they could have a major influence on how Americans think about nuclear war.

But before long, the PSR veered off to a bunch of other issues unrelated to medicine or even nuclear war. To me, the move seemed unproductive. A lot of us have convictions as individuals about all kinds of matters, such as apartheid in South Africa or who should be president, but physicians don't know more or less about most of these issues than anyone else does. I made a note to myself about the importance of focus and sticking to what worked.

I tried to keep this in mind when, in the spring of 1978, I decided to start an organization from scratch: NIRS, the Nuclear Information and Resource Service. I gave enough money to fund it, recruited a crack executive director, and opened an office near my apartment in Washington.

I didn't have a clear idea about what I wanted NIRS to do. At first it was basically antinukes, especially antireactors and antiproliferation. After a few months, however, I decided we shouldn't be anti- anything. We should instead simply give out reliable information about the nuclear age so that citizens could decide for themselves what they wanted. As naïve as this might seem in retrospect, it worked for a while, particularly during the near-catastrophe at Three Mile Island in March 1979, when a combination of mechanical and human failures—a few stuck valves, a few misread gauges—led to the partial meltdown of the reactor core of a nuclear generating plant in Pennsylvania and the release of dangerous radioactive gas into the air. As health officials worked to determine whether the gases were harmful, NIRS seemed to be the only channel for people to get accurate reports about what was happening.

By early 1981, however, NIRS was going off on tangents at odds with its role as a source of objective information. Like PSR, it shifted sharply to straight-out advocacy. It supported disarmament and opposed specific nuclear weapons in Europe. It turned into one more adversarial voice in the raging quarrel between Left and Right. Its heated and ideological rhetoric undercut its influence. Seeing how easy it was to lose sight of one's goals, I eased out of the organization I had created.

That spring Lisa and I went to a conference at the University of Groningen in the northern Netherlands. For three days a couple hundred European and American academics, activists, retired military officers, strategic experts, clergy, and politicians sliced and diced the problem of how to prevent a nuclear war in Europe. The issue was addressed from almost every professional point of view. Except one.

No one from the vastly successful business communities of Western Europe or the United States had been asked to contribute.

My entrepreneur's eye began to see what wasn't there: a business organization that would work on security issues with businesslike pragmatism.

⚭

FOR YEARS THE BEST in American business had earned the public's trust for their skills that made our economy flourish. Time and again, American entrepreneurs were praised for seeking innovation and producing results. But that classic American pragmatism, the key to our best business executives' success, was missing from our debates about how to secure our nation. I thought that if their influence and talents could be mobilized, they could help make Americans safer in two critical ways: by improving the management of our defense resources and by reducing the threat of nuclear war.

I had witnessed the squandering of defense dollars in the 1960s. Our government kept stores of strategic raw materials in a branch of the Defense Logistics Agency at Fort Belvoir, Virginia, called the National Defense Stockpile (NDS), to use in case of war. The government stocked manganese because steel couldn't be made without it and enough couldn't be mined in America. The General Services Administration (GSA), charged with supplying federal agencies, managed the buying and selling of these stores. The first time we heard they wanted to buy manganese, we bid an enormous price. I was surprised when GSA accepted our offer.

A few months later, GSA had wanted to sell manganese. We offered to buy it at a very cheap price, and again they agreed. They repeatedly bought high and sold low, sometimes for the same manganese. We didn't even need to transport it. We did this for years. At the time, I thought it was great business for my company.

But now, years later, I began to consider the larger implications of my dealings with GSA. I didn't know much about how our nation's security agencies worked, so during my year at Harvard I picked the brains of some people who did. I concluded that, by and large, many of our defense bureaucracies were as screwed up as the managers of the NDS. The US needed an organization of skilled business executives to help persuade the Department of Defense to operate in a more businesslike way.

It took me a while to see that business leaders might also help stop the spread of nuclear weapons and make their use less likely. My concern about these nuclear dangers had only deepened, broadened, and intensified in the three or four years since I first studied them at Harvard. After the Three Mile Island incident, I increasingly worried that nuclear reactors might melt down. I became even more troubled about the possibility that countries might build reactors for peaceful purposes but then use them to make nuclear weapons. I feared the proliferation of such bombs could lead to nuclear terrorism from rogue states and other crazies.

My novelist friend, Larry Collins, whom I got to know during the glamorous ski-and-sun vacations in Austria and Mexico in the mid-1960s, had made such threats seem real in his 1980 thriller, *The Fifth Horseman*. The best-selling novel imagines that Libyan dictator Muammar Gaddafi has secretly used materials from a civilian reactor to build an H-bomb, which Libyan agents then sneak into New York City, threatening to blow it up. Collins's piece of fiction scared the hell out of a lot of us in real life, including the French president, who called off plans to sell a civilian reactor to Gaddafi.

Real-world threats disturbed me even more. A new friend, Ted Taylor, a nuclear physicist at Princeton, had designed very small nuclear bombs at the Los Alamos National Laboratory in New Mexico, where a group of brilliant scientists led by the physicist, Robert Oppenheimer, had designed, developed, and perfected the first atomic bomb as part of the Manhattan Project thirty years before. Ted told me terrorists could now build such miniature nukes using quite small amounts of fissile materials. These bombs would be easier to build, move, hide, and use than big strategic weapons.

What troubled me most was the domination of our nuclear policies by a priesthood of specialists who thought about these issues in the abstract and in theoretical ways unconnected with real-world human consequences. As President Eisenhower had warned in his famous Farewell Address on January 17, 1961, our policies were now "the captive of a scientific-technological elite." Most of these so-called policy experts paid little attention to the "offbeat" threats, and their crazy ideas about the use of nuclear weapons distressed me even more. Their sweeping doctrine of mutual assured destruction, or MAD—the idea that we should bet everything on deterring a Soviet nuclear attack with the threat of an all-out nuclear response—indeed seemed downright mad.

This idea of adding an entrepreneurial voice to the nuclear debate was still cooking in my mind when I made a trip to Cuba a few weeks after the University of Groningen conference. I went mostly for the hell of it, simply because it was hard to get permission to go there. I traveled with David Hunter and a dozen other Americans, including two stellar businessmen: George Pillsbury and Larry Huntington.

George was a director of the Minnesota food company that carried his family's name, a revered American brand. He was an active Republican, a state senator, and a close friend of Vice President George H. W. Bush.

Larry, the CEO of Fiduciary Trust, was using his impressive mix of character and entrepreneurial creativity to grow his investment bank into one of the most trusted in New York. He was tough. A few years later he would climb Mount Everest—twice—up to a thousand feet short of its summit. He was also shrewd. He turned around both times to avoid risking his life in the murderous weather. He had a quiet authority about him. When he spoke, people listened.

Both men habitually acted out of conviction and a sense of public duty. They personified the qualities that would make the business group I had in mind effective. I tested my idea with them. They loved it and said they would join. Now I just had to start it.

ONE EARLY MORNING IN late March 1982, I stood gazing at Central Park from my suite on one of the highest floors of the Sherry-Netherland

Hotel. My suite was mostly one huge living room with high ornate ceilings, lots of lights, and wide windows for walls. Its bedroom was bedecked with mirrors. I had used the suite during my year at Harvard and loved it so much, I'd bought an owner's share.

I hadn't drunk alcohol for two weeks and had been moody and not sleeping well. But that day I'd woken up feeling good and rested. I was happy to be alone with my thoughts.

Standing there, I realized I was at last poised to start the organization I had been dreaming of. I mulled over how to make this new venture succeed. I tried to think of what I had learned from my fits and starts with the groups I had sampled over the years.

I didn't want another talky organization like the Institute for Policy Studies. I wanted one that would push for concrete results.

I didn't want another Citizens Party. I wanted a nonpartisan group of business leaders who would use their influence for real change, for their country, not for the profits of their companies.

I didn't want NIRS or PSR. I wanted a sharply focused set of pragmatists who would speak only about what worked so well for them in business.

I had learned to put a higher value on my natural strengths as a businessman. I knew myself better now. I was more confident. I had stopped trying to find my identity by osmosis. I no longer lusted for a seat at some academic's seminar table. I had found my own "deep base," not like the ones with scholarly credentials my old psychoanalyst Michael Maccoby had in mind, but one I earned myself: one tailored to my identity and natural talents, with its own power and effect, from which I could launch this new venture I envisioned.

I had come a long way to reach this place. My dream now seemed so close, I could hardly fail to grasp it. And that's how BENS was born.

THIRTY-FIVE

Being Dead Is Bad for Business

The organization I started in the summer of 1982 consumed me for the next twenty-five years. I invested the best of my energies, lots of my money, and all of my essential self in its success. I had no idea at the time how profoundly this new venture would change me.

From the first moments, I sensed it would be challenging. I didn't know any more about national security when I began than I had about ores when I wiggled down into my first hole in the ground. And this time, I didn't even have a manual.

I did know something, however, about working on a global scale. I had learned in Mexico how tenacious I could be when I absolutely wanted something done. I knew that the French typically require a master plan with layers of meticulous detail before they begin a project. I knew that I, like the British, preferred to muddle through instead. So I started with only a gut instinct about what I wanted to build. Then I improvised each of the organization's vital parts. I screwed up every step of the way and then adjusted until something worked. Muddling through was in my nature. It had worked well for me for decades.

I had learned from Frank Senkowsky almost thirty years before that my muddling worked best when I had someone to back me up. I needed help, and I knew just the right guy.

Jim Morrison was a clear-headed Texan, still in his thirties, full of conviction and smarts. He had been promoting a fresh policy agenda for independent businesses for over a decade, first at the Senate Small

Business Committee and then with a bipartisan quintet of congressmen who wanted the House to adopt these proposals. Although he had never run a company, he had the instincts and values of American business in his bones.

Jim had asked me to help him a few years earlier. He wanted to write a book to sell his ideas at a White House conference on small business in 1980. I was happy to support him. We spent a lot of hours talking about his views, so I got to see up close how his mind worked. Unlike many PhDs, Jim wrote clearly and unpretentiously, with a mix of authority, passion, and bite. He knew how to mount an argument. He was a good speaker, so he could make a case at the podium as well as on the page.

We partnered naturally and well. We both cared about language. We both despised bullshit and pomp. We liked to pick out strands of thought that intrigued us and play with them. We even collaborated on one chapter in his book, a synthesis of our ideas on business innovation.

I hadn't seen Morrison for a couple of years, but I ran him down in the summer of '82 and this time asked him to help me. Neither of us could fully picture yet the organization I had in mind, but we shared the same instincts about its character and purpose.

We agreed American business leaders had a real but still unrealized political power to influence security issues if we could just find a way to mobilize them. We both knew we needed to speak in a fresh, bipartisan voice tuned to their ears. Otherwise, to a business community suspicious of ideology, our message would be a hard sell. We both wanted to produce results, real improvements in the government's behavior.

Jim didn't have much experience in national security matters, and neither did I. We would both learn on the job. For the next eight years, we would muddle through together, working intimately to build from the ground up what wasn't there before.

✧

ONE AFTERNOON EARLY ON we huddled with a couple of friends in my Washington living room and kicked around ideas about what to call the organization. I finally decided on a name: Business Executives for National Security, or BENS. It clearly said what I wanted to say. I wanted to claim our unique business niche up front, where you couldn't miss it. I wanted executives to join as citizens and individuals, out of their personal convictions, because I thought corporations would be too timid to take positions that might roil their shareholders or customers. I also wanted to signal that we weren't just another pack of naysayers. We supported a strong defense and believed our country's security depended on avoiding nuclear war.

The name was a marketer's nightmare. It had so many words, you had to use the acronym to avoid running out of breath. But since "BENS" had no meaning by itself, you had to go back and unroll the full title. Yet the full title had no rhythm, poetry, or hook.

Over the years some of the country's most gifted advertising professionals offered to fix our name. They almost always suggested that we start over and find a new one. But I knew it didn't matter. The people we most wanted to influence—government officials and potential members—embraced BENS not because of our title but for what we did.

To become real and credible, BENS needed members most of all. For the next few years I tried one approach after another to recruit them. Like most homegrown start-ups, I began by signing up friends, such as Harry Hunt and Bernard Petrie, and family, such as my brother, Buddy. I even swallowed my pride and enlisted ancient foes, such as Kurt Reinsberg, the guy who had cheated me in the mercury business. Since I was a private person, however, I didn't know many business executives, nor did I have access to many people who did. My meager Rolodex didn't produce much of a crowd.

Our first tranche of fresh prospects came from Henry Niles, a retired chairman of a Baltimore insurance company. He had recruited business executives from all over the country to oppose the Vietnam War, and they continued to speak out about the dangers of a nuclear war. Niles was a lovely, gentle man with patrician tastes and Quaker convictions, a combination that landed him on Nixon's Enemies List.

I met with him and his wife at the stately Cosmos Club in Washington.

When we finished lunch, he quietly handed me the roster of executives he had recruited over the previous fifteen years. It was the symbol and substance of his finest work as a citizen, as well as an act of friendship to me and a gesture of faith in our young organization. I accepted it from him as though it were a kind of sacred document.

Niles's list became the starting point that BENS needed. I wrote a personal letter to every one of the two thousand names he gave me. A lot of them had moved or passed away. It was an old list. But I phoned or directly met with all the promising ones and pitched them one-on-one. About two hundred joined BENS, but we needed more.

I quickly learned the art of the fund-raising letter and put my unique twist on it. Just as I had applied myself years before to improving my vocabulary in the face of insults from Louis Marx, I pored over articles and stories to find the right kernel or phrase to touch on the potential donor's greatest passions. I was writing, after all, to some of the most respected business leaders in America. A simple "Please give us money because we need it" wouldn't do. Over time, I became proficient at making our fund-raising letters very, very personal.

One example was a letter I wrote many years later to the visionary founder of the Cable News Network, the first twenty-four-hour news network in America. Ted Turner, a daring and colorful man who had married Jane Fonda, had won the America's Cup sailing race, and was known for a sign he kept on his desk that read *Lead, Follow, or Get Out of the Way*. In my letter to him, I began by congratulating him on the success of his biography, *Call Me Ted*, before adding, "I'm thinking about writing my own biography, *Call Me Bens*." It was a little corny, but it was appreciated: Ted wrote a check and became a great supporting member of BENS.

This personal approach goes back to the lesson I learned many years before, growing up in Philadelphia: whether you are a day laborer or the CEO of a Fortune 500 company, everybody likes to feel appreciated. If there is an art to fund-raising, it's merely acknowledging that taking time to celebrate the person at the other end of the request isn't just important—it's everything.

When we exhausted Niles's list, I next targeted some independent groups of business leaders who had sprung up in several cities to oppose the Vietnam War locally, as Niles's crew had done nationally. Some executives had remained active and now spoke out against the dangers of nuclear war. I also hoped I could revive those whose passion seemed to have faded.

I visited them all, talked with their leaders, and invited them to affiliate with BENS while keeping their autonomy—a kind of federated relationship. I told them that hooking up with BENS would give them national reach to add to their regional clout. On the flip side, it would give BENS clusters of members who would otherwise have taken a long time to enlist one at a time. Here and there we hit pay dirt—as with a group in Boston, led by a mix of Quakers, high-tech tigers, and influential Brahmins, who enthusiastically signed up. They gave us a kick-start with their money, talent, and passion.

I gladly made such improvised deals wherever I could even though I knew I was taking a risk. Most of those we recruited from these groups and from Niles's list agreed with me about the danger of a nuclear war. But few were interested in improving the Pentagon's business practices, and many of them wanted BENS to speak with a stridency that I thought would turn off most business leaders. I had little choice. I had to work with what I had. I would deal with any downside later.

❧

I TRIED ANOTHER TACK in the fall of '82. I bought lists of businesspeople from brokers and tried recruiting through direct mail. We enlisted a handful of members this way. One proved to be a model of the kind of business executive BENS needed: Chuck Van Zoeren, the president of a flourishing trucking company in Kalamazoo, Michigan, and a staunch Republican. He and his wife later moved to Washington and ran the business side of BENS for an entire year—pro bono. Amazing!

Alas, Chuck was a rare find. My excursion into direct mail otherwise quickly turned into a fiasco. The lists were mostly bum.

Our first pitch was also out of tune with the business community. I had asked some veterans of the Citizens Party and other organizations with an ideological bent to help compose our message. I don't know what was in my head. Over Jim Morrison's objections and without my paying attention, they mailed material that sounded more like a street demonstration than a business offer. ("The only survivors of a nuclear war would be the cockroaches.") We got lots of nasty notes back from executives who didn't like to be shouted at.

By Christmas, I gave up on direct mail and began looking for another way to recruit.

In early 1983, I decided to speak directly to groups of prospects and tell them why they should join BENS. How could I expect them to commit to something that I, the founder, couldn't justify to them face-to-face? I owed them that. I also owed it to myself. BENS was a personal commitment for me, so I had to be able to articulate in public why it mattered so much.

The idea of speaking to large groups still terrified me. I was sure I would make a fool of myself, but I knew I had to try.

I scheduled my first speech for February 1, 1983, at an elegant penthouse on Manhattan's Upper East Side, the home of Bobo and Arthur, friends of Harry Hunt. Then, as if I were in some wild poker game, I brazenly raised the stakes. I flaunted my worst fears by inviting a hundred or so premier prospects to hear me.

I panicked and then tried to fight off my terror with several weeks of frantic preparation. I drafted a thirteen-page text. I compulsively rewrote it, again and again. Jim pleaded with me to shorten it. I refused.

I practiced my speech by myself so many times, it echoed in my ears. I presented it to Jim so many times, he got sick of listening to it. After hearing its first line over and over, he nicknamed it the "Thank you, Bobo!" speech. I rehearsed it in front of small groups of quietly suffering friends in Washington, but I never got any better.

The first day of February arrived all too soon. I entered Bobo's sumptuous home that night thoroughly intimidated by what lay ahead. She ushered me into her formal drawing room where a crowd of luminaries stood, waiting to hear me make my first public case for BENS. I shook with stage fright. I tried to it hide it, but the podium was too small.

Everything I said after "Thank you, Bobo!" turned into mumbo jumbo. I couldn't even read my prepared speech. I stumbled over every line. I tried to move away from the text a little bit and wing it, but I just sputtered. Jim had been right. The talk was too long, especially since everyone was standing. I blew it. I totally blew it.

Altogether, it was one of the most embarrassing experiences of my life. We didn't sign up one new member that night.

The next morning over breakfast, Francis Lear—the wife of my good friend, Norman Lear, the creator of *All in the Family*—gave me her unvarnished review of my opening night on Fifth Avenue: "You know, Stanley, you're smart, charming, and good-looking. I like you, and I like what you are trying to do with BENS, but *don't give any more speeches!*"

I was so depressed, I felt like taking her advice and slinking away. I was amazed to read in the *New York Times* the following morning: "A group of businessmen gathered in a Fifth Avenue apartment Tuesday night to support a new organization pledged to lobby for cost-effective management of military spending and for reducing the risk of nuclear war." The article went on to describe BENS exactly as I envisioned it. The piece made no mention of my miserable performance at Bobo's— which wasn't news, of course, except in my tangled psyche.

The *Times* story caught NBC's eye. At seven o'clock the next morning, I found myself on the *Today* show, chatting affably with cohost Jane Pauley. She liked my one-liner about the threat of nuclear war: "Being dead is bad for business." This is, of course, a twist of my Rule One: Don't die. When she asked why I was forming BENS, I eased into the conversation like her old friend and hit a cluster of key points, right in the camera's face.

I was still a rookie about how to promote BENS, but even I could tell that a piece in the *Times* and a pitch on *Today* paid off more than any speech I could have made at Arthur and Bobo's.

In less than seventy-two hours I had run the full gamut of emotions, first shaken to my roots by giving a terrible speech and then stirred in my heart by articulating my message on national television. This astonishing chain of events quickly made it clear to me that I had to get over my phobia. I had to learn how to speak to groups.

THIRTY-SIX

Finding My Voice

I left New York and hurried back to Washington armed with a new awareness and sense of purpose. To get potential members' attention, I would have to sit down directly with editors and reporters and tell them about BENS. I would also need to give them a news peg, an event for them to write about. This meant I had to give speeches, lots and lots of speeches all over the country. I needed to find some professionals who could show me how to do this.

I found a speech coach in Washington. She ran our sessions like a boot camp for Demosthenes, the great orator of ancient Athens. She gave me breathing exercises and told me to lower my pitch. She showed me how to say final consonants so they didn't come out slushy. She trained me to project my voice to a spot across the room. She warned me not to over-rehearse a speech, and she taught me to look the television camera right in the eye. She had me recite lines from the English poet Robert Browning's "The Pied Piper of Hamelin" to improve the rhythm of my delivery.

I took all this very seriously, and I worked hard. My sessions likely didn't improve my skills much, but they did give me more confidence. I became more relaxed about the prospect of speaking to groups. My strange, self-made British-Mexican accent had begun to fade by the late 1970s. With the lessons, it disappeared altogether. Perhaps my coach's drills for enunciating vowels—"spoo, spoh, spaw, spah, spay, spee"— finally tuned out any remnant overtones of my strange patois.

NEXT WE NEEDED A public relations pro, and Jim Morrison found one in the fast-talking, sharp-witted Steve Johnson. Steve had lots of moxie and really knew what he was doing. A former staffer in the US Senate, he had later moved to the National Association of Manufacturers. He was about the same age as Jim and had similar energy and smarts.

Steve was very sure of himself in a way that was reassuring to others. He was a perfect coach for a rookie like me who needed all the bucking up I could get. When I told Steve about my idea of a cross-country promotional tour, he tossed me a bundle of ways to make it work.

He sketched out a routine for me, and it worked. We picked a city. I found a local business executive to host a gathering of prospects. I gave the group my spiel. The next morning the city's newspapers featured stories about our meeting, usually told with Steve's slant and a picture of me. Steve had a knack for the press. He was clairvoyant about who to call, how to hook their interest, and how to frame a pitch. When I later met the town's best prospects one-on-one, they were already primed by the press's coverage. Then we moved to the next city and did it all over again.

My travels reminded me of how I had built my first network of manganese suppliers in Mexico. I went from town to town, listening carefully and directly connecting with people. For three years I crisscrossed the US in the same way, recruiting BENS members and expanding my network.

I had to learn how to chat with editors and pitch skeptical reporters about BENS. To my surprise, all this came rather naturally to me. It helped that the Pentagon, under President Ronald Reagan, had been exposed for a number of acquisition scandals that kept exploding from the president's military buildup, which gave me lots of hilarious material to play off. I usually began with a low-key show-and-tell, a rip-off from Walter Weiss's lovable vaudeville shtick. I pulled a twenty-nine-cent navigator's stool cap out of my pocket and kidded the crowd in Denver that we ought to mark it up to $1,118 and sell it to the Pentagon like Boeing had.

I welcomed prospects in San Jose at a $30 million breakfast, the amount the Department of Defense would spend while we met. I told a group in Kansas City that John Hechinger, the CEO of a chain of home improvement stores and a BENS member, featured toilets seats in his stores at a cut rate far below the $640 the Navy had paid Lockheed. I suggested in Chicago that we needed "a little old-fashioned capitalism" in the Pentagon.

I wasn't trying to bring the house down, but my gentle one-liners warmed up a crowd, sketched a vivid picture of BENS, and made it easy for lazy reporters to punch up their stories the next morning.

Newspapers across the country—from Pittsburgh, Pennsylvania to Orlando, Florida to Raleigh, North Carolina to San Jose, California —weighed in favorably on BENS and its results-driven, nonpartisan approach. The stories often went out of their way to argue that BENS wasn't "anti-military," but instead, was dedicated to "more effective defense spending." Seeing my words and ideas in print made them seem truer to me and reinforced my feeling I was on the right track.

The groups I spoke to were even more impressed when I listed the specific ways BENS wanted to improve the Pentagon's business practices: by increasing competition for military contracts, requiring warranties for new weapons, setting up an independent testing office to ensure new weapons would work, closing unneeded military bases. All these reforms made common sense to the business leaders and editors I met.

To my delight, the line that hooked more people than any other was, once again, my quip "Being dead is bad for business." Reporters put it in their leads, and editors stuck it in headlines and captions. Like Jane Pauley, they quoted it, nodded that it was okay to chuckle at it, offered a mild disclaimer ("Well, so much for the jokes"), and finally insisted that we recognize its rough truth. Planning to fight and win a nuclear war was utter madness.

I didn't score every time. I remember one talk I gave in Kansas City to a packed room of prospects at breakfast. As I rolled out my pitch, I could tell they weren't going to fall over one another to join BENS. None did.

Sometimes everything came together. I hit a trifecta when I made my first trip to Seattle in October 1983. A dynamic local entrepreneur, Bob Lamson, had joined BENS as soon as he had heard of us, and later helped run it. He'd gathered almost a hundred prospects for breakfast. I spoke for eleven minutes, and they lapped up my lines. When Bob urged his friends to "come on down" and sign up, a lot did.

Then Bob and I walked over to the *Post-Intelligencer*, Seattle's largest newspaper, to have coffee with its owners and editors in their boardroom. They loved BENS, and they repeatedly told their Seattle readers why. They splashed their story about Lamson's breakfast all over their business section the next day. They followed with an editorial praising BENS. A few days later their top columnist made our case all over again, in detail. Of course, I was delighted when he described me as "tall, dark, and handsomely tailored."

I was also delighted that they welcomed me as the personification of what I said BENS was. They told their readers I was a low-key, mild-mannered executive, not at all ideological—just a reasonable person in a three-piece suit, "as blue chip as AT&T."

I knew dashing back and forth across the country to promote BENS would be physically challenging, so in between trips I went to a Pritikin health center in Pennsylvania for a couple of weeks to get my body in fighting trim. I adopted its strict diet of whole grains and vegetables, exercised rigorously, and stopped drinking. I got in great shape. I stayed on Pritikin's regimen for a long time, eating healthy and not drinking. I felt like Superman.

Months later some of our members gave a big dinner for me in Denver. Before we sat down, I noticed people all around me were drinking a lot. I always noticed others drinking when I wasn't. Everyone else was having a great time. Except me. I felt bored, bored to tears with the whole thing.

The next day I went with several BENS members to one of the city's best Mexican restaurants, where I could get some Pritikin-approved beans and tortillas. I pushed my healthy fare around my plate for a while and mulled over the boredom I'd felt the previous night. Finally, I said to myself, "Stanley, is this really the way you want to live the rest of your life?" I ordered a double tequila, believing I would live happily ever after.

MY TOURS AROUND THE country during BENS's first two or three years eventually paid off. Although I never got great at public speaking, I got better, and I erased the last traces of my fear of talking to groups. My barnstorming also produced a credible national base on which we could build.

Even so, BENS needed more members. We especially needed more who could influence decision makers, and to make the organization work, we needed them right away. I realized I couldn't recruit enough of them by myself, no matter how many speeches I gave.

Then I stumbled onto a fresh way to increase membership.

David Arnold, an incredible skier who helped launch the Third Army Ski School in Germany at the end of World War II, invited me to a lunch in Boston, where he hoped to recruit an old pal to join BENS. David was one of Boston's most respected civic fathers, a top executive at the industry-leading Shipley chemical company, who had for years sparked almost every worthy cause in the city. He had thrown his weight behind BENS when I had first invited his local group of business leaders to partner with our new national organization.

David reserved an intimate room at the Harvard Club in the center of Boston's financial district. It overlooked the harbor where patriots had made much American history over the centuries. He seated his old friend on his right and placed a couple of BENS stalwarts on his flanks at the small round table. Thus the prospect found himself surrounded by a ring of peers, all of whom had partnered with him in many civic ventures over the years.

The conversation wandered genially, as if they were having a drink in the clubhouse after tennis. They eventually touched on BENS with typical Brahmin understatement, brevity, and clarity. By the time coffee was served, they had eased their friend into the fold with an invitation so genteel it didn't feel at all like a pitch.

I didn't decide that day to change my role in building BENS. I wasn't even aware that I should make a change. I just instinctively began to focus on recruiting strong, influential, and active members like David Arnold, one at a time, with the hopes they would sign up their friends, one at a time. Recruiting business leaders who would work with me to grow BENS in this way had more leverage than my trooping from coast to coast to make speeches. BENS became increasingly self-made—by its own members.

Once I targeted a key prospect, I zeroed in and found out everything I could about him: what he liked to read, his military record, his favorite ice cream. I looked for a mutual friend who would introduce me. Sometimes I called a person cold. I used what I had learned about making business deals to sign him up. Once we sat down, I invited him to tell me about himself. People liked talking about themselves, and I was a good listener. Getting him to join BENS was the easiest part.

This approach even worked in Kansas City. After I had bombed in my speech to the breakfast group, I walked over to the office of Landon Rowland, one of the most influential business executives in the Midwest, who had turned the railroad company Kansas City Southern Industries into a diversified conglomerate that included a financial services company—which became Janus Capital Group and grew into one of the largest asset managers in the world. Landon and I had never met, yet after an hour or so of one-on-one conversation, he enthusiastically joined BENS. He went on to recruit business leaders in the region and build a BENS operation that has flourished ever since.

This also worked with Dick Munro, the CEO of Time Inc., the first big national name to join BENS. He had served as a marine sergeant and ran his company with a gunny's grit. His Fortune 100 conglomerate, still in its glory days, had a distinctive prestige and panache. Dick was one of the most respected business executives in America. He joined on the spot and backed us to the hilt, stumping for BENS up and down the East Coast. He told the Princeton and Harvard Clubs that there could no longer be "detached observers in the nuclear age" because we're "all balanced on the same razor's edge." He urged them with the fervor of a Marine recruiter to see that "real patriotism" now required us all to make national defense "our business." I loved that he could state our vision more eloquently than I could. It meant he could enlist prospects who were beyond my reach.

Munro, Rowland, Arnold, and other BENS partners we recruited together came from a distinct segment of American business leaders. They burned with an inner fire, a passion for our country. They usually had served in uniform, often in combat. They typically were the engines, even the founders, of a host of local civic organizations and philanthropies where they lived.

These men were risk takers, entrepreneurs at heart, even if they were CEOs of large corporations. They either owned their own companies or ran them as if they did.

They were tough, pragmatic, successful business executives. They lived in the real world of concrete consequences and actions, and they wanted their country to stop chasing the flaky abstractions that might draw us into a nuclear war.

The first BENS members knew how to run a company, create a transformational product, turn around a broken enterprise, and deliver what they promised, on time, on price, on spec. Many were drawn to BENS because they thought the business side of the Pentagon ought to run as well as the country's best corporations. They joined BENS to help fix what they believed was broken.

Before long, other regional operations, like those in Boston and Kansas City, sprung up across the country. Each was built and led by executives who had earned a standing within their own network of peers whom I would likely have never met: Bernie Marcus, the cofounder of Home Depot, in Atlanta; Josh Weston, the CEO of one of the world's largest and most successful technology firms, the business payroll turned outsourcing giant, Automatic Data Processing (ADP), in New York City and New Jersey. Business leaders helped set up BENS in Seattle, San Francisco, the Twin Cities, Chicago, and Texas.

In the three decades since our start-up, these local offices have served as the wellsprings of BENS's membership and vitality. They are the foundation upon which we've built BENS—its federalist flavor notwithstanding—into a truly national organization.

THIRTY-SEVEN

Counselor

Now that we'd established BENS as a justifiable concern, we sought to distinguish ourselves from other advocacy groups in the public square. One person—Larry Smith—would push us forward in ways I had neither imagined nor prepared for. But my pitch seemed to bounce right off him at first. I could almost hear him yawn as he asked, "Why in the hell do we need one more organization in this town?"

I'd first learned of Larry from Ed Deagle, a key player at the Rockefeller Foundation, one of the many foundations through which I was trying to raise cash for BENS. Ed was a West Pointer, a combat veteran in Vietnam, a PhD from the Harvard Kennedy School, and a guy who had a seasoned sense about where he wanted to place his bets. He liked what we were trying to do, but he told me, "We're not going to give you any money. I'm going to give you something better than that. I'm going to introduce you to a guy who will help you build your organization."

I thought that was nice, but Larry and about $10,000 would have been even better.

I tried to tell Larry over the phone about my dreams for getting the business community involved in national security. "Why don't you come to lunch with me, and we'll talk about it?" I said.

When he finally agreed, we met for brunch at the Jockey Club at the Ritz-Carlton. We talked and talked until the room emptied in the late afternoon.

Larry mostly shared hilarious tales about how Washington functioned. I learned that he'd worked his way through a little liberal arts college on the Ohio River, the first in his family to earn a degree. He'd painted houses to pay for graduate school at Yale. He'd taught history at Dartmouth, where the students loved him so much, they created an award for distinguished teaching just to celebrate him and a colleague as he left academia for politics.

Larry had then thrived for almost fourteen years in the US Senate, serving as chief of staff to two members of the powerful Armed Services Committee and as a professional staff member on the committee as well. It seemed to me that during that time he had learned from direct experience almost everything that mattered to BENS.

For one, he had grappled with the danger of nuclear war, my gravest concern. He had been in the thick of the fight in 1979 for SALT II—a follow-up to the 1969 SALT I arms control treaty negotiated between the United States and Soviet Union—which was never ratified by the US Senate, due to Moscow's invasion of Afghanistan. He had also worked at the center of the Senate's major debates about new nuclear weapons under development: strategic missile defenses, cruise missiles, a new class of missile-armed submarines, the MX missile, B-1 bombers, and then the B-2 stealth bomber.

Most impressive to me, Larry had taken on—right in the belly of the beast—the insane idea of trying to fight a limited nuclear war. He had learned about the real-world effects of such a war from seasoned military professionals who would have had to try to fight it. The Strategic Air Command's planners had shown him how the US targeted its nuclear forces. He had climbed down into missile silos, deep under the plains of North Dakota. He had quizzed skippers of nuclear submarines and, while submerged on one, had felt the eerie bump of a missile launch.

Larry had also mastered practical politics. He knew how to frame an argument and how to speak to senators. This mattered, because BENS hoped to use our members' influence politically to move our agenda. Washington was filled with policy wonks who disdained elections, and political operatives who had no interest in government. Larry's fusion of politics and policy set him apart.

He could count votes in a committee or on the floor of the Senate, a special political art. He had grasped the mysterious arts of the Senate's deep inside games where so many decisions were made outside of the public's view.

Larry had also practiced electoral politics, from precinct to presidential. This was important to BENS, because we believed our political clout came from where our members lived and voted. In 1972, he had managed the reelection in New Hampshire of the first senator he worked for, a smashing win by a Democrat in a Republican state in a Republican year. He had also helped well-respected Colorado senator Gary Hart design his first run for the White House in 1984.

I wanted to get Larry to help BENS as much as I could, right away. Harvard had already recruited him to a big job in their top think tank on arms control. He moved to Boston with his family that summer, but I got him to fly down to Washington on and off for the next three or four years. I especially needed his help to deal with two kinds of growing pains at BENS.

For one, we needed to clarify our true and distinctive identity. Some of our members and some of our staff thought they had joined a liberal advocacy group, indistinguishable from the rest, except that we were business executives. I hadn't argued with them at first. I'd needed their support at the time. Even Larry had initially groaned at the prospect of "one more organization," because he too feared BENS was just like so many others.

He believed our future effectiveness and appeal depended on spelling out our special character. Again and again he gave us language to do this. He had a knack for coining a crisp phrase. He repeatedly took our approach to a problem and distilled it to its essence.

Larry labeled BENS a "do tank." This set us apart from think tanks that just issued reports or "talk tanks" that just listened to speeches or each other. The label appealed to business leaders who wanted to help make real improvements in the Pentagon's business practices and nuclear policy.

Larry also urged BENS to focus on "preventing the use of even one nuclear weapon." After years of working on such issues, he worried most that a missile might be launched accidently, out of misunderstanding, or by crazies on their own. He suggested that we promote crisis control centers here and in Moscow to prevent any such nuclear version of Murphy's Law.

Preventing the use of even one nuclear weapon underlined our rejection of the crazy idea of fighting a limited nuclear war. It distinguished us from traditional arms control groups, whose best dreams still would have left thousands of weapons poised to be fired. It differentiated us from theorists who obsessed about the comparative size of the superpowers' arsenals and about abstractions such as "essential equivalence." It had the concreteness and practicality of the way a business executive thought.

I especially loved Larry's haiku-like mantra that set us apart on defense spending: "More isn't better. Less isn't better. On the battlefield only better is better." Larry captured exactly what shrewd business leaders understand: how much you invest, and where, depends on what you were trying to do. BENS wanted powerful armed forces, second to none, and we believed the best way to build them was to think through a well-conceived strategy, a five-year defense plan, which the Pentagon didn't have at the time. We had the right idea. We just needed the right language to say it.

Larry's catchphrases helped position BENS as unique among your run-of-the-mill advocacy groups. They clarified not only what we were but also what we were not. As the organization became better defined, some of our early supporters soured on us. We weren't as liberal, partisan, or ideological as they wanted. I met with these individuals one-on-one. Some dropped out. I invited several others to leave. Altogether we lost a couple dozen members and the money they were giving. It was worth it. Otherwise the BENS I now understood more clearly and wanted to grow would have withered on the vine.

As it was, the organization I envisioned then would not have survived without Larry's counsel, and over the years his work was critical to building a BENS that blossomed far beyond my imagination. Ed Deagle had been absolutely right.

BY THE SPRING OF 1984, it was obvious I needed someone to run the place. I had enough self-awareness by then to realize I wasn't the right fit, even though I was CEO and chairman. I was on the road most of the time, and I still commuted from London and Gstaad. BENS needed a manager, a chief officer of operations. I knew just the man.

I flew to Boston and knocked on Larry's door at the Kennedy School. He was very polite and very clear. The answer was no.

I needed Larry, but I couldn't find a way to hook him. He didn't seem to care much about money or title. As we chatted, I finally realized that what intrigued him most was the challenge of figuring out how to make BENS work.

The more I told him about BENS's disarray, the more interested he became in finding ways we could fix it. He was a compulsive problem solver. I finally persuaded him to do a full-scale assessment of our operations and tell us what we needed to do.

I should have been careful what I wished for.

Larry embedded himself at BENS, watched us work, studied stacks of internal documents, and interviewed everyone on the team. He was a great listener, a shrewd interviewer, and a perceptive observer, noting every detail of what was said and not said.

> You have a mess. The way you do your work is a tangled, self-generated, self-defeating, self-feeding, self-enraging mess.
>
> Your habits drain energy, sap confidence, reduce effectiveness, produce tensions, and make tasks much more difficult than necessary.
>
> Your daily operations are herky-jerky. Your work is not focused, sustained, integrated, or clear. You rush into tasks ill-prepared and with insufficient lead time. You don't define concretely what you are trying to accomplish or how you will know whether you have succeeded.

Then Larry cut to the bone and claimed the primary source of our problems:

> Much of BENS's operational mess comes from the way Stanley manages. He directs BENS unilaterally, personally, and on his own authority. He insists on putting his stamp on everything. He bitches post hoc about bobbled details out of proportion to their importance.
>
> He gets impatient. He never trusts a task will be done and therefore asks several people, even those who have nothing to do with the matter, to do the same thing.
>
> He has a pattern of starting a program, followed by a rush of doubts about it which then makes it less likely it will be well executed.

Larry's prescriptions were as stark as his diagnosis. As Frank, Mendoza, and I had discovered in Mexico, he said I needed to focus on what I did best and extract myself altogether from the day-to-day operations. Things I could do: raising large money, helping design BENS's strategic plan, and serving as the lead spokesman to the press, Congress, and groups around the country.

Larry said we needed a collegial way of running BENS. He specified a checklist of crisp commonsense remedies:

1. Divide our work into six sets of critical tasks.

2. Form a team for each.

3. Define concrete goals for each.

4. Agree on specific but simple ways each would get their job done.

5. Integrate their interdependencies collegially under the aegis of a new senior leader.

Clearly, Larry was not a muddler.

I knew I wasn't the best administrator, but I hadn't thought of such a radical change in my role. I believed we just needed a strong COO to fix the mess. After all, I had partnered well with good managers in my businesses.

Larry claimed that this would not be enough. He told me that whatever titles another BENS leader and I might have, the crucial test would be whether I would actually withdraw from the daily details of BENS work and devolve unencumbered authority to someone else to run it. That was the "nub of the matter." He wrote:

> BENS is not one more business venture. BENS consumes you. It's your darling. It's the summation of your citizen's life thus far. Its emotional weight for you may make it difficult to relinquish its operations to other hands.
>
> One of the most difficult acts in life is to willingly yield power over what we love. One of your closest friends doubts you will.
>
> BENS is so full of promise. But as of now, your baby is strangling on its own umbilical cord. If you can't free it so it can breathe on its own, I fear it won't exist a year from now.

In all my life no one had ever told me such important, hard truths with such unrelenting candor.

I was conflicted. On the one hand, I wanted BENS to succeed more than anything, and Larry's assessment of its chaos and my role in it seemed right to me. But to extract myself altogether? Really? Part of me, deep inside my psyche, couldn't imagine BENS would ever have another CEO. It *was* my darling. I wanted to run it forever.

It took me a while to resolve my internal conflict. The turning point came a few months later in front of our most promising potential contributors. I had gathered them in Denver to raise big bucks. I got Larry to rewrite his findings in an upbeat way. He deemphasized our operational problems. He touted BENS as a once-in-a-lifetime opportunity. He said we just needed a fresh flush of cash to finance what he called our "tooling up."

Larry and I sat on opposite sides of the conference table, touting BENS's promise to our prospects with overlapping arguments from both flanks. I wanted him to make our case, because he knew how to rouse a group, excite them, and move them to act. I felt we were doing pretty well.

Then, unexpectedly, our differences about my role somehow popped out. The two of us went back and forth with unflinching candor. I think our prospects liked what they were seeing, an authentic disagreement about a central issue, between two men who clearly respected and cared for each other. They seemed to appreciate that each of us made our points on the merits without getting personal or miffed.

Finally, Larry closed his case. He offered the parable of George Steinbrenner, the capricious, domineering owner of the New York Yankees, who was credited with restoring the winning tradition of a great franchise, but whose personal style had alienated many talented managers and players. "Steinbrenner should hire the manager, recruit the players, and negotiate their contracts," Larry argued. "But he shouldn't order his field manager to bring in the lefthander from the bullpen in the bottom of the seventh."

That got me. It still took me a year or two to see that a chairman and a CEO play different roles. I had to realize that although I was the best delegator in the world in my business life, my passion for BENS was indeed suffocating it. Larry was right.

As Larry and I worked together in these and other ways, we developed a lifelong friendship. For all our differences, we shared an ineffable appetite for each other's company, for working together, and for getting something worthwhile done well.

THIRTY-EIGHT

There's Something About Charley

For the first two or three years after starting BENS, I paid for most of the costs from my own pocket. I could do this because my business had taken off in new ways. In 1981, about the time my idea of BENS had been jelling, I decided—along with my longtime partners, Ralph Feuerring and Frank Senkowsky—to form a new enterprise with a new partner. For me, it was a partnership that was more than twenty years in the making. That's how long it felt, as though Charley Gehret and I had circled around one another, going all the way back to my days in Mexico.

Charley is the only other person I've known who grew up in the Philadelphia area and made a career in the minerals business. Born and raised about twenty minutes northwest of me, in the Pennsylvania borough of Norristown, he was six years younger than me. A baseball player and cross-country runner intent on pursuing an Ivy League education at Dartmouth College, Charley saw his fortunes reversed one day when the director of admissions at local Lafayette College, a small liberal arts college about an hour's drive to the east, came to his house and convinced his father that he should attend. Choosing a military scholarship over athletics, Charley joined the ROTC, earned a degree in industrial engineering, and went into the army immediately after graduation.

While stationed as an ammunition supply officer at the Aberdeen Proving Ground in eastern Maryland, where the US government had once manufactured poison gas for use in French and British artillery shells during World War I, Charley heard about a job at a mineral trading company in Philadelphia called Frank Samuel. When he got out of the army in the spring of 1956, he interviewed and was quickly hired. On his first day on the job, the owner of the company handed him an English-Spanish dictionary and told him that he was leaving the next morning for Mexico, to follow up with a guy with whom the company had invested money in manganese. Like me, Charley had never heard of manganese, had never been to Mexico, had no idea what he was doing, and had no idea where he was going.

But the next morning, he flew to Chihuahua to search for Charley Barnet, a prospector, part-time crop duster, and would-be supplier of manganese who also didn't speak Spanish and thus had difficulty buying from the locals. The two Charleys found one another, and during one particularly memorable afternoon, Barnet took Gehret out flying on a Piper Cub and proceeded to fall asleep, nearly killing them both. He explained that he wasn't having much luck in the minerals business, but confessed there was another guy from Philadelphia—a competitor—who was buying the manganese dug by small suppliers at the local rail stations and then exporting it.

That competitor was me.

Although we didn't meet then, Charley remembers leaving Mexico three weeks later wondering who Stanley Weiss was and how this other Philly son had ended up in the business. At about the same time, our future partner, Ralph Feuerring, arrived in Mexico on Nelson Kusner's recommendation to buy manganese ore from me. Although we couldn't have known it then, our paths were already beginning to merge.

Coincidentally, around the time Charley was in Mexico, another one of my competitors actually sent an employee to Mexico to see what I was doing. I saw him following me around one week, and finally went up and asked him if he was a spy. He told me that he worked for the Philipp Brothers, a New York–based mineral company. They had asked him to watch me and see whether they could get into the same business.

I told him that he should have just asked me.

He was embarrassed, and we became friends. He eventually returned to New York and set up a huge oil business for the Philipp Brothers. When they didn't pay him the bonus he expected, he left, took half of the company, and set up across the street. He went on to make billions in global commodities. His name was Mark Rich, and he became a public figure after President Bill Clinton pardoned him years later for making illegal oil deals with Iran during the hostage crisis.

Over the following decade, Charley stayed with Frank Samuel as it was bought by a French company called Howmet. He began to earn a reputation in the industry as a thoughtful and forward-looking engineer who had a knack for seeing market trends before they developed. I don't remember when I first heard his name, but it came up from time to time in conversations I had with industry suppliers. I was intrigued enough during a trip back to Pennsylvania in 1966 to look Charley up and invite him to lunch.

We met at a restaurant in Conshohocken, Pennsylvania, an old mill town on the Schuylkill River in suburban Philadelphia, where Frank Samuel had a brick plant operation. With similar backgrounds and careers, we hit it off right away. We talked as much about the Phillies and growing up in Philadelphia as we did about importing and exporting minerals. Over the years, I've come to believe that in the first five minutes, you usually know whether a person is somebody you want to do business with or not. With Charley, I just knew. He struck me as a person whose judgment could be trusted, whose understanding of the industry ran deep, and whose loyalty to friends and allies was unquestionable. By the end of the lunch, I did something that I hadn't expected to do when I walked into the restaurant: I told Charley Gehret that I wanted to be in business with him. He confessed that he never thought of going into business with me, or really anybody, but he was intrigued. We both filed that idea away and went our separate ways.

After Lisa and I moved to London in 1971, Charley would call me from time to time and we'd have friendly conversations. I didn't see him again until 1976, when both of us attended the Second International Congress on Industrial Minerals, which met that year in the

West German city of Munich. Charley was there with his wife and a former football star for the Philadelphia Eagles named Chuck Bednarik. I'll never forget going to dinner with the two of them one night, when Bednarik tried to order using garbled German that he had learned back in high school. Whatever he had ordered didn't translate: the waiter came back and handed him a roll of dental floss.

The one experience Charley and I had together then that solidified our friendship was a trip we took to the Dachau concentration camp, located just outside the town of Dachau, about eleven miles north of Munich. The first of the extermination camps in Nazi Germany, opened by the man who oversaw the camps for Hitler—Heinrich Himmler, who personally directed the killing of six million Jews—Dachau was a place where more than thirty thousand prisoners had lost their lives. Charley and I disagree to this day about whose idea it was to go. What we'll both never forget is that there wasn't a single person in the town of Dachau who could tell us where the camp was. At one point, we were a block away, and still nobody knew how to get there. It said a lot about how hard the German people tried to ignore what took place there.

Once we found and entered the camp, all of us got very quiet. My usual instinct to make jokes or lighten the moment had completely left me. I had read about the horrific things that the Nazis had done in the camps to people just like me. I had dozens of Jewish friends who had lost family members in these camps, many of whom had gone years and even decades before learning the truth. I was as prepared as I could have been for the experience. But in truth, there is no way to prepare for the feeling you get while standing in the middle of the same roll-call square where starving prisoners—some of whom shared my last name—were counted every morning, and where "troublesome" prisoners were often hung. There is no way to prepare for the sight of the railroad tracks, where the Americans who liberated the camp in April 1945 reported finding boxcars full of corpses. There is no way to prepare for how moving it feels to read the stories of solidarity between prisoners who knew this was likely the last place they'd ever see on earth. It was an experience that all of us visiting lived quietly, without a word between us.

Charley and I left Germany as good friends. Little did we know that within five years, we'd be business partners.

⁂

I CANNOT REMEMBER A time when I looked forward more to hitting the ski slopes and spending time with good friends in Gstaad than in the winter of 1980–81. With the bad taste of the Citizens Party in the 1980 election just weeks behind me, Switzerland was a much better place to be than Washington, with the inauguration of Ronald Reagan opening the gates to a flood of conservative politics. As always, I was ready to have fun, and my favorite alpine resort town was the place to do it. Warm fires and cold drinks were waiting for me at the Eagle Club, which, as my friend Taki once wrote, "lies at the top of the Wasserngrat mountain because its members have reached the top of society." I had spent the past year in the pits of America's electoral system—I was ready to be up there with my pals once again.

One morning, I was brushing my teeth and looking out the window of our chalet when my gaze was met by that of Charley Gehret, who was looking at me from the other side. He had come to Gstaad and walked up the hill to my house to find me. It was startling to see my friend there, but I had an inkling of why he had come.

In 1968, the French company that Charley had gone to work for decided to spin off Frank Samuel as a mineral refracting business, and asked him to broker the deal. He had heard that a New York–based firm called Combustion Engineering (CE), which developed both fossil and nuclear steam supply power systems, wanted to get into the business, and reached out. Charley arranged the sale and included himself in the transaction, going to work for Combustion Engineering. He helped move CE into other successful businesses, but in 1970 he decided to leave the engineering giant and start his own company with his twenty-three-year-old son, John. They called it Industrial Minerals and, in partnership with a German company and a South African company, moved iron ore and chrome ore around the world.

By the late 1970s, it was clear that Combustion Engineering had never really developed a mentality for the mineral processing business, and CE decided to sell off a number of its plants. Charley, who by this point had decided that Industrial Minerals didn't meet his expectations, was between jobs and deciding what to do next. At age forty-nine, he didn't have the resources he needed to retire, but he saw something in the marketplace that made him believe there was an opportunity just waiting to be exploited. China was beginning to enter the world mineral trade, and Charley believed that if we could find a plant that was big enough to handle diverse shipments of bulk ore to compete with the Chinese—that would enable us to bring in ten-thousand-ton lots and then store it, grind it, and ship it out ten to twenty tons at a time—we could become a prime producer in the industry. We could make a killing.

Charley was focused on one manufacturing plant in particular: a state-of-the-art facility that he had helped design in Wilmington, Delaware. I had told Charley a few years before in Munich that we were beginning to think, given the steady but limited global market for manganese, American Minerals should diversify as a company. Iron ore and chrome ore would fit the bill. Through a former employee of his who now worked for Ralph and me, named Jessie Miller, Charley floated the idea of purchasing the plant together. His house call in Gstaad that winter morning was to pitch the same proposal in person.

Intrigued, I agreed to visit the facility with Charley when I returned to Washington a few months later. I was very impressed by what I saw: the plant was extraordinary, and would allow us to diversify our business beyond manganese. But I couldn't convince my partners to buy it. We already had a profitable plant running in Philadelphia, and Frank in particular didn't see the point in buying another, bigger facility.

But fate or luck or carelessness—you could make an argument for any of the three—intervened. The Reading Railroad, which leased the land on which our Philadelphia plant stood, decided it needed to build a new facility of its own. And as it turns out, we had forgotten to renew our lease for the land. So, shortly after we told Charley that American Minerals wasn't interested in partnering, Reading kicked us out of our plant. The only realistic option we faced to avoid a severe interruption of our operations was to purchase the Wilmington plant.

By default, I was able to get Frank and Ralph's acquiescence, and for the next three weeks, I spent every day at the plant in Delaware—which, Charley joked, was probably the longest continuous amount of time I've ever spent in one place in the mineral business.

Charley put me in touch with his former boss at Combustion Engineering to negotiate a deal, which is something I knew how to do. As usual, the key was to make the other person feel good about himself, to feel important, so he felt good about me. CE was so eager to part with the plant that we pretty much stole it. We agreed on a sales price that was a fraction of the facility's real value, and as an additional sweetener, we didn't have to put a penny down—instead, it would be paid out of profits. We shut down our operation in Philadelphia and moved to Wilmington.

Charley and his son, John, joined as our partners. We used the American Minerals name that I had used since 1960, and Charley created a side company called Mineral Development to handle the sourcing of our minerals. He and his son served as sales agents and equity partners.

From the get-go, Ralph and Charley were at loggerheads. Their personalities were so similar, I joked that while Ralph used to worry every day, he now had to worry only on odd days and Charley would worry on even days. Ralph retaliated amiably that the best part of our new partnership was Charley's son. But I trusted each one of them and trusted their judgment. We soon became a great team. Ralph crunched the numbers, Frank made things work, I handled the relationships, and Charley found new ways for us to make money. In fact, I've never been in business with anybody who was as good at making us money as Charley—with the possible exception of his son, John.

꙳

OUR PUSH TO DIVERSIFY American Minerals paid off immediately. The money started to roll in.

One element on which we made an unexpected killing as the 1980s wore on was zirconium silicate, or zircon, which is naturally occurring beach sand. When subjected to very high heat, zircon is converted into a glaze that makes porcelain tiles more durable. When it is subjected to refraction, its stability at high temperature is perfect for creating things like the bricks that line furnaces that make steel. For a variety of reasons in the mid-1980s—primarily the debut of high-end zircon-crafted tiles, for which customers were willing to pay more—global supplies ran short and prices went through the roof. Thanks to Charley's foresight, we had agreements and inventory of zircon already in place, and our earnings nearly doubled.

More important to our long-term success was another market that Charley saw before everyone else, one that nobody had ever really imported into the United States: magnesium. Most of us associate magnesia, used as a curative in ancient civilizations, with modern household health items such as milk of magnesia and Epsom salts. Depending on how magnesium is processed, however, its uses are endless, stretching from water treatment and animal feed to oil and gas, construction, agriculture, and rubbers and plastics. Having worked for nearly three decades in the manganese business, I was used to people confusing the two and even had a stock set of "manganese, not magnesia" jokes to deploy.

After purchasing the Wilmington plant, we began importing shiploads of magnesia using Charley's contacts in Greece, storing it, and grinding it up for different customers. Recognizing that our earnings were limited by the fact that our facility could grind and produce only a set amount each day, we ended up buying a second plant—this one in Camden, New Jersey—from Combustion Engineering for even less than we had bought the first, also without putting down a penny.

This eventually lent itself to a funny story.

Camden was a plant in which we regularly discharged zircon. Since it's a mineral that doesn't do as well when it's wet, we worked hard to keep it dry. Charley used to joke about the pre-Columbian figures I had collected in Mexico and fixated specifically on my "friendship" with Tlaloc, the Aztec rain god sitting outside of Mexico's National Museum of Anthropology. He used to tell me that when we were off-loading zircon, it was my job to handle the weather.

One day, when we were unloading a ship in Camden, Charley was driving across the Ben Franklin Bridge in Philadelphia when it started to rain. He called me on his car phone and said, "Stanley, it's raining in Camden. What are you going to do about it?"

I said, "I'll talk to Tlaloc right away."

By the time Charley arrived in Camden, the sun was shining.

AS THE 1980S CAME to an end, we began to look for more growth. While walking along the ocean in Palm Beach, Florida, with Ralph's daughter, Nicole Hill, Charley wondered out loud if we had maxed out our business and should consider selling it altogether. An extremely talented graduate of the University of Pennsylvania and its Wharton School of Business, Nicole was a rising star in the private equity world. As thoughtful and deliberate as her father, she worked at the prestigious Capricorn Investors in the wealthy New York suburb of Greenwich, Connecticut. Nicole recognized an opportunity: Capricorn owned Premier Refractories, another leading importer of Chinese magnesia, which it had bought from Combustion Engineering. What Premier needed more than anything was strong management. Combining its operations with ours would make us the largest single importer of Chinese magnesia in the United States.

We combined the businesses in 1989 and—after working through some old asbestos lawsuits—officially merged in 1991. The new company was renamed American Premier, Inc. Charley, Ralph, John, and I owned half, and Capricorn, through a subsidiary, owned half. There was only one drawback: I wasn't especially enamored with the founder of Capricorn, Herbert "Pug" Winokur, because he didn't strike me as trustworthy.

In February 1993, I circulated a one-page memo to the American Premier board. I called it "SAW's Rules for Success," and it listed seven items learned in the four decades that I had been in business:

1. Don't run out of cash.

2. Look out for stupid competition (i.e., cut price).

3. No product or market lives forever.

4. Partners are necessary; people need to share your success.

5. Professionals are advisors, not decision makers (experts are like perfume—sniff, don't swallow).

6. Taxes are forever.

7. Don't run out of cash.

We followed those rules to a tee. We reaped the rewards until 1997, when Capricorn began selling off its interests to cover other losses in the marketplace. One day, Pug proposed bringing in a French company, and I hit the roof. I said, "You bring in the French, and we'll be dead."

I argued that the reason we worked so well together was because we were a small group and made decisions sitting around a table. I said if we brought in the French company, it would take six months for every decision because they would run endlessly through the logic of whatever was being discussed. I knew I had a great deal of insight on how things worked in France and other parts of Europe as opposed to in the US. To me, it was just this simple: The French weren't entrepreneurial in the same way as Americans.

I was outvoted, and we were screwed, for precisely the reason that I had predicted. With the French at the table, by the time we decided to get something done, somebody else had already done it.

Frustrated beyond belief, we decided to simply sell our shares in the entire company to the French in 1998, who then sold it all to a British company that they had blocked from buying us a few years before.

But there was one part of American Premier that Charley insisted we had to buy back from the British: an underperforming magnesium mine and processing plant located about three hundred miles northwest of Las Vegas in the unincorporated mining community of Gabbs,

Nevada. It was an orphaned division of a big company, and Charley and John both insisted that the Brits had no idea what they had in that Nevada mine, and they were right: they ended up selling it back to us for a song.

It turned out to be the smartest business decision we ever made. Under Charley and John's leadership, our new company—which eventually settled on the name Premier Magnesia—became the largest domestic producer of magnesia in the United States and, as we say on our website, "one of the world's leading manufacturers and suppliers of high-purity calcined magnesium oxide and magnesium hydroxide products."

As we took over the mine, we made a handful of small acquisitions to help round out our portfolio. Then in 2007 came the second-smartest business decision we ever made.

One of the companies that we supplied magnesium to was Giles Chemical. Founded in North Carolina in 1950, Giles was the largest supplier of Epsom salts in North America, meeting the individual needs of customers in everything "from bath and beauty to pulp and paper to agriculture and animal feed," as its website says. In the early 2000s, China began making noise about shifting from being a mere provider of raw materials to making end products. Fearful that China was going to cut back its exports, companies began stockpiling magnesia, and global pricing went through the roof. It was enough to scare Giles owner Rick Wrenn, a terrific manager, who was reminded—in an industry with no long-term contracts—how dependent he was on magnesia. As we talked about the problem with him, we realized it was such a natural extension of our business that we decided to combine our two companies. Rick became the president and COO of our new entity. For Giles Chemical, it meant a steady supply of its most important raw material. For Premier, it meant the addition of real day-to-day management talent on the ground that would complement John and Charley Gehret's genius as strategic visionaries—along with branding and marketing talent we could use.

The merger came at a perfect time: precisely the moment when 75 million baby boomers began retiring at a rate of ten thousand a week, and the fitness movement in America began to take off in new ways.

Every week there seemed to be another fitness magazine with a story about how good it was for your body to soak in Epsom salts. Since 2007, we've had tremendous growth. What started as a health craze is now primed to be institutionalized, as physicians increasingly recommend Epsom salts for their real health benefits. And I'm thankful for this every quarter that a significant amount of revenue appears in my account.

⁂

OF COURSE, THE MOST rewarding part of my partnership with Charley Gehret is the friendship that has endured for more than half of our lives. Charley is a great wit who has always been quick with a joke, but has never taken himself too seriously. A few years back, he sponsored a women's tennis team in Florida that he called, naturally, Charley's Angels. He had hats made and everything.

Charley and I played tennis whenever we were together, well into our seventh decade. One time, he took me to the prestigious 160-year-old Germantown Cricket Club in Philadelphia, which is reputed to be the place where tennis began in America. The forerunner to the US Open, known as the National Tennis Championship, was played on the club's courts in the 1920s. It is, needless to say, as Waspy as a club gets in America. When I was growing up, people with the name Weiss weren't allowed in.

As we were driving up to the club, I asked Charley, "Are you sure this is a good idea? Isn't it restricted for me to go in there?"

"What are you talking about?" he said. "Sixty percent of the members are Jewish."

"Is nothing sacred?" I replied in jest.

Charley now lives in Florida, and has poured just as much energy into finding a cure for Parkinson's disease as he once poured into creating new opportunities for our company.

One of the great pleasures of our business is that his son, John, now runs it as CEO. He's every bit as brilliant as his father, with that magic ability to see into the future. He's more than adventurous—a champion outdoorsman who embraces everything that moves fast, including ciga-rette boats, in which he once famously beat *Miami Vice* actor Don John-son in a championship race in Miami. Under his leadership, Premier Magnesia has prospered.

Just as Charley ran the company hand in hand with Ralph, John runs the company hand in hand today with Ralph's daughter, Nicole. She complements John perfectly while making sure the company keeps its books and maximizes its profits—in the same exact way that Ralph did until his death in 2007. I simply adore her.

At some point, my daughter, Lori Christina, and my son, Anthony, will inherit Lisa's and my shares. Anthony will take my place on the board, managing relationships and bringing his considerable charm and deal-making skills to the business. And then the business that began more than six decades ago—not long after Charley Gehret first heard my name and Ralph Feuerring first reached out to me in Mexico—will come full circle, with the children taking the place of the parents.

That's more than a success story. That's my legacy.

THIRTY-NINE

Coming of Age

On November 20, 1984—thirteen years after she had lost her husband and just twelve days after what would have been Hans's eightieth birthday—Gretl Popper died in San Francisco. I was honored to deliver the eulogy at her funeral, where I said:

> Gretl was like a twinkling star. She sparkled. She made one feel good to be with her. She had enormous old- and new-world charm and vivaciousness, and no vanity at all. She was a magnet that attracted to her the young and old, the rich and poor, the sophisticated and the simple. She brought joy and a rare sense of her love for life to those who knew her for three generations and to those who met her only in passing. She made everyone she touched a richer person . . .
>
> But most of all, she knew how to love. Her love asked nothing in return. It was the core of her beauty, her warmth, her selflessness, her caring, her courage, her independence. The void she leaves in all of us lucky enough to have known her can never be filled. But all of us fortunate to have learned from her, to have grown from her example, to have been loved by her, will have Gretl with us forever.

I knew there were few things that could fill the emptiness Lisa felt when she lost her mother. She wanted to get as far away as possible, to find new experiences that would occupy her mind, even while she grieved. Our good friends Paul Hamlyn, a German-born British publisher, and his wife, Helen, a successful designer—who, a few years later, would start a foundation that became one of the largest independent grant-givers in London—had recently told us about the spectacular Indonesian island of Bali. While in Mexico two years earlier, I had read the classic book *Island of Bali*, published in 1932 by Mexican painter Miguel Covarrubias about a trip he had taken to the island with his wife, Rosa. Lisa and I decided to follow in their footsteps and take a trip to Bali, along with our children. It was love at first sight.

That first trip to Bali was the start of annual three-month treks to Asia over the following three decades. We'd begin with a visit to the beautiful beaches and unmatched elegance of the renowned Amanpuri resort in Phuket, Thailand, over Christmas and the New Year. Then we'd move on to the exotic and ancient beauty of Yangon and other cities in Myanmar, also known as Burma, at the end of January. We would spend three or four weeks in India in March, starting in New Delhi and ending up among the lavish palaces of Udaipur in the western Indian state of Rajasthan. Then we'd return to Bali, with side trips to the Indonesian capital of Jakarta, in the summer. Every year we stay in many of the same places, often in the same rooms, and renew friendships with expats and local residents we've gotten to know as family through the years. These trips began a new chapter in our lives.

Lisa's Danish first cousin, the very funny Torben Lenzberg, reflecting approvingly on our annual trips to Asia (not to mention Paris, Venice, Gstaad, the US, and so forth), delivered a line for the ages: "When it comes to Lisa," he said, "vacation is her vocation."

⁂

MEANWHILE, MY EXTENDED TRIPS to Washington from London to tend to the work of BENS were beginning to pay dividends. Recruiting became easier. Every quarter I updated a one-page roster of our most prominent members, because I knew their prestige mattered more than anything I could say.

We were growing financially stronger too. We found some big backers who gave money at an underwriter's scale. Don Carlson, a hugely successful entrepreneur in the East Bay near San Francisco, fell in love with BENS at first sight; he wrote big checks and made sure his crowd of friends did too. Tom Ford, who had built 3000 Sand Hill Road—the nerve center of Silicon Valley—recruited some of its elite venture capitalists and wrote his own big checks. Peter Grace, one of America's wealthiest men, who spent a record forty-eight years running the diversified chemical company of the same name started by his grandfather—the first Roman Catholic mayor of New York—was a kindred spirit. President Reagan had tapped him in 1982 to head a new agency, eventually known as the Grace Commission, which brought together two thousand business executives to find ways to eliminate waste in the federal government. Grace lent an air of prestige to the marriage of business and public service that later served BENS well.

Michael Sonnenfeldt jumped in after reading the first piece I ever published about BENS, in *Inc.* magazine, a hot journal for entrepreneurs like him. He was a whiz kid with an MIT degree, not yet thirty years old, who had gone on to make a fortune in commercial real estate in the New York area. He gave BENS major money and used his brilliance for raising more from others. He suggested we offer prospects different levels for contributing, with different names, like the Directors Club and the Chairman's Club. It worked.

About three years into BENS, these early investors were giving the organization an income with enough breadth and depth to build on. We had new financial muscle.

Our influence on Capitol Hill began to blossom. I didn't want to preach about military reform; I wanted to make it happen. We needed Congress to pass laws that required the Pentagon to adopt the business practices we had been touting. Our members' number and stature gave us political clout. Fortunately, both Jim Morrison and Mike Burns, a new partner he had recruited, knew how to use it.

Mike had worked for Georgia congressman and future House speaker Newt Gingrich, who would later become the architect of the first Republican House majority in forty years, and for the Heritage Foundation, a conservative think tank that supplied many of the ideas that helped fuel the Reagan Revolution. Yet he was neither a partisan nor an ideologue, and his professionalism and temperament reinforced BENS's credibility as an independent, nonpartisan organization. Mike was another PhD who spoke clearly and persuasively, and he brought his own network of key congressional staff allies to add to Jim's.

Both Jim and Mike had mastered the art of legislation. They were especially adept at teaming. They worked closely with firebrand Republican reformers in both congressional houses, such as Chuck Grassley, the conservative senator from Iowa, and the larger-than-life new congressman and future House majority leader from Texas, Dick Armey. They partnered with the bipartisan Military Reform Caucus, which supported our agenda and which found BENS's business credentials politically helpful.

Before long, most of our initial menu of business reforms for the Pentagon had been passed into law. We didn't do this by ourselves. We couldn't have. Getting anything worthwhile done in Washington is a team sport. Still, military reformers from both parties, in and out of office, gave us a lot of credit. One Republican senator told me our contributions to defense acquisition reform were "essential." A member of the House Armed Services Committee said to me that BENS's efforts to improve the Pentagon's business practices "really made a difference."

And some of the greatest early praise we received came for the lead role we played in developing a process for closing and rehabilitating obsolete military bases across America. Based on a concept first proposed by BENS member Bill Tremayne, the Base Realignment and Closure (BRAC) process was created in the late 1980s to remove politics from the difficult process of closing bases.

We maintained our focus even after the legislation passed. In 1994, BENS issued a report that contained damning evidence that twenty-six of the sixty-seven major bases recommended to be shut down by BRAC either hadn't closed or had reopened under new names and with new federal tenants. In other words, the Pentagon was getting around the intent of the base closing law by closing an Army base one day and opening it the next day as a Navy or Air Force base, something the public wasn't remotely aware of. The story caused such a sensation that I was invited to appear on *60 Minutes*, the award-winning CBS show, to tell the story. On October 9, 1994, I did, calling the Pentagon's actions "political pork at its worst." The report helped get the BRAC process back on track while shining a prime-time spotlight on BENS and its work, which felt good.

Since 1988, there have been five rounds of base closings, with actions approved at more than 450 obsolete locations, saving American taxpayers billions of dollars. As Dick Armey, who sponsored our history-making, base-closing bill, told us, it "would not have passed without the help of Business Executives for National Security."

♌♌

SINCE I HAD NO skill at the arcane inside game of legislative tactics, I stayed out of it and left it to Jim and Mike. My role was to champion our agenda before congressional committees. In early 1984, I appeared for the first time in a public hearing with real big shots, yet another sign that BENS was becoming a player.

I testified along with four senators: two Republicans, Kansas moderate Nancy Kassebaum and Chuck Grassley; and two Democrats, Max Baucus from Montana and future vice president Joe Biden of Delaware. BENS backed their bill to freeze federal spending across the board. Their proposal drew fire from both left and right. Conservatives, who opposed any cuts in defense, labeled it the "KGBB" freeze. I liked the moniker for its flavor and irreverence.

Others in Congress, like the "KGBB" senators, were impressed that such prominent executives were giving their time and money to push for reforms in which they had no corporate interest. When I met the Democratic senator from Georgia, Sam Nunn, revered in both parties for his foreign policy expertise, he said to me, "Mr. Weiss, you are the first businessman who ever came to see me who wasn't asking for something for himself." He and others respected us not just for what we were trying to do, but also for what we were not doing.

The national press was similarly fascinated that BENS wasn't another trade association chasing pork. It was a man-bites-dog story. The *New York Times* ran a series of front-page stories that praised our legislative agenda and emphasized that our only interest was to make our country's military stronger. The editors of the *Wall Street Journal* were especially intrigued. They asked us to meet with them in their boardroom to explain what we were doing, leading to a feature story on BENS that focused on our work to help the Pentagon get its house in order.

I chewed on the irony. BENS was getting respect because we didn't play Washington's usual self-interested games.

By the fall of 1985 I thought BENS had come of age. We were still young, at most adolescents, but our members gave us adult muscle. We had bested hardened defense lobbyists in big-guy fights, winning a fistful of defense reforms. Hard-nosed members of Congress and the press respected our character, distinctiveness, and public purpose.

Yet it wasn't enough for me. I wanted to make sure everyone who mattered knew about our work and recognized its importance. I wanted to celebrate it, trumpet it, and hear about it in revered places. I weighed the pros and cons of holding a special event commemorating our achievements so far.

I realized, however, that putting on an ambitious black-tie dinner congratulating ourselves would hardly set us apart from the usual self-serving gatherings in Washington. Instead I decided that we should give a tribute to President Eisenhower and celebrate his Farewell Address. Its twenty-fifth anniversary came in January of 1986. Ike's warnings and call to action had led me to found BENS. I felt we could indirectly carve out a more distinctive and valuable niche by commemorating Ike and the beliefs we shared with him.

I hoped Eisenhower's family would join us. I hadn't met any of them, but I wrote a letter to his son, John, explaining what we wanted to do and why. A retired army brigadier general and military historian, John enthusiastically wrote back that I was the first person who had really understood his father's speech. He resented the suggestions that Ike had called for "unilateral disarmament." Like his father, and like us, John wanted our country to simultaneously have strong armed forces and avoid "frivolous" military spending. Of course, we featured his love letter about BENS in the front of the evening's program. The president's two grandchildren, David and Susan, both articulate, accomplished professionals, personalized our connection with the Eisenhowers by agreeing to speak at the dinner.

The family's commitments to join us worked like the first olives out of a bottle. Once it was clear that the Eisenhowers were blessing our dinner as an authentic tribute to the late president, all three of his living successors—Presidents Nixon, Ford, and Carter—added their endorsements. An all-star lineup of Ike's cabinet officers and other key players in his White House followed their lead and jumped in too. We were on our way.

I reached for other stars. I wanted Tom Watson Jr. to headline the evening. I thought he was the most distinguished business leader in the country. Not only had he made IBM the icon of American invention and financial success, but he also shared BENS's convictions about the danger of nuclear war. He had used his business judgment and pragmatism as the American ambassador to the Soviet Union, thereby demonstrating BENS's vision that such practical ways of thinking could help make our country more secure. Watson agreed to speak that evening, after which he became a major backer of BENS and a personal friend for years to come.

I wanted Lesley Stahl to serve as our emcee. At the time, no star burned brighter in television and political journalism than she. She covered the White House for CBS and moderated its Sunday talk show, *Face the Nation*. She had earned her stardom in a new-fashioned way—with sparkling intelligence, unrelenting drive, and a confident luster the camera loved. She had what she once confided to Larry Smith was the secret to winning audiences: "It's energy, Larry. Energy."

Although we had never met, I just called her. She loved the idea.

I mentioned Tom Watson was speaking, of course. She said she had gone to the same school as Watson's mother. She couldn't have been more gracious.

We also wanted a diverse crowd of sponsors and guests who would both signal their support of our work and personify our distinctive mix of purposes. We touched every component of our identity. We had a bipartisan roster of thirty-nine senators who cosponsored the dinner: twenty Republicans and nineteen Democrats, spanning the full ideological spectrum, from staunch conservative Barry Goldwater to liberal stalwart Ted Kennedy. We featured our allies among the military reformers in the House from both parties. We recruited a galaxy of nuclear scientists, all of Eisenhower's and Kennedy's top science advisors, including physicist and Nobel laureate Isidor Isaac Rabi; James Killian Jr., a former president of the Massachusetts Institute of Technology and lead architect of America's space program; Jerome Wiesner, also a president of MIT; and even the widow of Eisenhower science advisor George Kistiakowsky. They had helped build our nuclear arsenals and now, like BENS, were haunted by the danger of their use.

Everything seemed in place as we approached January 29, 1986, the night of our dinner. We had the right cast and the right script. We had the right place, the finest hotel, the one closest to the Capitol. Then a last-moment problem threatened to dash our hopes.

The morning before our dinner, America's space shuttle, *Challenger*, blew up, leaving the country in abject grief. We listened to President Reagan's powerful eulogy. Like all of us, he wrestled out loud with what Americans should do next in the face of such tragedy. Then he told us, "Nothing ends here; our hopes and our journey continue." We took his fatherly words to heart and decided to go ahead with our plans.

We awoke the morning of the dinner to a mix of fog and snow that darkened our hopes for a packed house. Washington always gets spooked by even a hint of snow. We feared the worst.

In spite of everything, however, BENS's first Eisenhower dinner turned out to be a smash hit, the hottest ticket in town. Five hundred notables jammed into the largest ballroom on Capitol Hill. Lesley Stahl lit up the room with her grace and energy. The two young Eisenhowers did their grandfather proud. Tom Watson bestowed his gravitas on the festivities. The *Washington Post* gave us a huge valentine the next morning. It told our story the way we wanted and trumpeted a joyous headline: "They Still Like Ike."

The *Post*'s story rightly dwelled on our salute to Ike's Farewell Address. We had treated it like scripture. We put its full text at everyone's place along with an op-ed I had written about the address for the *Wall Street Journal*. David Eisenhower told us how he had parsed Ike's early drafts in the Eisenhower Museum in Abilene, Kansas. Watson gave us a reverent description of it in detail.

The climax of the night moved us all. The room fell dark as a huge screen rolled into view. The crowd hushed as President Dwight David Eisenhower himself appeared. We were transfixed as he delivered his prophetic seventeen-minute Farewell Address. It was one thing to read the text, yet another to hear and see him talk to us directly.

He spoke to and for all of us that night, but I felt he was especially speaking to and for me. He voiced a litany of convictions that were at the heart of BENS and that I had come to believe deeply. He wanted our country's arms to be "mighty" and "ready." Yet he worried about the "unwarranted influence" of an unprecedented "military-industrial complex." He was proud that American technical creativity had made us more secure. Yet he warned that we needed to be alert to the "danger that public policy could itself become the captive of a scientific-technological elite."

Above all, like some stirring recruitment officer, Ike told us, "Only an alert and knowledgeable citizenry can compel the proper meshing of the huge industrial and military machinery of defense with our peaceful methods and goals so that security and liberty may prosper together."

I closed the evening with a succinct coda that made explicit BENS's connection with Ike's warnings and challenge. I wanted everyone there to know that we had created BENS to do exactly what Eisenhower said the country needed.

Though I didn't realize it then, my celebration of BENS's coming of age had turned into a kind of civic bar mitzvah. I wanted to gather a congregation who shared our beliefs. I wanted us to recite a revered text that expressed our convictions and purpose. I wanted a ceremony where elders would explicitly certify our maturity and importance. I wanted us to declare to them, to everyone, the secular equivalent of "Today I am a man."

It wasn't just BENS that had come of age. I had come of age too. I had never felt more articulate, self-knowing, or purposeful than I did that night. That night, in a new and deeper way, I became a man myself.

FORTY

Crossing a Ravine on a Rope

There were many more such events to come over the years, of course, and whenever John Whitehead and I found ourselves at the same big dinners, he loved to tell the story of how we slept together. That is, if I didn't tell it first.

John was born in Evanston, Illinois, the son of a man who set telephone poles and strung electrical wires. As a naval officer, John delivered the first wave of American soldiers to hit the beaches at Normandy on D-Day. He survived the bloody battles of Iwo Jima and Okinawa in the Pacific. He went on to become a Wall Street legend, leading Goldman Sachs into global markets while creating a new standard for philanthropy among American bankers.

John came out of a comfortable retirement to serve as the deputy secretary of state in the Reagan administration, the State Department's number two job. More than a decade later, as he neared eighty, he came out of retirement again after the devastating terrorist attacks of September 11, 2001, and oversaw the restoration of Lower Manhattan, helping it return to a beautiful and powerful symbol of American resilience and strength.

I met John and his pal Arthur Levitt, the soon-to-be chairman of the United States Securities and Exchange Commission, when I was recruiting new BENS members in the late 1980s. Unbeknownst to me, Arthur was also a founding member of a very rare tribe of Jews known as the Association of Jewish Outdoorsmen. I imagined a logo with a tall mountain peak covered by a yarmulke. Every year, Arthur would invite a nonsectarian group to join him in the spectacular wilderness of the Rocky Mountains for whitewater rafting or mountain climbing. He made these trips under the aegis of Outward Bound, a nonprofit that sought to promote personal growth through extreme outdoor adventures. Outward Bound also provided guides, mainly to make sure that none of the middle-aged, blistered, and oxygen-deprived business executives fell into a ravine.

Arthur invited me to join him in June 1991. He knew I skied, but I didn't tell him I found hurtling down a mountain on skis a lot less terrifying than standing on a mountain cliff in hiking boots. I had a severe fear of heights—acrophobia—and we were going to climb to fifteen thousand feet. But I had remembered reading somewhere that a local gym offered classes on how to climb. So I channeled my inner Sir Edmund Hillary, packed a few sandwiches, and signed up. It turns out that rappelling down a rock, since you're basically looking at a rock wall the whole time, wasn't too bad. Climbing up, on the other hand, was really tough. But I was in good shape, and during the several days of the class, I developed a little bit of confidence that I wouldn't make a total fool of myself.

So I went on the trip with Arthur and absolutely loved it. What I learned about camping at high altitudes in Colorado is that it gets so cold at night, you literally have to get near somebody to get warm or you'll freeze to death. That's how I ended up sleeping for five days in a tent with John Whitehead, often called the "chairman of the establishment."

The exhausting climb felt good, and I loved the adventure. For our last exercise, the guides invited each of us to pull ourselves along on a rope across a ravine, crossing an open space about a quarter-mile long and more than three football fields deep.

Most people opted out of it, but I decided to do it, even though I was the oldest guy on the mountain, except for John. It was one of those moments when you face your greatest fears. I was scared shitless the entire time and thought for sure they'd soon be scraping me off the rocks. But I made it.

At the very end of our trip, we all had to pick the member of the team we most respected and award him an Outward Bound pin. At the ceremony, John Whitehead tapped me to receive the pin. This was a guy I profoundly admired, even idolized. And he chose me. We were close friends for the rest of his life.

ONE OF THE UNEXPECTED side benefits to the recruiting and evangelizing I was doing for BENS was that from time to time, different entrepreneurs for whom I had great respect asked me whether I was interested in investing in their ideas and providing seed capital for their companies. For instance, Silicon Valley venture capitalist Neill Brownstein—one of the original funders of both the Internet and voice mail back in the 1970s, and a co-investor when Sidney Harman repurchased his company from Beatrice Foods—invited me to invest in an idea he had to create one of the first early-stage venture capital funds based in India, which I did. More than three decades later, Footprint Ventures is still going strong and still run by Neill and his brilliant wife, Linda.

Another opportunity came to me through the friendships I struck up at BENS with motivational speakers Jack Canfield and Mark Victor Hansen, who wrote the iconic book *Chicken Soup for the Soul*, a collection of inspiring stories from the lives of ordinary people they had met. Canfield and Hansen had used the success of the book to launch their own media and publishing company, Chicken Soup for the Soul Publishing, dedicated to turning the book into a series of books targeted by audience. It caught the eye of a close friend and fellow BENS board member, Bill Rouhana, a hugely successful media CEO who had created Winstar Communications and turned it into a billion-dollar brand in less than seven years. He was also deeply involved in global affairs as vice chairman of the United Nations Association, through which he led eight citizen inspection tours of UN peacekeeping operations in the 1990s. Bill saw untapped potential in Chicken Soup for the Soul Publishing and asked me to help him acquire it. My daughter, Lori Christina, who believed deeply in the message of the book, and I became two of Bill's earliest investors. I'm glad we did: under Bill's leadership, the company has become a fast-growing global life improvement brand, with more than two hundred titles around the world. It's not just a success, it's a cultural phenomenon—one that Lori is still involved with today as a member of the board.

During the presidency of George H. W. Bush, I even got involved in an effort to improve America's schools. A 1983 report by the Reagan administration had sounded alarm bells that schools weren't preparing students to compete in the global economy. One BENS member who was deeply involved in education reform was David Todd Kearns, the CEO of Xerox. Wesray Capital Corporation founder Ray Chambers, CEO Josh Weston of ADP, and I had driven together to Xerox headquarters in Connecticut to recruit him. After joining BENS, Kearns began reaching out to fellow business leaders, including me, to get involved in a private nonprofit called the New American Schools Development Corporation, which was supported by the Bush administration.

Over the course of a few years, we met regularly—including meetings at the presidential retreat at Camp David—to identify and fund what we called "break-the-mold designs" to reform America's public schools. A key part of our approach was to empower teachers to take even more responsibility for all school functions, and to work with design teams as change agents to reinvent everything from the parent-teacher-school relationship to quality standards. We also created new approaches to increase local discretion over school budgets and staffing. The ideas showed so much promise that Bush nominated Kearns in 1991 to become deputy secretary of the US Department of Education.

But I quickly learned that the Pentagon wasn't the only public institution resistant to change. Holding teachers accountable for higher standards proved to be too much for America's teachers unions, which opposed our proposals at every turn and ultimately killed them.

MY WORK AT BENS produced lots of ripple effects in my life like my Outward Bound trip, side businesses, and work on education reform.

Such unlikely encounters often triggered friendships with people I deeply respected, people whom I had not known prior to BENS but who were models of citizenship for me. They had succeeded wonderfully in business and then resolved to give something back to the world.

One of those people was Roswell "Ros" Gilpatric, who had joined BENS in our early days and who, until his death in 1996, was one of the most respected BENS members in the country. A New York lawyer, Ros had been the deputy secretary of defense in the Kennedy administration and an enormously important man in American history. At the height of the Cuban Missile Crisis in October 1962—when the US confronted the Soviet Union over ballistic missiles it had installed just ninety miles off the Florida coast in Cuba—Ros was the man who dissuaded President Kennedy from invading Cuba, which most military advisors wanted to do, despite the risk of nuclear war. As Kennedy speechwriter Ted Sorensen would later write in *Kennedy*, his memoir of those years, at the most crucial moment of the debate:

> Gilpatric, who was normally a man of few words in meetings with the President when the Defense Secretary was present, spoke up. "Essentially, Mr. President," he said, "this is a choice between limited action and unlimited action, and most of us think that it's better to start with limited action."

Convinced by Gilpatric's reasoning, Kennedy ordered the blockade instead.

In 1993, we honored Ros with an Eisenhower Award Dinner. Among the guests who joined us was one of his closest friends, Jacqueline Kennedy Onassis, who had reportedly dated Ros for a while in the years after President Kennedy's death. At one point during the dinner, she sat next to me to thank me and BENS for honoring her good friend. During the conversation, the former First Lady said something to me that I'll never forget: she told me I was very handsome. I was probably too tanned for people to tell, but I'm sure I was blushing.

For so much of my life, I didn't find much in myself to admire. If

I'm honest, one of the reasons the friendships with people like John Whitehead and Ros Gilpatric have meant so much to me is that they have confirmed my best idea of myself. They revalidated for me the kind of person I have long dreamed of being. Without consciously knowing it, through the relationships opened up by BENS, I've come to understand that having a sense of my own worth—knowing that I was able to attract these kinds of people in joining me to do something worthy—is deeply satisfying to me. I'm sure that sounds awful. After nearly nine decades on this planet, I still don't know where feeling good about yourself or revalidating yourself ends and braggadocio begins.

I'm sometimes embarrassed by my own need for that kind of valida-tion. On the bookshelf behind my desk in Washington sit two beautiful leather-bound volumes. The first was presented to me on the tenth anni-versary of BENS; the second, on the twenty-fifth anniversary. Each is a compilation of letters from other accomplished men and women, all cel-ebrating me and what I did at BENS. Here's one from the legendary John Kenneth Galbraith. There's one from Tom Watson Jr. Here's a beautiful poem about me by Bostonian businessman poet Peter Karoff. Former sec-retary of defense Les Aspin, former World Bank president Jim Wolfen-sohn, legendary television producer Norman Lear . . . and on and on.

Another item I keep close by is a note I received from one of my closest friends in the world, Simon Murray, whom I met on the beach in Phuket. Simon's life story reads like an adventure movie. A British businessman and adventurer, he was, like me, rejected by the parents of the love of his life at age eighteen because he had nothing to offer. Want-ing to prove himself, he joined the French Foreign Legion, serving for five years and fighting in the Algerian War, rising to the rank of colonel. Upon leaving the Legion, he returned to the love of his life, Jennifer, and they were married. He made a fortune in banking and investing, and then wrote a memoir of his time in Algeria, called *Legionnaire*, which is one of the greatest military memoirs I've ever read.

At the age of sixty-three, Simon decided to walk across Antarctica to the South Pole. I saw him the day before he left, at the 21 Club in New York, and I was convinced he was going to die. But two months and 750 subzero miles later, having lost forty pounds, Simon became the oldest man in history to reach the South Pole unsupported.

There's something about that combination of courage and moxie that I really admire. Nick Spencer, a close friend of mine and Simon's, celebrated his seventieth birthday by climbing Argentina's 23,000-foot Mount Aconcagua to raise money for children living in poverty in Asia. Nick's terrific wife, Kai, helped him distribute the funds. Another friend, Scottish-bred British diplomat and scholar Rory Stewart, spent two years walking six thousand miles across rural and often dangerous areas of Afghanistan, Pakistan, Iran, Nepal, and India—the thirty-two days he spent in Afghanistan are captured in his fantastic book, *The Places in Between*—before becoming a member of Parliament. To me, Nick, Rory, and Simon embody a kind of adventurism that never grows old. That's why it meant the world to me when Simon sent me a note that read:

> Hope is the greatest source of energy in our lives, and you unintentionally provide it to everyone who hears about what you have done. You remind me of Ulysses in old age, standing with the windy plains of Troy behind him, with his words brought to us through the moving prose of Tennyson: "Though much is taken, much abides . . . and though we are not now the strength which in old days moved earth and heaven . . . that which we are, we are . . . One equal temper of heroic heart made weak through time and fate, but strong in will to strive, to seek, to find, and not to yield."

Like a retired athlete who looks at his trophies from time to time, or a soldier who polishes his medals, I find that vanity compels me every now and again to flip through these keepsakes.

FOR DECADES, ONE OTHER source of affirmation for me has been a tradition that Lisa and I began in Mexico and San Francisco and carried over to London: hosting dinner parties and inviting interesting people who represent a range of different views and backgrounds. Always small and intimate—ideally, with no more than ten or twelve people—these parties encourage conversations around our table that are far-ranging and almost always unforgettable. And it's all because of Lisa.

My wife plans every single dinner party with a kind of thoughtfulness, attention to detail, and eye for beauty that is rare. When we're in London, she often plans two dinners and one brunch each week with different friends. She actually keeps a log going back for decades of every party we've ever hosted, what was served, which flowers we had on the table, and who sat next to whom. She always brings me in to help decide the mix of guests, a process I loathe and never have patience for, but she never fails to shine: it is one time when others get to see the remarkable elegance and grace that she inherited from her parents, which of course I see every day. It makes me very proud that Lisa's dinner invitations are always one of the hottest tickets in town.

What I like most is that many of our dinner guests have become some of our closest friends. On any given night, we might have the comedian Barry Humphries, playing his alter ego Dame Edna, and his wonderful wife, actress Lizzie Spender. They may be seated near Lord Charles Powell, who served as the private secretary of British prime minister Margaret Thatcher, or Lord Carrington, Thatcher's foreign secretary and the last surviving member of Winston Churchill's cabinet.

Other dinner guests might include the venerable British publisher David Campbell, who relaunched the iconic Everyman's Library series and not only is the curator of some of the world's great books, but can discuss them at length. He does so often, with some very famous authors who have become close friends to Lisa and me—including master storyteller and former spy Freddie Forsyth; British historian Sir Alistair Horne, whose work on Algeria, *A Savage War of Peace*, is an all-time classic; *Wild Swans* and *Mao* author Jung Chang, who is probably the best writer in the world on the evolution of modern China; best-selling British historian and author Adam Zamoyski, who is descended from Polish royalty and has written what is arguably the most comprehensive history of Poland ever; the brilliant author and award-winning former ABC correspondent in the Middle East, Charlie Glass, who was held hostage by Shia militants in Lebanon for sixty-two days in 1987, and who is a frequent houseguest of ours in both London and Gstaad; British journalist, historian, and war correspondent Simon Sebag Montefiore, author of popular histories of Russia and the Middle East that are routinely nominated for top prizes; and Nigerian novelist, poet, and short-story writer Ben Okri, the youngest-ever winner of the Booker Prize for fiction, for his book *The Famished Road,* and one of the best African authors in history, whose work has been compared to that of Salman Rushdie, who is another occasional dinner guest of ours. Ben comes to dinner with his free-spirited partner, the charming British painter and printmaker Rosemary Clunie.

These distinguished guests are sometimes accompanied by my pals Simon Murray and Nick Spencer, who can always be relied on for engaging dinner conversation. They may also find themselves in the company of the gifted Hong Kong businessman and concert pianist Sir David Tang; the celebrated Polish portrait painter Barbara "Basia" Hamilton, who has sketched everyone from Lech Walesa to the Queen Mother to Pope John Paul, and who calls me "Big Stas"; the chief prosecutor at the Nuremberg trials and the long-established historian for the Royal Family, William Shawcross; Alexander Yakovenko, the Russian ambassador to the United Kingdom, and his beautiful wife, Nana; and the globally renowned hotelier Adrian Zecha, who built the Aman brand, starting with the iconic Amanpuri Hotel in Phuket. Also joining us might be famous actress of stage and screen Janet Suzman; former British Army officer, spook, and security firm CEO Tim Spicer, who sometimes plays the part by wearing sunglasses through dinner; Russian Len Blavatnik, who made billions in the aluminum business, and whom I met through veteran British diplomat and former ambassador Sir Michael Pakenham and his wife, Lady Mimi; or Claus von Bülow, one of the best lawyers in the world, who is exceedingly charming and has an endless supply of fascinating stories. He, of course, was the subject of one of the most famous murder trials of the past hundred years, so there is nobody now whose opinion of him is neutral: some people believe he was guilty, and others (like Lisa and I) believe he was innocent and rightly acquitted of all charges. What most people don't know is that von Bülow is a brilliant writer.

Two Americans we've gotten to know better since we've lived in London and I started BENS are recognized for their political work supporting big—and diametrically opposed—ideas: George Soros and David Koch.

Whenever he is in town, the business magnate, financier, and philanthropist George Soros either comes to dinner at our house or invites us to dinner at his. We first met at a cocktail party hosted at the New York apartment of the Bulgarian political refugee and author Stephane Groueff, when Soros was making a name for himself as a hedge fund manager before most people even knew what hedge funds were. After that, we got together from time to time at his place in the Hamptons. I remember him once telling me that he was really bothered by the fact that he couldn't see any head of state anytime he wanted, so he decided to break the Bank of England. And that's exactly what he did, by putting in $2 or $3 billion (the equivalent of $20 to $30 billion today) against it in favor of the German deutschmark, causing the British pound to drop precipitously. After that, he could see anybody he wanted to.

Unfortunately, we were never business partners. George, of course, went on to fund a number of candidates and projects for the Democratic Party. I admire him immensely for the work he's done through his Open Society Foundations to advance transparency, democracy, rule of law, and government accountability in more than one hundred countries around the world. We share the same concerns about nuclear danger. He constantly sends me books to read when he's on the road.

Another American whom we've gotten to know is businessman David Koch, who turned the family business he took over with his brother, Charles, into the second-largest privately held company in the US. David was the Libertarian candidate for vice president of the United States in the same 1980 election that I ran Barry Commoner for the Citizens Party, with about the same result. As a younger man, he was a frequent presence in London, often dating young and attractive women, which I used to give him a hard time about. He's become a great supporter of BENS, and we get together in New York. Like Soros, he gives away hundreds of millions of dollars to worthy causes, from cancer research to the ballet. But all he's known for in America is his support for conservative causes. I tell David that he and his brother should let people see more of the good they do in the world, to serve as an inspiration to others.

The countless interesting and important characters Lisa and I have come to know since moving to London and since starting BENS are a constant reminder to me of the long journey I've traveled from my childhood in Philadelphia. But they also do something more: they inspire in me a desire to throw that rope across the next ravine—to constantly do my part, to give back in any way that I can—which has led me into unexpected new places over the past decades.

FORTY-ONE

Growing Our Footprint
Across the World

I n the late spring of 1994, I was invited to breakfast at Henry Kissinger's home in New York. I wasn't really sure why I was invited. Our paths had crossed from time to time over the years, and we were friendly, but we weren't close. When I arrived, I was even more surprised to find there were just four of us present.

I quickly realized why we were there: Kissinger had just returned from South Africa, where he and Lord Carrington were invited to mediate a fierce dispute between the African National Congress and the Zulus, who wanted an autonomous homeland. The discussions had paved the way for Nelson Mandela to be chosen as the first president of post-apartheid South Africa by the country's newly elected Parliament, just four years after Boer president F. W. de Klerk had overseen his release from the jail where he'd spent twenty-seven years as a political prisoner. Kissinger had gathered us there so he could tell Mandela stories.

I guessed that my friend Lord Carrington had said nice things about me to Kissinger and told him that Mandela was a personal hero of mine. That's how I found myself listening to the former secretary of state talk for more than an hour with very few interruptions. He kept saying, "Can you imagine what a thrill it was to meet with Nelson Mandela, Zulu leader Mangosuthu Buthelezi, and President de Klerk? Isn't that extraordinary?"

I'm not sure what compelled me to speak up, but I did—and it ruined his whole fun. "Well, I've met them all, too," I said.

Kissinger shot me a decidedly unfriendly look and said, "You did? When? Where?"

"In 1992, at the World Economic Forum in Davos," I replied. It had been their first joint appearance outside of South Africa and the place Mandela had come to make his first speech on his country's economic future. "I had to pee, and that's where I met them."

Kissinger's look turned quizzical.

I continued, "While I was there, at the next urinal was Nelson Mandela. And next to him was Chief Buthelezi. And next to him was Mr. de Klerk."

On our way out of the men's room, I had mentioned my friend Anthony Sampson, a celebrated writer who was a pal of mine in London and a close friend of Mandela's. At the time, he was working on the icon's authorized biography.

Mandela had immediately asked, "Is Anthony here?"

"No," I'd replied, "but he said I should say hello to you if I got the chance. And I can't tell you what a great honor it is."

After that, Mandela shook my hand, said a few nice things about Anthony, and then left. "And that's my Nelson Mandela story," I finished for Kissinger.

In response, I got only a blank stare.

Granted, my experience wasn't nearly the same as mediating a dispute. But as for anybody who meets a personal hero, it's a moment that was important to me. Maybe I shouldn't have said anything. Either way, I'm still waiting for my next invitation to Henry Kissinger's house.

⁂

IT WAS TOM WATSON who first suggested, in 1991, that I attend the World Economic Forum at Davos, Switzerland. The annual conference had been started two decades earlier by German economist Klaus Schwab as a gathering place for world leaders and elites from finance, business, philanthropy, and entertainment to focus on pressing global challenges. Tom didn't just tell me to go—he suggested both the hotel and the room I should stay in. His insistence persuaded me to see what all the fuss was about.

The group was much smaller in those early years at Davos, and I met a lot of fascinating people in the five or six years I attended, until I stopped going because it became too big. I enjoyed sitting through the discussions, but as usual, Lisa and I loved the social gatherings more— where you might find yourself in a deep discussion on the European Union with Bono, the global activist and lead singer of the pop group U2, or trading views on the economy with the current head of the World Bank. One year, I was even invited by Schwab, who knew and liked what I was doing with BENS, to give a talk on nuclear weapons, which I did.

I also attended, for about four years, the Bilderberg conference, named after the hotel in Oosterbeek in the Netherlands where the first meeting was held. Founded in 1954 in response to growing anti-Americanism in Europe in the wake of the Korean and Cold Wars, the very secretive annual meeting sought to "bolster a consensus around free market Western capitalism and its interests around the globe." Not a word of these discussions every reaches the public. The difference between Davos and Bilderberg is that in recent years almost anybody who paid enough money could go to Davos, but not to Bilderberg. Invitations are extended to about 150 experts from government, industry, academia, and media circles in Europe and North America. I was invited because John Whitehead headed the US delegation and Lord Carrington was in charge of the British delegation.

While Business Executives for National Security—as an organization—does not involve itself in foreign policy issues, governments have relied on organizations and individuals for centuries as alternative channels of upper-level communication. Often foreign government officials will share information with the private sector that they won't share with the US government. At Bilderberg, we are free to ask any questions without creating a diplomatic incident. BENS members are some of

the leading CEOs, financiers, and entrepreneurs in the United States—
people who operate at the highest levels every single day. Weren't these
exactly the kinds of people that foreign leaders wanted to know? Why
couldn't we be a force for positive change in other countries?

At least one other officer at BENS agreed: Josh Weston, who had
given BENS its first entrée to the leaders of the country's major corporations. Like the others who helped BENS begin to take off financially, Josh has always been an entrepreneur at heart, despite the size
of his organization. He is a master fund-raiser for good causes and
became my closest, most relentless long-term partner in making sure
that BENS remained self-funded by our members. He is also one of the
most energetic, public-spirited, and creative persons I have ever met.
Josh believed we could do more to affect policy at the source of conflict
around the world, rather than simply helping America prepare for its
consequences. It was Josh who introduced me to one of the most interesting men I've ever known, a man who not only shared that vision, but
would become one of the central players in helping BENS grow our
footprint around the world: Raphael Benaroya.

An Orthodox Jew who was born in Jerusalem, Raphael fought in
two Israeli wars in the 1960s before making his way to America. He
graduated from the University of Minnesota with business and computer science degrees, and then went on to make a fortune in retail,
fashion, consumer brands, wealth management, and financial services.
His list of humanitarian and other civic commitments is more than two
pages long. He is the absolute model of a modern citizen-soldier, a man
who has never stopped giving back, not only to his home country but
to his adopted one too.

When we first met, Raphael and I talked for more than three hours
straight about foreign policy and national security, spending half of that
time discussing why and how the United States chooses to sanction certain nations, and why those sanctions so often are self-defeating. Not
long after, on a flight aboard a KC-10 refueling tanker to visit the US
Air Combat Command at Nellis Air Force Base in southern Nevada,
Raphael asked me, "How do you define national security?"

This kicked off another debate, of course, and we settled on four pillars: a strong military, a strong economy, strong foreign relations, and the quality of discourse within a country (although I made a strong push for including intangibles such as a strong education system too). As BENS had proven over the previous decade, we knew that our members could make an impact on all of those pillars—both at home and around the world.

We talked about where BENS might focus our attention. At the time, the United States military was positioned to fight and win battles simultaneously in two major regional conflicts. The real-world test for the White House and top policy makers proved more troublesome in Iraq and Afghanistan in the twenty-first century and certainly left more questions unanswered than answered. But as an organization, we agreed that it made sense for BENS to understand more about the high-sensitivity areas around the world. Those hot spots were the Middle East and India–Pakistan.

One thing we all agreed on: BENS was not going to be a travel agency for globe-trotting CEOs. Each BENS trip would have a specific purpose. The goal was to connect with people of influence, to create relationships that could be multiplied and expanded later in ways that advanced America's national security interests and goals. It wasn't enough to seek out meetings with other industry groups just because we were businesspeople. If we wanted to have real impact, we needed to come in at the level of the national security infrastructure of the nation we were visiting.

On the way back from Nevada to Washington, Josh and I asked Raphael directly: "Why don't you organize a trip to Israel?"

He agreed. It was that trip that set the tone for every other BENS trip to follow.

⁂

BEFORE LEAVING FOR ISRAEL, Raphael looked intently at Lisa, who was not taking the trip with us, and said, "I'll protect him. Don't worry."

It was the only time I ever remember getting furious with him. I said, "I don't need your protection." I might have even thrown in a few more colorful words. But I knew he meant well—and in truth, there are much worse people to have defending you than a six-foot-two-inch former commando of the Israel Defense Forces.

It was April 1996. The very hopeful new beginning between Israel and the Palestinians that came out of the landmark Oslo Accords signed on the White House lawn—and the unforgettable handshake between Israeli prime minister Yitzhak Rabin and PLO chairman Yasser Arafat—was two and a half years behind us. Seven months earlier, in September 1995, another agreement signed by Rabin and Arafat at the White House had given Palestinians control over the vast majority of the West Bank. A little more than a month later, on November 4, Rabin had been assassinated in Tel Aviv by an Israeli ultranationalist crazy who deeply opposed the peace initiative and the Oslo Accords. The acting prime minister, Shimon Peres, vowed to continue Rabin's efforts toward peace.

We arrived at the same time that Israel and Lebanon were negotiating an agreement, brokered by the US, to end a sixteen-day border conflict that had seen Hezbollah missiles launched into Israel. In keeping with our goal to engage at the highest levels, our first meetings were with Israeli president Ezer Weizman, Prime Minister Peres, and Defense Minister Moshe Arens, among a dozen other statesmen—not a bad lineup for the first few days of the first trip. In our meetings, we listened and learned, emphasizing the role that industry could play in advancing our joint security. It was plain how much these men all loved and respected Raphael.

The most remarkable part of the trip was a two-day joint patrol we spent with Israeli and Palestinian soldiers on the West Bank. The soldiers were buddies. The Israelis were speaking Arabic; the Palestinians were speaking Hebrew. They laughed and joked with each other. It was a really, really hopeful time.

There was one guy on the trip who stayed on to see more of the country. I ran into him five months later and asked, "How was it?"

Here is what he said:

> Oh, it was wonderful. But I have to tell you a funny story.
>
> When I was leaving—at the airport, of course—they were very careful about interrogating us. An Israeli security agent stopped me and said, "Can you tell me who you saw?"
>
> I said, "Well, I saw the president, the prime minister, the minister of defense . . ."
>
> The woman said, "Look, this is Israel. This is no joke. Who did you see?"
>
> I said, "I saw the president, the prime minister . . . ," and went through the whole thing again.
>
> So she calls a tough guy. He comes over and says, "I don't care if you're an American. This is no joke. Who did you see while you were here?"
>
> I said, "I saw the president, the prime minister . . ."
>
> He said, "Well, listen. You're either going to go to jail or to the VIP room."

By that point, everything had begun to change. A month after we were there, the leader of Likud, Benjamin Netanyahu, narrowly defeated Peres in the Israeli elections by opposing the Oslo Accords. "Land for peace" was dead for three years—until Labor swept back into office in 1999. In the final months of Bill Clinton's administration, Prime Minister Ehud Barak came close to realizing the promise of a peaceful two-state solution imagined by Oslo. In negotiations that started at Camp David and continued in the Egyptian town of Taba, Palestinians were twice offered a solution that met 97 percent of their demands. Both sides declared that they had "never been closer to peace."

But Arafat would never commit. Israel then had an election, negotiations stopped, and the new prime minister had no interest in restarting. Hamas won the loyalty of Palestinians preaching violence and the end of Israel. Then the war in Iraq happened, Syria exploded, and the Islamic State was born. The hope of Taba—which I saw later from the Golan Heights—died. Years later, near Gaza, I returned to hear shells falling on Israel. In the fifteen years that have passed since the failure of Taba, more than 1,200 Israelis and 9,400 Palestinians have been killed, a continuing tragedy made all the more heartbreaking by the memory of how close the two sides came to ending the conflict altogether.

But if and when Israelis and Palestinians decide to try again, they will face the same land, the same choices, and the same history they faced in 1995. When they do, I know we will be there to help—as we've quietly done in numerous ways for more than twenty years since that first trip. And Raphael Benaroya will be first in line.

⁂

IN MY OFFICE, I have a copy of a story that ran in the *Calcutta Telegraph* in India on September 26, 1997. The lead reads, "Why did the United States president, Bill Clinton, undoubtedly one of the busiest heads of state, seek a meeting with the Indian prime minister, I. K. Gujral, in New York (at the United Nations)? The answer is a four-letter word: BENS. Business Executives for National Security."

That's my kind of four-letter word. Our trip to India in the summer of 1997 was the most successful of our BENS trips and the ultimate validation of why we began taking them in the first place. It was also on this trip that we came the closest to getting the US ambassador fired.

Four years before the end of the millennium, the United States still treated India with a contempt unbecoming the oldest democracy in the world. The Cold War was to blame: India was the archenemy of Pakistan, America's pal during our fifty-year standoff with the Soviet Union—helpfully providing a base for America's U2 planes to spy on Moscow and to smooth relations with China, while unhelpfully giving birth, with Saudi Arabia's help, to the Taliban. Meanwhile, India was Russia's pet. But even though India and Pakistan had been literally separated at birth back in 1947, half a century later, India, as I wrote back in 2000, had "one foot firmly planted in the twenty-first century" whereas Pakistan had "both feet planted in the past."

A little more than a year after our trip to Israel, BENS arranged for a delegation to spend what the *Calcutta Post* would later call "a week of give and take with almost every major military and political figure in India." When we arrived in Delhi, I insisted that we begin by visiting the American ambassador, Frank Wisner. A longtime member of the US foreign service who had previously served as the US ambassador to Zambia, Egypt, and the Philippines, Frank was a close friend of a good friend of mine, author Larry Collins. Larry had introduced me to Frank and his wife ten years earlier, when Frank became America's ambassador in Cairo, and we had been friends ever since. I knew that if anybody in the country could tell us what was what, it would be Frank.

We had heard that the Bharatiya Janata Party (BJP), seen as an extreme-right Hindu group, might soon assume power in India, and we wondered what Frank thought. He told us that the BJP wasn't as bad as its reputation suggested, and that he could help arrange a meeting with Jaswant Singh, who was soon to become the finance minister in the new administration of Atal Bihari Vajpayee. In fact, Frank was very helpful in introducing us to many Indian leaders, including Commodore Uday Bhaskar, a veteran commander in the Indian navy who was still deeply involved in the natural security infrastructure. While Frank opened many doors for us on the political side, Uday helped introduce us to current and retired military leaders, many of whom remain our very good friends to this day.

But then I asked Frank a more pointed question: "I don't know very much about any of this, but why does America have India and Pakistan hyphenated?" Every time the US sends a representative to one of the countries, we have to send someone to the other. They are not Siamese twins. On the contrary, they're totally different, and lumping them together is a great mistake.

Indeed, Pakistan and India still battle along the Line of Control, the de facto international border between the two in the disputed Kashmir region, which some of us were hoping to visit. Jim Kimsey, the cofounder of Internet service pioneer America Online, wanted to travel there to see where all the fighting happened. A West Point graduate who had served three combat tours of duty as an Airborne Ranger, two in the Vietnam War, Jim was as tough as they come. But Frank wouldn't approve the visit.

Jim was also a lovable rogue. Finally he said to me, "Let's hijack a helicopter. I can fly it, and we'll go out there."

Frank got word of Jim's idea and said, "Stanley, tell Jim not to do that. You're going to make me lose my job."

I had to tell Jim, and he was genuinely hurt. But he finally stopped threatening to steal a chopper.

The more people we met with, the more it seemed crazy that no American president had visited India in nearly twenty years. We suggested that Frank should send word back that the president should come for India's golden jubilee celebration of its independence that year, and that we would work for the same change from inside Washington.

When we returned home, Raphael and I both felt that we could help change American policy. In March of 1997, I began writing a series of columns on India, arguing that "the elephant is beginning to move"; asserting that it was long past time to "de-hyphenate India and Pakistan" and treat them as separate countries; and lobbying the White House with the perspective that history would remember Bill Clinton fondly if he restarted the United States' friendship with India. We argued that the place to start was a meeting in New York during the United Nations General Assembly in September.

It would take three years—and a tense standoff between the US, Pakistan, and India in 1998 as Delhi successfully tested its first nuclear weapon—but the administration would eventually accomplish exactly what we hoped it would do.

During a follow-up trip to India during the Bush administration in the early 2000s, one of our tasks was to find out why the Indian Parliament was balking at approving a civil nuclear agreement Bush had negotiated with India's government. It was a breakthrough agreement with a nuclear power that was one of only four nations that had not joined 191 other signatory nations on the Nuclear Nonproliferation

Treaty, created in 1968 as a means to prevent the spread of nuclear weapons while promoting cooperation on nuclear energy. Again, the BENS trip proved the private sector can often learn things that our government officials cannot. We were able to report valuable information back to Washington that ultimately led India to approve the deal.

In 2009, the new US president, Barack Obama, made good on one of our earlier calls to action and restructured the State Department to remove the hyphen between India and Pakistan. Some of the most prized possessions that Raphael and I share are letters from officials and friends in India thanking us for playing an important role in changing American-Indian relations. I've been proud to return to India every year since 1997 with Lisa, meeting with old friends and new friends while writing more than fifty related columns in that time span.

I worry increasingly about Pakistan, which, with the help of China, will soon be the world's third-largest nuclear power and the only one with Islamic terrorists routinely roaming freely around questionably guarded nuclear facilities. I believe Islamabad must get on with the work of pulling itself together and stop using India as an excuse for investing billions of dollars of US aid in its military at the expense of hospitals and secular schools.

Did we really make a difference in India? Yes, I think we did. At the very least, we proved that members of BENS have a reach that goes well beyond the United States—and will continue to play an important role in the years to come.

∞

SINCE 1997, I'VE TAKEN many trips privately and with BENS to hot spots around the world. I saw ugliness in Afghanistan and some of the saddest human tragedies in Rwanda. BENS made emergency trips to help Haiti, and Lisa and I sought to understand the changes sweeping across Iran. We've seen Indonesia grow into the largest and strongest Muslim-majority democracy on earth. Some of the most memorable moments came during trips to Europe and Africa, hosted by the

European Command, the US military's authority in the region. One traveling companion I always enjoyed on those adventures was Ramon Marks, a retired senior partner and influential attorney at Washington powerhouse Arnold & Porter, and—from my perspective—the full package: the perfect combination of brains and fun. Ramon, who once obtained a record amount in punitive damages against Saddam Hussein for fraud and abuse, brought top-notch strategic insight as a member of the BENS board for more than two decades.

One memorable experience was a trip Ramon and I took to Africa with Andrew Young, a hero of the civil rights movement, who had served as the US ambassador to the United Nations during the Carter administration. On the plane between stops, Young and Ramon bonded over a long conversation, which Ramon later recounted for me. Young told him about visiting the home of his future wife, Jean, in Marion, Alabama, while they were college students in the early 1950s. Young was sitting at the kitchen table with her good friend, Coretta Scott, when in walked Coretta's boyfriend, a young man named Martin Luther King. That day, at the kitchen table, Young and King started talking for the first time. Young would go on to serve as one of King's principal lieutenants throughout the 1960s.

He also shared memories of what it was like to be with King on the day he was assassinated. Young had been at a Memphis court much of the day, where he was the point person negotiating an end to the restraining order that had halted a march for striking local garbage workers. Young said that when he returned to the Lorraine Motel to debrief King and the Reverend Ralph Abernathy on his progress, they both attacked him with pillows, which launched a huge pillow fight. A few hours later, Young was dressed for dinner and waiting for King in the parking lot when he heard what he believed to be a car backfiring loudly. He looked up to see King slumped on the room's balcony. It was, he said, the worst day of his life.

While Ramon grew fond of Andy Young, I can't say that I shared the same feelings for the man. I couldn't have been less impressed. While sitting together on the plane, Young told me about his admiration for

Zimbabwe's dictator, Robert Mugabe, who was known for committing horrific human rights abuses. I asked how he could defend a man who drove thousands of white farmers off land they had owned for generations—killing many—while turning what had been Rhodesia, the breadbasket of Africa, into a country that had to import food to feed its own population. When Young angrily replied that many fewer whites were killed in Zimbabwe than in neighboring South Africa, any personal relationship between us disappeared. I couldn't believe that this civil rights hero was a bagman for one of Africa's most despicable autocrats.

Later, at a dinner for the president of Cameroon, we all sat at a long table and I heard Young suggest that we change our name to Business Executives for *Global* Security. I couldn't resist. "Sure," I said, "BEGS!"

SINCE THE TERRORIST ATTACKS on the United States on September 11, 2001, BENS has also traveled repeatedly to the Middle East, including Turkey and Iraq.

We first visited Turkey in 2002, just months before the US led an allied invasion of Iraq to topple the government of dictator Saddam Hussein. The Turkish Parliament was signaling that should there be war, Turkey would not permit US troops to use the northern border it shared with Iraq, or to stage attacks from America's Incirlik Air Base in southern Turkey. Despite being a longtime ally and NATO partner, Turkey—which had been a secular democracy since the end of World War I—was increasingly falling under the sway of strident Islamist Recep Tayyip Erdoğan, who identified more with the Muslim Brotherhood than with Western powers and who would begin a decade-long run as prime minister in 2003 before assuming the presidency in 2014.

As with previous trips, because we belonged to the private sector, we were free to ask questions without creating a diplomatic incident. We received valuable insights on an evening dinner cruise along the Bosphorus with senior officials. A frequent and valued participant on many BENS trips, including this one, was another trusted member of the BENS board named Mary Boies, the chair of our Executive Committee and half of the formidable power couple that she made up with her husband, David Boies, one of America's most prominent and respected attorneys. At dinner parties hosted at Mary's house, I have gotten to know a number of America's defense leaders—including four-star General David Petraeus, the former commander of US Central Command and the successful commander of US forces in Afghanistan, and four-star General Jim Jones, who served as Marine Corps commandant, Supreme Allied Commander Europe, and President Obama's first National Security Advisor. A whip-smart trial lawyer in private practice, Mary would prepare in advance and study everything she could find about the people with whom we met. She had a gentle—and lethally playful—way of asking questions.

At one point during our trip, we met with senior leaders from the Turkish military. It quickly became clear to us that the Turkish general in charge of the meeting thought Mary was only there to pour coffee. He made a statement about US and Turkish capabilities, and Mary gently asked a question. When he answered in the most condescending, dismissive way possible, she responded with more detailed information about Turkish military capabilities than our entire delegation put together could have done. The Turkish general then gave us a straight answer.

Mary had spent the previous three decades being underestimated by adversaries until they had dug a hole too deep to escape. It was no accident that when the trip ended, we were able to pass along information to Washington that helped policy makers understand the changes that were under way in the Turkish government.

⁂

FOR MANY YEARS, MARY was one of the only women to join us on our trips, and we didn't hesitate to haze her. In Algeria, a dinner hosted by the government included a whole roasted goat displayed on a large table. After we were instructed to tear off parts of meat with our hands, several of us noticed that Mary initiated any conversation she could, as far from the table as she could.

The first BENS trip to Iraq occurred shortly after the country was invaded on March 20, 2003, and the government of Saddam Hussein had fallen on April 9. General John Abizaid, then commander of the US Central Command, which oversaw military operations in a twenty-seven-country region including the Middle East, had asked us in late March to visit. When we invited Mary to join us on the trip, she asked, "Yes—but what for?"

We responded that General Abizaid said he was receiving only good news from his staff and wanted an independent evaluation to determine, as he put it to us, "whether we are getting drunk on our own whiskey." As America and the rest of the world soon learned, his fears were well founded.

We went to Iraq hoping to learn that the war was going well. Whether we supported the war or not was irrelevant. We wanted US policy to succeed. It was apparent to us within an hour that Iraq was "about to blow," and we reported back as much, with specific recommendations, to the State Department, the Defense Department, General Abizaid, and the White House. Some were even adopted—but not enough to prevent President George W. Bush, less than a month later, from delivering a speech while standing on the deck of the USS *Abraham Lincoln* in front of a giant banner that read *MISSION ACCOMPLISHED*. US combat operations in the war would stretch on, officially, for another seven years—and unofficially, to this day.

Five months later, during an October 2003 trip to northern Iraq, BENS was in the field at Mosul. We were running behind schedule for a quick trip planned to Baku, Azerbaijan, a few countries to the north of Iraq, to visit its new president, Ilham Aliyev. By late afternoon, everyone was still in field dress and very dirty. Early prototypes of the army's new armored fighting vehicle, known as the Stryker, had just arrived in Iraq, and we had spent the day in areas that were very hot and sandy. When the group finally boarded the plane, it was so behind schedule that there was no chance to clean up and dress at the hotel before meeting with the new president.

It was decided that everyone would change into proper suits on the plane, without showering. The president and CEO of BENS at the time, General Charles Boyd—a highly decorated combat pilot, a veteran of the Vietnam War, and the only former Vietnam prisoner of war to earn the rank of four-star general—directed Mary to go to the cockpit so we gentlemen could change clothes, which she promptly did.

On her return she said it was her turn to change into a dress.

"Impossible," said General Boyd. "We can't all fit in the cockpit."

"But, General," Mary replied, "you can direct all eyes forward, and I can change in the back. I don't meet with country presidents while wearing pants, let alone dirty ones." And that is exactly what happened: she changed clothes in a planeload of men.

Four years later, on another trip to Iraq, sponsored by then chairman of the Joint Chiefs, Admiral Michael Mullen, we participated in a briefing he received about the lack of progress in setting up a banking system in Iraq. Joining us on the trip was Hank Greenberg, a BENS member and former chairman of the New York Federal Reserve Bank, who was then head of the head of global insurance giant AIG. Hank asked whether anyone had contacted the New York Fed, reminding the group that when the Russian banking system had collapsed in the early 1990s, the Fed had sent experts to help the banks quickly reestablish function. Admiral Mullen responded and, within moments, Hank was on the phone with the New York Fed, which immediately dispatched experts to Iraq.

The Iraqi banking system improved for a while, and if today Iraq has no functioning banking (or any other) system, it wasn't for the lack of expert advice and effort.

⁂

WHAT I REMEMBER MOST about the trip we took to Kosovo, during a dreadful time in that nation's history, is that we spent an evening on patrol wearing our pajamas under uniforms.

All of us on that trip had served in the military. Landon Rowland, my good friend from Kansas City and a legendary philanthropist and entrepreneur, and I were asleep in our bunks when we got called out of bed to go on patrol. We put on fatigues, and the next minute we were marching. We called it the pajama parade. We weren't even armed.

As is the case with all of these trips to hot spots, we enjoyed meeting American soldiers in Kosovo, but Raphael Benaroya has always been the one who stays in touch. He has huge binders full of emotional letters from soldiers around the world. Over the years, he has helped more than a few of them with college and even with scholarships for their kids. After Kosovo, he brought three local soldiers to America so they could experience our democracy for a while.

Raphael has fulfilled the original vision of our trips abroad in ways that are hard to comprehend today. He is regularly contacted by high-ranking officials in countries like Egypt, where he is often trusted to pass along sensitive information that is in America's national security interest. He occasionally even meets with foreign leaders; one memorable meeting was with Syrian leader Bashar al-Assad, years before Syria's horrific civil war began in 2011, when Assad was begging for interaction with Washington and America no longer had an ambassador in Damascus.

Raphael said to Assad, "You should know that I was born in Israel."

To which Assad responded, "Did you think I didn't know?"

I guess word gets around when you're making a difference. I like to think that BENS—and the personal trips taken by Mary, Ramon, Raphael, and many others—had something to do with that.

FORTY-TWO

Looking in the Mirror

I looked into the mirror, readying myself for the evening. I was in a reflective mood as I reached for my favorite cuff links, a gift from Lisa long ago.

The invitation had gone out months before on white linen paper embossed with gold lettering. It read: *Please join us for the twenty-fifth anniversary celebration of Business Executives for National Security as we honor our founder, Stanley A. Weiss.* My role as BENS's chairman had consumed me for a quarter century. Now, on May 7, 2007, I was stepping aside, handing my baby to successors I trusted, and taking the honorary title of founding chairman.

It was hard to believe that twenty-five years had gone by so fast. We had lived through the end of one era and the beginning of a remarkable new one. The Cold War had come to an end with young Germans wielding pickaxes atop the Berlin Wall. As former communist nations sought to build a future apart from the crumbling Soviet Union, the governments of Europe sought to build their future together, joining in a historic union for the twenty-first century—a new union that was quickly challenged by the familiar specter of war driven by ancient hatreds in the Balkans.

A world defined for half a century by two superpowers had given way to a world driven by one, with America emerging as the strongest economic and military power the world had ever seen. At the end of a millennium that stretched from William the Conqueror to William

Henry "Bill" Gates, American genius sparked a new global information revolution, as the Internet and digital technology brought us together in ways we had never imagined before. That revolution gave rise to emerging economic giants such as China and India—but also to a dangerous new generation of radical Islamic fundamentalists who targeted the West in deadly new ways.

As a man who very likely would have met an early end six decades before, had two atomic bombs not fallen first, I felt very lucky to have lived long enough to see a new century. I also felt the sting of irony that the preceding twenty-five years of that life would have been dedicated to eliminating these very kinds of weapons. Nor was it lost on me that a quarter-century journey that began for BENS during the presidency of Ronald Reagan was now marking its silver anniversary under the vaulted glass ceilings of the Ronald Reagan Building and International Trade Center in Washington, DC.

More than anything, I felt a profound sense of gratitude. Organizations come and go in Washington, but to last a quarter century during a time of such immense change was something that made me proud. I felt extremely fortunate to have worked with five terrific CEOs in that time.

Lieutenant Colonel Ty Cobb, who had served as part of the National Security Council during the Reagan administration and was highly regarded as an expert on the Soviet Union, was the first to lend his experience and prestige to our then fledgling organization.

Lieutenant General Tom McInerney, a deeply respected pilot who had flown more than four hundred combat missions during the Vietnam War before serving both Vice President Al Gore and the secretary of defense in leadership positions, helped see us through the end of the millennium.

General Chuck Boyd, our first four-star general, had a reputation as a terrific strategist and an insightful leader who had recognized new terrorist threats taking shape before most others did.

Still to come after the silver anniversary evening in 2007 would be General Montgomery C. Meigs—a decorated thirty-five-year veteran of the US Army who had served with distinction as a reconnaissance troop commander in Vietnam, as commander of the Iron Brigade of the First Armored Division in Iraq during Desert Storm, and later as commander of the US Army in Europe and commander of NATO's peacekeeping force in Bosnia—offered his vast knowledge and experience on national security to BENS's work on new threats.

General Norty Schwartz, our second four-star CEO, would follow General Meigs in that role. Norty had served as the chief of staff of the Air Force, where he was responsible for more than 680,000 airmen, and brought his talent for leadership and organization to BENS in 2013.

It filled me pride to know that some of our nation's greatest leaders would move from the Pentagon to BENS—and that a few truly remarkable men and women would make the same journey in reverse. Little did we know on the evening of our silver anniversary dinner that within a decade, BENS would achieve what is a rare and historic achievement for a non-governmental organization: that two former BENS staffers would receive Senate confirmation and simultaneously run branches of the United States military. In 2013, former BENS executive vice president and chief operating officer, Deborah Lee James, would be confirmed as America's twenty-third secretary of the Air Force. Three years later, former BENS senior vice president for strategic development, Eric Fanning, would be confirmed as the twenty-second secretary of the Army.

I also felt gratitude for the remarkably talented professionals who had lent their time and experience to advancing the BENS mission while serving on our board. Investment advisor Denis Bovin had mastered defense policy with the same skill he had conquered Wall Street, which he left to oversee MIT's $17 billion endowment. Denis was also named one of the world's forty Most Influential People in global defense, aerospace, and national security by *Defense Daily*. Bill Murdy, the former CEO of Comfort Systems and chairman of the Thayer Leader Development Group, dedicated to building future leaders grounded in the US Army leadership philosophy, had brought the same commitment to BENS that he gave to America as an officer in

392 STANLEY A. WEISS

the 173rd Airborne, where he had served two tours in Vietnam, and the 82nd Airborne, where he served in the Dominican Republic. Meanwhile, Bruce Mosler, the chairman of global brokerage for Cushman & Wakefield, the world's largest real estate services firm, and a founding member of JP Morgan's 100,000 Jobs Mission—which has helped more than 100,000 US veterans get hired by some of America's most influential companies—had guided BENS as chairman of the board. Along with board members Mary Boies, Raphael Benaroya, Ramon Marks, and Norty Schwartz, they were a group worth celebrating.

But what, exactly, were we celebrating? What difference had we made in our time? "We do not remember days," the Italian novelist Cesare Pavese once observed. "We remember moments." As I fiddled with the knot of my tie in preparation for the evening ahead, it was moments that came rushing back to me.

I remembered the slide show presented by Bill Perry, a brilliant engineer and businessman who had served as the secretary of defense under Bill Clinton from 1994 through 1997. Perry had used the Nunn-Lugar Cooperative Threat Reduction Program to denuke the former Soviet Union's strategic missile force. He had come to a BENS dinner eleven years earlier to celebrate the two senators, Sam Nunn and Richard Lugar, for creating the program and to thank BENS for supporting it. I remembered sitting between Nunn and Lugar as the lights dimmed so we could see the snapshots Perry had taken on his many visits to Ukraine. They made clear, step by step, how Nunn-Lugar worked.

The first slide showed a fully armed SS-18 intercontinental ballistic missile, still in its silo, still aimed at us, still armed with the Soviets' most powerful nuclear warheads.

The second slide showed us the same silo a year or two later, empty, its missile carted off and destroyed, its warheads gone, disarmed.

The third slide showed a patch of sunflowers growing where the silo had been filled in.

Perry, a master of clarity, explained how he used American cash from the Nunn-Lugar program to support the process of irreversibly dismantling a major part of the Soviets' nuclear threat. This effort ensured that not even one of those nuclear weapons could be ever used by accident or in anger.

As I listened, I remembered that twenty-five years earlier I had hoped business leaders could help reduce the danger of a nuclear war by insisting that our policy makers think about this threat in more pragmatic ways. I didn't know how we would do this. I just intuited that we could. I certainly hadn't imagined then an approach as practical as Nunn-Lugar. But as soon as we saw it at BENS, we embraced it and promoted it. It was a perfect business solution.

As John Kennedy reminded us, victory has a thousand fathers. That night, Bill Perry, Sam Nunn, and Dick Lugar all said BENS had been one of them in this case.

⚬⚬⚬

THAT EVENING, I ALSO remembered the moment Fred Webber said, "We're in."

Fred was a Yale graduate and Marine Corps colonel who had served five years of active duty in the 1960s, first as an officer during the Dominican Crisis in 1965 and then as an artillery battery commander in the Second and Third Marine Divisions. He later served as the CEO of the Chemical Manufacturers' Association (CMA), which is the role in which he would become known to me.

I had given no thought to the threat of chemical weapons when I started BENS. But by the 1990s they were proliferating, and bad guys were using them. Iraqi dictator Saddam Hussein had used chemical weapons to kill many Kurdish people in his own country. For the first time since World War I, our own troops in the first Gulf War faced chemical threats. I realized that chemical weapons were the poor man's nukes, and I thought BENS should help ban them.

In early 1997, the US Senate was about to decide whether to ratify the Chemical Weapons Convention, a treaty that would prohibit their production and use. President Reagan had negotiated it. The first President Bush had championed it. The Clinton administration supported it, but then delayed it, ignored it, and politically mismanaged it. So for over four years the treaty had been ensnarled in partisan politics, a presidential election, bitter quarrels among Republicans, and the very personal opposition of Senator Jesse Helms, the chairman of the Senate Foreign Relations Committee, where its ratification had to begin.

When I started BENS, I had wanted the organization to be absolutely political and positively nonpartisan. Now here was an opportunity to use the political clout our members had with lots of senators across the party line, and to draw on the standing we had earned among senior uniformed and civilian defense officials.

We also had the political skills of two premier veterans of Senate debates on national security, one from each party: Larry Smith and his friend, preeminent lobbyist and strategist Jeff Bergner, who had served as staff director of the Foreign Relations Committee and as Senator Lugar's top hand. They came up with a two-pronged plan: an outside game to make the public case for the treaty that the White House hadn't, and an inside game that targeted key senators for our members to lobby.

As muscular as these political assets were, we lacked a critical credential regarding the treaty. From the beginning, I'd wanted BENS to work primarily on matters our members understood professionally. But we had no special credibility about the technical aspects of chemical weapons.

The Chemical Manufacturers' Association did. Fred Webber and the CMA (which is now the American Chemistry Council) had worked closely with American negotiators and helped draft much of the treaty. It was a smart, effective group supported by companies like DuPont and Dow, businesses that knew chemical weapons best and had their own political clout. I thought CMA would be the perfect partner for BENS.

I proposed to Fred that we join forces. I told him each of our organizations had strengths the other didn't. I suggested that merging our efforts would make us more effective than working separately.

When I finished, he shot his hand out to me and said, "We're in."

Our alliance worked wonderfully. Together, BENS and CMA produced a crisp, persuasive case for the treaty. Our combined force highlighted how our organizations were credible in separate and reinforcing ways. We targeted different lists of senators, and our members pitched them with distinct methods and means. The CMA spoke as employers in the senators' states. BENS worked with an impressive set of three- and four-star generals to make the military case for getting rid of chemical weapons.

CMA's support of the treaty had enormous weight, especially with Fred as its primary spokesman. In addition to his credentials as a Marine officer, he was a devout conservative and had worked in the Ford administration and the Nixon White House. He was a formidable advocate, a striking mix of competence and character.

Fred was so effective, the treaty's opponents tried to stifle him. They attacked him from the rear by pressuring his member companies' brass to shut him down, but to no avail. He was tough as nails. He didn't flinch.

The fight came to a climax in April 1997. The outcome of the final vote was uncertain. Republicans stayed sharply divided. It was clear that the treaty's ultimate fate would be decided by Trent Lott, the colorful Republican majority leader from Mississippi. Senator Lott remained uncommitted, and a handful of undecided senators waited for his signal until the very end. Vice President Gore dashed to the Senate, sirens in full cry, as the roll call was being taken, in case his vote was needed.

BENS worked with other supporters to help make the final decisive move. Through a chain of trusted friendships, Senator Lott came to learn that General Norman Schwarzkopf—the United States' field commander in the first Gulf War in 1990—believed "the boys need it." General Schwarzkopf wanted to protect our troops in the future from the kind of chemical weapons that could have been used against them in Iraq.

That did it. Lott and his allies voted for "the boys," and the Senate ratified the treaty.

When I started BENS, my hope was that "alert and knowledgeable" business leaders, as President Eisenhower had pointed out, could politically influence national security decisions. In 1982, this hope was vague, unformed, and amateur. Twenty-five years later, as I mulled over what we had done in solidarity with the chemical manufacturers, I still found much of the politics of the chemical treaty and our role in it a mystery.

But as I reminisced that night in front of the mirror, I knew in my heart that somehow we had helped make our troops and our country safer, as I had originally hoped. And I knew I would always remember Fred Webber as a model of moral courage.

⁂

ANOTHER MEMORY CAME TO me as I faced myself in the mirror: of a cryptic phone call I received from Buzzy Krongard in the late 1990s. At the time, Buzzy—a legendary collegiate lacrosse player who had served as an infantry officer in the Marine Corps—was the third- or fourth-highest-ranking officer at the Central Intelligence Agency. I had met him at a Redskins football game one Sunday some years earlier, where we were both guests in the box owned by AOL cofounder Jim Kimsey, and we had become friends.

"Listen, I'm calling because I'd like you to do me a favor," Krongard had said over the phone.

"What's that?" I'd replied.

"Well, we're interested in setting up a small venture capital fund at the CIA."

"Venture capital fund?" I asked. "Why would you want to create a venture capital fund?"

"Well, this idea is too small for the banks and others to do, but we think it would be kind of fun."

I was curious. "Explain it to me. What would you do?"

"Well, have you ever seen a James Bond film?"

"Of course."

"Do you know the character Q?"

"Of course," I answered. Like every red-blooded American male over the previous half century, I was well aware of Q, the scientific genius who ran the lab that created all the cool weapons and gadgets that James Bond used in every movie, from exploding pens to cars that had rotating razors coming out of the wheels.

"We want to set up something like that," Buzzy said. "And we were wondering if some of your BENS members might be interested in helping."

I told Buzzy that it was the most ridiculous notion I had ever heard. And I promised to help. Within a few weeks, I had brought together twelve BENS venture capitalists. They all loved the idea.

I called Buzzy and said, "Never mind my initial thoughts about it. They think it's a great idea and want to be involved."

Buzzy invited them out to CIA headquarters in Langley, Virginia, just a short distance outside Washington. BENS members agreed to provide the seed money. And that's how the CIA's James Bond–like weapons lab, In-Q-Tel, was born. And now it can be told: the "Q" in "In-Q-Tel" literally stands for "Q" from the James Bond films.

Since then, In-Q-Tel has dreamed up and delivered hundreds of gadgets, innovations, and technology advancements to the CIA and US intelligence agents across the world. My favorite part of the story is that after the company was created, the CIA went to Hasbro—one of the top toy companies in the world—and recruited a longtime friend of mine, the brilliant owner and executive Alan Hassenfeld, to run the operation. After all, they were going to be making toys, so why not recruit the head of a toy company?

*

AS I REMINISCED BEFORE the big event that evening, another moment came back to me. I'd been sitting in an ornate hearing room of the Senate Appropriations Committee one morning ten years earlier, in October 1997, when I saw my original dream of how BENS should work fully realized.

I sat in the middle of a dozen or so leaders of some of America's most innovative companies: Fred Smith of Federal Express, Bernie Marcus of Home Depot, John Morgridge of Cisco Systems. This was a new generation of corporate giants who had created transformational businesses and were igniting a fresh burst of American growth that was reshaping the world's economy.

Secretary of Defense Bill Cohen, the longtime senator from Maine, sat among us at a long conference table that morning. He had been sworn in earlier that year. He leaned forward and told us that although the Department of Defense had reduced its spending almost 40 percent in recent years, its support structure remained bloated. He said he wanted BENS to play an "instrumental role" in reforming the way our military did business. He wanted us to find the best business practices of the country's smartest companies, and he wanted us to help him to get the Pentagon to adopt them.

It was just what we'd been waiting for, and we were ready. Over a year earlier, BENS had created a Tail-to-Tooth Commission at the urging of Josh Weston, who loved the concept of citizen commissions and had served on some influential ones. Josh saw the need for a commission to work with change agents in the Pentagon to install world-class ways of doing business. Our title inverted a familiar military term: the "tooth-to-tail ratio." It meant that we wanted to reduce the costs of support activities (the tail) and invest the billions saved into combat capabilities (the tooth).

The commission was made up of prominent BENS members, especially those who were inventing revolutionary new business practices in their own companies. We recruited as advisors two former secretaries of defense, Bill Perry and Frank Carlucci (who had served under Reagan from 1987 to 1989), and several former members of the Joint Chiefs, all of whom had tried to reduce the costs of the "tail." The former US senator from New Hampshire, Warren Rudman, and Josh served as cochairs.

We knew the challenge of improving the Pentagon's ways of doing business had been studied to death. In the previous fifteen years, there had been eighteen task forces and panels that recited more or less the same list of needed changes. Our commission was different. We focused on how to get these reforms adopted.

When we sat down with Secretary Cohen that morning, we gave him a fistful of action plans for eleven specific reforms. Each was a detailed road map through the maze of bureaucratic and congressional pockets of resistance. Each proposed concrete steps he could take to make the needed changes happen. After all, BENS was a *do* tank.

The session we had with Cohen that morning illustrated the kind of direct exchange I had hoped for from the beginning of BENS. We had executives who knew better than anyone what the secretary and the country needed to understand. Cohen personally picked their brains and tested his own ideas with them. Everyone focused on solving a problem that the country needed to fix. We concentrated on producing results, not just talking.

At one point, Cohen, a published poet and novelist, said he welcomed BENS's help and partnership, because he saw us as "loving critics." His phrase stuck with me. In our early years, some BENS members had wanted us to take a harshly critical line against the Pentagon. I remember the precise words I used in arguing against this approach: "We have to make a decision about whether we're going to throw rocks at the Pentagon or have a seat at the table. If we don't have a seat at the table, we're nothing."

Cohen adopted our work. He called for a "revolution in military business affairs," a play on the "revolution in military affairs," the buzz phrase at the time for smart weapons and the computerization of the battlefield. I was told that people had posted our road map on their walls at the Pentagon.

Secretary Cohen made some progress, but business reform at the Pentagon will always need more work. When the Clinton administration ended, BENS members made a fresh pitch to the new secretary of defense, Donald Rumsfeld, who was equally inspired. On September 10, 2001, Rumsfeld gave a speech in the Pentagon courtyard that contained almost all of what BENS had proposed. It was to be his platform for change for the following four years.

Then fate intervened.

The next day, two planes flew into the World Trade Center in New York, another was flown into the Pentagon, and a fourth crashed into a Shanksville, Pennsylvania, field while on its way to the capital city. The terrorist attacks of 9/11 changed America forever, and with it, the focus of our national security.

⚬⚬

NEXT I REMEMBERED THE moment Ray Chambers told me what he did after 9/11.

Ray had lost friends in the attacks. He was grieving. He was sitting at home across the river in New Jersey, searching the Web. Ray had already made his fortune in private equity, and had been involved with BENS since the late 1980s. Within the next seven years to come, he would raise billions of dollars to try to bring the scourge of malaria to an end in Africa. But that night he was looking for some way that he, as a businessman and citizen, could help make his home state safer. He found what he was looking for: an effort BENS had begun more than two years earlier.

In 1999, although the Cold War had been over for a decade, there were still lots of leftover controversies about how to keep our country safe from the dangers we had known since World War II. Like most engaged citizens, BENS members wanted to weigh in on this cacophony of causes, all well intentioned but largely rooted in the world as it had been, not the world as it was becoming. There was very little fresh thinking in policy circles about the dangers America now faced and what to do about them.

I asked Larry Smith to help us sort this out. He came back with a fresh agenda for BENS, which he labeled the New Tools and New Teams for New Threats project.

Larry warned that our country was now facing new threats that were qualitatively different from those we had confronted for most of our lives. These groups didn't operate as governments or regular armies. We couldn't continue to rely primarily on diplomacy and deterrence as we had in the Cold War, because these bad guys didn't calculate risks and didn't make deals in the same way as the rational actors we were used to.

He said we needed to search for new tools to deal with these new threats. As we did, we would learn that many such tools would require public-private partnerships to work together in nontraditional, unfamiliar ways. BENS's combination of business standing and history of working with government decision makers positioned us to help form these new teams.

We kicked off the project in April 1999 and focused on a targeted list of emerging dangers that fit our model. Banks could help the government refine how we tracked terrorists through their financial transactions. Most cyber systems, even those on which the government depended, were privately owned. Politics as usual wouldn't let you just pass a law to protect them. Cyber security wasn't just the purview of government. The protection of America's energy grid and our ports similarly required the expertise of the private sector.

BENS bluntly warned that the threat of major terrorist activity in the United States was no longer hypothetical. We said it would take the unprecedented cooperation of public and private organizations to protect Americans against such terrorism.

We road-tested these ideas around Washington. No sale. We found that it was difficult, perhaps impossible, for most people to get their mind around the idea that we now faced threats that were categorically different from those we had always worried about. They couldn't conceive that there might be groups of individuals—not countries—who wanted to hurt our country.

Looking back, I guess that wasn't so crazy. It was hard to imagine that a madman, hidden halfway around the world, could direct nineteen other madmen to commit suicide by flying airplanes into some of America's most iconic landmarks. But then it happened for real.

A couple of nights after 9/11, Ray Chambers sat down as his computer, searched for the BENS website, and found our New Threats report. He saw immediately what he could do. He commissioned BENS to design and build a public-private partnership to help New Jersey mobilize for future disasters. And he paid for all of it.

We called it the New Jersey Business Force. We recruited corporations to commit physical resources they used in their business to help communities recover from an attack or other disasters. The state of New Jersey couldn't afford a fleet of trucks to move food to needed areas or a string of depots to distribute lifesaving water and other supplies to families. But McDonald's could. Walmart could. Verizon could. The Business Force worked directly with the governor's office and his emergency preparedness officials to make sure the right resources were prepositioned and exercised.

A decade later, in 2012, the Business Force would help the state recover after Sandy, the largest Atlantic hurricane in history, devastated large parts of New Jersey and New York. Today, this model of a local public-private partnership is at work and spreading in other state business response cells across the country.

Back in 2007, though, I took one last look in the mirror. I was pleased that my original vision for BENS had worked. The idea that we might create something like the Business Force had never entered my mind twenty-five years earlier. I never could have imagined that our country would be attacked the way we were. I was amazed that we had been able to find such entirely new ways to help our country in such a changed world.

I straightened my coat. It was time to leave for the dinner.

PART OF ME SAT back in my chair that night at the packed banquet hall and enjoyed the waves of congratulation that washed over me. I enjoyed being recognized for my role in starting BENS, and I was proud to hear our first twenty-five years of work lavishly celebrated.

Then a wiser part of me realized that what mattered most was not what BENS or I had done in the past, but what our example suggested for the future. I recalled Ike's warnings in 1961 about what threatened us in the Cold War. He seemed eerily prescient about the dangers that now bedeviled us and would do so for years to come: America today is "threatened by the conflict now engulfing the world." We continue to "face a hostile ideology global in scope, . . . ruthless in purpose, insidious in method . . . and of indefinite duration."

I believed this meant that, as far as we could see ahead, we would need citizens who know how to do things government officials and policy wonks don't understand. Our country's security would continue to require the talent of all, in Eisenhower's words, "alert and knowledgeable" citizens.

I knew that we had always depended on the strengths of all Americans and their passion to serve our country in troubled times. But I also knew firsthand how hard this would be to do now. It's out of fashion. We're out of practice.

I hoped others could learn from BENS how to do this in the future. I thought we could be a model for citizens of all walks who want to mobilize what they can distinctively contribute on their own initiative, without waiting for government to ask. I believed this would be BENS's most enduring legacy and its most profound promise.

That night, I went home with something more than a bow-tie around my neck: the Distinguished Civilian Service Medal, given to me by the Department of Defense. I couldn't have felt more proud.

I wished my master sergeant at Fort Knox had been there when I received it. The burly Italian-American from Hoboken had earned his medals the hard way, in combat in North Africa. He saw something in me before I did. He would have been so pleased for me and so proud of me. He would have said, "I knew you could do it."

FORTY-THREE

Bleeding on the Keyboard

When legendary sportswriter Red Smith was asked if turning out a daily column was a chore, he replied, "Why no. You simply sit down at a typewriter, open your veins, and bleed."

Like most people who write, I have certain quirks or ingrained habits for organizing and arranging material. In my case, I have a special affection for brightly colored plastic paper clips (small only), transparent plastic folders (light blue), and red pens (medium point). You'll find all these items scattered across desks, kitchen tables, nightstands, and floors wherever I am staying around the world, usually surrounded by a few dozen newspapers, magazines, and books in various stages of distress.

Long before I ever wrote a single word, I was a read-aholic. I still am. I read between ten and twenty newspapers, magazines, and think tank reports every day, alongside countless ongoing books. But I can't read a single page without underlining important points with my red pen, tearing out articles, paper-clipping them by subject, and then assembling them in their own blue plastic folders.

It's still odd for me to hear friends refer to me as a writer, because for more than half of my adult life, I didn't really write at all. I have written columns for thirty years but didn't write my first one until I was in my fifties. It's not that I didn't want to write. I did, since the time I was a young man. I admired Hans Popper's eloquent way with words. I traded stories with some of America's best columnists and novelists at Trader Vic's. I flirted with buying *Ramparts* partially in the hope that I might get to write. I have listened to and learned from, at my home in London, many best-selling authors who have become close friends to Lisa and me over the past five decades—including Freddie Forsyth, Sir Alistair Horne, Jung Chang, Charlie Glass, Simon Sebag Montefiore, Adam Zamoyski, and Ben Okri.

Although I desired to write throughout all those years, I just didn't. I think I was simply too intimidated. I hadn't even finished college. Trying to write something serious took more courage than I had. As Kenneth Galbraith explained in an interview, the art and skill of writing "involves the terrible problem of thought combined with the terrible problem of composition—and only by the third or fourth draft can [one] really escape that original pain." Many years before, I had inflicted the opposite kind of pain on my English teachers at Central High, who had to endure my artless teenage essays and book reports. I just couldn't express myself very well. I had millions of ideas, but they all seemed to prefer to stay jumbled, and that's usually how they came out.

In earlier years, I did write intimate and thoughtful letters to my family and close friends. I would offer just a line or two, a clever turn of phrase or joke, as though I were at lunch with my columnist pals Herb Caen and Art Hoppe in San Francisco. And when called upon, I never hesitated to write a farewell to a departed loved one. As a last gesture of love in 2001, I wrote the eulogy for my sister, Janice, whom I adored. It began:

> Janice was always late for everything. So, Janice, what was the hurry to get here so early for your next adventure? Well, you always had your own timepiece and compass and marched to your own drummer. This must have been just the right moment to say good-bye.

In 1975, I achieved a personal breakthrough when I wrote and published my book on manganese, a subject I had mastered. It was hard work. But neither my book nor my amusing letters required me to tell a story, construct an argument, develop a theme, or prove a larger point. Unexpectedly, I learned how to do all these things—and got to practice them—during my many trips around the world, both with BENS and with Lisa. Everything I had learned so far, and continued to learn, seemed to equip me for writing persuasive essays and editorial letters.

And newspaper editors began to publish them.

✣

WHEN WE STARTED BENS, I realized that one of the tools we had to use to spread our message was the opinion pages of influential newspapers and journals. If we wanted to attract some of America's most respected leaders while shaping some of its most important debates, it wasn't enough to wait for them to come to us. We had to go to them.

In 1983, as the Reagan administration's tough talk and tough actions when confronting the Soviet Union were about to reach their zenith, I worked with BENS staffer Jim Morrison, a good writer and a patient coach, to put together an op-ed piece for *Inc.* magazine. It described our vision of the world and shared our hope that not even one nuclear weapon would ever be used again. It was well received and even helped attract a major new partner in young entrepreneur Michael Sonnenfeldt, who had graduated from MIT and gone on to make a fortune in commercial real estate in New York.

Three years later, to coincide with the January 1986 BENS dinner celebrating the twenty-fifth anniversary of President Eisenhower's Farewell Address, I wrote a piece in the *Wall Street Journal* on Ike's legacy. Taking issue with those I thought were misinterpreting the speech's most quoted line—which warned that America "must guard against the acquisition of unwarranted influence, whether sought or unsought, by the military-industrial complex"—the piece argued that Ike was making a much deeper point:

> In discussing the military-industrial complex, Ike urged, characteristically, balance of its enormous latent power.

He concluded that section of the speech with an admonition admirable in its clarity and insight: "Only an alert and knowledgeable citizenry can compel the proper meshing of the huge industrial and military machinery of defense with our peaceful methods and goals so that security and liberty may prosper together."

That's not a call for the destruction of the military-industrial complex, any more than it's a call for giving them a blank check. Ike simply reminded us of the need for improved checks and balances, which is as central to our national experience as the Constitution.

The response to the piece was overwhelming. The nicest reaction came from Eisenhower's son, John, who said the piece captured the true meaning of his father's words better than any writer had done before.

Less thrilling, however, was the process of writing the op-ed itself. I came to understand Red Smith's admonition a bit better, because I felt like banging my head against my keyboard. Over time, I would come to learn that there is a formula for the op-eds that run on the editorial pages of our leading publications. You start with a colorful news hook or lead paragraph that engages the reader, establish your argument by the third paragraph, then build out the "spine" of the argument with three additional points before closing with a memorable kicker. If you wanted it to run in one of the big four—which for many years consisted of the *Wall Street Journal*, *Washington Post*, *New York Times*, and *USA Today*—you did it all in 750 words.

After the Ike piece, I began writing about the issues that BENS focused on, from nuclear weapons to defense spending to the need for the Pentagon to stop paying $900 for hammers and start running like a business. That focus continued until the start of the Clinton administration in 1993, when President Bill Clinton introduced the North American Free Trade Agreement, known as NAFTA, which sought to better harmonize the US, Canadian, and Mexican markets. Almost immediately, the labor unions screamed bloody murder, liberal Democrats in

Congress abandoned the president in droves, and the debate over the treaty became a rallying cry for business. It continues today.

Much of the debate focused on the largely tariff-free manufacturing zones in Mexico, known as the "*maquiladoras*," just across the border from Texas. Democratic leaders opposed to NAFTA had found ads in trade publications there urging businesses to move operations from the US to Mexico to take advantage of workers, as the ads claimed, "like Rosa, who will work for thirty-nine cents an hour." Having lived and run a business for years in Mexico, I really know this country and I had a different view: I believed that NAFTA would be good for the United States—as well as Mexico and Canada—and wanted to help it pass.

So, in 1993, I wrote an article making the case for NAFTA. The *Los Angeles Times* agreed to run it. A few months later, I wrote another piece and was thrilled when it was accepted by the *International Herald Tribune*—which at the time was jointly owned by the *New York Times* and the *Washington Post*. The editorial page editor, Bob Donahue, told me he liked the way I used personal and historical stories to make the case, something that would become a hallmark of my writing. Not long after that, the *IHT* solicited a third piece, and then a fourth, and then a fifth—all on Mexico—and I began to become a regular contributor. I would continue writing for the *IHT* for the next sixteen years.

Writing for me was still, as President Bill Clinton once said of Internet censorship in China, "like trying to nail Jell-O to the wall." I'm a very slow learner. I worked endlessly to hone the jumble of stories and facts in my head into a legible column that others would find interesting.

⁂

IN LATE 1997, BOB DONAHUE called and asked me a simple question: "Don't you know about anything other than Mexico?"

I had to laugh. Not only did I know about other countries, but I had noticed a pattern beginning to develop in global reporting—a pattern that began to alter the course of my recurring column. With the economies of Asia asserting themselves more in the global economy, the attention of the West was beginning to shift eastward. But most of the articles being written at the time focused either on the big players, like China, or on the economics of the region, as occurred after the 1997 Asian financial crisis. Less attention was being paid to the geopolitical trends and stories that impacted US national security and foreign policy in countries that were, to American audiences, more obscure. However, those happened to be the exact countries—such as India, Myanmar (which the British and others call Burma), and Thailand—where Lisa and I were now taking annual trips. Bob Donahue's call came just as I was set to head to another country with Lisa, a country that would soon be engulfed in its own crisis: Indonesia.

Lisa and I had been back to Bali more than a dozen times since our first trip in 1984 after Gretl's death. But we had very different ideas about what constituted "fun" on vacations. She had a fondness for things and places; I liked people. While I loved the exotic culture of Indonesia, unlike Lisa, I found there were only so many beach chairs and cremation ceremonies that I could take. So over the years, I decided to become a student of Indonesia. I not only read every book and article about the country that I could get my hands on, but also reached out to contacts I had made through BENS and friends I had gotten to know through my prior trips, to set up meetings with influential people in Jakarta and across the country. It turns out that the talent I'd discovered for making friends and establishing a wide circle of contacts while starting BENS served me well as a columnist too.

I also had, once again, my old friend Luck on my side. After three decades of dictatorship under the strongman Suharto, a military coup in 1998 began a new future for Indonesia, one that I was very eager to help Americans understand. I wrote my first piece on Indonesia for the *New York Times* in the summer of 1998. It sought to explain the key to understanding Indonesian politics while focusing on what the US should and should not do in Indonesia. It began:

> The key to understanding Indonesian politics is the Java-
> nese shadow play called wayang—stories about mythical

battles between gods and kings, good and evil, with the common people standing aside in powerless awe.

A shadow play is more than mere entertainment; it is a deeply ingrained way for Indonesians to view events in their world. The driving force behind each performance is the dalang, the puppet master. He has control over the destinies of the characters.

For 32 years, President Suharto was the dalang, a king who possessed wahyu, the divine light signifying a Javanese leader's power. He ruled his nation as a benevolent despot, consulting frequently with his spiritual advisor and tapping the deep cultural roots of the wayang.

Last year, he lost his wahyu. There were fires, droughts, locusts, and plane crashes. This year, the economy crashed. Now he is gone.

He has been replaced by B. J. Habibie, who appears to be trying to open the way to democratic reform. This new puppet master does not hold all of the strings and seems to be making up his stories as he goes along.

It wasn't a bad piece, and it covered a lot of important ground. But it wasn't until some two years later, in the winter of 2000, when everything finally clicked for me as a writer, in a piece I wrote about an ailing, nearly blind stand-up comedian, and leader of this country's largest Muslim organization named Abdurrahman Wahid—known to all as Gus Dur—who had recently become the new president of Indonesia.

I had met Gus Dur through Dennis Heffernan, an American expat living in Jakarta. During a memorable breakfast on his porch at the presidential palace, he had told a handful of us—including Lisa and my fellow BENS board members Ramon Marks and Raphael Benaroya—about his dreams for Indonesia, speaking in spiritual terms about his plans as president. His idealism was palpable, and while we all wondered how a nation of over 200 million would make the jump from rule by military to rule by spiritualist, I left feeling very optimistic. Turning to my keyboard shortly after our breakfast, I searched for a metaphor that I could use to carry the piece.

Gus Dur was a revered and crafty politician who some believed was a living saint, while others believed he was a puppet—but everyone agreed that he knew how best to work the system. It occurred to me that he was like a chess master, moving pieces around a board. So I brushed up on my chess and ended up writing an article in which each chess piece became someone in Indonesian politics, which I then used to explain the various political machinations of the system.

The piece received a lot of attention and was a huge hit. The important lesson I learned is that good writing is really about good research—and that every article is made stronger when you not only tell stories but take time to explain the history and relationships behind every situation.

Since those first pieces ran, I've become friendly with dozens of ambassadors, journalists, thinkers, businesspeople, students, and politicians across Indonesia—all of whom give me insights and quotes either on or off the record, often telling me stories that they'd rarely relay to a journalist. The opinion pieces I've written about Indonesia in that time, tracing the history of the world's largest Muslim-majority democracy, number nearly fifty, which I have to guess is more than just about any other Western journalist has written. Most of these columns bring the voices and perspectives of Asian leaders to Western readers in ways they haven't seen before. At least one of them got me—or, more accurately, got a future president of Indonesia—in trouble.

The future president was General Susilo Bambang Yudhoyono, known as SBY, and the issue that got us in trouble was America's International Military Education and Training program, or IMET. As I've written repeatedly over the past decade, and said in a column in 2014, IMET was "created in 1976 to strengthen ties between the US and foreign militaries, [and] gives bright young officers from friendly nations the opportunity to study in the US, which, for many, is the first exposure to what a vibrant military-civilian relationship looks like in a free society." When I was running BENS, we became a huge supporter of the IMET program, because in many regions like Southeast Asia that

don't have a long tradition of democracy, it helps expose new generations of potential leaders to the principles of civilian governance, democratic values, and human rights. In its absence, too often, militaries
like the one in Myanmar turn instead to China or even Russia, which
embody very different values that often are the exact opposite of Western principles and interests.

In the early 1990s, the US Congress—led by the senior senator
from Vermont, Patrick Leahy—tied IMET more overtly to promoting
human rights. As I've written more than a dozen times since then, that
decision has ultimately created a catch-22 that undermines our foreign
policy. In many nations where we'd like to influence human rights,
such as Myanmar, the presence of the very behavior that IMET was
set up to change is now a litmus test that *prevents* IMET from being
applied in the first place. I understand that we don't want US tax dollars to support death squads in foreign countries. But in the twenty-first
century, the zealotry with which IMET is being applied by Senator
Leahy and others—which friends in Indonesia refer to as "the selective
self-righteousness of US politicians who deny access to help profession-
alize the militaries of nascent democracies while throwing billions at
serial human rights abusers like Saudi Arabia and Pakistan"—has been
self-defeating at best and delusional at worst.

I got to know SBY when he had become a general and a leader in
the Indonesian military. He had been a young military officer from
Indonesia training in the United States from 1988 through 1991, where,
as I later wrote for the *Huffington Post*, "he parachuted out of planes
with Fort Benning's storied 82nd Airborne and attended the U.S. Army
Command and General Staff College." When he was being talked about
as a candidate for president of Indonesia in 2003, we had lunch together
with our mutual friend and his fellow general, Agus Widjojo. Jakarta
had just experienced a terrorist bombing that killed ten people and
wounded more than 150 others. Talk turned to the IMET program as
a potential antidote for the kind of Islamic radicalism that was growing
across the world and threatening Indonesia. In the *New York Times*,
I wrote:

Lieutenant General Agus Widjojo fondly recalls training with the U.S. Army Rangers, whom he describes as "warriors with a respect for human rights." Susilo Bambang Yudhoyono, a retired general who is now coordinating minister of security and political affairs, speaks of America in glowing terms: "I love the United States, with all its faults. I consider it my second country."

As it wages a global campaign to win Muslim hearts and minds, Washington needs as many Widjojos and Yudhoyonos as it can get. And as Jakarta wades through the dangerous terrain ahead, it needs as much help combating terrorism as it can get.

After that column ran, I learned something about unintended consequences. I had used the quote from SBY because he gave me permission to use it. During the presidential campaign that took shape over the following year, SBY did indeed become a candidate, and the woman who was running against him—former president Megawati Sukarnoputri, the daughter of Sukarno, the country's first president after Indonesia won independence from the Netherlands—used the quote to bludgeon him, repeatedly insisting that it meant he preferred America to Indonesia. SBY won anyway, and went on to serve two terms as president.

When I next saw him in the presidential palace, we had a wonderful discussion. As I was leaving, the president turned to me and said, "Oh, by the way, Stanley—can you do me a favor?"

I said, "Sure, what?"

He replied, "Please don't write about me."

꧁꧂

WHEN I WASN'T GETTING presidential candidates in trouble, I used the same approach to writing that worked in Indonesia in other countries: I ask friends made through my trips with Lisa and through my BENS contacts to secure high-level interviews, and then I write about the interviews. My goal has been to help Western readers understand more about Myanmar, Thailand, China, India, Israel, Palestine, Pakistan, Afghanistan, Turkey, Iraq, Iran, and other countries and governments throughout the entire Middle East and Southeast and Central Asia.

In fact, shortly after I wrote my maiden piece on Indonesia back in 1998, I wrote what would be the first of many columns over the following two decades on the threat posed by radical Islamic terror, tracing the roots of the historic confrontation between Sunni and Shia Muslims and their mutual enmity for the Western world. In 1993, a truck bomb had been detonated by terrorists below the North Tower of the World Trade Center in New York City, taking six lives while injuring a thousand. Two years later, in 1995, a Kuwait-born operative who had spent time in Afghanistan, Ramzi Yousef, was arrested and charged with masterminding the bombing. For the first time, an American president, Bill Clinton, signed a directive that labeled terrorism not just a crime, but a national security issue. That same year, authorities identified a connection between Yousef and a Saudi national who had fought with Pakistan's Muslim warriors in the mujahideen against the Soviet Union in Afghanistan in 1979, and who was believed to be the leader of a Saudi-financed terrorist group called al Qaeda. His name was Osama bin Laden.

In August 1998, bombings at the US embassies in Kenya and Tanzania were linked to al Qaeda, drawing a swift US response, as sixty-six cruise missiles exploded on and around bin Laden's suspected hideout in Sudan, narrowly missing him. I coauthored a September 16, 1998, op-ed with General Tom McInerney, then BENS's CEO, with the headline "The Hunt Is On for Osama bin Laden," which opened with the line, "The United States wants terrorist mastermind Osama bin Laden dead—or alive." It still chills me to think that just three years later, US President George W. Bush would utter those words in the aftermath of the bin Laden–directed attacks of September 11 on the World Trade Center and the Pentagon, in the worst terrorist attack in US history.

A CLOSE FRIEND WHO has read my columns for years likes to say that I work hard to be a provocateur. I'm not much for labels. I work hard to write articles that will, hopefully, inform readers, promote interest, and provide a platform for thoughtful debate and discussion.

After visiting Iran, I argued that engaging Iran politically was good when others said it was bad. More recently, I've said this approach was bad when others said it was good.

I've argued that Turkish president Recep Tayyip Erdoğan was a "brilliant fraud" and an insult to Turkey's secular, democratic tradition, when others still believed he desired to have Turkey join the European Union. I've also continually made the case that America's true friends in the region are the Kurds, whom Turkey has been trying to destroy for forty years.

I've made the case that Russian president Vladimir Putin becomes dangerous in tolerating talk of nuclear warheads as offensive weapons, but I've also written that America should make him feel as important as he needs to feel so that Russia restarts our mutual work to reduce nuclear stockpiles.

I've argued that the United States should reconsider its habitual relationships with "allies" Saudi Arabia and Pakistan, which are two of the most dangerous countries in the world, flagrantly violating human rights in the most vicious ways while sending billions in aid, support, and shelter to violent jihadists across the world.

I've also maintained, since his first year in office, that President Barack Obama has been overmatched in foreign policy, squandering America's historic leadership position around the world and confounding many of our allies while leaving the world a more dangerous place. His failure to intervene in the Syrian tragedy is exacting an even higher price than George W. Bush's interventions in Iraq and Afghanistan.

I suppose the most obvious contrarian position I've staked out over the past decade is in my frequent and consistent criticism of the leadership of Myanmar's Aung San Suu Kyi, who was awarded the

1991 Nobel Peace Prize for her opposition to her country's military long-running junta, which kept her under house arrest for fifteen of twenty-one years after winning and then being denied the presidency in 1990. Barred from running for the presidency by a constitutional provision disqualifying any Burmans with foreign spouses or children (which was drafted specifically for her, since her late husband and sons are British), Suu Kyi won a seat in parliament in 2012 and led her party to win an overwhelming majority of seats in 2016, making her the de facto leader of the country. Many, including Obama, find "the Lady," as she's known in Myanmar, to be one of the world's most inspiring symbols of freedom. All I've seen is a person whose political judgment has been badly flawed and who, to this point, has refused to lift a finger to help any of the nation's 130 ethnic minority groups, including the persecuted Muslim Rohingyas, some of whom have been at war with the Burman majority nonstop since the end of World War II.

Denied basic rights, ethnic groups in Myanmar have seen a slow-motion apartheid develop over the past six decades, one that Suu Kyi has yet to prove she will address with any kind of priority. As I wrote in 2015:

> Suu Kyi's pursuit of the political spotlight has been relent-less—but her use of that spotlight to advocate for some-thing other than herself has been absent. . . .
>
> Maybe being hailed as her nation's savior is more pres-sure than she, or many of us, could live up to. Or maybe the substance of Aung San Suu Kyi never really matched the symbol—and the West would do well to see that Myanmar is much more than The Lady.

It does appear, finally, that Suu Kyi is trying to pick up where her father, national hero General Aung San, left off. In the days after World War II, he convened a tribal summit in the village of Panglong which led to an agreement committing Myanmar to a spirit of equal represen-tation—a future path that was frozen in its tracks when Aung San was assassinated within weeks of the conference. Nearly seven decades later, his daughter will reportedly chair the so-called 21st-Century Panglong

Conference, an all-inclusive round of peace talks and political discussion aimed at making Myanmar a federal state. For the sake of the dozens of friends I've made in Myanmar over the past few decades, I hope Suu Kyi proves me wrong, and becomes a leader as good in practice as in promise.

EVEN WHILE TAKING CONTRARIAN stands, there are three principles I've consistently advocated during the thirty-plus years I've been writing.

The first is that global business can and should be a force for progress, and that economics can overcome rifts between and within countries.

The second is the vital need for US leadership around the world. I believe that the US is still the indispensable nation. I'm not a knee-jerk interventionist, but I am an internationalist who believes the world is better off when America is out in front—whether in the form of dialogue, through trade, by leveraging our investments to achieve outcomes, or just in setting an example through our moral authority. It's impossible to imagine China playing a role even remotely as global as the one America has played over the past seventy years.

The third is that I believe national borders should respect historical realities, and in some cases, we shouldn't be afraid to redraw the map to encourage self-determination. I've argued in many columns and contexts that the world's greatest geopolitical headaches—in the Middle East, Asia, and elsewhere—were caused by colonial powers arbitrarily creating nations with no regard for ethnic or religious background. I realize that there are many people who don't feel it's practical to engage in such discussions, but I believe strongly that a number of ethnic groups should gain their own countries—including Kurdistan for the Kurds, Pashtunistan for the Pashtuns, and even an Iraq that is split up once again along the religious lines that divided it a century ago, when it was ruled by the Ottoman Empire. I argued this line of reasoning in 2014 in a piece titled "Gertrude of Arabia and Her Kurdish Mistake":

> In addition to being a remarkable mountaineer, Gertrude
> Bell was also an Oxford-educated historian, adventurer,

archaeologist, British foreign officer, and spy—a female
Lawrence of Arabia . . .

It was Bell, as an officer of Britain's post–World War I
Arab Bureau, who helped fix the region's boundaries after
France and Britain carved it up in the 1916 Sykes-Picot
Agreement. ("I had a well-spent morning at the office
making out the southern desert frontier of the Iraq," she
once wrote to her father.)

It's a stark reminder . . . that Iraq as it is presently
constituted has had only a brief and haphazard existence.
. . . Astonishingly, if the whole history of Iraq was con-
densed into a single day, modern Iraq—Gertrude Bell's
Iraq—would have existed for only 5.5 seconds.

Since 1983, I've written hundreds more articles on dozens of different topics. I've had the special opportunity to be one of the few Western writers to have consistently written about long-ignored parts of the
world as they go through dramatic change while the attention of the
world pivots to the East.

Without BENS, without my travels around the world with Lisa, I'm
not sure I ever would have found such a public voice. Years ago, the son
of a friend, whom I remember as something of a twerp, wrote a letter to a
newspaper after one of my columns had run, asking the question, "What
the hell does Stanley Weiss know about Asia, and why are you running
his columns?" At the time, it was a good question. Today, however, I'm
proud that I've had the opportunity to essentially enjoy a third career
that tied together elements of the previous two, and to advance the public
debate—all while doing my part to keep up sales of multicolored plastic
paper clips, light-blue plastic folders, and red medium-point pens.

Have my articles made a difference? I'd like to think so. I get a lot
of nice notes every time a column runs. I'm also pretty sure that my
freshman-year English teacher back at Central High would have been
happy to know that all the time she spent trying to teach us to write
eventually paid off for at least one of us.

FORTY-FOUR

Finding Gold After All

One quirk that Lisa and I have always had in common is that we pay little attention to birthdays and anniversaries. But there have been moments that I insisted on celebrating.

Anybody who knows Lisa knows that no secret, detail, or surprise ever gets past her. Yet against all odds, I managed to pull off a surprise celebration of our twenty-fifth wedding anniversary, in Paris. With stealth assistance from our daughter, Lori Christina, who was living in Paris, we organized a terrific evening with family and friends at the super chic à la mode restaurant, Maxim's. It seemed appropriate to celebrate in the city that was practically part of my wedding vows, where I had upheld my promise to take Lisa every year we were married.

On our fortieth wedding anniversary, I went for an encore, this time in Venice—which by then had also become an annual destination of ours. With the help of Lori and two of Lisa's Venetian girlfriends, we conspired with 140 friends, who waited in a darkened room in my wife's favorite palazzo, an incredible old building being sold by our very close friend, Edward Lee Cave, who agreed to lend it to us for the occasion. Inviting Lisa to join me on a romantic gondola ride from our hotel, down our favorite canal, to the palazzo, I then convinced her to sneak inside one of her favorite rooms as though we were teenagers—only to have our friends shower their love on her when the lights came on. We then had dinner at the magnificent Hotel Monaco and Grand Canal, where the terrace was underwater by the time we sat down to eat. It was an evening so memorable that it inspired my son, Anthony, to get married there a few years later.

As our fiftieth wedding anniversary approached in 2008, I felt a strong desire to celebrate once more. Figuring that if I was going to push my luck, I might as well go all the way, I suggested that since we celebrated our twenty-fifth with one celebration, we should commemorate our fiftieth in two different cities. Once she got past her surprise and then amusement and then revulsion at the idea, she agreed. I'm glad she did, because she really shined in both cities.

The highlight of the two nights was the speaking program and the toasts Lisa and I delivered, one after the other, that looked back on our fifty years together. For good measure—*Measure for Measure*, to be exact—I framed mine around a Shakespeare theme. Lisa chose a classic narrative. A friend later observed that hearing them separately was a scream, but thinking about them woven together was a poignant way to think about our relationship, since they were the same, but different.

I liked the idea. When I was working on this memoir, I actually put the two together for the first time. It turns out that my friend was more right than he knew.

Here's what we said the first night, in Paris:

> Stanley: Let's take it from the top. I love all of you, so let me be straight with you. It all started one day when I said, "Lisa, wouldn't it be lovely?" Since she pays no attention to birthdays and anniversaries, she had no idea I wanted to celebrate fifty years. Can you imagine the horror? Fifty years! Having celebrated our twenty-fifth here in Paris, it seemed twice as appropriate to celebrate our golden anniversary—in both New York and Paris.
>
> *Lisa: I am in complete, total denial. This cannot possibly be happening to me. I am reading this because I am not here. I have crawled under the bed. This gathering was Stanley's idea.*

So once I got Lisa to agree, screaming and kicking, it meant sending invitations to the people we love, and that's when the troubles began—finding the place, flowers, music, menus. So I have a confession to make to all of you: Enjoy your meal. It's good wine. I think it's only fair to tell you that Lisa told me just before arriving here, she's filing for divorce.

> *How did these incredible years begin? Well, in 1957, I joined my parents in Mexico City, when two different friends suggested I call a Stanley Weiss. I thought, A total stranger? Never.*

A Marriage, in five acts. You've heard Lisa's version: *A Comedy of Errors*. Now here's my version: *Love's Labor's Won*.

Act I—Mexico City, December 1957.

> *But after three days with my parents, I changed my mind. My timing was exquisite. He was off to New York in two days, and he had just broken up with a girlfriend—I think a bullfighter. We played it safe and agreed to have a drink. He came to my parents' hotel, and I thought,* Pas mal. *(Translation: "Not bad.")*

Enter a man from Philadelphia: daring, dashing, digging for treasure. He discovers that "all that glitters is not gold"—it's *manganese*. Enter a young beauty from San Francisco, a Sarah Lawrence graduate.

> *It turned out my father and Stanley were in similar businesses, liked each other immediately, and two hours later (!) we finally went out for dinner!*

He meets with her parents. Her father approves. Her mother . . . well. From the moment he meets her, he knows—her grace, intellect, and love of life—"this is the woman I'll marry."

> *Off he went to New York, by car and train. He didn't fly. Ironic to think of that now.*

He imagines a life together: *All's Well That Ends Well.* She returns to San Francisco: *Much Ado About Nothing.*

> *Once there, he called and asked if I'd like him to return for New Year's Eve. Yes! So he got back on the train to San Antonio, Texas, then drove twenty-four hours nonstop to Acapulco, arrived, and passed out. I stayed on five more days.*

She wonders: *To marry or not to marry?* That was the question. And he thought: *The lady doth* not *protest too much.* Then a correspondence, love letters, a March visit. On the advice of her father, he starts French lessons.

> *In March, Stanley drove to San Francisco. I think he was there three days. He proposed. I started Spanish lessons.*

Act II—San Francisco, the Palace Hotel, May 23, 1958.

The young bride is stunning, radiant. The groom knows his good fortune. "We are such stuff as dreams are made on."

> *In May, I married this gorgeous stranger. I highly recommend doing it, although if my daughter or son had, I would have killed them.*

She had only two stipulations: He had to learn how to ski. And he had to take her to Paris every year. And to these he would remain ever faithful—starting with the honeymoon.

And then the great adventure began.

In Paris, she introduced him to her old French boyfriends. In Venice, to her old Italian boyfriends. At which point he insisted on a cruise around the Cyclades.

Then, twelve very happy, very fun years in Mexico. Stanley building his minerals business, adding a company in the Soviet Union—even making a film.

Act III—Mexico and Beyond.

His business grew, and so did their family.

We had lovely children.

They were blessed with sugar and spice and everything nice, Lori Christina; and snips and snails and puppy dog tails, Anthony.

Stanley thought the children should have the best education possible.

Their mother insisted they learn Spanish and French. And while you're at it: German, Italian, Russian, Mandarin, Arabic, Farsi, and Hindi. Their father—to understand them—insisted they speak English.

He asked me where I would prefer to live: New York or London? I didn't know London, but I knew it was much, much closer to Paris. Off we went on our merry-go-round.

"All the world was a stage," from Mexico to San Francisco to London to Gstaad. Proud parents: of Lori Christina the filmmaker, of Anthony the executive. And, as we grew older, but never old—"Grandmother?" Never. "Call me 'Mumsie.' Call him 'Pop Pops.'"

More busy years. A friend and another mentor, John Kenneth Galbraith, suggested a year at Harvard's Center for International Affairs. (Not crazy about that one.) Not bad for someone who had never graduated from anywhere. Then Stanley's political journey went on to the birth of BENS.

Act IV—Washington and the World.

When he felt it was time to give back, he created BENS. And since she couldn't stand Washington, she stayed back—in London. Which just goes to show, opposites do attract. She's an introvert. I'm not. She's refined and cultured. I'm not. She's a teetotaler. I've been known to have a drink.

Along the way, I, fortunately or unfortunately, discovered Asia. And Stanley—probably in self-defense, after too many temples and ceremonies—started another career: writing.

On our trips, my idea of a good time? Work. Meetings with ministers and military. Her idea of a good time?

Enjoyment and pleasure. Culture, cuisine, and if we're in Bali: processions, rice paddies, dances, cremations, cremations, cremations.

If I say the following, I might have hysterics.

Act V—well, still to be written.

Lisa, looking back over fifty springs and all the seasons. I call it *A Midsummer Night's Dream*. You might call it *The Tempest.*

What I love and admire Stanley for—aside from intelligence, curiosity, great sense of humor, and being so handsome—is that he really did it. He went, penniless, to Mexico and succeeded. He went, let's say semi-blind, to Washington and achieved what he set out to do, and more.

I can't imagine life without you. I can only wish for twenty-five more springs together. To Lisa, after this fifty-year love affair (as the Bard wrote in Sonnet 104): "To me, fair friend, we can never be old. For as you were when first your eye I eyed, such seems your beauty still."

I feel like we were married about six months ago. It has been, and it is, and it will be—perfect.

So, let's have a wonderful evening. Lisa doesn't file the divorce papers until the morning.

Thankfully, she didn't. As I write this, we now approach our sixtieth wedding anniversary. Many people have asked me, "What's the secret to a long and happy marriage?" It's a question I actually answered in

New York, at our second fiftieth anniversary celebration. The answer still holds true.

People have asked us: "50 years—what's the secret?"

Well, there's no one secret or rule.

There's the Ogden Nash Rule, which goes:
"To keep your marriage brimming
With love in the marriage cup,
Whenever you're wrong, admit it;
Whenever you're right, shut up."

There's the Henny Youngman Rule:
"My wife and I take time to go to restaurants
two times a week.
A little candlelight, dinner, soft music, and dancing.
She goes Tuesday, I go Fridays."

And there's the Stanley Weiss Rule:
"Don't marry for a sense of beauty.
Don't marry for a sense of adventure.
Marry for a sense of direction."

It's an iron rule, maybe evolutionary,
for the sake of survival.

Two people with a good sense of direction?
They'll never stop arguing.

Two people with a bad sense of direction?
They'll never find their way home.

Fortunately, for Lisa and me, we have the perfect balance:

There's no city, no scene, she can't navigate.
From the Champs-Elysées to the silk markets of Asia.

When I say I made my fortune by stumbling onto a mine,
I mean stumbled.

Once, in Mexico City, I took the children to the zoo;
Lori Christina—7. Anthony—3.
I showed them the lions, the zebras, the chimpanzees,
the elephants.
The lions, the zebras, the chimpanzees, the elephants.
The lions, the zebras, the chimpanzees, the elephants.
And they realized—Daddy's lost.

They both squeezed my hands and led me out.
They've been blessed with their mother's sense
of direction.

So, Lisa, Lori Christina, Anthony, believe me when I say:
I wouldn't be here without you.

That's never been more true than it is now. Today, I'd only amend
it to include Lori's children, Milena and Julian, and Anthony's lovely
wife, Natacha, and their children, Sacha and Tessa.

I'm not sure what I ever really did to deserve all this. But thank you,
my dear family, for making the latest and greatest and happiest chapters
of this improbable American story come true.

Thank you for helping me, after all these years, to finally strike gold.

Seventy Years to a Better Vocabulary

I guess you could say it was an act of historical foreshadowing that I was born into this world in the same year that Hirohito became emperor of Japan, Hitler published the second half of *Mein Kampf*, the book that laid the groundwork for Nazi Germany, and Robert Goddard launched the first liquid-fueled rocket with technology that would help usher in the nuclear age.

If the atomic bomb hadn't been dropped on Japan to end the war that Hirohito had helped begin—and if Hans and Gretl Popper hadn't managed to escape from Vienna with their newborn baby daughter, Lisa, just before the Nazis eliminated most of the Jewish population of Austria—the story that unfolds in this book over forty-four chapters and ninety years would have ended in chapter 4. It's a sobering thought when I imagine the stories that *could have* been told by hundreds of thousands of my fellow GIs and millions of Jews if they'd been given the same chance I've had to, as the Irish say, "comb gray hair."

But I didn't realize until I began research for this book that I was also born at exactly the same moment that the author of *The Treasure of the Sierra Madre* was putting the finishing touches on the book, published in 1927, that would eventually become the John Huston movie that would change my life. I didn't realize what I would come to share with the author, known by the pseudonym B. Traven, who is one of the most mysterious figures in the history of literature.

On one detail, there was no denying: he was a man who believed that Mexico was a place where a person could completely reinvent himself—where, his widow would later recall, he "lived something like ten lives."

I had gone to Mexico because I wanted to be the man in the white hat. But as it turns out, the man in the white hat was actually a stand-in for the author, B. Traven, himself. I wonder how many times I might have passed Traven in the street, or sat next to him in a café in Mexico City, where he lived until his death in 1969. I would have told him that he was right about Mexico: it was a place where I not only reinvented myself, but began what would become at least ten different lives lived over the following decades—in places and with people that I, or he, scarcely could have dreamed about when we were very young men.

⟡

SOCRATES SAID, "AN UNEXAMINED life is not worth living." For a really long time, I thought Socrates didn't know what he was talking about. I have lived most of my life to the fullest. I have had more fun in more places and with more people in more ways than almost anyone else. I've laughed and played, dared and danced, all without much examination, and still found every bit of it worth living, and wonderfully so. I started out following my instinct and desire more than making decisions based on reflection and reasoning. No wonder Socrates's words weren't at all meaningful to younger versions of myself.

I originally intended to write this story of my life as a gift for my grandchildren. I wanted to tell them about our family's roots, and regale them with the funny and colorful stories I had offered friends for decades. It didn't occur to me at first to think what these episodes, if examined carefully, might reveal about me and my life's worth.

But there were moments during the drafting of the book that caused deep reflection in me. The death of my brother, Buddy, at the age of ninety-four in October 2015 was one of those moments. It was hard not to think back on our long lives together. In my eulogy of Buddy, I recalled how our parents wanted him to be perfect in school and how my grandmother wanted him to be perfect at Hebrew School—which he was, along with being a terrific husband to his wife of nearly seventy years, Harriet, and a wonderful father to his children, Amy, Cindi, Dan, and Rick, all of whom spoke movingly at the service. I concluded my remarks by saying:

> Buddy was also a perfect friend to everyone he met—always giving, never taking. I'll tell you a story that may get me in trouble (because I'm not sure Harriet knows about this to this day), but what the hell.
>
> In 1950, I came back from Europe broken and broke. I needed help. Our father had died. Our mother was penniless. Buddy had recently married and started his career as a certified public accountant. When I told him I needed a car to get around, he bought me one. It was in this black Chevrolet that I drove to Mexico and changed my life.
>
> Bud, you will be in my thoughts as long as I live—and in our hearts forever.

As I wrote about stories and experiences like these, I became curious about their deeper meaning. I was drawn into considering my inner life, my unexplored feelings about the purpose of my life, with the same mix of unease, mystery, and wonder I felt when I first crawled into Mexico's mines to search for precious minerals and metals.

Examining my life helped me understand myself more clearly in many ways. For the first time I can see how I developed as a person. I can see which fundamental parts of me were there from birth. I can also see how I struggled later to find a worthy purpose for my life and thereby developed my most mature self, the one who writes this story.

Maybe more than anything else—more than being saved by the bomb, or having a movie change my ambition, or finding the love of my life in Lisa—I now realize that most of what I became in life grew out of a single moment of humiliation that changed me forever. When Louis Marx gave me that vocabulary test on his patio in 1948 with the

sole intention of shaming and embarrassing me in front of his daughter—slowly calling out the scores of the other participants, "100 . . .
98 . . . 90-something . . . 90-something . . . ," before winking at me,
clearing his throat and declaring for all to hear, "And Stanley . . . ahh . . .
Stanley. You got . . . twelve"—I felt like crawling under a rock. An instant
later, I felt like doing him harm when he stared intently at his daughter
as if to say, *So, is this the kind of guy you want?* I was even angrier later
when I found out the bastard had a book that he studied before giving
every one of those tests, to make sure he got 100 every time.

I remember that book because I still have the copy his daughter gave
to me to brush up on my words. It's a small paperback called *30 Days
to a More Powerful Vocabulary*, and it still sits on a bookshelf in my
London home. The front cover and a handful of the opening pages are
gone now, and its yellow spine is crumbling. But nearly every page is
filled with notations, underlines, and answers to sample tests written in
my twenty-one-year-old hand. It sits on the shelf next to *2,300 Steps
to Word Power*, whose cover is falling off, and the completely intact
ruby-red laminated *How to Build a Better Vocabulary*. Each book was
a constant companion of mine throughout the 1950s, each with more
and more underlined words written smaller and smaller in the margins.
What Louis Marx did to me that day drove me to try to put him out of
business—and also to learn everything there was I could possibly learn.
I still think of him as a monumental son of a bitch. But then again, I
owe everything to him. He changed my life. He made me want to be a
better person.

Have I achieved that goal? On balance, I'd say I have. I haven't
always been the best husband or father. I haven't always been the
nicest guy. I haven't always had my priorities in the right place. But
looking back at the sweep of nine decades, I'd say I did more good
than not—for my friends, for my family, and I hope, for the world I'll
leave behind.

My personal crisis is over. I now know myself better than ever. I've
become more comfortable and at ease with myself. I have more peace in
my life. My new sense of self has helped my marriage with Lisa achieve

more clarity, more harmony. I love her now in a much stronger way than I ever did. She's so much a part of me that I can't tell where one of us ends and the other begins.

༠༠

DURING THE TWENTY-FIVE YEARS I was chairman of BENS, I hosted a fiesta every December at the best Mexican restaurant in Washington. I gathered all my friends who had ever worked with me at the BENS headquarters to celebrate the season and each other. We reveled in shared pride about what we had accomplished together. I felt their love for me. I loved them. Still do. Always will.

Each year when our party reached its full height, I would take the floor, quiet the room, lift a tumbler of tequila, and salute life by reciting my favorite poem:

> There was a very cautious man
> Who never laughed or played.
> He never risked, he never tried.
> He never sang or prayed.
> And when he one day passed away,
> His insurance was denied.
> For since he never really lived,
> They claimed he never died.

The room would laugh and cheer. They understood me. They knew I had lived every single day of my life to the fullest and was urging them to do that same.

In nine decades on earth, I've found that being dead is bad for business and being boring is bad for life. To friends who want to laugh, who want to have fun, who want to enjoy all that life has to offer, I give the same response today that Humphrey Bogart's character gave in *The Treasure of the Sierra Madre* when asked if he was interested in prospecting for gold:

"Of course . . . Any time, any day . . . I was only waiting for you to ask."

Acknowledgments

As long as I can remember, the most important day of the year for me has been Thanksgiving. It's the one day when you say thank you—with no gifts or strings attached. Generally, the twenty or so people around Lisa's Thanksgiving table get bored having to hear my same thank-you's year after year. So, many, many years ago, I started a tradition making one "victim," usually someone new, recite a column that the late, great Art Buchwald wrote in 1953 while living in France and working for the Paris edition of the *New York Herald Tribune*. In the piece, Buchwald tries to explain Thanksgiving—"Le Jour de Merci Donnant" as the French refer to it—concluding that it's the one day each year where "American families . . . eat better than the French do." The table usually falls apart listening to the pronunciation of the many French phrases that make the piece so memorable.

When I look back on my life, I'm thankful to more people for their friendship than any book could possibly contain. If I tried to list them all, we'd be here for another ninety years. But suffice it to say that when it comes to those who have impacted my life—from Philadelphia, Mexico, San Francisco, London, and Gstaad to Thailand, Myanmar, Indonesia, India, and all BENS trips in between—you know who you are. As a wit whose name is lost to history once said, "I want to say thank you to all the people who walked into my life and made it outstanding, and all the people who walked out of my life and made it fantastic."

But there are a few people who deserve special recognition for their help and patience (not necessarily in that order) during the years I've worked on this memoir.

My thanks begin with the person whose help has been immeasurable these past eight years, not only to keeping this book on track, but to keeping my life on track as Lisa and I travel around the world: my executive assistant Kathryn Fox. How I got so lucky, I will never know. She's always been a step ahead. Without Kathryn there would be no book.

Among my colleagues who contributed, there is one without equal—my friend and long-time counselor Larry Smith. For years I've joked that my memoir would be the first three-word book in history. I'd simply write, "He doesn't remember." But it was Larry who helped shake the cobwebs—who helped me remember people and places by arranging the interviews, guiding the conversations, piecing together the narrative, and challenging me to confront the meaning of it all.

I'd also be remiss if I didn't mention my seven-year partnership with Paul Orzulak, a former foreign policy speechwriter for President Bill Clinton and a founding partner of the widely respected West Wing Writers. He has been a sounding board for me on both my memoir and my columns since the beginning of the Obama Administration. I know I can rely on him to play devil's advocate, even if he doesn't always like what I have to say about Barack Obama and Hillary Clinton.

Lastly, my thanks end where my life begins—with Lisa, for her endless patience; with Anthony and Lori Christina, for their eternal love; and with my grandchildren.

As for all of the friends who traded stories, sat for interviews, read early drafts, read later drafts, let me annoy you from time to time, and who have long known me, as Buchwald wrote, as "*un vieux Fanfan la Tulipe*"—a man not of words but of action—I hope my words match your memories and that our time together has been worth it. I know it has been for me. Not being boring is good for living.

About the Author

STANLEY A. WEISS was formerly chairman of American Premier, Inc., a mining, refractories, chemicals, and mineral processing company. He is founding chairman of Business Executives for National Security (BENS), a nonpartisan organization of senior executives who use the best practices of business to strengthen the nation's security.

Mr. Weiss has written widely on public policy matters. His work has appeared in the *Huffington Post*, the *International Herald Tribune*, the *New York Times*, the *Wall Street Journal*, the *Washington Post*, and the *Washington Times*. His book, *Manganese: The Other Uses*, is the definitive work on the non-metallurgical uses of manganese.

A former fellow at Harvard's Center for International Affairs, Mr. Weiss is the recipient of an honorary Doctor of Humane Letters from Point Park University in Pittsburgh, Pennsylvania. He currently serves on the Board of Directors for Premier Chemicals and is a member of the Council on Foreign Relations, the American Ditchley Foundation, the International Institute for Strategic Studies, and the Royal Institution of Great Britain. Mr. Weiss has served on the Board of Directors of Harman International Industries; the Board of Visitors of Georgetown University School of Foreign Service; and the Advisory Boards of the RAND Center for Middle East Public Policy and the International Crisis Group.

Mr. Weiss is married with two children. He divides his time between his residences in London and Gstaad, and his office in Washington, DC.